Beauty AND BUSINESS

COMMERCE, GENDER, AND CULTURE IN MODERN AMERICA

EDITED BY PHILIP SCRANTON

Routledge

New York • London

A volume in the series Hagley Perspectives on Business and Culture, edited by
Philip Scranton and Roger Horowitz. Volumes in this series to date include *Beauty
and Business: Commerce, Gender, and Culture in Modern America* and *Boys and
Their Toys: Masculinity, Class, and Technology in America.*

Published in 2001 by
Routledge
29 West 35th Street
New York, NY 10001

Published in Great Britain by
Routledge
11 New Fetter Lane
London EC4P 4EE

Copyright © 2001 by Routledge
Routledge is an imprint of the Taylor & Francis Group.

Printed in the United States of America on acid-free paper.

Library of Congress Cataloging-in-Publication Data

Beauty and business : commerce, gender, and culture in modern America / edited by
Philip Scranton.
    p. cm. — (Hagley perspectives on business and culture)
Includes bibliographical references and index.
ISBN 0-415-92666-1 — ISBN 0-415-92667-X (pbk.)
    1. United States—Commerce—History. 2. Beauty, Personal—United States—History.
3. Clothing trade—United States—History. 4. Fashion—United States—History. I. Scranton,
Philip. II. Series.

HF3013 .B42 2000
391.6'0973—dc21   00-036781

Contents

Part 2 BUSINESS AND WORK

Part 3 CONSTRUCTING COMMODITIES

Preface

PHILIP SCRANTON

*I*n March 1999, more than a hundred scholars, students, museum staffers, and intrigued individuals gathered at the Hagley Museum and Library to participate in a unique conference focused on the intersections of beauty and business in the United States. The energy and enthusiasm generated by researchers' presentations set in motion the process that yielded this collection, which initiates a Routledge series, Hagley Perspectives on Business and Culture. These prefatory paragraphs will offer a few background remarks and brief sketches of the essays that follow.

In an effort to promote productive connections between gender history and business history, Hagley's Center for the History of Business, Technology and Society organized a symposium on the theme "Gender and Business" in November 1996. Wendy Gamber (Indiana University) and Kathy Peiss (University of Massachusetts–Amherst) delivered papers linking their research on dressmakers/milliners and the cosmetics trade, respectively, to prospects for future inquiry. Joan Scott (Institute for Advanced Study) provided a wide-ranging, provocative response. Suitably revised, their essays reached a broader audience when included in the Summer 1998 issue of *Business History Review*.[1] In the interim, the center's Associate Director, Roger Horowitz, and I considered possible venues for extending this initiative. Appreciating that Kathy Peiss's book-length study of cosmetics in America was nearing publication,[2] we invited her to join in developing a conference on beauty and business since the late nineteenth century. Our call for papers drew a mass of proposals, in itself a signal that this was a timely theme. Having devised the program, headed by Professor Peiss's keynote, we were delighted when Routledge editor Deirdre Mullane contacted us, expressing interest in publishing a collection of the papers, perhaps supplemented by engaging collateral work. The near-term result of these interactions is this volume; the longer term outcome will be a Routledge series, Hagley Perspectives on Business and Culture, anchored by research presented at other Hagley conferences. At this juncture, two additional collections are "in the works," and we presently are planning three more for the years ahead. Now, a quick summary of what you will find in the pages that follow.

Kathy Peiss's "On Beauty. . . and the History of Business" sets out a thematic agenda for current and future research, emphasizing that a sizable segment of the American economy has become centered on selling beauty and fashion, that beauty is integral to multiple business strategies, and that culturally, beauty has been attached to a wide range of "goods," from art to bodies. Part I, "Images and Reforms," presents four papers that capture complementary elements of the interplay between gender, business, shifting values, and social practices from the 1870s through the 1920s. Drawing on designs and museum-conserved garments, Sarah Gordon analyzes the controversies triggered by women's rising participation in sports and active leisure, whereas Nancy Bowman illuminates the gendered constructions of smoking and the cultural tensions sparked when fashionable and young women adopted cigarettes. Next, Carole Turbin's examination of the "collar wars'" class and gender implications after 1900 shows how contested notions of masculinity became entwined with innovations in shirt designs. Looking directly at businessmen, in part through too-rarely consulted trade journals, Jill Fields revisits corset makers' panic attacks when they believed women's widespread rejection of their products was surfacing after 1910, as fashionable clothing and body images shifted away from Victorian ideals.

In Part II, "Business and Work," we encounter women as entrepreneurs and employees in the beauty trades from the 1920s through the post–World War II era. Katina Manko goes "inside the firm" at California Perfume (later Avon) to explicate a business strategy that yielded steady profitability during the century's most economically troubled decade. Reconstructing the social relations and political dimensions of African-American beauty shop culture, Tiffany Gill establishes the critical role these businesswomen (and their organizations) played in creating free spaces, sustaining communities, and battling discrimination. Having mined company newsletters and union correspondence, Vicki Howard documents how a shared beauty culture shaped the work experiences of women operatives at Maidenform just as the company undertook to commercialize its postwar image of the ultrafeminine body. Closing Part II, Nancy Koehn's business biography of Estée Lauder employs a classic historical form to illustrate the interplay between ambition and contingency that underlay one female entrepreneur's rise to international prominence.

"Constructing Commodities," the collection's final section, treats the commercial nexus between business and beauty during and after the 1950s, focusing most directly on the female body. Susannah Walker explains that although in the sixties African-American women's adoption of the "natural" hairstyle represented both a radical departure from customary practice and a political statement, in time the Afro also became a business opportunity for salon operators and beauty product manufacturers. At the same time, gender, ethnicity, and the Cold War intersected in complex and surprising ways, as Judy Tzu-Chun Wu demonstrates in her close examination of the Miss Chinatown U.S.A. beauty pageants, sponsored by San Francisco's Chinese American business association. Beginning in the 1950s, as Kirsten Gardner notes, information about breast cancer and mastectomies began circulating widely, helping create a niche market for prosthesis makers whose devices embodied the notion that concealing surgery's effects meant a survivor's return to "normal." Gardner here explores the marketing of breast replacements as well as these commodities' contested psychological and cultural messages.

In these twelve essays, as so often with a relatively new area of cross-disciplinary research, historical inquiries proceed in multiple directions, using a variety of approaches and sounding common themes but in a range of keys. Bringing these voices together in this volume has not involved pressing them toward harmonizing, for the dissonances and the diversities well express the rich possibilities of exploring the beauty-business relation. It is our hope that encountering the work that follows will prove as thought-provoking for you as experiencing the conference and producing this collection has been for us.

NOTES

1. *Business History Review* 72:2 (Summer 1998), Special Section: Gender and Business, 185–249.
2. Kathy Peiss, *Hope in a Jar,* (New York: Metropolitan Books, 1998).

Acknowledgments

The editor owes multiple debts of gratitude to those institutions and individuals who have made this collection possible. Glenn Porter, Hagley's director, has provided crucial institutional and personal support for the center's efforts to encourage creative scholarship concerning business and technology in American society. Roger Horowitz, my colleague at Hagley and the series' coeditor, is the sharpest yet most relaxed intellectual partner I could wish for. Together, Carol Lockman, the center's indefatigable coordinator, and Roger built a conference from scraps of paper and piles of proposals, then managed the endless details necessary to making it happen. As ever, Hagley's experienced staff helped the sessions flow flawlessly.

Kathy Peiss has been an invaluable colleague before, during, and after the "Beauty and Business" sessions, joining the program committee, delivering the lead paper, commenting on a session, and helping select the essays for this collection. There is more. In 1997, the Business History Conference had commenced the process of creating a new journal, *Enterprise and Society,* a quarterly that debuted in March 2000. Its editor, Will Hausman, invited Roger, Kathy, and me to select several of the "Beauty and Business" papers to form a special issue during its inaugural year. Kathy took principal responsibility for working with these four authors and their essays, assisted by Sally Clarke (University of Texas–Austin) and Will (College of William and Mary). My thanks to them for hard work well done and to *Enterprise and Society* for permission to reprint articles from that issue (Vol. 1, No. 3, September 2000) by Kathy Peiss, Carole Turbin, Vicki Howard, Susannah Walker, and Kirsten Gardner.

Roger Horowitz recollected reading Judy Wu's Miss Chinatown U.S.A. article in the Fall 1997 *Journal of Social History*. Happily, Professor Wu accepted my invitation to include it, and the journal's editors kindly permitted its being reprinted here, along with Jill Field's conference paper, which first appeared in the *JSH's* Winter 1999 issue. At Routledge, Deirdre Mullane's enthusiasm for this project and for the series has been gratifying and invigorating. Derek Krissoff's assistance with the complexities of permissions was timely and priceless. Most important, it is essential to acknowledge the twelve authors of *Beauty and Business*, all of whom gracefully endured my nattering about schedules and deadlines, and my many critical and trivial comments on drafts as well. I thank each author for presenting her work in the first volume of the Hagley Perspectives, and, as many of these essays preview books-in-progress, I look forward to the shelf of monographs these studies will generate.

On Beauty . . . and the History of Business

KATHY PEISS

*W*hat can business historians learn by making beauty a subject of research and investigation? Beauty and business—one might as well say: beauty and the beast. These terms conjure up distinct domains, different images, and contrasting values. Beauty is seemingly frivolous, superficial, and female, the subject of aesthetics, art, poetry, and most recently, feminist criticism. Business, in contrast, connotes serious, consequential, indeed manly activity, the intellectual domain of economists and social scientists.

Until recently, business historians have not yielded to beauty—at least as a subject of scholarly inquiry. The field has been so much defined by studies of heavy industry and corporate power that the activities of hairdressers, fashion designers, and Avon ladies have largely gone unnoticed. But beauty is big business, with large-scale production, international distribution networks, media-saturation advertising, scientific marketing, and sales in the billions of dollars. And business historians have begun to take notice. Placing business within the broad narratives of American history, they increasingly investigate how economic enterprises interacted with cultural and social developments, responding to and influencing them in turn. They have opened new directions for research on gender, race, the creation of markets, and the role of consumers. Interest in beauty, style, and fashion is a logical development in the new business history.[1]

And what of those who write about beauty? They pay much more attention to the power of representation—paintings, poems, prescriptive literature, and advertising images—than to the strategies of business. Critics of the commercialization of beauty tend to treat business as a monolith, an industry whose motives are uniform, actions syn-

7

chronized, and effects transparent.[2] The papers in this collection go beyond such approaches to investigate closely the relationship between beauty and business practices. They explore the assumptions and decision-making of entrepreneurs, manufacturers, retailers, advertisers, and consumers. They consider how changing ideals of beauty, notions of fashion, and attitudes to the body shaped business strategies. Just as important, they show how businesses profited from their attention to beauty and influenced cultural ideals and social identities embodied in faces, figures, and fashion. These case studies demonstrate that beauty and business are worth pondering further.

A broad look at the historical relationship between beauty and business points to several key approaches to this subject. One concerns the emergence of a large sector of the economy devoted to selling beauty aids, fashions, bodily care, and style to American women and, increasingly, to men. Another is the deployment of beauty as a business strategy in creating brands, sales, and marketing, in managing the workplace, and in projecting corporate identities. A third considers the sale of beauty itself as a value added and attached to a wide range of goods, from art to bodies. These approaches offer new directions for future research.

A SHORT DISQUISITION ON BEAUTY

The word *beauty* requires a closer look at the long-standing intellectual and cultural traditions that have defined its meaning. Beauty is an aesthetic category applied to art and objects, faces and bodies, nature and souls. In the Western tradition of aesthetics, at least since the eighteenth century, beauty has been understood as a quality apart, dissociated from history and social contingencies. For philosophers, poets, and artists, the aesthetic was an autonomous and transcendent realm outside the ordinary, the mundane, and the utilitarian. The contemplation of beauty—whether the sublimity of Niagara Falls, the sensuousness of a Rubens painting, or the charm of a young girl's face—took one out of the self into a higher realm of appreciation and discernment. Much ink was spilled in the nineteenth century in the effort to identify those qualities of female beauty upon which everyone could agree. There were "celestial" beauties—often tubercular or close to death—and robust pulchritude, classical Venuses and oriental exotics, blondes and brunettes, all placed in a moral order and physical hierarchy based on complexion, hair, and symmetry of face and form.[3]

This aesthetic tradition, with its assertion of universal standards and perceptions, has been challenged on many grounds by sociologists, feminist critics, postmodernists, and artists, among others. One especially useful critique insists upon the centrality of the historical and social contexts in which beauty takes form and achieves meaning. That,

Kathy Peiss

in turn, requires a consideration of how meanings are ascribed to a wide range of cultural products, and by whom. How do particular societies or social groups define beauty? What categories of taste do they employ? How do they discern the qualities of the beautiful? When is an object "art" and when is it a "tchotchke"? What makes a beauty queen? This approach asks us to consider vernacular aesthetic forms as well as the Old Masters. And it requires us to study viewers' perceptions, their cultural frames of reference, and their social locations so as not to assume a universal subject.[4]

Beauty signifies difference in a number of registers, making distinctions between high and low, normal and abnormal, virtue and vice. In so doing, beauty helps to define morality, social status, class, gender, race, and ethnicity. Ideals of beauty, in turn, are fundamentally shaped by social relations and institutions, by other cultural categories and practices, and by politics and economics. Even so, beauty should not be reduced to any one of these: if not autonomous, the aesthetic is a realm with its own language and logic. One need not be a sociobiologist tracing contemporary attitudes toward beauty back to our evolutionary heritage and genetic hardwiring to think this.[5] Rather, one only need recognize that beauty ideals, as well as our perceptions and reactions, develop in complex ways.

Each historical period has its own culturally specific standards of beauty: the hourglass figure of the 1890s, the boyish flapper of the 1920s, the unisex look of the 1960s. Yet conceptions of beauty are quite long-lived, their referents going far back in time: in the West, the classical beauty of Greece and Rome remains a governing beauty ideal; many Americans still consider African appearances beautiful only if exoticized. At the same time, beauty is destabilizing because perception, which constructs beauty, occurs in complex individual and cultural circumstances. Beauty turns heads, stops the action, and evokes emotions from lust to piety. Once we have analyzed the social constructions, cultural practices, politics, and economics, we still may not fully understand what beauty does in people's lives and what it means. In its largest sense, aesthetics offers us a way of knowing the world around us in a different key from, say, science or religion. Beauty is, in Suzanne Langer's evocative phrase, "significant form." And it is a form that in the past century has been increasingly mobilized and informed by business enterprise.[6]

THE BEAUTY SECTOR OF THE ECONOMY

Beauty and business seem most closely related in the modern era, but beauty has always been for sale. Whenever and wherever markets arise, beauty has had a commercial value. Art markets developed among elites, whether Renaissance princes, Gilded Age robber barons, or Cold

War corporate leaders. As patrons to artists and buyers of beautiful objects, they claimed and projected cultural power. Romanticist ideals of beauty in nature, from the pastoral to the sublime, became the currency of real estate and tourism: a splendid view turned a profit.[7]

Beauty added exchange value to women, whether in the market in slaves, in prostitutes, or in wives. Abolitionist writer and former bondswoman Harriet Jacobs noted how beauty was a misfortune for African women sold as commodities in slavery, since it made them the sexual prey of their masters. Women who bargained their sexual services as prostitutes worked in a hierarchy. Beauty, youth, and fashionability were for sale in "high-class" brothels; women without those attributes toiled in factorylike "cribs" and walked the streets. And as feminists from Mary Wollstonecraft to Emma Goldman charged, *marriage* was a market in which beauty, not brains, found the highest bidder. It is no coincidence that cosmetics and paints were viewed in the nineteenth century as particularly pernicious symbols of commerce, linked to prostitution, female con artists, and tainted goods.[8]

If beauty ideals and practices were shaped by earlier exchange values, they in turn set limits and created opportunities for the modern fashion and beauty industries. Despite similar emphases on style and appearance, beauty and fashion actually followed different logics, and the businesses that sold them developed on separate tracks. In distinct ways, entrepreneurs, local firms, national businesses, and mass media projected beauty and fashion as representations, sold them as tangible goods, and promoted them in the name of service to women.

The "fashion system" predated the emergence of a widespread commercial beauty culture. Fashion transforms clothes as material objects through a process of style creation and information dissemination; it requires news about "what's new" to be spread in print, through images, and by word of mouth. The nineteenth-century publishing industry, especially the genteel women's magazine, created and interpellated women readers in part by promoting new styles and taste. Making fashion the centerpiece of its appeal, *Godey's Lady's Book* contained the latest news from Paris, London, and New York, ran engravings and fashion plates, and offered instructions for updating older clothes with trimmings, embroidery, new sleeves, and other techniques.[9]

In the nineteenth century, genuine beauty was considered different from fashion—a timeless, inner, and natural quality, not mutable, external, or socially driven. Still, magazine and book publishers made advice, illustrations, and fiction about beauty a salable product that helped fuel the publishing boom after 1830: Don't buy cosmetics, went the sales pitch, but do buy the book on how to achieve moral beauty. *Godey's* and handsome gift books disseminated ideals of appearance to affluent women, while low-cost beauty manuals reached factory hands and domestic workers. Expanded literacy, faster and cheaper printing technologies, and new book distribution systems fostered a market for beauty advice across the socioeconomic spectrum.[10]

What scholars call "prescriptive literature"—in contrast to such private writings as letters and diaries—was often, in fact, a product of business and should be examined in that light. In *Godey's* and the advice manuals, emergent genre conventions, representational strategies, and narrative structures developed to keep women buying and reading. The fashion plates and gossip about Parisian and New York high society promised the *dernier cri* to American women in the hinterlands. Magazine fiction gratified readers' interest in good looks while implicitly praising their good sense and good names: short stories featured willful beauties who painted and primped in pursuit of husbands and fortune but died of lead poisoning from toxic face powder or developed consumption after dancing all night in sheer, low-cut ball gowns.[11]

If nineteenth-century beauty ideals tended to naturalize gender differences and legitimate the new cultural authority of the middle class, they also spurred the growth of a women's market in publishing. This early commercial dissemination of feminine ideals and images was critical in the making of mass-market beauty and fashion industries. It began a long-term process of educating the eye, channeling desires, and creating an identification between representation and viewer that would serve the sale of goods and foster new perceptions of beauty in the culture at large.

Just as important was the web of small-scale proprietors, entrepreneurs, manufacturers, and retailers who, by the late nineteenth century, had established fashion and beautifying as cultural practices linked to commerce. Their stories have been especially important to recover, for they complicate our historical understanding of the beauty and fashion sector of the economy and suggest some new directions for business history. Perhaps most significant is the role of women in these businesses: seamstresses, hairdressers, beauticians, department store buyers, and cosmetics saleswomen all made beauty and fashion integral to the lives of women. As Wendy Gamber shows, dressmakers and milliners were ambitious, independent, and skilled craftswomen who often became proprietors of their own shops, secured a competency, and achieved some standing in their communities. They had to be highly responsive to information about what was stylish, respectable, and attractive, and became authorities themselves, translating high style and fashion plates for local tastes and pocketbooks.[12]

The beauty business has also been and remains intensely personal. What began as domestic service—the hands-on care of the hair, face, and body by maids or slaves—became organized into businesses by individual proprietors and entrepreneurs in the late nineteenth century. These beauty enterprises began to appear in cities across the country: a manicure shop tucked away in a multifloor walk-up, a storefront hair salon, a "beauty college" in a loft, cosmetics counters front and center in department stores.[13]

These businesses opened opportunities for some women by aligning commercial enterprise with the very ideals of femininity and beauty that had long justified women's exclusion from most lines of work. In a culture that celebrated inner, moral beauty, they placed a new emphasis on external appearance and its cultivation through the purchase and use of cosmetics and other beauty aids. They directed their business and marketing efforts not only to the affluent but to working women, African Americans, and immigrants, drawing upon the cultural practices and institutions familiar to women in their everyday life.

The beauty business joined the sale of goods to the provision of services in innovative ways. Avon saleswomen went into homes to teach women about beauty products and how to use them. Unlike selling vacuum cleaners and encyclopedias door to door, selling beauty often involved a long-term, continuous relationship between seller and buyer. Salons were based in specific localities and their hands-on approach offered the pleasure of touch, the promise of makeover, and the enjoyment of sociability. Franchising operations and beauty schools spread across the country what began as local, personal endeavors; women went to a Madam C. J. Walker or Marinello shop for a particular experience of hairstyling, grooming, and social interaction. In African-American salons, the small talk between hairdresser and client sometimes turned to matters of economic and political import and even nourished community activism and the Civil Rights movement.[14]

Woven into the "house calls" of the Avon Lady and the wash-and-set at the beauty parlor was an ongoing conversation about appearances that opened out in many directions. These businesses encouraged a high degree of self-consciousness of the face and body. Operating in a local context, they reinforced yet mediated the barrage of advertising, motion pictures, and national magazines that fostered an external, visual standard for self-assessment.

Selling beauty itself as a product became much more systematic, self-conscious, and widespread after 1920. Historians have only begun to research the full dimensions of this effort across the economy and society—not only in specific cosmetics, hair care, clothing, and accessories firms, but in modeling agencies, commercial beauty contests, cosmetic surgery, weight camps, the health club business, and other enterprises. Scholars have delineated the role of beauty and fashion in furthering the development of national and mass markets. They have written extensively, for instance, on the "tie-in" as an integrative business strategy in cosmetics and fashion marketing by which local retailers, national advertisers, mass-circulation magazines, and movies aligned their interests. Film producers built moments of female display and spectacle into the movies not only for the male gaze but also for women viewers—the obligatory "how do I look" scene in front of the mirror or the staging of a fashion show. Movie studios struck agreements with clothing manufacturers to highlight new styles. If a dress received particular notice from fans—like one worn by Bette Davis in *Letty Lynton*—it was quickly manufactured at popular prices and featured in department stores.[15]

These cooperative strategies and nationalizing tendencies stand in contrast to the ongoing conflicts among local businesses, national media, and mass manufacturers. The local and regional remain salient in the modern beauty and fashion business. Although the rise of ready-to-wear fashions put many dressmakers out of business or turned their activity into alteration work for stores, women with an understanding of clothes often became specialty shop owners or department store buyers. Buyers made and continue to make decisions about New York or Paris fashions based on their understanding of hometown constituencies. Specialty shops have sought the trust of customers through personal service and sensitivity to local standards of beauty and style.[16] That sensitivity is not just a matter of price but an awareness of taste— what color palette, design elements, and accessories appeal to the eyes of women in their communities, whether middle-class African Americans, Jewish retirees in Florida, or working-class secretaries in Dallas. Beauty shops also mediate the national and the local. Salon operatives promote trends created by product manufacturers, trade associations, and celebrity hair designers while remaining attentive to the particular practices and views of their patrons.

If beauty is a signifier of difference, beauty businesses—whether national, regional, or local—have continually made choices about what differences to emphasize, reinforce, or efface. Hairdressers have long been trained in different techniques that reinforce a racial distinction between "black" and "white" hair. Instructions on permanent waves in the 1930s, for instance, emphasized marcelling for white clients, croquignole waves for African-American women. Even after the desegregation of beauty schools and beauty shops in the 1960s, these customary distinctions continued. Hair is most obviously a potent symbol of gender difference. The rise of "unisex" salons and men's hairstyling in the 1960s was an important development in the beauty business that challenged the dominance of the barbershop as the bastion of male appearance. Unisex styling salons capitalized upon the larger questioning of traditional notions of masculinity by men in the "youth revolt," counterculture, and antiwar movements of the time.[17]

These examples suggest how much beauty businesses have shaped the social definitions and physical attributes of femininity and masculinity as well as race and ethnicity, age and generation, and class. They have done so not only through advertising but through product design, sales strategies, and in the daily operations and practices that underlie brand and company identity. For instance, in oral history interviews conducted by the Smithsonian, the Noxell (originally Noxzema) corporation and its advertisers were extremely forthcoming about their choices when developing and marketing Cover Girl makeup in the late 1950s and 1960s. Noxzema was already established as a maker of a medicated cleansing and moisturizing cream when it decided to create a makeup line. The product was in its initial development, intended for both young adult women and teenagers with "problem" skin, and the challenge was to make the product acceptable to both groups as well to parents of teens anxious about their daughters' use of makeup. Mary Ayres, an advertising executive handling the account, developed the idea of Cover Girl as a medicated makeup, with the advertising stressing both glamour and health. Among the early slogans were "glamour that's good for your skin" and "clean makeup." [18]

By the mid-sixties, the agency had consciously decided upon a particular vision of female beauty to sell this idea: a young, fair-skinned, sun-bleached blonde, fit and active yet absorbed in her own beauty. Modeled by Cybill Shepherd and Cheryl Tiegs, this "California look" was specifically intended to appeal to Middle America, the mass market and cultural mainstream. The ad designers perceived the light skin of models and white space in the ads as a "clean" look, and "cleanliness" was a message that they believed would appeal to girls and parents alike. The manufacturer had its own concerns, including keeping the price of the product competitive, simplifying packaging, gaining shelf space in drugstores, and managing consumers' choices in a self-service environment; for all these reasons the firm created at first only three, then seven shades of foundation, none of them appropriate for deep olive, brown, or black complexions. This example illustrates how a mass-market company, through a complex process of decision-making and a deeply engrained set of cultural biases, produces and reproduces racialized and gendered beauty ideals.

AESTHETICIZATION AS A BUSINESS STRATEGY

The perception that "beauty sells" became commonplace in business after 1920. Scholars have studied how manufacturers and advertisers have long used representations of beautiful women and handsome men both to sell specific products and to promote consumption-oriented lifestyles. The "beauty appeal" as a self-conscious commercial strategy went further by promising consumers the psychological and social benefits of better looks. The beauty appeal went well beyond the cosmetics and fashion industries, and was used to sell virtually any product that could be connected in some way to the body, self-presentation, and personal identity. Toothbrushes made by the Prophylactic brush company, once sold on the basis of health and hygiene, were now guaranteed to beautify one's smile; Wrigley's touted chewing gum as a five-minute facial for secretaries; automobile ads encouraged women to buy their cars to match their frocks. Articles on "beauty, the new business tool" appeared throughout trade journals, in-house newsletters, and the popular press.[19]

To many manufacturers, beauty was a measurable value added to goods, a quantum that could alter the perception and placement of products. Lever Brothers, maker of a popular laundry detergent, stressed the value of glamour when it introduced Lux toilet soap in 1925. It hired the J. Walter Thompson Company to develop a marketing and advertising campaign. When Thompson offered its proposal for ads that promoted Lux as a "new form" of soap, Lever's president complained that the ads would confuse consumers into thinking that the soap was simply another kind of laundry detergent. "Our idea," he said, is that the toilet soap "should be placed on a pinnacle, removed from any suggestion of laundry or dishpan use." He urged the ad agency to replace the word "suds" with "lather" and depict the soap in the boudoir, not the kitchen. "We must throw more glamour around our new product to justify the price in the consumer's mind of 9c to 10c per cake. . . . Remember, we are lifting a laundry product up to a toilet plane."[20]

Aesthetic categories helped businesses define and build their markets. Cosmetics manufacturers relied heavily on package design and targeted advertising to reach particular consumers. African-American businessman Anthony Overton wanted the packaging of High Brown Face Powder to be elegant and respectable, and he chose the face of a woman with light brown skin and European features to adorn the label. The French perfumer Bourjois sold Java face powder in a traditional loose-powder container with a floral design, touting it as a "natural" beauty aid for conservative, older women who balked at looking made up; Bourjois placed the same powder in a jazzier package, named it Manon Lescault, and marketed it to flappers as a tool for man-hunting and romance. Businesses that used aesthetic codes to convey social and moral messages would find "it is quite possible to reach two mutually antagonistic classes of prospects," as one trade journal observed.[21]

Businesses worked with older aesthetic categories, updated and shaped them for commercial purposes, and made them relevant to the perceptions and tastes of consumers. Sales campaigns used typologies of beauty—dark and fair, foreign and exotic, ethereal and physical—to differentiate products and markets. Max Factor and other cosmetics firms created complexion analysis charts to help women choose their "beauty type" and the best array of products. Earlier aesthetic dictates show up repeatedly in advertising. William Hogarth's "curve of beauty"—a sinuous S shape identified by the eighteenth-century writer as the most beautiful line—inspired an advertisement for Zip depilatory: The model's pose, one arm curved above her head to reveal a hairless underarm, rendered the otherwise indelicate subject artistic and tasteful.[22]

Business leaders also adopted new artistic movements they perceived as having commercial value. The forward-looking aesthetic of Art Moderne was attached to many products with varying degrees of success. Everything from trains to toasters was streamlined to convey a sense of speed and modernity. The beauty firm Marinello even packed face cream in jars that looked like set-back skyscrapers. Retailers looked to artists and museums for aesthetic inspiration and design trends for store layouts, show windows, and special events. Advertisers, too, used new artistic elements to position their products in the marketplace, hiring such leading photographers as Edward Steichen to take modernist shots of hands for Jergens Skin Lotion. Coordinated designs and ensembles, inspired by clothing fashion, could be seen in products ranging from cosmetics to furniture to bathroom fixtures. Today this principle informs the lifestyle marketing of such stores as Pottery Barn and Rooms to Go.[23]

Beyond marketing and sales, beauty and appearance have played an important role in employment, conveying through the body a set of messages about a firm. Formal uniforms, customary dress codes, hairstyles, makeup requirements, and weight restrictions became visual cues that served to unify the corporate or brand identity, put forward a pleasing face to the public, and manage employees. This has been especially true in white-collar and service-sector jobs, in which people are, in a sense, part of the company's product. After World War II, when airlines chose women over men to work as flight attendants, rules stipulating appropriate appearance became commonplace. By the 1960s flight attendants were required to wear nail polish, lipstick, hats, gloves, and girdles; hair dye, bleach, Afros, and cornrows were banned. Limitations on body weight had nothing to do with overloading the plane and everything to do with projecting an image of svelte, youthful beauty. National Airlines' infamous "Fly Me" advertising campaign of the 1960s sold the vicarious experience of flight attendants' sexuality and beauty along with air transportation. Such requirements have increasingly become the source of individual and collective conflict in the workplace. In the 1970s, the flight attendants' union successfully fought both marital status and weight requirements as discriminatory; both requirements constructed "the stewardess" as youthful and attractive. African-American women have challenged employers who bar cornrows, dreadlocks, and other hairstyles from the workplace: designating an appropriate corporate identity, they argue, has the effect of enforcing a "white" appearance. Even more widespread are the gender-, class-, and race-based assumptions about appropriate looks at different levels and kinds of business. These differences were evocatively captured in the 1988 film *Working Girl*, in which makeup, hair, and clothing styles distinguished the women managers from the secretaries. As Melanie Griffith's upwardly mobile and newly shorn character explains, "if you want to be taken seriously, you need to have serious hair."[24]

Aestheticization has also proven to be a powerful business strategy in establishing corporate identity. Since the 1930s, but especially after World War II, corporations have projected their economic and political power through a "corporate aesthetic." Henry Luce intentionally made *Fortune*, a general magazine for businessmen, into a beautiful physical object at the very moment—the onset of the Depression—when many publishers were cutting the quality of paper and illustrations and shrinking the size of magazines. Despite the high cost, Luce printed *Fortune* in large format and on heavy paper stock, hired modernist artists to design the covers, and commissioned renowned photographers to take the pictures that appeared inside the magazine.[25]

Individual and corporate ownership of art collections also became an important means of projecting cultural and economic authority. Helena Rubinstein had an extensive art collection, which she showed in her New York salon and loaned to museums; it underscored Rubinstein's belief that beautifying was not a practice of the vulgar and vain but a "decorative art," part of a celebrated aesthetic tradition. Some business leaders, such as Walter Paepcke, the head of the Container Corporation of America, patronized abstract artists as representatives of free enterprise and the free world. More generally, arts patronage, public sculpture, and commissions to renowned architects have been used in corporate, white-collar settings to project a sense of common mission and elevated status: the "corporate sublime."[26]

BEAUTY FROM HIGH TO LOW

Business may promote the "corporate sublime" to express its higher aims but it has also used beauty for "lower" purposes. The exploitation and sale of sexualized beauty and its larger impact on the economy and society remain largely unexamined by business historians. Yet "smut-peddling"—as *Hustler* owner Larry Flynt quaintly calls it, evoking a bygone era of shrewd, sweet-talking men carrying packs full of trinkets—is in fact big business. Changing beauty ideals and images affected the contours and growth of this industry, including its movement from illicit trade to legitimate enterprise.

The modern invention of pornography has been linked to the development of printing and consequent distribution of books, magazines, pamphlets, and ephemeral literature, a development associated, interestingly, with the emergence of a Habermasian "civic" public sphere in the eighteenth century.[27] Beauty became more important to smut peddling as new image-making technologies developed. By the 1860s, the unique image of the daguerreotype gave way to *cartes-de-visite,* stereographs, and other reproducible formats. A lively trade resulted, not only in the manufacture of personal portraits, but also in the sale of the pictures. Photography studios, peddlers, and department stores marketed the faces and figures of actresses, dancers, burlesque performers, self-styled beauties—and naked women. Photographers embraced specific styles of posing, camera placement, and lighting that regularized images of beauty, including those intended to be sexually arousing. And they drew upon conventions of display and spectacle developed first in burlesque and musical reviews and later in body-building and beauty pageantry. Images of beauty used to sell products explicitly to men, especially those connoting a male "sporting" culture, emphasized female physical attributes. Bosomy, dark-featured women regularly appeared on cigar boxes, for instance.[28]

It is striking indeed how frequently businesses based on new image-making technologies have found in sex and sexualized beauty a means of gaining a foothold in the entertainment and information economy. In the early days of the motion pictures, most films were projected on screens in vaudeville shows, nickelodeons, and traveling exhibitions, but dime museums and "peep shows" featured kinescopes of women flirting and disrobing. Radio and television were tightly regulated for sexual content, but both the videocassette format and the new Internet commerce have depended heavily on sex as a source of profit. Blockbuster and other video outlets have, in fact, seriously undermined the older forms of sexual entertainment in vice districts, the peep shows and triple X theaters; what had once been largely a male viewing habit and male-defined product has changed dramatically with the striking numbers of women renting X-rated videos. In the early years of Internet commerce, high-tech smut peddlers have profited the most in this new medium of communication and entertainment.[29]

Until the last twenty-five years pornography was an illicit enterprise, and its history is still largely uncharted. These businesses were run by entrepreneurs who did not want their activities documented. What we do know comes largely from the traces of smut peddlers, lowlife printers, nude-model photographers, and others appearing in trial records and government-led crackdowns. The legal repression of obscenity, such as the Comstock Act, was fundamentally a restraint on trade, and pornographers fought to preserve their businesses, not just their speech rights. Occasionally these firms did leave records, and one, at least, suggests the complex network of under- and aboveground transactions. H. Lynn Womack, a mail-order publisher of gay pornography, had contacts in photography studios, in the armed forces, and in the gay community who sent him snapshots and portraits of young men, either fully clothed or in briefs or bathing suits. From these he selected the images that best fit the appearance requirements of his publications—and he commented on them: the bodybuilder, a winsome "chicken," a "well-hung" model.[30] In this way, Womack actively constructed masculine beauty directed to the gay male market.

Since the 1950s, ideals of beauty have helped the pornography business redefine the line between licit and illicit, between "smut" and "adult entertainment." *Playboy* pioneered the way by calling itself a "men's magazine," with fiction, advice columns, and interviews, as well as naked women. The Playmate blurred the boundary between sex queen and girl-next-door. The magazine's photographers drew upon pictorial conventions from fashion photography and "pinup" posing. Airbrushing, makeup, and lighting perfected the beauty of the female image; layout further domesticated the sexualized image by juxtaposing the Playmate's naked body, personal biography, "everyday" snapshots, and portrait. The magazine's imagery was more similar to the style of the Miss America beauty pageant than to underground X-rated photographs. As courts chipped away the obscenity standard and many Americans embraced the "sexual revolution," the adult entertainment industry was born. This industry used familiar business strategies of legitimation: it started trade journals and associations, rationalized distribution and marketing, used genre narratives and visual conventions, and differentiated beauty ideals to appeal to different consumer tastes.[31]

Beauty, fashion, and style are threaded through the history of American business as products for sale, as systems of representations, and as categories of taste and discrimination. The implications of beauty in business are complex and contradictory: beauty images simultaneously promise and withhold, elevate and degrade. They are sanitized and sexualized, aspirational and arousing. Beauty has advanced modern business at many levels. It represents and projects corporate identities. It has opened entrepreneurial opportunities for women, even as it fosters the exploitation of women's bodies. Indeed, it has ignited the commercial potential of information and entertainment businesses.

Nor is this only an American story: the face of global capitalism is not so much streaked with sweat as carefully made up. The fall of the Soviet Union, for example, led to the resurgence of commercial beauty culture among Russian women, many of whom embraced a self-consciously feminine beauty image that departed from the communist ideal. In China, India, and even Amazon rain forests, women sell Avon, Mary Kay, and other beauty products; as was the case a hundred years ago in the United States, these "microbusinesses" have given some women a foothold in the developing market economy.[32] Selling, marketing, and projecting beauty have become more important to the workings of a global, media-oriented economy. Commerce, in turn, links goods, looks, status, and identity to influence how cultures define the norms of appearance for women and men. Beauty and business may seem to exist in different domains but, as the new scholarship shows, their relationship grows ever closer and more significant.

ACKNOWLEDGMENTS

I thank Sally Clarke and Peter Agree for their comments on an earlier version of this essay. Discussions with Philip Scranton, Roger Horowitz, Will Hausman, and the participants of the Hagley Conference on Beauty and Business (March 1999) aided my thinking on this subject.

NOTES

1. Kenneth Lipartito, "Culture and the Practice of Business History," *Business and Economic History* 24 (Winter 1995): 1–41; "The Future of Business History" special issue, *Business and Economic History* 26 (Fall 1997); "Gender and Business History" symposium, *Business History Review* 72 (Summer 1998): 185–249.

2. See, e.g., Susan Bordo, *Unbearable Weight: Feminism, Western Culture, and the Body* (Berkeley, CA: University of California Press, 1993); Dean MacCannell and Juliet Flower MacCannell, "The Beauty System," in *The Ideology of Conduct*, ed. Nancy Armstrong and Leonard Tennenhouse (New York: Methuen, 1987), 206–238. For a popular version, see Naomi Wolf, *The Beauty Myth* (New York: Anchor Books, 1991).

3. For a brief description of the aesthetic tradition, see Peggy Zeglin Brand and Carolyn Korsmeyer, eds., *Feminism and Tradition in Aesthetics* (University Park, PA: Penn State University Press, 1995), 1–22. A foundational text is Immanuel Kant, *The Critique of Aesthetic Judgement* (Oxford: Oxford University Press, 1952). On nineteenth-century beauty ideals, see Lois Banner, *American Beauty* (Chicago: University of Chicago Press, 1984); Karen Halttunen, *Confidence Men and Painted Women: A Study of Middle-Class Culture in America, 1830-1870* (New Haven, CN: Yale University Press, 1982).

4. Brand and Korsmeyer, eds., *Feminism and Tradition in Aesthetics*; George E. Marcus and Fred R. Myers, "The Traffic in Art and Culture: An Introduction," in their anthology, *The Traffic in Culture: Refiguring Art and Anthropology* (Berkeley, CA: University of California Press, 1995), 1-51. For an excellent study of vernacular aesthetics, see Judith Goldstein, "The Female Aesthetic Community," in Marcus and Myers, eds., *Traffic in Culture*, 310–329.

5. For the sociobiological perspective, see Nancy Etcoff, *Survival of the Prettiest: The Science of Beauty* (New York: Doubleday, 1999).

6. Susanne Langer, *Feeling and Form: A Theory of Art* (New York: Scribner, 1953). For a feminist psychoanalytical perspective, see Griselda Pollack, "Woman as Sign: Psychoanalytic Readings," in her *Vision and Difference: Femininity, Feminism, and the Histories of Art* (London: Routledge, 1988), 120–154.

7. On art markets, see Marcus and Myers, eds., *Traffic in Culture*; Edward Goldberg, *After Vasari : History, Art, and Patronage in Late Medici Florence* (Princeton, NJ: Princeton University Press, 1988); Paul DiMaggio, "Cultural Entrepreneurship in Nineteenth-Century Boston: The Creation of an Organizational Base for High Culture in America," *Media, Culture and Society* 4 (1982): 33–50; Judith A. Barter, "The New Medici : The Rise of Corporate Collecting and Uses of Contemporary Art, 1925-1970," Ph.D. diss., University of Massachusetts, 1991. On tourism, Dona Brown, *Inventing New England:*

Regional Tourism in the Nineteenth Century (Washington, DC: Smithsonian, 1995); Karen Dubinsky, The Second Greatest Disappointment: Honeymooning and Tourism at Niagara Falls (New Brunswick, NJ: Rutgers University Press, 1999).

8. On beauty and the market in women, see Harriet A. Jacobs, Incidents in the Life of a Slave Girl ed. Jean Yellin (Cambridge, MA: Harvard University Press, 1987), 11; Timothy J. Gilfoyle, City of Eros: New York City, Prostitution, and the Commercialization of Sex, 1720-1920 (New York: W. W. Norton, 1992); Emma Goldman, "The Traffic in Women" and "Marriage and Love," in The Traffic in Women and Other Essays on Feminism, ed. Alix Shulman (New York: Feminist Press, 1971).

9. On nineteenth-century fashion, see Halttunen, Confidence Men and Painted Women, 56–91; Banner, American Beauty, 17–27, 45–65. On the clothing industry in the United States, see Claudia B. Kidwell and Margaret C. Christman, Suiting Everyone: The Democratization of Clothing in America (Washington, DC: Smithsonian, 1974); on France, Philippe Perrot, Fashioning the Bourgeoisie: A History of Clothing in the Nineteenth Century (Princeton, NJ: Princeton University Press, 1994). On fashion as a symbolic process, see Roland Barthes, The Fashion System (1967; Berkeley, CA: University of California Press, 1990); Gilles Lipovetsky, The Empire of Fashion: Dressing Modern Democracy (Princeton, NJ: Princeton University Press, 1994).

10. Banner, American Beauty, 28–44; Kathy Peiss, Hope in a Jar: The Making of America's Beauty Culture (New York: Metropolitan Books, 1998), 9–36.

11. This discussion of genre conventions is informed by the work of Janice Radway, Reading the Romance: Women, Patriarchy, and Popular Literature (Chapel Hill, NC: University of North Carolina Press, 1984). For an example of this literature, see Caroline Lee Hentz, "The Fatal Cosmetic," Godey's Lady's Book 18 (June 1839): 265–279.

12. Wendy Gamber, The Female Economy: The Millinery and Dressmaking Trades, 1860–1930 (Urbana, IL: University of Illinois Press, 1997).

13. The following discussion relies on my book, Hope in a Jar, chapter 3.

14. On Avon, see Katina L. Manko, "'Now You Are In Business for Yourself': The Independent Contractors of the California Perfume Company, 1886–1938," Business and Economic History 26 (1997): 5–26. On the politics of African-American hair salons, see Tiffany Melissa Gill, "'I Had My Own Business. . . So I Didn't Have to Worry': Beauty Salons, Beauty Culturists, and the Politics of African-American Female Entrepreneurship," in this volume.

15. On the systematic sale of style, see William Leach, Land of Desire: Merchants, Power, and the Rise of a New American Culture (New York: Pantheon, 1993); Peiss, Hope in a Jar, 122–133. On tie-ins, Charles Eckert, "The Carole Lombard in Macy's Window," in Fabrications: Costume and the Female Body, ed. Jane Gaines and Charlotte Herzog (New York: Routledge, 1990), 100–121; Charlotte Herzog, "'Powder Puff' Promotion: The Fashion Show-in-the-Film," in Ibid., 134–159.

16. Sarah Elvins, "Selling Hinterland Style: Fashion Retailing in Upstate New York, 1920–1940," paper presented at the Hagley Museum and Library Spring Conference on Beauty and Business, March 26-27, 1999.

17. Julie Ann Willett, "Making Waves: Race, Gender, and the Hairdressing Industry in the Twentieth Century," Ph.D. diss., University of Missouri, Columbia, 1996; Susannah Walker, "Black is Profitable: The Commodification of the Afro, 1960–1975," in this volume.

18. Peiss, Hope in a Jar, 262–263; Cover Girl Make-Up Advertising Collection, 1959–1990, Archives Center, National Museum of American History, Smithsonian Institution, Washington, DC; see especially interviews with L. C. "Bates" Hall, George Poris, Malcolm MacDougall, and Peter Troup.

19. For one example, among many, see Ernest Elmo Calkins, "Beauty the New Business Tool," Atlantic (August 1927).

20. J. A. Countway to Stanley Resor, January 27, 1925, Client Files, Lever Brothers, Sidney Bernstein Papers, J. Walter Thompson Advertising Collection, Duke University, Durham, N.C.

21. Roy W. Johnson, "Copy Strategy Sells Face Powder to Flappers and Anti-Flappers," Printers' Ink 120 (September 28, 1922): 89; Peiss, Hope in a Jar, 215.

22. See William Hogarth, The Analysis of Beauty, ed. Ronald Paulson (New Haven, CT: Yale University Press, 1997); Zip depilatory pamphlet, n.d., in author's possession.

23. Jeffrey Meikle, Twentieth Century Limited: Industrial Design in America, 1925–1939 (Philadelphia: Temple University Press, 1979); Leach, Land of Desire. On the business and cultural problems packaging and design posed for manufacturers, see Glenn Porter, "Cultural

Forces and Commercial Constraints: Designing Packaging in the Twentieth-Century United States," *Journal of Design History* 12 (1999): 25–45.

24. Georgia Panter Nielsen, *From Sky Girl to Flight Attendant: Women and the Making of a Union* (Ithaca, NY: ILR Press, 1982), 10, 98–101; see also Dorothy Sue Cobble, *Dishing It Out: Waitresses and their Unions in the Twentieth Century* (Urbana, IL: University of Illinois Press, 1991). On African-American women and discrimination cases based on appearance, see Paulette M. Caldwell, "A Hair Piece: Perspectives on the Intersection of Race and Gender," *Duke Law Journal* (April 1991): 365–396. Griffith quote from *Working Girl* (Mike Nichols, director; Twentieth Century Fox, 1988).

25. Kevin Reilly, "Corporate Stories: Fortune Magazine and the Making of Managerial Culture," Ph.D. diss., University of Massachusetts, in progress. On the connections between the post–World War II economy, politics, and aesthetics, see Jackson Lears, "A Matter of Taste: Corporate Cultural Hegemony in a Mass-Consumption Society," in his *Recasting America: Culture and Politics in the Age of Cold War* (Chicago: University of Chicago Press, 1989), 38–57.

26. For an excellent discussion, see Neil Harris, "Designs on Demand: Art and the Modern Corporation," in his *Cultural Excursions: Marketing Appetites and Cultural Tastes in Modern America* (Chicago: University of Chicago Press, 1990), 349–378. See also Parke-Bernet Galleries, *Modern Drawings and Watercolors: The Collection of Helena Rubinstein* (New York: Parke-Bernet, 1966); Barter, "The New Medici"; Serge Guilbaut, *How New York Stole the Idea of Modern Art: Abstract Expressionism, Freedom, and the Cold War* (Chicago: University of Chicago Press, 1983).

27. On the history of pornography, see Lynn Hunt, ed., *The Invention of Pornography: Obscenity and the Origins of Modernity, 1500-1800* (New York: Zone Books, 1993); Walter Kendrick, *The Secret Museum: Pornography in Modern Culture* (New York: Penguin, 1988); Linda Williams, *Hard Core: Power, Pleasure and the "Frenzy of the Visible"* (Berkeley, CA: University of California Press, 1989).

28. On photography, Abigail Solomon-Godeau, "The Legs of the Countess," *October* 39 (Winter 1986). On sexualized women, display, and spectacle, see Robert Allen, *Horrible Prettiness: Burlesque and American Culture* (Chapel Hill, NC: University of North Carolina Press, 1991); Lois Banner, *American Beauty*, 120–127.

29. Charles Musser, *The Emergence of Cinema: The American Screen to 1907* (New York: Scribners, 1990). Jonathan Coopersmith, "Pornography, Technology, and Progress," *Icon* 4 (1998): 94–125; Nick Ravo, "A Fact of Life: Sex-Video Rentals," *New York Times* (May 16, 1990): C1.

30. See H. Lynn Womack Papers, Human Sexuality Collection, Division of Rare and Manuscript Collections, Kroch Library, Cornell University.

31. On *Playboy*, see Barbara Ehrenreich, *The Hearts of Men* (Garden City, NY, 1983); Joanne Meyerowitz, "Women, Cheesecake, and Borderline Material: Responses to Girlie Pictures in the Mid-Twentieth-Century U.S.," *Journal of Women's History* 8 (1996): 9–35. On *Esquire*'s related, early effort to define male consumers in part through aesthetic categories, see Kenon Breazeale, "In Spite of Women: *Esquire* Magazine and the Construction of the Male Consumer," *Signs* 20 (1994): 1–22.

32. On global beauty culture, see Colleen Ballerino Cohen, et al., eds., *Beauty Queens on the Global Stage: Gender, Contests, and Power* (New York: Routledge, 1996); Sarah Banet-Weiser, *The Most Beautiful Girl in the World: Beauty Pageants and National Identity* (Berkeley, CA: University of California Press, 1999). On the global sale of cosmetics, see Gabrielle Glaser, "In Poland, Studying the Fine Art of Chic," *New York Times* (September 11, 1991): C9; Nicholas Kristof, "Let a Thousand Lipsticks Bloom," *New York Times*, May 3 1992): Section 9, 2; Ron Harris, "Avon Ladies Find Success in Jungles of Brazil," *Springfield Union-News* (September 6, 1994); Alessandra Stanley, "New Face of Russian Capitalism: Avon and Mary Kay Create New Opportunities for Women," *New York Times* (August 14, 1996): D1.

Part 1

IMAGES AND REFORMS

"Any Desired Length"

NEGOTIATING GENDER THROUGH SPORTS CLOTHING, 1870–1925

SARAH A. GORDON

At the age of 53, Frances Willard, leader of the Women's Christian Temperance Union, learned to ride a bicycle. When she rode her two-wheeler—which she named Gladys—she wore a tweed suit with the skirt three inches from the ground, and walking shoes. In her book, *How I Learned to Ride the Bicycle,* published in 1895, Willard critiqued women who claimed their conventional dress was comfortable, and wrote that: "reason will gain upon precedent, and ere long the comfortable, sensible, and artistic wardrobe of the rider will make the conventional style of woman's dress absurd to the eye and unendurable to the understanding."[1]

Toward the end of the nineteenth century, at a time when definitions of femininity were being challenged from many different directions, women, together with an emerging industry, invented, debated, criticized, and celebrated an entirely new category of women's clothing. The physicality of newly popular sports demanded a genre of costume that would challenge prevailing ideas of decorum and women's fragility. Through the process of inventing and adapting clothing to suit new activities, both women and the fashion industry helped to produce a new conception of what it meant to be feminine.

This essay will explore the role of invention and negotiation in the development of a new category of clothing. It argues that the novelty and marginality of clothing for sports provided a space in which women contested notions of "feminine" and "appropriate" bodies, behavior, and appearances. Using sources such as sewing patterns, surviving garments, magazine articles, and advertisements, I will suggest that an interactive relationship between producers and consumers emerged in which the choices women made helped reinvent turn-of-the-century femininity.

The cultural climate of the late nineteenth and early twentieth centuries heightened awareness of changing gender ideals. One aspect of this climate was a growing acceptance of women's participation in athletics and physical culture and a gradual rethinking of the meanings attached to the female body and womanhood. A new understanding of health and leisure, while tempered with caution, informed ideas of proper female behavior. Middle-class observers—the cultural rule-makers—now accepted women at beaches, in single-sex gymnasiums, on the recently invented bicycle, playing tennis, golf, fencing, and walking in the woods. Though once discouraged, girls now were encouraged to be "athletic" and seized opportunities to play and exercise at schools, playgrounds, and settlement houses. This new physical culture infused and informed the emerging concept of the "New Woman."[2]

Athletics and leisure challenged ideas of gentility and female delicacy as they offered new arenas for women to find personal satisfaction. Moreover, while affluent and middle-class women had the most time for sports, this athleticism was accessible to working-class women as well. As these new activities redefined notions of propriety, some of the distinctions between white, middle class women and the working women against whom they had defined their respectability were challenged.

Many women found that their clothing did not accommodate these new activities, and so embraced a series of innovations that defined a new form of clothing that was appropriate yet practical.[3] Unlike the dress reform movement, marginalized since its beginnings in the 1840s and 1850s, clothing for sports engaged a wide variety of women in a discussion about their relationship with their garments. At a time when mainstream women rarely challenged fashion's dictates, the novelty of sports offered an opportunity to rethink women's clothing. Meanwhile, the idea that the clothes were only for play made them less of a threat to anyone who perceived them as challenging traditional women's styles. Embodied in the new activities and the clothing worn for them was a new but problematic concept of femininity, one that did not hide but instead celebrated women's bodies and opened new arenas for women's participation in public life. As women considered what *they* thought was appropriate, useful, and comfortable, as they read magazines describing the clothing, as they chose patterns and sewed garments, and as they wore the garments to participate in new leisure activities, they both questioned and embraced inherited ideas of what it meant to be female.

A variety of businesses engaged in this debate. Magazine articles asked what made a good sports outfit, offered a variety of options, and acknowledged the sometimes conflicting issues of comfort, aesthetics, and modesty. Ready-to-wear catalogs insisted *their* bathing suits wouldn't *dare* cling. Advertisers played with language and imagery that associated their clothing with women's liberation. Meanwhile, pattern makers sold patterns designed to be interpreted in different ways, allowing readers to create their own definitions of what was appropriate and feminine.

All forms of women's clothing reflected cultural shifts and tensions as middle-class women moved from domestic to more public roles. Yet sports clothing is especially interesting because of its close relationship with changing ideas of the female body as well as with women's participation in leisure activity that undercut prevailing domestic norms. Clothing for sports functioned as a middle ground between the "New Woman," who was economically independent, physically active, and sexually autonomous, and older ideals of femininity.

The rules for "acceptable" clothing for sports changed over time, until a relatively uniform idea of sports clothing emerged in the 1920s. With this near-consensus came both the most revealing sports and mainstream clothing ever worn in America—along with a very different concept of femininity. The ideological shift from "Victorian" to "modern" cultural values included a rethinking of the outward manifestations of gender. Perhaps sports clothing actually caused this larger change, as some historians have proposed, but I do not seek to establish causality.[4] What I will argue is that clothing for sports offers a unique way to understand this cultural transformation. Clothing for bicycling, swimming, walking, and gymnastics provided a space where women actively contested and rethought femininity.

Because I am interested largely in the *process* of fashioning this new way of thinking, the actual design, feel, and construction of garments are as important to the story as are the magazines that discussed and promoted them. Moreover, the means by which women interpreted styles can be understood as participation in this renegotiation of gender. Did women sew or purchase the items they read about? Did they make modifications? How did the construction and material of the garments affect how they were received? In time, how did the move to ready-made garments change this process?

This era's mainstream fashionable clothing provides the context for understanding the turn-of-the-century discussion over clothing for sports. Women's clothing in the late nineteenth century was hardly conducive to even the gentlest of physical activity. The popular silhouette of the 1870s and 1880s included floor-length skirts worn over petticoats or hoops, often drawn tightly across the front and gathered in the back in a bustle that emphasized a woman's curves. Collars were high and sleeves were long and tight. Women wore boned corsets that emphasized their breasts and hips. By the 1890s, shoulders swelled with the giant poufs of "leg-of-mutton" sleeves, and while skirts lost bustles they remained long. Depending on their occupation, working women were less likely to wear tight corsets or heels when on the job, but as historians Kathy Peiss, Elizabeth Ewen, and Nan Enstad have suggested, many went to great effort and expense to buy or sew fashionable styles.[5]

Clothes were the insignia of women's respectability. Women were supposed to be delicate, curvy, and soft—and hidden by yards of fabric. One reason middle-class observers often portrayed poorer women, both white and African-American, as morally slack was because their finances did not allow for suitable clothing.[6] Moreover, physical labor did not always allow women to wear corsets, which to some implied a certain laxness or even easier sexual access.[7] For those who could afford more than a few outfits, complex rules governed what was to be worn when and where. Modesty was paramount. Most middle-class women would rarely expose even their arms, at least during the daytime, and it was considered rather shocking to show an ankle. Pants were associated with dress reformers, children, laborers, and even prostitutes.

Women rarely questioned these designs and expectations. Those who did were often dress reformers or proponents of "rational" dress, whom mainstream writers considered marginal, even radical. Reformers criticized tight corsets and long skirts, which they saw as restrictive, dangerous, and unsanitary, citing examples of women tripping over skirts, going up in flames, and sweeping street debris into their homes. The dress reform movement, spearheaded by Amelia Bloomer in the mid-nineteenth century, was associated with the Women's Rights movement; early feminists sometimes wore the "Bloomer costume" of long, full pants and a knee- or calf-length skirt. Often ridiculed, reform clothing represented a threat to gender distinctions held by both men and women.[8] Cartoons lampooned "Bloomer girls," showing a woman in bloomers involved in masculine work, while her husband, emasculated, wore a dress and cared for children or cooked. Elizabeth Stuart Phelps, a dress reformer and novelist in the 1870s, acknowledged how women felt threatened by suggestions for change, seeing in reform dress an erosion of respectability and gender distinction. She wrote that: "[t]hrough your vaguest suggestion as to the healthful-ness of shoulder-straps, she sees herself walking up the aisle at church in the scantest of bloomers, and a stovepipe hat."[9] With notions of gender so deeply embedded in clothing, changes in styles portended changes in the social structure.

The emerging interest in physical culture proved a serious threat to a fragile gender structure, not only because of the physicality and mobility of new sports but also due to the form of new clothing styles.

The popularity of sports in the late ninteenth century grew from a long history. Trips to the seaside and hot springs, footraces, and riding and walking for pleasure had been popular among colonists (and then Americans) since the eighteenth century, as they were in England and Europe. More organized and "scientific" activity arrived, in the form of games with strict rules or timed races, with the Industrial Revolution and urbanization. German and Swedish immigrants brought with them gymnastics methods and established men's exercise clubs. "Mixed" or coed bathing became acceptable in the 1840s and 1850s, as resort areas such as Cape May and Newport became vacation destinations; and bathing was, as one historian describes, "transformed from a medicinal treatment to a pleasurable pursuit."[10]

However, as sports became increasingly accepted, women were often excluded due to "separate sphere" gender ideals. Whereas middle-class masculinity was predicated largely on being socially dominant and competitive, middle-class femininity became defined by domesticity.[11] These social ideals informed physical ones; what Lois Banner calls the "Steel Engraving Lady" ideal—with her "delicate constitution," pale skin, birdlike bones, sloping shoulders, and narrow waist—embodied Victorian femininity.[12] Some also thought sports threatened (middle-class) women's reproductive functions. Doctors warned of collapsed uteri or other "female complaints," advising that too much activity, physical or mental, would sap women of their limited supply of vitality.[13] Moreover, propriety demanded that women not expose their bodies, even their ankles. Thus up to the 1860s or so, women's "respectable" sports and exercise could find an outlet only in croquet, archery, or calisthenics. Even seaside bathing, rarely strenuous in the first place, required elaborate "bathing machines" in which elite women would change clothing and be transported to the water.

Even as sports and "physical culture" for women became increasingly accepted, they remained problematic. Although some experts encouraged women to exercise, others warned of its dangers. Well into the twentieth century, magazine articles that praised healthy "modern girls" would in the same breath ask "Are athletics a menace to motherhood?" Too much exercise, especially unsupervised, could threaten a girl's future health and fertility; the "free out-of-door life, so priceless when properly conducted, may prove to be the path to pain and weakness, if not to permanent invalidism."[14]

At the very least, writers argued, too much sports could leave women with masculinized bodies. Contemporary fiction and magazine articles indicated a fear that sports would masculinize women, either in specific physical ways or by means of subtle behavioral changes. In Edith Wharton's *The Age of Innocence,* set in the 1870s, a society matron complains that a younger woman's hand is large (and by implication,

Sarah A. Gordon

masculine) due to "these modern sports that spread the joints."[15] Either in self-defense or because they had invested in the same values, exercise proponents eagerly assured readers that athletic women would not develop hard muscles or other "masculine" traits. An 1890 article promoting fencing warned against the dangers of too much tennis, claiming that among tennis aficionados: "big, knotty biceps are found to have become all too prominent in a white, rounded arm, and gloves for the left hand refuse to fit over the broadened palm."[16] Another article glowingly praised a new women's health club but quickly assured readers that the club's gymnastics instructor was "not at all the typical athlete, with specimen biceps and iron integuments, according to the popular notion, but a thoroughly womanly and refined personality," thereby implying that she would teach with moderation and not threaten the femininity of her pupils.[17]

Yet the concern for women's health could also serve as an argument for greater acceptance of women's participation in sports. In 1850 the *Massachusetts Teacher* warned that girls would not be "fit" mothers if they did not exercise.[18] Proponents of calisthenics such as Catharine Beecher claimed that exercises such as gentle stretches and push-ups against a table would render women healthier for childbirth and housework. Etiquette books proposed that mild exercise was good for women's health; one manual from the 1860s claimed that "[c]alisthenics, and the Indian sceptre, as taught on the improved scale by our present professors, are also highly beneficial as exercises," and that "ladies of every age" who participated "gained increased strength and stature, improved the state of their health, and added grace, ease, and firmness to their motions."[19] Exercise was therefore acceptable as long as it promoted health and preserved feminine qualities such as grace and posture; it might even encourage a "rosy glow" that would make young women more attractive to appropriate men.

Despite such fears, during the 1870s and 1880s, schools and colleges began to teach physical education, and seaside and mountain vacations became more affordable. By the 1890s, innovations such as the bicycle became wildly popular. A day trip to the beach was accessible to people of all income levels—contemporary articles about Coney Island described how both rich and poor enjoyed the beaches (although they did note a "descending scale of fashion" among the beach resorts)—while private gyms and colleges were more middle- and upper-class oriented.[20] Although a special outfit for a private gym was more a middle-class concern, working women who went to Coney Island also sewed, purchased, or even rented bathing suits. The ideas of femininity and respectability central to white, middle-class ideology therefore affected any woman who joined in the discussion over clothing for sports.

Sports became increasingly associated with ideas of modernity. Athletics offered new sources of personal gratification and social interaction based more on consumption and entertainment than on production and traditional class and family ties. Charles Dana Gibson, illustrator of the famous "Gibson girl" images that epitomized for many Americans the "New Woman" and who in his illustrations often critiqued Victorian control of women, frequently portrayed women involved in sports. The "New Woman" had become heavily intertwined with the new physical culture.

As sports and leisure became increasingly common, women began to ask what could be worn to preserve modesty and femininity, yet allow for ease of movement and comfort. While mainstream clothing changed slowly, clothing for sports, in its specificity and novelty, was open for debate. Moreover, given its marginality, it was considerably less threatening. Starting around the 1870s and accelerating through the turn of the century, cultural vehicles such as magazines and etiquette books recognized that sports required a rethinking of clothing design. Articles in mainstream publications asked what women should wear for specific activities (an extension of what affluent women had already done for decades with their morning, afternoon, and evening dresses, for example), and fashion magazines offered suggestions and images. Meanwhile, schools and clubs proposed their own uniforms, and etiquette writers, dress reformers, fiction writers, and sports enthusiasts joined the discussion.

While magazines are often perceived as vehicles for prescriptive information, they can also serve as an arena to discuss cultural change. From general-interest magazines such as *Scribner's Monthly* to "women's" magazines such as *Ladies' Home Journal* to the topic-specific *Outing*, magazines presented an important dimension of a larger discourse about the future of American culture, health, femininity, and representation.[21] On a more practical level, at a time when many women still made much of their own clothing or paid a seamstress to make it for them, magazines and paper pattern designers offered patterns and instructions for new styles. When more clothing became available ready-made, retailers advertised endless permutations of gymnasium and bicycling clothing, and catalogs sold more models of bathing suits as the years went on. These magazines therefore both raised the question of what was appropriate, and suggested how to make and wear these new and alien garments. Still, because of the garments' novelty, there was no *one* way to think of them. Through a process of discussion and direction, the magazines helped form a new understanding of women's clothing.

Some articles raised the issue of how the new styles were improvements upon older garments. Others asked outright how to fashion new

Sarah A. Gordon

clothing for new activities. Materials from colleges and private clubs demonstrated that women had to learn what a "gymnasium costume" or a "bathing costume" actually was, and how to make it. Advertisers, primarily of bicycle clothing, not only proposed numerous possibilities but justified clothing appropriate to the activity. Sports clothing was so unfamiliar that it warranted repeated questioning, discussion, and explanation.

One of the earliest American fashion magazines, *Godey's Lady's Book*, printed an article in 1871 entitled "Ladies' Bathing Dresses" which addressed the "great reforms" made recently in the dress worn for bathing. These developments came just in time, apparently, since "great reform was needed—for the preservation of modesty as well as of health and comfort." Previously, women would wear a long chemise or simple dress, which had the nasty habit of both clinging to the legs and ballooning around the bather like a giant jellyfish; indeed, "swimming in such a garment was very nearly something miraculous."[22] The new costume, which consisted of a combination of trousers and a tunic or dress, offered both modesty and mobility.

The picture in *Godey's* showed varying lengths of sleeves, pants, and skirt. The bathing dress design was so novel that few rules had been made as to the exact coverage required. Individuals could negotiate their own version of "appropriateness" when they sewed their new costume; in fact, the author commented that "there are a good many different ways and fashions for making these" and explained that women of different ages and sizes might want to adapt their suits to their particular bodies and taste.[23]

The *Godey's* article is intriguing, but how did women respond? One way to approach this question is to use surviving garments as evidence about how actual people behaved. Real clothes are problematic, since most items that survive to enter a museum collection were those of middle- and upper-class people; poorer people usually reused their clothes until they disintegrated or were torn up for rags. Nonetheless, working with a garment opens up new questions and possibilities. Fabric and construction affected how people moved, how they thought about their clothing, and how they interacted with others. Surviving garments offer invaluable insights for gauging the choices women made and how they responded to the advertisements, articles, and patterns they read.

A bathing costume in the collection of the Metropolitan Museum of Art bears a striking resemblance to those in the *Godey's* illustrations. Dated by the museum as 1870–1873, this black-and-white-striped wool garment consists of a calf-length dress with long, full sleeves and ankle-length bloomers.[24] The costume, most likely made at home on a sewing machine, is somewhat more conservative than those illustrated in the

Figure 2.1. Surviving garments provide clues as to how people responded to a magazine's suggestions. This bathing costume from the 1870s is a conservative version of a design suggested in *Godey's Lady's Book and Magazine* in 1871. Bathing costume, American, ca. 1870–1873, Metropolitan Museum of Art, gift of the New-York Historical Society (1979.346.18ab), photograph by the author.

magazine, perhaps suggesting the wearer's taste.[25] Evidently, someone, somewhere, read *Godey's* or a similar journal and chose to make and wear such a garment. She must have really wanted to swim, or at least wear a stylish costume at the beach, since the wool would have been hot, heavy, and itchy. (See Figure 2.1)

That the feel of the fabrics and construction of the garments were not always as comfortable as one might hope suggests another reason for wearing such clothing—that of display. It is quite possible that women not only sought amusement and exercise but saw in sports a new way of displaying their bodies. In making and wearing her striped bathing costume, our imagined woman announced her ability to participate in a newly fashionable leisure activity, with all of its cultural and class implications. Swimming cut across ethnic and class boundaries while unifying participants in a leisure culture. Swimming, and sports in general, were not only entertaining or healthy but also a way to participate in a modernizing process. They were, in a sense, a statement about joining a social movement.

Clothing for calisthenics and the new "Swedish gymnastics" also embodied this process of innovation and reception. Early calisthenics manuals show women in ordinary clothing, but later a specific "gymnasium costume" was invented. Women students wore the earliest gym suits at colleges and schools that issued instructions for making a suit. In 1883, the gymnastics instructor at Mt. Holyoke issued written directions for a suitable "Gymnastic Dress" (which consisted of a dress worn over bloomers) complete with how long it should be (7 inches from the floor). The designs for such suits were hardly uniform; some specified a dress with separate bloomers, some attached bloomers to a blouse with a separate skirt, and some required no skirt at all. Many years later, in 1908, Mt. Holyoke was still offering detailed instructions, by then for a suit with a divided skirt, including the exact dimensions of the split and the crotch; the seamstress was to first make the more familiar skirt and then sew it into two gusseted legs.[26]

By the 1870s and 1880s, instead of copying a very schematic pattern from a magazine, readers could purchase inexpensive but complex tissue patterns through the mail.[27] These patterns were unlike their predecessors in that they were produced in specific sizes and contained detailed instructions with perforations, fold lines, and numbers. One of the early and most successful pattern companies, E. Butterick Co., promoted itself as offering up-to-date and easily followed styles. Butterick sold its patterns through the magazine the *Delineator*, which began in 1872 as a simple vehicle for selling patterns but became a more general magazine with articles on subjects such as homemaking, women's clubs, and girls' activities in addition to offering dress patterns.

The *Delineator* followed a specific format in which the suggested use of the garment was followed by a careful description of its design. The patterns specified yardage, suggested what types of cloth and trim to use, sometimes recommended colors, and showed an illustration of the front and back of the finished garment. The reader would then write to Butterick requesting a pattern by number and size and enclosing payment. Many women may have ordered the patterns to be sewn by a dressmaker—and the Butterick archives contain letters from aristocratic Europeans who surely didn't do their own sewing—but most women ordering the patterns probably made the garments themselves.[28]

In addition to everyday styles such as skirts, blouses, coats, and undergarments, the *Delineator* marketed patterns for sports clothing. Patterns for gymnasium suits, walking and biking skirts, and knickers to wear under skirts for "all outdoor sports" were frequent offerings.[29]

It was, after all, Butterick's business to sell patterns, and the novel sports clothing styles provided a new product line. Butterick thus understandably promoted sports and sports clothing as desirable. An entire spread on "New Styles for Bicycling," for example, introduced one outfit as "a new three-piece cycling skirt . . . combined with a perfectly adjusted jacket in a most pleasing and up-to-date cycling costume that is equally appropriate for golfing and general outing wear."[30] The magazine, and the pattern company behind it, sought to convince women that such clothes and activities were socially acceptable.

While the very nature of sewing with a pattern makes for a certain degree of conformity, the patterns described in the *Delineator* allowed for a great deal of personal interpretation. Each pattern offered numerous options to the reader. For example, number 1727, for a "Ladies' Gymnastic Costume," could be made "high-necked with a standing collar or open-necked with a sailor collar and with elbow or full-length sleeves." A "practical and becoming gymnastic costume," it was shown in "navy-blue serge and trimmed with black braid" but could be made in numerous other combinations of color, trim, and fabric. No matter what fabric and style the reader chose, Butterick promised it would be "exceedingly comfortable for wear while engaged in gymnastic exercises."[31] (See Figure 2.2)

This language of options and interpretation carried over into the physical pattern. A paper pattern for a costume very similar to the one described above (it is in fact intended for use as a bathing costume but strongly resembles the gymnastics costumes) came with eleven separate pieces of printed tissue paper with which the sewer could cut out the top and attached bloomers, short sleeves, long sleeves, scoop and V necks, a high collar, a skirt and peplum, and a ruffled "bertha" for around the shoulders. Each piece was marked with lines and perforations so that the sewer could follow the instructions while making her own choices. The rapidly growing business of paper patterns was therefore producing specific designs that nevertheless contained a great deal of room for personal interpretation.[32]

As its reputation became established, Butterick published a series of sewing manuals that included instructions for altering patterns. Most adjustments were aimed at those whose measurements strayed from the average, but they also indicated how to make changes in styles. For example, one manual included specific instructions for a sailor-style blouse, but explained how to create variations such as a front opening "if front openings are desired, and are not provided for in the pattern."[33] Like patterns, sewing manuals suggested and even promoted changes to a particular design.

We can observe the process of personal interpretation by examining two costumes. The Metropolitan Museum of Art costume collec-

Figure 2.2. This pattern for a gymnastic costume from 1898 allowed for multiple options. Courtesy, the Butterick Company Archives, New York.

tion holds a navy wool one-piece gymnastics costume that bears a striking resemblance to the *Delineator* pattern number 1727; the person who made it chose a sailor collar and long sleeves.[34] Whoever wrote out the collections card at the Met noted the similarity and gave a reference to the magazine; it is quite possible that the costume was sewn according to the *Delineator* pattern. That suit is woolen, but women had a range of fabrics to choose from, adding another dimension to their ability to shape their own suits. A costume sewn in black silk with short sleeves and long bloomers in the collection of the Hermitage Museum in Ho-Ho-Kus, New Jersey, was fashioned with a separate skirt which hooked on to the waist.[35] It dates to a few years after the *Delineator* gymnastic suit patterns and navy wool suit, and demonstrates a different interpretation of what was appropriate for gymnasium use. While using silk makes it lighter in weight as well as cooler and not itchy, the skirt nonetheless added more layers and therefore more cloth around the legs.

Gymnastic costumes provide valuable insight into the process of invention, negotiation, and interpretation of sports clothing at this time. But gym suits were almost always worn in private, single-sex settings. In comparison, bicycling clothing, like bathing costumes, was meant to be worn in public and therefore triggered especially intense discussion. The invention of the "safety bicycle" with brakes and soft rubber wheels in the mid-1890s meant that bicycling, previously a rather macho sport, was now marketed to and acceptable for women. Moreover, unlike colleges or private clubs, the bicycle was accessible to working-class women as well, who could rent a bicycle in a park for the afternoon.

Bicycles were seen by many, including Frances Willard of the Women's Christian Temperance Union, as offering new mobility and freedom to women. Willard called her bicycle an "implement of power" and wrote that through bicycling she "found a whole philosophy of life."[36] In addition to being worn in public, the designs for bicycling clothing were also rather daring. While bathing and gym costumes included bloomers, they were often hidden under a skirt. Now some women wore bloomers or knickers in plain view without the skirt on top. The new clothing for bicycling, like the activity itself, was associated with modernity and independence.

Advertisers took advantage of these associations and used a rhetoric of liberation to sell their merchandise. Magazines teemed with advertisements for bicycles, bicycle cloth, cycling corsets, skirts, and knickerbocker suits (knickers or knickerbockers were pants that extended below the knee, were worn with stockings, and were narrower than bloomers). Not only did magazines like the *Delineator* offer numerous skirt designs, but magazines, advertisers, and bicycle proponents suggested that women could also wear knickerbockers for cycling.

Manufacturers and merchandisers explicitly connected bicycling to modernity and freedom. An advertisement for Victor bicycles in the May 1895 *Ladies' Home Journal* compared images of a woman sitting at a spinning wheel to a happy cyclist and offered the following verse: "The Spinning Wheels of days gone by / Give way to Spinning Wheels that fly. / And damsels fair do lightly tread / The graceful Victor now, instead."[37] Another advertisement claimed that "Physicians recommend bicycling. Dame Fashion says it is 'good form.'" This overruled two common objections to women's athleticism: perceived threats to feminine health and to appearance. Furthermore, the ad promoted daring costume styles when it offered a women's bike with a high bar that was "especially designed for the many ladies who prefer to wear

Sarah A. Gordon

The Spinning Wheels of days gone by
Give way to Spinning Wheels that fly.
And damsels fair do lightly tread
The graceful Victor now, instead.

Overman Wheel Co.,
Makers of Victor Bicycles.

Boston.   New York.   Chicago.   Detroit.   Denver.
Pacific Coast: San Francisco.   Los Angeles.   Portland.

Figure 2.3. Bicycle advertisements in the 1890s associated their product with liberated, modern women. Advertisement for the Overman Wheel Company, *Ladies Home Journal*, May 1895, p. 30.

knicker-bockers rather than cumbersome skirts."[38] It is possible to see these advertisements as co-opting and cheapening the language of independence and freedom, but nevertheless they promoted athleticism as a modern and liberating activity. (See Figure 2.3)

While that manufacturer appealed to women's perceived need to be fashionable and healthy as well as comfortable, a third advertiser cut to the chase. The Sterling Cycle Works company ad read: "For Bloomers: Ladies who cycle in bloomers will find The Sterling the ideal Bicycle. Very light; very strong; very easy running."[39] Women were thus identified by their choice in clothing styles, as Sterling cashed in on the association of the word *bloomers* with the dress reform movement. However, this rhetoric of liberation was still limited by traditional norms—witness an advertisement for "Cyclist and Athletic Corsets," which promised "perfect freedom."[40]

This association of sports clothing with freedom was not just a retail strategy. Dress reformers were vocal about the freedoms offered by sports or "outdoor" costume; what they had failed to popularize through their rhetoric of health and politics, sports made well known.

Willard was certain that the costume worn for bicycling would serve as the test case for dress reform ideas and finally "convince the world that has brushed aside the theories, no matter how well constructed, and the arguments, no matter how logical, of dress-reformers."[41] During the 1870s, as bloomers and related sports costumes were just becoming familiar, one writer recognized in them the key to change in dress:

> [s]omething of the nature of the American costume—the gymnasium suit, the beach suit, the Bloomer, call it what you will—must take the place of our present style of dress, before the higher life—moral, intellectual, political, social or domestic—can ever begin for women.[42]

A later reformer wrote excitedly that liberating dress was preferable to economic or political independence and influence:

> Talk about the emancipated woman! The right to earn her own living on terms of equality with man, to vie with him in work, sport or politics, to vote, to hold office, to be president as well as queen and empress, would never bring the blessed sense of freedom that an outdoor costume, sans trailing skirts and entangling folds and plus a short skirt and bloomers, gives to the average woman . . . .[43]

While many would have objected to her proposition that freedom in dress was preferable to economic or legal independence, her words make it evident how thrilling it must have been to wear such clothing. Sports clothing gave women the opportunity to experience and discuss the meaning, design, and feel of their clothing in a way previously left to political radicals. Moreover, the emerging physical culture allowed them an acceptable, if marginal, space in which to wear these styles.

Still, women felt some trepidation when it came to actually wearing pants for bicycling, so the pattern and retail companies, eager to sell the new styles, came up with alternatives. With articles such as "New Styles for Bicycling," the *Delineator* patterns offered the consumer numerous designs: skirts that had extra pleats so they acted and looked divided, divided skirts that were full enough to look undivided, and even divided skirts, such as pattern number 2044, which had an extra flap of fabric to cover the split in front. Style number 2044 was billed as a "Ladies' Divided Cycling Skirt, Having deep side-plaits at the back and the division in front concealed by lapped gores (to be worn on diamond or drop-frame wheels and to be in any desired length)" and was described as "a decidedly stylish divided cycling skirt planned on simple, graceful lines."[44] The feature that the "division" of the skirt is hidden is repeated twice in the design description, while the illustration shows it in two lengths. Evidently the pattern designers sought to reach readers who were shy about wearing a divided skirt but who were less reluctant to be seen in shorter hems.

The Museum of the City of New York has conserved a similar suit. Made of cream-colored linen, from the back the skirt worked like pants, allowing the rider to sit on the bicycle saddle; from the front it appeared to be a skirt, which looked more modest and feminine.[45] Other women wore knickers with a skirt over them; at least one manufacturer offered ready-made suits with a matching removable skirt for "stylish women everywhere"; the bicycle costume cost $7.50, the skirt, $2.50 extra.[46] Two identical examples of such a costume are in the collection at the Metropolitan Museum of Art; custom-made for two sisters, the skirts are wool while the knickerbockers are linen (perhaps they wore the warmer skirts in cooler weather?).[47] Because of their solid construction and the good condition of the skirts, it is possible that the knickerbockers were worn by themselves and the skirt put aside.

However, either because of budgets or personal taste, not everybody wore the latest look in bicycle clothing when riding. One photograph in the collection of the Hermitage Museum shows a woman, dressed in a skirt and shirtwaist, climbing onto a bike with a diamond frame (or "man's style") as a friend steadies the bike. A second photo shows her riding confidently down the field with her skirt bunched up around the crossbar, exposing her stockings and high boots.[48] The magazines don't show this slice of reality; all the women in advertisements wear knickerbockers on a high-frame bike and skirts on a drop-frame or "ladies'" model. Contemporary etiquette writers would have fainted dead away to see her expose her stockings. Nonetheless, *she* had evidently decided it was acceptable to wear what she did.

Like the bathing costumes proposed by *Godey's* in 1871, which could be made "with or without sleeves" and which were shown in various lengths, the *Delineator* patterns for bicycling skirts explicitly stated that the reader could make the skirts "in any desired length."[49] This element of consumer choice is very much in keeping with the idea that the unfamiliar realm of sports and sports clothing allowed, even required, a significant degree of improvisation. In some areas, such as in bicycle clothing, even basic designs were contested and discussed. As styles were conceived and chosen as appropriate by the media and by retailers, women could make their own suits or purchase different versions. All of these activities involved a rethinking and an invention of basic styles of clothing and their relationship to the female body.

While women were willing to show more of their bodies, they had hardly abandoned older ideas about propriety and modesty. Most were still wearing corsets, even to swim, and opaque tights. A constant theme in advertisements and articles is a sense of maintaining *correctness*. Consumers were very concerned that the garment uphold ideas about feminine modesty and attractiveness. This concern often manifested itself in terms of esthetics or decoration but also extended to the actual construction of a garment. Since many of the designs for sports involved divided skirts or bloomers, which were the most shocking, manufacturers stressed their "grace" and convenience.

This anxiety over bloomers is evident in an 1889 article from *Outing* magazine describing a women's athletic club. The female author, who was clearly enthusiastic about women's participation in sports, nevertheless demonstrated some ambivalence about the design of the club uniforms. The costume consisted of a dark-blue blouse and divided skirt or bloomers, the "severance" of which, she noted carefully, was "scarcely perceptible." After a long and detailed description of the construction of the bloomers, she decided that "the effect obtained is extremely good, granting all the necessary freedom to the legs and presenting, at the same time, a graceful and modest garment."[50] It was therefore important, even in a publication devoted to sports and in an article praising women's participation in athletics, to convince readers that both the activity and the clothing worn for it did not threaten ideals of feminine bodies or "graceful and modest" clothing.

The severity of the challenge to propriety posed by new activities was itself under debate. In addition to articles, patterns, and advertisements, fiction provided another arena for discussing the relationship of athleticism to femininity. Ellen Gruber Garvey discusses the role of fiction in popular magazines in teaching women "correct" bicycling etiquette. Most of the stories she describes involve a young woman returning to the home after a brief rebellion; such stories, she contends, "contained" the threat posed by the mobility and perceived sexual nature of the bicycle. In one such story, the girl dresses as a boy to go biking, is discovered by a suitable boyfriend, and switches to female clothing. Another describes a young woman who rebels against a too-strict father; she tells her father that "girls ride them things . . . in trousers and breeches like men." The father claims such attire isn't "commonly decent," but she rides off anyway.[51] (According to Garvey, her rebellious behavior was acceptable to readers because of the parochial attitude of the father.) In both stories there is a degree of uncertainty about what behavior and dress are acceptable.

Authors of etiquette books were more certain about the proper place for cycling clothing, and tended to promote a rather conservative view. Unlike retailers, etiquette writers were, after all, less interested in promoting new styles than with preserving customary ideas of femininity. One writer suggested having a "bicycle tea" complete with bicycle-shaped sandwiches; the party "should be given out of doors, where outing costumes would not be incongruous."[52] Another author suggested that "[i]t is the Correct Thing . . . to wear a short tailor-made skirt of cloth or other heavy material, when riding the bicycle, or playing golf"; however, "[i]t is not the Correct Thing . . . to wear a bicycle or rainy-day skirt when making a formal call."[53] Thus the guidelines for just where and when to wear clothing for sport were also a part of the debate.

In addition to their concerns about the radical nature of pants and where to wear such clothing, women did not want to reveal the contours of their bodies. This was especially true when it came to bathing costumes. Both etiquette books and retail catalogs emphasized the modest nature of the fabric out of which bathing suits were made, and some emphasized modesty over comfort or mobility. One etiquette book instructed readers that "[b]athing calls for a costume of some material that will not cling to the form when wet. Flannel is appropriate, and a heavy quantity of mohair also makes a successful dress, as it resists water and has no clinging qualities."[54] The 1908 Sears, Roebuck & Co. catalog addressed the same concern, offering three models of women's bathing suits, all with skirts, attached bloomers, and short puffy sleeves, to be worn with dark stockings, described as "very pretty" and not "clinging to the figure."[55] Despite such hopeful promises, a photograph of bathers up to their knees in the Maine surf in which the women wear suits similar to those in the Sears catalog shows that they did in fact cling.[56] It may be that this rather uncomfortable reality was a secondary concern, and that both retailers and consumers presumed that it was nonetheless necessary to use yards of wool fabric to find the right balance of modesty and practicality. (See Figure 2.4)

Other articles, and other activities, likewise balanced the issues of practicality and esthetics. An article entitled "A Costume for Lawn Tennis" in an 1881 *Lippincott's Magazine of Popular Literature & Science* highlighted this dilemma. The female author praised tennis as offering an "exciting" alternative to "staid croquet," but wrote that due to the:

> movement, the alertness, the agility, required in the game, a light, easily-fitting costume, which, above all things, will leave the feet free to run, is necessary and must be instituted, or women will finally give up lawn tennis as they have given up so many games because they could not cope with men in playing them.[57]

But despite her eagerness, the author dismissed a very practical design consisting of a tunic over pants proposed by a male friend, claiming: "there is something essentially unaesthetic in any combination of petticoats and pantaloons." Instead, she proposed a more complicated embroidered skirt and full trousers. In designing what she considered a "charming, appropriate, and modest dress" the author sacrificed some practicality for the sake of appearance.[58] In a similar vein, an article on fencing described how men's fencing attire was easily purchased but that: "for women no such convenience is known, and she must perforce tax her ingenious brain to fashion a dress that must

Figure 2.4. Their bathing suits may have clung "immodestly," but people enjoyed them anyway. Bathers at Ocean Beach, Maine, August 1906. Courtesy of private collection.

combine the three virtues of adaptability to the exercise, modesty, and—above all!—attractiveness."[59] Women were asked to invent something new, something that combined practicality with conventional ideas of feminine beauty.[60]

Articles praising women's involvement in sports reminded readers that the new activities and clothing need not compromise their delicacy. One *Delineator* article claimed that while sports "give the body perfect freedom of action and engender a courageous spirit, they detract nothing from that womanliness which is always woman's greatest charm."[61] The same piece described outfits for different sports as "trim," "graceful and comfortable," "jaunty," and "attractive." This language of esthetics can be read as a strategy to preserve symbols of femininity and reduce the threat to gender norms posed by athleticism, while encouraging readers to buy, sew, and wear such clothing.

Many patterns and garments from the 1870s to about 1915 demonstrate this need to maintain a sense of "prettiness" or traditional femininity, often following trends from mainstream styles. In doing so, the garments reconnected the wearer with the traditionally feminine (and "frivolous") world of fashion. Gym suits were trimmed with silk bows, bathing costumes, with nautical insignia. One skating sweater has the high neck and enormous leg-of-mutton shoulders stylish in the 1890s, complete with stuffing to hold the shape.[62] Some gymnasium suits had extra fullness in the bust, in the blousy "pouter pigeon" style of the early 1900s.[63] At other times, cycling, golf, and tennis styles were more "mannish," with straight ties and boater hats. Many garments were styled to resemble children's clothing. The sailor collar, a design associated with children's playsuits, is found repeatedly in both bathing and gymnasium costumes. Perhaps encouraging grown women to dress like little boys and girls was a way to reduce the threat of their changing behavior.

None of these details related to the technical function of the garment. Instead, as decoration they symbolically associated the wearer with feminine appearances and at times infantilizing styles. In the case of the men's ties, they served to contrast with the wearer's gender, reinforcing to both wearer and spectator that the activity was temporary. The costume allowed for new activity, but the design reminded the wearer of her true identity.

Around 1910 women's sports became more widely accepted; concurrent with this acceptance was a more uniform appearance of clothing and fewer "feminine" details. Articles spent less time justifying athletic behavior and describing clothing as if to newcomers; the designs had become a part of the mainstream vocabulary. Advertisers continued to use a rhetoric of modernity, leisure, and liberation, and designs became less concerned with frilly or girlish detail and more abstract and streamlined.[61]

Mainstream clothing was changing significantly as well. Arguments as to exactly why are numerous, but one view is that an orientalist esthetic, spurred by modernist costumes worn by the Ballet Russe and high-fashion designs by Paul Poiret, generated interest in bright colors, soft draping, and narrow skirts.[65] Ironically, the shorter (1 to 2 inches above the ankle) yet narrow "hobble skirt," all the rage in 1910, limited movement even more than earlier, fuller skirts.[66] Lower necklines became popular in 1913 despite denunciation by religious leaders and doctors who claimed exposing the neck was indecent and unhealthy.[67] Poiret supposedly outlawed the corset around this time as well, but most women continued to wear them, albeit in more tubular and less curvaceous models. Overall, variety was more acceptable, and women increasingly ignored traditional voices of caution and "decency."

An *Independent* editorial about the new popularity of divided "harem skirts" in 1911 commented on the process by which styles became popular: "if working girls had adopted it first it would have stood no chance of popular favor, but being taken up as a fad of the idle rich it may ultimately reach those who need it most."[68] Despite this view that fashion works "top-down," working-class women were very much a part of the greater popularity and modernizing sensibilities of sports clothing. Wage-earning women's experiences with sports in the late nineteenth century would probably have been limited to trips to Coney Island and similar resorts, rented bicycles in a park, and factory lunch-break calisthenics. These women may not have owned many specialized items of clothing, but they would have worn certain elements, especially bathing suits—as early as 1880, Coney Island had facilities to clean thousands of bathing suits a day.[69]

Working and African-American women had more recreational opportunities after the turn of the century in the form of community leagues, settlement houses, and Y.W.C.A. gymnasiums, pools, and summer camps. Susan Cahn writes that "[y]oung black and white women of small or average means for the first time found significant opportunities to engage in athletic activities, from basketball and baseball to tennis and track and field."[70] In 1901, the Brooklyn Y.W.C.A. offered gymnastics classes in addition to more practical and work-oriented courses in sewing, millinery, and cooking.[71] Classes were held at night to accommodate work schedules, and despite the fact that it lost money, the Brooklyn Y offered a free summer home for working girls. While there is no evidence as to what members wore in the Y gymnasium, the *Annual Report* includes an advertisement for a shoe store that sold the "'Regulation' Gymnasium Oxford such as used in the Y.W.C.A. Gymnasium."[72] There were therefore certain expectations for gym attire at the Y, and the activities were evidently important enough to some women to warrant a special expense.

The national Y.W.C.A. continued to offer summer camps for working women, or "industrial girls" as the Y literature called them, well into the teens. Photographs from the camps show happy-looking girls in swimsuits, bloomers, and middy blouses. One Y held what it called a "Health Pageant"; "[t]he purpose was to set forth in a symbolical [*sic*] way, right ideals about living, eating and clothing." The pageant included women representing allegorical goddesses called "Zeal, Knowledge, Good Taste, etc."; the Y.W.C.A. newsletter wrote that, of those who acted and watched:

> [m]ost of these girls are Industrial girls . . . they took keen interest in the sports, which were portrayed and in the kind of clothing which Good Taste approved for sport wear. They were enthusiastic over the sport shoes and the clothes which lent themselves to the best advantages that could be had from outdoor sport.[73]

Women could also participate in sports at the workplace; for example, turn-of-the-century department stores offered rooftop calisthenics at lunchtime, and a 1923 photograph of a women's basketball team at a textile plant in South Carolina shows them wearing matching uniforms.[74] Because they had the time for leisure and the resources to spend on special outfits, white, middle-class women were responsible for much of the redefinition of femininity due to sports and sports clothing. But working women, white and African American, were active participants. Just as their appearance and behavior had long served as a foil for the definition of middle-class respectability, the fact that they now participated in some of the same leisure activities—and dressed in some of the same styles to do so—demanded a rethinking of that respectability.

Questions of modesty continued to be a part of the discussion about sports clothing, but the boundaries of modesty shifted dramatically after World War I.[75] During the war, women wore pants in munitions factories and short-skirted nurses' uniforms in ambulance corps; one costume historian notes that "[s]ome Land Army girls abandoned their restrictive corsets, almost literally, in the field."[76] The visibility of the Suffrage movement and its success in 1919 may also have played a role. The idea of "choice, " central to the debate over sports clothing, is evident in articles concerned with mainstream fashion—for men's clothing as well as women's. Dominant paradigms of modesty in clothing were becoming unstable.[77] Charlotte Perkins Gilman, well known for her feminism and support of nontraditional lifestyles, criticized women's narrow range of choice in their dress.[78] A discussion that had previously been limited to sports clothing had now expanded to mainstream dress.

By 1916, a male author writing for *Outing* was ready to dismiss the idea of modesty altogether. He compared the relative merits of skirts, bloomers, riding breeches, and knickerbockers for walking and hiking. There was no longer any need to blush over the description of bloomers; in fact he dismissed all options except for knickerbockers, writing that "they have all the virtues and none of the vices [of other styles]. On the woman of average build they look neat and trim, mask rather than exaggerate or display the figure. . . . They are the thing to use for every reason."[79] Modesty had become a question of suitability, not of simple bodily coverage.

By the 1910s and twenties, when public discourse included notions of "modern women" who worked, were independent, and were openly sexual, clothing for sports as well as everyday fashions had changed from symbols of girlishness to streamlined, more functional styles. Bifurcated garments for sports were no longer a threat but a given, and comfort and ease of movement superseded ideas of feminine modesty. At the same time, however, women had less agency as *producers*. Now that sports clothes were considered to be "normal" and more likely to be purchased than sewn at home, personal interpretation through sewing gave way gradually in the face of increased consumer options.

Gymnasium and bathing suits reflected this changing sensibility. Gym clothing was relatively standardized by this time, with women wearing black or navy bloomers, tights, and white "middy" (sailorstyle) blouses with short or long sleeves. Photographs of a basketball team at the National Training School for Women and Girls (a school for African-American women in Washington, D.C.) in 1915 and from a Y.W.C.A. summer camp for "industrial girls" demonstrate this uniformity.[80] The young women's blouses aren't entirely uniform, which suggests that they were told what *type* to buy or make but were not given exact details. The blouses all follow a general style, some have bows or ties, some have longer or shorter sleeves, but on the whole they use less fabric and decoration than previous designs. This clothing was evidently available to working as well as middle-class women, and to African-American women as well as whites.

Likewise, bathing suits became more streamlined and revealing; having worn short sleeves by about 1905, women were wearing sleeveless suits by 1910. Advertisements in 1916 spoke of the suits as "striking" or "attractive" and said little about modesty, although they mention a "knitted underpiece" that came with the suit.[81] Two charming 1910 suits at the Hermitage Museum have dramatic white piping on black cotton sateen cloth; they are considerably lighter than their earlier sisters, would not itch, and have no classically feminine bows, poufs, or ruffles.[82] Advertisements continued to distinguish between such woven, skirted "bathing suits" and sleeker, more revealing, knit "swimming suits" as promoted by Annette Kellerman, a well-known swimmer and diver, but even the more conservative cuts were considerably more revealing than ever before.

Claudia Kidwell, a curator at the Smithsonian Institution's National Museum of American History, describes a tension between the knit suits and the skirted ones; Kellerman herself wrote that "anyone who persuades you to wear the heavy skirty kind is endangering your life."[83] She was presumably referring to the amount of fabric used in the "skirty" suits which, when wet, could become unwieldy. In comparison, the newer style of knit suits, sleeveless with attached shorts, small skirts, and striped hems, used much less fabric. They closely resembled men's styles of recent decades; in fact, it is often nearly impossible to tell the two apart. A deep-purple sleeveless suit with a V neckline and attached shorts at the Metropolitan Museum of Art would fit tightly, yet stretch with the body; its tightly knit fabric is a lightweight mix of wool and silk. The color and some braid are concessions to ideas about decorative femininity, yet the overall look and feel is phenomenally different from the 1870s suit described at the start of this essay.[84]

Kidwell writes that the knitted suits, associated with even greater athleticism, became linked with flappers and modernity; she describes how this distinction was made in fiction. In one story, a villainess sits on the beach in a taffeta sleeved suit, whereas the modern heroine wears a knit suit as she plays in the water; in another, a woman wearing a "scanty" suit describes herself as modern.[85] Compare an earlier woven silk suit that looks like a party dress, complete with square neckline, short sleeves, and princess seams, to the purple knit suit; the new suits would have looked, felt, and even *sounded* different on the wearer.[86] In 1924, Sears, Roebuck offered a "flapper style" knit suit; the model was photographed in a provocative "movie-star" pose.[87] The style had become embedded in the idea of the "modern woman."

Once again, advertisers and retailers were an important part of the process of change as they promoted new looks and cashed in on this changing attitude. An advertisement in a 1923 *Ladies' Home Journal* described black pleated bloomers and white sailor tops that were "roomy in cut and free as the wind."[88] A Vassar College gym suit at the Metropolitan Museum of Art reflects this style and sense of new feeling—unlike its wool predecessors, it is made of lightweight cotton twill with minimal trim.[89] At least one sports organization followed the example of clothing retailers and made a direct appeal to the new political rights of women: an African-American women's baseball team called "Madame J. H. Caldwell's Chicago Bloomer Girls" advertised for opponents with an ad that asked "our women are voting now, so why not be able to play a real game of baseball?"[90] Not only had sports and sports clothing become clearly associated with new ideas of femininity and women's rights, but older restraints of modesty had diminished in favor of being as "free as the wind."

Clothing provides a place to negotiate, both verbally and through images, different ideas of womanliness. The novelty of women's sports opened up a space in the discussion of women's clothing, and in that space women and the fashion industry negotiated different representations of femininity. Advertisers, retailers, magazine writers, and pattern makers played a significant role in this ongoing discussion by offering opinions, playing to women's desires and insecurities, and providing multiple options. But women were the ones who actually wore the styles—so their views were central to the process.

At a time when sports posed a challenge to notions of womanhood, clothing for sports both smoothed and exacerbated the paradox of "sporting women." Throughout this period, the clothing worn for sports displayed what can be seen as a social ambivalence over changing gender ideals. The tension between traditional female roles and bodies and modern ideas of womanhood manifested itself verbally—in the rhetoric used by advertisements, articles, and patterns—and visually—in the form of images and actual clothing. I do not suggest that the new clothes themselves *caused* changes in femininity, although it is arguable that the clothes helped women experience their bodies in new ways. But I do insist that the *process* through which the clothes were invented and popularized helped women, along with a diverse fashion industry, to rethink what it was to be feminine. At a time of significant gender flux, the tension between traditional female roles and bodies and modern ideas of womanhood was created, negotiated, and at least partially resolved through the discussion and appearance of clothing.

NOTES

1. Frances E. Willard, *A Wheel within a Wheel: How I Learned to Ride the Bicycle, with Some Reflections by the Way* (New York: F. H. Revell, 1895), 38.

2. In *American Beauty* (New York: Knopf, 1983), 135, Lois Banner claims that women who had access to college educations and professions or who "claimed the prerogatives of husbands and fathers" were first viewed with suspicion and labeled "advanced" during the 1880s. By the 1880s, as their numbers grew, they were seen as less of a threat and were labeled "new." Banner, 146.

3. Of course, women had been working in long skirts for centuries, but as middle-class women became interested in sports, they led the search for a new style of clothing. However, I argue that working-class women were also a part of this innovation.

4. Patricia Warner, "Clothing the American Woman for Sport and Physical Education, 1860 to 1940: Public and Private," Ph.D. diss., University of Minnesota, 1986. Warner claims that it was "private" gym clothing that made "sportswear" or more relaxed and comfortable clothing acceptable by the 1920s. Others, such as Barbara N. Noonkester, "The American Sportswoman from 1900–1920," in *Her Story in Sport*, ed. Reet Howell (West Point, NY: Leisure Press, 1982), also suggest that sports clothing was directly responsible for changes in women's styles.

5. Banner, *American Beauty*, 135. Kathy Peiss in *Cheap Amusements: Working Women and Leisure in Turn-of-the-Century New York* (Philadelphia, PA: Temple University Press, 1986) and Elizabeth Ewen in *Immigrant Women in the Land of Dollars: Life and Culture on the Lower East Side* (New York: Monthly Review, 1985) both address the importance of fashionable clothing to working and immigrant women. Nan Enstad in *Ladies of Labor, Girls of Adventure: Working Women, Popular Culture, and Labor Politics at the Turn of the Twentieth Century* (New York: Columbia University Press, 1999) writes that working women included arguments about their right to wear fashionable clothes as part of their demands for improved labor conditions; during the shirtwaist strike of 1909, Clara Lemlich told reporters that the women needed places to hang their hats, claiming that "we like new hats as well as other young women. Why shouldn't we?" Enstad, 8.

6. In her work as a visiting nurse, Lillian Wald noted that poor families often lacked even basic clothing and so stayed at home or kept children out of school. She and other settlement house workers often distributed clothing to these families. Beatrice Siegel, *Lillian Wald of Henry Street* (New York: 1993).

7. This was such a widespread cultural assumption that it made its way into idiomatic expressions—witness the "loose woman" as opposed to one who is "straightlaced."

8. While some women wore the bloomer costume for its practicality, especially while traveling or moving West, fewer women wore them than might be expected. This was in part because they could not afford such an outfit, but also because wearing a dress was one way to preserve fragile gender distinctions threatened by the physical demands and social isolation of the West. It was also a way to distinguish between white and Native American women. Lillian Schlissel, in *Women's Diaries of the Westward Journey* (New York: Schocken, 1982) writes that "Frontier women resisted any form of dress that would accommodate their daily life and work. No change that might seem to bring women closer to the dress of men or Indian women was tolerated. . . . In their steadfast clinging to ribbons and bows, starched white aprons and petticoats, the women suggested the frontier, in a profound manner, threatened their sense of social role and sexual identity." Schlissel, 85.

9. Elizabeth Stuart Phelps, *What to Wear?* (Boston: n.p., 1873), 31.

10. Allen Guttman in *Women's Sports: A History* (New York: Columbia University Press, 1991) provides a social history of sport in the U.S. and places the emergence of organized sport in a context of industrialization. Similarly, Norbert Elias argues that as society became increasingly "civilized" and restrained, overt emotionalism was discouraged, but sport was one place where people could express extreme emotions. He writes that "[i]n advanced industrial societies, leisure activities form an enclave for the socially approved arousal of moderate excitement behavior in public." See Norbert Elias and Eric Dunning, *Quest for Excitement: Sport and Leisure in the Civilizing Process* (Oxford: Blackwell, 1986), 65.

11. In her classic article, "The Cult of True Womanhood: 1820–1860," *American Quarterly* 18 (1966): 151–174, Barbara Welter argues that middle-class women of the nineteenth century were expected to lead domestic lives as a means of providing a constant in the face of social and economic change. A more recent work that discusses the development of middle-class culture and gender norms is Mary Ryan, *The Cradle of the Middle Class: The Family in Oneida County, New York, 1790–1865* (New York: Cambridge University Press, 1981).

12. Banner, *American Beauty* (New York: Knopf, 1983). Karen Halttunen also addresses physical ideals and their relation to class identity in *Confidence Men and Painted Women: A Study of Middle-Class Culture in America, 1830–1870* (New Haven: Yale University Press, 1982).

13. Several authors have written about the perceived health risks of sport, especially to reproduction. For example, Caroll Smith-Rosenberg and Charles Rosenberg write of the preoccupation with women's reproductive health and the idea that the body was a "closed system" with a finite amount of energy in their article "The Female Animal: Medical and Biological Views of Women and Their Role in Nineteenth-Century America," in *From "Fair Sex" to Feminism: Sport and the Socialization of Women in the Industrial and Post-Industrial Eras,* ed. J. A. Mangan and Roberta Park (London: Frank Cass, 1987), 13–37. It is now known that female athletes who reduce their body-fat ratio to extremely low proportions stop menstruating, but it is highly unlikely that Victorian-era women were exercising to that extreme. It is much more probable that poor women would have had insufficient nutrition or body weight to become pregnant or maintain a healthy pregnancy, yet these doctors and writers were predominantly concerned with middle-class women's reproductive capacity.

14. Annette Parry, M.D., "The Athletic Girl and Motherhood," *Harper's Bazaar* (August 1912): 380.

15. Edith Wharton, *The Age of Innocence* (New York: Scribners, 1996), 25.

16. Margaret Bisland, "Fencing for Women," *Outing* (February 1890): 342.

17. Eleanor Waddle, "The Berkeley Ladies' Athletic Club," *Outing, An Illustrated Monthly Magazine of Sport Travel and Recreation* (October 1889): 58–59.

18. "Some Defects in Education," *Massachusetts Teacher* 3 (1850), 67, 68, cited in Roberta Park, "Healthy, Moral and Strong: Educational Views of Exercise and Athletics in Nineteenth-Century America," in *Fitness in American Culture: Images of Health, Sport, and the Body, 1830–1940,* ed. Kathryn Grover (Amherst, MA, and Rochester, NY: The Strong Museum and University of Massachusetts Press, 1989), 123–168, quotation at p. 139. Park also notes that Darwin's theories influenced the move to support exercise for women.

19. Anonymous, *Etiquette for Ladies and Gentlemen; or, The Principles of True Politeness, To which is added The Ball-Room Manual* (London: Milner and Sowerby, 1862), 82–83.

20. "To Coney Island," *Scribner's Monthly* (July 1880): 357.

21. In *The Dream of a New Social Order: Popular Magazines in America, 1893–1914* (New York: Columbia University Press, 1994), Matthew Schneirov suggests that magazines promoted utopian views and, as one of first truly national media forms, can serve as a reliable source for understanding the evolution of American culture.

22. "Ladies' Bathing Dresses," *Godey's Ladies' Book and Magazine* (July 1871): 43.

23. Ibid., 44.

24. Bathing costume, American, ca. 1870–1873, Metropolitan Museum of Art, gift of the New York Historical Society (1979.346.18ab).

25. I am basing this assumption on the size of the stitches; most are small machine-stitches, but there are larger hand stitches as well. Sewing machines were becoming popular at this time and were relatively affordable.

26. Warner, "Clothing the American Woman," 69, 73–74.

27. While the origins of the paper pattern are disputed, paper patterns that offered different sizes and detailed instructions became commercially available during the late 1860s and early 1870s. The two largest pattern companies were the E. Butterick Company and Madame Demorest, which sold patterns largely through their publications *The Delineator* and *Mme. Demorest's Mirror of Fashions.* For more on the evolution of the pattern industry, see Claudia B. Kidwell, *Cutting a Fashionable Fit: Dressmakers' Drafting Systems in the United States* (Washington, DC: Smithsonian, 1979); Margaret Walsh, "The Democratization of Fashion: The Emergence of the Women's Dress Pattern Industry," *Journal of American History* 66 (September 1979): 299–313; and Carol Ann Dickson, "Patterns for Garments: A History of the Paper Garment Pattern Industry in America to 1976," Ph.D. diss., Ohio State University, 1979.

28. In her fascinating study of clothing through photographs, *Dressed for the Photographer: Ordinary Americans & Fashion, 1840–1900* (Kent, OH: Kent State University Press, 1995), Joan Severa argues that "ordinary" people were interested in and followed fashion to the best of their ability. She writes that if they could afford to do so, many women had professional seamstresses sew or at least cut and fit a garment for them. However, unless they were copying another dress or the dressmaker was skilled at using one of the many "grading" or pattern drafting systems available to them, these women still purchased commercial patterns for the dressmaker to use.

29. The *Delineator* is especially interesting in that it appears to have had a diverse readership, and promotional materials for the *Delinator* claim that it reached women from a range of economic classes. It was relatively inexpensive, ran ads for sibling magazines in Spanish, German, and French, and included numerous ads for "respectable" ways for "ladies" to earn money. *Souvenir of the Butterick Exhibit at the Pan-American Exposition*

(New York: Butterick, 1901), 2, in the collection of the Hagley Museum and Library, and "Remarks on Current Fashions," *The Delineator, A Journal of Fashion, Culture, and Fine Arts* (May 1890): 361.

30. "New Styles for Bicycling," *Delineator* (October 1898): 484.
31. "Up-to-Date Bicycle and Gymnastics Fashions," *Delineator* (August 1898), pattern No. 1727, 165–167.
32. Lady's Bathing Costume, Butterick Pattern Company Pattern No. 6838, May 1894, in the collection of the Butterick Company Archives, New York. A peplum was a part of the bodice that formed a small ruffle around the hips, and a bertha was a wide collar.
33. *The Dressmaker* (New York: 1911), 57. The manual also includes a chapter entitled "The Best Method of Altering Patterns."
34. Gymnastic costume, American, 1890s, Metropolitan Museum of Art, gift of the Jacqueline Loewe Fowler Costume Collection (1981.149.10).
35. Gymnastic costume, American, ca. 1904, Hermitage Museum (84.16.9ab).
36. Willard, *A Wheel within a Wheel*, 73, 25.
37. Advertisement for Overman Wheel Co., *Ladies' Home Journal* (May 1895): 30.
38. Advertisement for Columbia Bicycles, *Ladies' Home Journal* (May 1895): 30.
39. Advertisement for Sterling Cycle Works, *Ladies' Home Journal* (May 1895): 30.
40. Advertisements for Edward B. Grossman & Co. and WB Corsets, *Ladies' Home Journal* (April 1896): 29.
41. Willard, *A Wheel Within A Wheel*, 39.
42. Phelps, *What to Wear?* 39.
43. Mary Sargent Hopkins, "Out of Doors," *The Ladies' World* (February 1896): 10, cited in Warner, "Clothing the American Woman," 159. Some women did in fact wear gymnasium suits for purposes other than sports, notedly for travel. A young woman traveling west after the Civil War admired the practicality of suits with skirts and bloomers worn by some women; see Schlissel, *Women's Diaries,* 141.
44. "New Styles for Bicycling," 484.
45. Bicycle costume, American, ca. 1908, Museum of the City of New York, gift of Mr. John Noble (72.20.1ab).
46. Advertisement for Edward B. Grossman & Co., *Ladies' Home Journal* (April 1896): 29.
47. Bicycle costumes, American, ca. 1900, Metropolitan Museum of Art, gift of Miss Mathilde E. Webber (CI.55.41.5ab).
48. Photographs, ca. 1895–1900, Hermitage Museum (RG 1.7.1 Item No. 8 [Mary Elizabeth Rosencrantz I,"Aunt Bess," 1855–1943] and RG 1.71 Item No. 9).
49. "Ladies' Bathing Dresses," 43, and "New Styles for Bicycling," 484.
50. Waddle, "The Berkeley Ladies' Athletic Club," 61.
51. Ellen Garvey, "Reframing the Bicycle: Advertising-Supported Magazines and Scorching Women," *American Quarterly* 47 (1995): 87.
52. Maude C. Cooke, *Social Etiquette or Manners and Customs of Polite Society* (early 1900s), 304.
53. Florence Howe Hall, *The Correct Thing in Good Society* (Boston: Dana Estes and Co., 1902), 232–233.
54. Cooke, *Social Etiquette*, 425.
55. Sears, Roebuck & Co. catalog (Chicago: 1908): 1112.
56. Bathers at Ocean Park, Maine, August 1906, photograph in private collection.
57. M.H., "A Costume for Lawn Tennis," *Lippincott's Magazine of Popular Literature and Science* (November 1881), 522.
58. M.H., "A Costume for Lawn Tennis," 522.
59. Bisland, "Fencing for Women," 344.
60. There were even contests for designs. Mrs. Marie Reidesdale won $50 for a bicycle costume in a contest run by the *New York Herald* in 1893. Her design was for a split skirt of black cashmere worn with leather gaiters from ankle to knee. Contest noted in Warner, "Clothing the American Woman," 155.
61. "Dress for Summer Sports," *Delineator* (June 1894): 670.
62. Gymnasium costume, American, 1890s, Museum of the City of New York, gift of Mrs. Henry James Spencer (44.66.1ab), and skating sweater, American, ca. 1895, Museum of the City of New York, gift of Mrs. John Hubbard (38.149.16).
63. Gymnasium costume, ca. 1904, Hermitage Museum (84.16.9ab) and gymnasium costume, American, ca. 1905, Museum of the City of New York, gift of Miss Margaret D. Leverich (63.186.5ab).
64. In "The American Woman's Pre-World War I Freedom in Manners and Morals," *Journal of American History* 55 (September 1968): 315–333, James B. McGovern argues against historiograhical claims that dramatic shifts in manners and morals happened due to World

War I. Instead, he suggests that, in part because of increased urbanization and birth control, such changes had begun well before the war. He includes more risqué and mannish clothing as examples of these changes.

65. Costume historian James Laver writes that: "There has been much argument as to what brought this [fundamental change] about, but it was plain that the Russian Ballet had something to do with it, and so had Paul Poiret . . . what is certain is that there was a wave of Orientalism following the extraordinary excitement caused by the production of Schéhérezade. . . ." James Laver, *Costume and Fashion: A Concise History* (London: Thames and Hudson, 1969), 224. In a similar vein, Nancy Bradfield writes that: "by 1913, designers turned to the East for their inspiration. . . . Paul Poiret had already moved away from the then orthodox styles." Nancy Bradfield, *Costume in Detail, 1730–1930* (New York: Barnes and Noble, 1997), 378.
66. Alison Carter, *Fashion History* (New York: 1992), 72.
67. Laver, *Costume and Fashion*, 227.
68. "Bifurcation," *The Independent* (March 16, 1911): 581.
69. "To Coney Island," 356.
70. Susan Cahn, *Coming On Strong: Gender and Sexuality in Twentieth-Century Women's Sport* (New York: 1994), 36.
71. *Thirteenth Annual Report of the Young Women's Christian Association of Brooklyn* (New York: Y.W.C.A., 1901).
72. Advertisement for J. & T. Cousins shoe store, Fulton and Bond Streets, Brooklyn, in *Thirteenth Annual Report of the Young Women's Christian Association of Brooklyn* (New York: Y.W.C.A., 1901), unnumbered back pages.
73. "The Health Pageant," *War Work Bulletin* (July 25, 1919): 2.
74. Photograph in Cahn, *Coming On Strong*, 86b, c.
75. I agree with McGovern (see note 64) that this was neither an immediate change nor caused entirely by the war. Nevertheless, many fashion historians do cite the war as having at least some effect on changing clothing styles.
76. Carter, *Fashion History*, 72. Fashion historians have also noted that the double-skirt fashion of right before the war evolved into shorter skirts as nurses, intent on increased mobility, removed the longer and cumbersome underskirt. This was perhaps sanctioned because of the immediate need for their services and the need to conserve material.
77. An article by Paul Poiret promoted styles that suited the wearer, not "fashion." Paul Poiret, "Individuality in Dress: The Secret of the Well-Dressed Woman," *Harper's Bazaar* (September 1912): 451. Another article questioned why men should continue to wear jackets and hats even in sweltering weather: John B. Huber, M.D., "What To Wear—and Why," *The Independent* (August 7, 1916): 206–207.
78. Charlotte Perkins Gilman, "Concerning Clothes," *The Independent* (June 22, 1918): 478–483.
79. William J. Whiting, "Skirts or What? Should the Woman in the Woods Wear Skirt, Bloomers, Riding Breeches, or Knickerbockers?" *Outing* (October 1916): 33.
80. Photograph of African-American basketball team in Cahn, *Coming On Strong*, 86b, c; photographs of Y.W.C.A. summer camp in "Laboratories of Work, Worship and Play—Summer Conferences," *Blue Triangle News* (July 1920): 2–3.
81. Sears, Roebuck & Co. catalog (Chicago: 1916), 077.
82. Bathing costumes, American, ca. 1910, Hermitage Museum (H75.415 and 94.11.59)
83. Annette Kellerman, *How to Swim* (New York: George H. Doran Co., 1918), 47, cited in Claudia B. Kidwell, "Women's Bathing and Swimming Costume in the United States," *United States National Museum Bulletin* 250 (1968):2–32 [repaginated as 169–200], 26 [194].
84. Bathing suit, American, ca. 1915–1925, Metropolitan Museum of Art, gift of J. Robert Hoffman (1979.124.3).
85. Jane Pride, "Pick-Up," *Delineator* (May 1927): 15, cited in Kidwell, "Women's Bathing and Swimming Costume in the United States," 29.
86. Bathing costume, American, ca. 1900, Hermitage Museum (88.19.19).
87. Sears, Roebuck & Co. catalog (Chicago, 1924), 731.
88. Advertisement for Jack Tar Togs, *Ladies' Home Journal* (September 1923): 62.
89. Gymasium uniform, American, 1929, Metropolitan Museum of Art, gift of Sadie E. Scudder (1980.193.1ab).
90. Cahn, *Coming On Strong*, 38.

Questionable Beauty

THE DANGERS AND DELIGHTS OF THE CIGARETTE
IN AMERICAN SOCIETY, 1880–1930

NANCY BOWMAN

*H*enry Ford banned the "little white slaver" from his factories and shops; Carl Werner dedicated a book to "the Daintiest and most Delectable . . . the fairest form in which My Lady Nicotine has wooed and won us."[1] Clearly the cigarette has been adored and abominated, savored and censured, but it has never been an object of indifference in American culture. Neither has the question of *who* samples Lady Nicotine's wares.

A century ago, middle-class, cigarette-smoking women were the most controversial and castigated element in America's ever-growing population of tobacco users. By the 1920s, however, though some critics remained, their cigarette-smoking daughters were readily accepted, even celebrated and glamorized by their peers in popular culture. Changes in Americans' cultural understandings of gender and beauty between 1880 and 1930 permitted this dramatic reinterpretation. Women themselves, drawing on newly acquired opportunities in the college, marketplace, and court, and taking liberal cues from the burgeoning consumer and popular cultures, gradually refashioned social standards of beauty and meanings of womanhood that, by uncoupling notions of morality from definitions of physical comeliness, permitted a range of new freedoms, including cigarette smoking.

In exploring women's association with cigarettes at the turn of the century, this article complicates somewhat the historical understanding of the contemporary relationship between women and the advancing consumer culture. The case of cigarette smoking shows women driving the manufacturers and the advertising industry (the most obvious and ubiquitous element of consumer culture), rather than vice versa. Not until the late 1920s did leading cigarette manufacturers appeal directly to the female market, by which time millions of women had taken up the habit and made it their own. Here then, consumer culture was not always or necessarily the conservative force in women's lives that scholars often suggest.[2] Of course, the consumer culture influenced women in this as in other habits, but the give and take of the relationship was more subtle than an advertising campaign that encouraged women to smoke. Between 1880 and 1930, certain messages and interests of the larger consumer culture coincided with the interests and impulses of New Women to transform notions of beauty and womanhood in such a way that cigarettes were finally both appealing to and appropriate for women. What had been anathema to Victorian womanhood in smoking—its explicit contribution to personal, as opposed to communal, pleasure and satisfaction, and its associations with sexuality—was privileged in consumer culture and by the newest of New Women in the 1910s and 1920s, the flapper, ultimately rendering the act a marker of modern womanhood.[3]

At the turn of the century, the cigarette itself was relatively new, intruding on established patterns of tobacco consumption, and its use even by middle-class men was often contested. Self-appointed guardians of morality, however, not only contested middle-class women's use of the cigarette, but found it unthinkable. They knew that prostitutes, demimondaires, and actresses used the cheap smokes, but assumed "respectable" women to be entirely outside the community of smokers.[4] When reality indicated otherwise, cultural conservators depicted the errant females as mannish or as unattractive impediments to social progress and civilization. (See Figure 3.1.) One particularly vehement opponent, journalist Ella Wheeler Wilcox, described the smoking woman quite memorably and unattractively as "a fungus growth on the tree of time."[5]

Yet between 1880 and 1930 millions of those otherwise "respectable" women took up the cigarette habit. By the end of the 1920s, women could and did publicly display an enjoyment of tobacco. Men's enjoyment of tobacco had for most of the past century been very much associated with sensual pleasures and sublimated sexual desires; as the high-Victorian "Steel Engraving Lady" passed in favor of the late-Victorian Gibson girl, and the Gibson girl in favor of the flapper, women's appreciation of smoking recognized and took on some of those same associations. These successive waves of new women first acknowledged, then positively embraced, and finally openly expressed their personal opinions, desires, and sexuality.[6] In 1926, *Life* magazine published on its cover an image of the smoking woman quite at odds with that of "fungus growth": the "sweet girl graduate" who, cigarette and diploma in hand, was representative of rather than a drag on modernity. She was the product, beneficiary, and proponent of the

424 HARPER'S NEW MONTHLY MAGAZINE.

WOMAN'S EMANCIPATION.
(BEING A LETTER ADDRESSED TO MR. PUNCH, WITH A DRAWING, BY A STRONG-MINDED AMERICAN WOMAN.)

Figure 3.1. The author and illustrator of "Woman's Emancipation" (*Harper's Weekly*, August 1851) envisioned the fashionable scene should the fairer sex engage in "unwomanly" behaviors like smoking. Courtesy of Department of Archives and Manuscripts, McKeldin Library, University of Maryland at College Park.

Figure 3.2. The essence of modernity. Courtesy of Illustration House, New York City.

ongoing reconfiguration of beauty and womanhood. Feminine fingers cradling a cigarette as rouged lips exhaled its delicate smoke marked the ultimate of modern standards. (See Figure 3.2.)

In the 1920s, women openly enjoyed the sensual treats of cigarettes, but they did not establish the association in the public mind between tobacco, women, and sex. Throughout the eighteenth and into the early nineteenth century, both men and women used and enjoyed tobacco.[7] In the antebellum era, however, authors of new social and gender models suggesting female purity and passionlessness, and separate spheres for men and women, proscribed middle-class women's use and enjoyment of tobacco. Simultaneously, producers, advertisers, and devotees of tobacco redefined and feminized the product—giving it a feminine character and designating it for masculine use only. Indeed, tobacco, as described and advertised, figured alternately as a substitute for and rival of women in men's affections and attentions.[8] Tobacco embodied a sexuality and sensuality, and promised an availability and languor that the normative literature directed at the middle class told "true women" to deny or suppress. This is not to say that Victorian women were, in fact, bereft of sexual passion or desires, but that they were discouraged from its open acknowledgment, and insofar as tobacco in its various forms took on any erotic connotations in the nineteenth century, it had to be forbidden to respectable women if they were to approach the ideal.[9]

Literary figures great and (mostly) small paid homage to and anthropomorphized tobacco as the glorious "Queen Nicotiana" or "Lady Nicotine." Whether in the form of loose tobacco, chewing tobacco, the stout but sultry cigar, humble briar pipe, or newfangled cigarette, tobacco figured as romantic muse, haunting reverie, and coquette. Novelist J. M. Barrie devoted an entire monograph to "My Lady Nicotine" so that he might weigh the respective benefits of smoking and matrimony. He ultimately resolved to give up his pipe—"my most delightful solace . . . for no other reason than that the lady who was willing to fling herself away on me said that I must choose between it and her." But this ultimatum "deferred our marriage for six months."[10] A contributor to the *Atlantic Monthly* vowed himself "a bachelor husband of the Goddess of Nicotine," content to share his life with pipe and books.[11] The *Gentleman's Magazine* published a poem that perfectly captured the gendered and wonderfully sensual aspects of tobacco and the competitive, if ephemeral, relationship between women and tobacco:

Choosing a Wife by a Pipe of Tobacco

Tube, I love thee as my life;
By thee I mean to choose a wife.
Tube, thy *color* let me find,

In her *skin*, and in her *mind*.
Let her have a *shape* as fine;

Let her breath be sweet as thine;
Let her, when her lips I kiss,
Burn like thee, to give me bliss;
Let her, in some *smoke* or other,
All my failings kindly smother.
Often when my thoughts are *low*,
Send them where they *ought to go*;
When to study I incline,
Let her aid be such as thine;
Such as thine the charming pow'r
In the vacant social hour.
Let her live to give delight,
Ever *warm* and ever *bright*;
Let her deeds, when'er she dies,
Mount as incense to the skies.[12]

Rudyard Kipling likewise made clear that women and tobacco often vied for men's affection in the verse "Maggie vs. Smoke." His "old friends" were the occupants of his cigar box, and to them he was determined to be true. The (in)famous line ". . . a woman is only a woman, but a good cigar is a Smoke" is followed in that poem by the assertion that he will "Light me another Cuba; I hold to my firstsworn vows; If Maggie will have no rival, I'll have no Maggie for Spouse." Masculinity, as Kipling understood it anyway, entitled men to the sensual pleasures of both woman and tobacco.[13]

Beginning at mid-century, advertisements, too, attested to the feminization of tobacco. In the majority of these advertisements, in which women symbolized the tobacco product, the female figure represented an accepted ideal or type: the appealing, yet demure and beautiful "true" woman; a mythical or symbolic figure—Liberty or Columbia, for example; or an "exotic" type—well outside the confines of white, middle-class womanhood, and thus a permissibly sensual tease. In the first case, the idealized figure embodied the traits of chaste Victorian womanhood, marking tobacco as a good and appropriate companion and helpmeet to the male user. In the second, she represented strength and honor and seemed thereby to equate tobacco use with qualities of American manliness. Last, the "exotics" were often dark-skinned women or fair women in foreign, usually construed as "Eastern," locales that connoted alternative sexual standards, suggesting that some sort of lawful seduction lay within reach.[14] In all cases, the tobacco claimed to share the exaggeratedly beneficent or pleasurable qualities embodied by the image—although in almost no instance did the tobacco product itself appear; only the manufacturer's and brand names announced that tobacco was being sold.

Such advertising and poesy rendered women, visually and rhetorically, the objects rather than the agents of tobacco consumption. Moreover, by representing tobacco through attractive women yet suppressing or displacing white women's sexuality, these cultural productions constructed its leaf and by-products as admirably desirable commodities. The prevailing understanding of beauty among Victorian America's anxious moralists and opinion-makers, however, did not admit of commodification, and the dictates of Victorian womanhood demanded that women not just eschew but condemn their rival as most *unlovely* and join in efforts throughout the nineteenth century to prevent the spread of tobacco use.

To be sure, competing notions and images of beauty existed at every point along the continuum from the mid-nineteenth to the early twentieth century: the pale, frail "Steel Engraving Lady" competed with the hale and hearty voluptuous woman at mid-century; the vigorous and statuesque yet refined Gibson girl eclipsed the voluptuous woman at the end of the century; the gamine flapper unceremoniously dismissed the Gibson girl from the stage in the 1910s and 1920s. The very real, physical embodiment of beauty associated with those "types" is not unrelated to my project of explaining the ultimate acceptability of women's smoking, but I focus on what I believe was the greater centrality of an *abstraction* of beauty that intertwined spirit and form, inner and outer loveliness, to proscribe behavior. This ethereal conceptualization privileged woman's moral conduct as a determinant of "true" beauty, and seems to have been shared by a plurality of editors and authors of the middle-class press, reformers, and feminists. This is what I characterize as the Victorian model of beauty that had to give way before women's cigarette smoking could be culturally sanctioned.[15]

In this Victorian model, then, beauty was not just, or even primarily, a visible, physical attribute of women, and not a saleable good, but rather was contingent on a woman's internalization and successful embodiment of the qualities of "true womanhood." Obviously resting on the presumption of separate male and female spheres that marked Victorian culture, beauty was said to be "eloquent of the higher plane to which woman has been raised."[16] It both promised and bespoke success in her "proper" role as a wife and mother: beauty was a woman's tool before marriage but after marriage was evidence that she was properly fulfilling her social obligations. A clear complexion, wrote Susanna Cocroft, indicated a clear and clean life; blemishes "symbolize[d] imperfections within."[17] Whatever one's outward appearance, only by modeling all the virtues and adhering to the proscriptions for one's sex could an individual be reckoned truly lovely; respect and admiration in society demanded close observation of a rigid, moral code. If blessed with an attractive face and form, "right living" guaranteed retention of those gifts. "[L]et us realize," wrote beauty "expert" Harriet Ayer in 1902:

> that perpetual beauty and virtue are synonymous, because it has been proved that even physical beauty, if maintained in its proper sense, after maturity, means purity and temperance, and without these two attributes no power on earth can preserve a woman's loveliness beyond the early thirties.[18]

By the same token, if indeed one exemplified the virtues, then society reckoned one lovely. "To become lovely," wrote another "expert" and critic Robert Tomes, one must overcome "unlovely traits of disposition." And in becoming lovely, one could enhance or even transcend physical beauty. "Let us remember," he continued:

> that a beautiful woman is not always a lovely one, and that a lovely woman is often a very plain one; that a beautiful woman who is not lovely is like a rose without perfume whose charm is gone when its petals are faded. . . . Loveliness is the sum total of beauty and may or may not include perfection of feature and form.[19]

This and other essays and handbooks on beauty thus conflated sincere personal beauty (or loveliness, in Tomes's words) with proper performance of gender roles. Female beauty was most quickly implied through fairness of form and visage, but physical gifts (or the lack thereof) were augmented by conforming to the demands of "true womanhood." By the same token, this beauty or perfection of womanhood could be destroyed by unwomanly or "unlovely" behaviors; it could be sullied by improper associations. What actions and items might properly be connected with a "lady" came into question, however, when industrialization begat a consumer culture in which a plethora of new goods were made available to all without distinction. At the turn of the century, the Victorian authors of chaste perceptions of beauty and rigid distinctions between the sexes found their ideals endangered by modernizing forces that they themselves unleashed.

The mass-produced cigarette was a good example, from the Victorian perspective, of "progress" gone awry. Manufacturers were too efficient in their production and distribution of this new consumer good; the American public too willingly embraced this slight smoke.[20] This delicate product of industrialization, this representative of an emerging consumer culture and ethos, was too successful. Its popularization among men, women, and children challenged the dominant perceptions of gender, beauty, and virtue, and, in the 1890s, reignited in their defense a moribund crusade against tobacco among some members of the middle class.[21]

These late-nineteenth-century antitobacco crusaders preached that excessive tobacco use threatened the nation's very soul. The cigarette was a "little white slaver"; habitual tobacco use was "bondage."[22] For proof of what would befall America if cigarette use, at least, was not condemned, antitobacco reformers looked to the experience of countries such as Turkey, Spain, and Mexico, which they believed to have an inordinate fondness for the leaf. The "narcotic" tobacco, they claimed, "demoralize[d] nations and change[d] their type . . . and tends to ruin . . . on a fearful scale."[23] If Americans persisted in lighting up at such an alarming rate, every indication seemed to be that like the once-mighty Ottoman Empire, the United States would sink into political decay and moral slothfulness.

Reformers made an effort to prick men's consciences concerning tobacco use; particularly as cigarette use spread, men were asked to set a good example for their sons and other youth whom they might influence by not smoking—especially in their presence or proximity.[24] Men were lectured that tobacco use, and especially cigarette smoking, "derange[d] the whole system" of the individual, family, and society[25] Editors of antitobacco journals offered damning images of cigarette smokers as men who were:

> deliberately giv[ing] up respectable female society to indulge the solitary, enervating vice of smoking until their broken-down constitutions clamor for careful nursing; then they cooly ask some noble girl to exchange her health, strength, beauty and unimpaired intellect for their sallow face, tainted blood and heart, irritable temper, and mental imbecility.[26]

Clearly, such men were abandoning manhood and sacrificing womanhood to become "tobacco fiends," and a spate of commercial "tobacco cures" trailed in the wake of the cigarette, appealing to consumers' concerns with (in particular) men's physical appearance and virility. Promoters of No-To-Bac, Tobacco Redeemer, and Narcoti-Cure, for example, all promised that their products made "Manly Men" who would "have the nerve to make [wives or sweethearts] happy."[27]

The reformers really expected women rather than men, however, to hold the line against tobacco use generally and the "progress" of the cigarette in particular, and thereby prevent the nation from taking "the down-hill road to social degeneracy."[28] Youth held the promise of the nation's future; women were their protectors and thus the guardians of the nation. For the antitobacco crusaders, preserving the nation from the evils of the cigarette meant preserving and reiterating Victorian models of gender as well. They referred repeatedly to women's purity, their morality, and the beauty that marked their particular nature and position in society. Women were expected to present themselves as natural allies of the antitobacco cause, and the advertisements for No-

To-Bac and the rest, then, were aimed at women as much as men, in the expectation that "wives and sweethearts" had a vested interest in using their powers of moral suasion to cleanse men—and increasingly, boys—of the tobacco habit. Should they not, the result might be "a lot of sickly, scraggly, scrofulous, cancerous liliputian children."[29] Women who ignored the cigarette evil, claimed reformers, would have failed in their womanly duty, sacrificed beauteous virtue, and risked the national well-being.

It should have been a glorious catfight—the fair mothers and maids of America against the dangerously alluring Lady Nicotine. Gradually, however, the antitobacco reformers realized that some women—their presumed allies—were actually adding to rather than ameliorating the "cigarette problem." There were grievous defections from the cause, as a burgeoning, if clandestine, cigarette habit developed among some otherwise "respectable," virtuous, and lovely women by the end of the nineteenth century.

In fact, the social ban placed on women's smoking earlier in the century was never completely effective. Some women took snuff; older women persisted in smoking their pipes; and, from the moment cigarettes became widely available, young women and girls in America's cities experimented with them as enthusiastically as did their brothers. Controversy surrounded the practice and was aired (among other places) in the popular press, as men and women wrote in for and against women's smoking: Was it a right? Was it an issue of morality? The general consensus arrived at by many (and especially younger) Americans, according to one of the most famous advice columnists of the early twentieth century, Marie Manning, was that "no nice girl smoked *openly*, unless she was 'fast.'"[30] Thus women who used tobacco at and before the turn of the century engaged in a variety of subterfuges to safeguard their public image.[31]

For if, in the eyes of anticigarette crusaders and Victorian cultural observers, a woman who ignored the cigarette habit in her loved ones was failing in her womanly duties, then the woman who herself smoked was forsaking her very identity as a woman. A variety of critics outside the organized movement against tobacco and cigarettes depicted the smoking woman as mannish, "fast," or fearsomely revolting. In 1851, *Harper's New Monthly Magazine* published an illustration of the excesses of "Woman's Emancipation"—including women's smoking petite cigars and a concomitant blurring of sexual identities. (See Figure 3.1) Returned from one of his Western expeditions in the 1870s, explorer and East Coast urbanite Clarence King described his encounter with Mrs. Newty, formerly of Pike County, Missouri, in the most unflattering and even frightening terms, leaving no doubt as to his thoughts on the dangers of female tobacco use. Upon approaching the family's campsite, King noted a:

confused pile of bedclothes, partly old and half-bald buffalo-robes, but, in the main, thick strata of what is known to irony as comforters, upon which, outstretched in wretched awkwardness of position, was a family . . . looking as if they had been blown over in one direction. . . . The mother was a bony sister, yellow, shrunken, of sharp visage, in which were prominent two cold eyes and a positively poisonous mouth. . . . She rocked jerkily to and fro, removing at intervals a clay pipe from her mouth in order to pucker her thin lips up to one side and spit with precision upon a certain spot in the fire. . . .

King clearly believed that this woman had forsaken all responsibilities and images commonly expected of American women: her physical person had deteriorated, and her behavior would likewise contribute first to the ruin of her family and then to general "social decomposition."[32] Scientific "experts" likewise reinforced the notion that smoking endangered a woman's health, beauty, and very identity in society. In 1900, sexologist Havelock Ellis, in his *magnum opus*, *The Psychology of Sex*, accepted the convention of smoking as a man's prerogative and a masculine trait. Ellis's caveat that "transvestism"—the taking on of behaviors, manners, or appearance of the opposite sex—"by no means necessarily involves inversion" did not dispel the notion that, at the very least, he viewed a woman's cigarette smoking as deliberately "mannish" behavior. He noted that "[t]he commonest characteristic of the sexually inverted woman is a certain degree of masculinity or boyishness," and there appeared to be in his records a correlation between a woman's smoking and her sexual inversion, or departure from true womanhood.[33]

The mass popular culture consolidating after 1890 persisted in associating tobacco-using women with negative, even criminal, images, although it also offered more positive alternative readings of the smoking woman as time went on. In Harold Frederic's 1896 bestseller, *The Damnation of Theron Ware*, for example, the morally dubious leading lady Celia Madden was a redheaded, cigarette-smoking freethinker who led the hitherto upright and respected Reverend Theron Ware down a path of intellectual and sexual confusion and emotional betrayal to the destruction of his career. Arthur Reeve made the weapon of choice in his World War I–era short story "The Murder Syndicate" a ladies' gold-tipped cigarette, spiked with pure nicotine— "Two or three drops on the mouth-end of a cigar or cigarette . . . fatal in a few minutes," as sleuth Craig Kennedy and any antitobacco advocate could tell you. As late as 1926, Helen Duncan Queen depicted one of her heroines, Flip Demarest, as sadly lacking in refinement and a comprehension of truth and meaningful beauty at the outset of her story "Change." This lack was signaled in the plot primarily through Flip's tawdry taste in home decorating, but also by her taste for cigarettes, which, by the end of the story, she abandoned as part of the "Change" into the type of woman who can satisfy her husband.[34]

All of this was fuel for the fire of the cigarette's organized opponents who, as time went on, noted not only that women were smoking, but that they and the rest of society were becoming more open about it. Indeed, as it became clear that more women *were* smoking, the cigarette's opponents painted a yet more unlovely picture of those transgressors and made ever greater claims for the evil consequences of their fascination with the "little white slaver." Ella Wilcox, remember, had so vividly characterized the smoking woman as a "fungus growth on the tree of time." Lucy Gaston, a feverishly devoted anticigarette reformer, demonstrated some restraint when she described "society girls who sit with their feet up and smoke with men" merely as a "disgrace to American womanhood."[35] Dr. Lauretta Kress, another staunch opponent of women smoking, was appalled by the number of women smoking cigarettes (she estimated in 1916 that there were at least 100,000 women smokers in New York alone) and feared women would no longer be a "redeeming" but a contributing factor to the problem of race degeneracy.[36] Mrs. Carrie Flatter wrote to the president of the Ohio State University to urge his attention to the habit among his coeducational student body, convinced that "upon the use or non-use of tobacco, depends the rise or fall of the American republic."[37] Temperance unions and antitobacco leagues warned that the United States was becoming a "nation of degenerates," dope addicts, and criminals, thanks to the increased use of the cigarette among women and youth.[38] Athletic coach Amos A. Stagg blamed smoking mothers for "the downfall of modern youth" insofar as they were failing to "set an example for them in . . . self-mastery."[39] Even the pope offered his opinion on the topic, asserting that women's use of the cigarette was evidence of their lowered moral standards, which, he went on to say, was one of the trinity of evils abroad in the world, hell-bent on "the deterioration and destruction of a Christian society and civilization."[40]

Given the fervor with which these opinions were expressed and disseminated, opponents cast about in some dismay and confusion for possible explanations of the weed's successful breach of convention and the increasing prevalence of cigarette-smoking women. They wanted to blame the cigarette manufacturers and their advertisers but, given that the leading manufacturers did not target women until the late 1920s, could not. Other explanations extended for women's smoking credited—or faulted—mass entertainment forms such as novels and the movies. Those who didn't think that women were mimicking celluloid vamps and flappers suggested that they were aping the manners of the Europeans and American "high society" to be "smart."

Others offered that the cigarette was first a substitute for and then an extension of the ballot. Another possibility ventured was that women smoked because they believed that men found it attractive.[41]

They had but an imperfect understanding of the ways in which two cultural currents—an emerging mass and consumer culture and the steady progress of New Women toward greater opportunity and equality—intersected after 1890 to effect a radical change in some "respectable" women's mien. Reformers could not explain women's behavior in picking up the cigarette habit because they were working from the false premise that their Victorian value system was and would remain dominant. Instead, slowly, some women were reconceptualizing beauty and femininity, unhinging them from the old dicta of domesticity and virtuous self-sacrifice and self-control on which reformers based their appeals. New standards—initiated by the working girls and Gibson girls of the 1890s, further enunciated by the flappers of the 1910s and 1920s, and reenforced and then exploited by purveyors of mass and consumer culture—uncoupled a woman's personal beauty from moral worth, inner goodness, or service to others, and linked it instead to the ability to purchase new commodities and to an attractive physical presence that exuded (at least) a glimmering awareness of sexuality and desire, bodily health, and individualism of spirit.[42]

After 1880, young women across class lines mounted an ever more forceful and successful challenge to the gender constructs that underlay the Victorian experience and worldview. Working-class young women pioneered the creation of alternative models of feminine beauty and behavior at least as early as the 1860s.[43] Already outside the narrow bounds of bourgeois expectations by the fact of paid employment, these working-class women created their own sense of style and set their own rules for behavior in their leisure hours. They frequented dance halls, dressed to please themselves and their pickups or dates, wore makeup, and generally scandalized middle-class reformers who offered them mostly unsolicited guidance, advice, and protection.[44]

By the turn of the century, however, not all members of middle-class womanhood were horrified by the prospect of a dance hall or more casual interactions with men. Young women of the middle class were also redrawing behavioral boundaries for themselves as they began storming the campus and corporate gates in the 1880s and 1890s. These latter women took a page from their working-class sisters and drew as well on decades of arguments for women's rights that demanded equality and condemned sexual double standards as they revisited old proscriptions and definitions of beauty. The Gibson girl was the prototype of certain of these qualities and inspired imitators in the real world and the pages of the popular press where artist Charles

Dana Gibson brought her to life. She was men's competitor, comrade, and lovely consort—an idealized embodiment of New Womanhood in the 1890s and 1900s. Undeniably a positive image, the Gibson girl nonetheless challenged the Victorian "Steel Engraving Lady" who preceded her. She was more educated, more active, and more self-aware. As expressed in a fictional debate between the two types, the Gibson girl was "not [of] a shy, retiring, uncomplaining generation."[45] She wanted to accomplish things—to broaden woman's sphere and improve the world. Most frequently this New Woman articulated demands for political and economic power and independence long denied her. The spirit and conviction of equality between the sexes that prompted such demands, though, permitted some women comfortably to adopt as well various social freedoms—like bicycling and cigarette smoking—that lay outside their scope.

In the 1910s, there were further changes in the feminine ideal. Lingering Victorianism competed not only with the politically oriented New Woman of the 1890s but with the emergence of a newer New Woman, dubbed the "flapper" in 1915 by H. L. Mencken. These young women not only abandoned the pose of selflessness demanded by the Victorian ethic, but reshuffled their priorities for women's liberation to privilege social freedoms and personal pleasures ahead of political and economic emancipation. There was under way in the first decades of the twentieth century, noted Marie Manning, a "feminine revolution which had nothing whatever to do with women's rights or wrongs."[46] They adopted increasingly frank conversational styles, a more open sexuality, free and easy interaction with men, shorter costumes and coiffures, and the use of cosmetics, alcohol, and tobacco, claiming the need to assert their independence from "the patent [and petty] absurdities of Victorianism."[47]

The flapper in particular, in the 1910s and 1920s, attacked the Victorian moral code that focused on narrow behavioral proscriptions while ignoring women's physical beings and broad realities. She was the "woman of the future" described by Swedish feminist Ellen Key in 1907, locating beauty and purity in passion and individualism. "Her greatest charm will lie in her ability to be true to her own self . . . and her imperishable youth, her ultimate beauty she will reveal solely to the one whom she loves."[48]

Young women claimed their sexuality, and older women (and men) had its recognition forced upon them by the younger generation and by experts of every stripe. Havelock Ellis had offered an often ambiguous interpretation of woman's smoking and her sexuality, but he was clear about his desire to separate facts "from all would-be moralistic or sentimental notions, and so spare the youth of future generations . . . trouble and perplexity."[49] Other sexologists advertised their how-to and information books in the pages of family magazines in the early twentieth century. Psychoanalysis had become, even by World War I, the "latest cult in America." Popularized versions of Freud's theories of sex and personality permeated the culture and sanctioned a "repeal of reticence" in the 1910s and 1920s.[50]

By the mid-1920s, young women were fully persuaded of their sexual birthright and the propriety of their new morality. Indeed, in retrospect, sex repression should never have had any place in defining womanly beauty or morality. Christian reformer Maude Royden cautioned against the "imbecile assumption" that women were not sexual beings, and asserted that you could read the negative effects of sex repression in a woman's face and spirit. "You know the type," she wrote: "you know the kind of person who becomes hard and narrow and uncomprehending. . . .You can read it in their faces. The pinched look, the cramped mentality reflects itself in the body and the face."[51]

Alyse Gregory seconded Royden while defending the changing morality of young women. Without denying the occasional excesses of "modern youth" in the 1910s and early 1920s, she nonetheless believed that:

> when one compares them to their Victorian spinster prototypes, so meek and petulant and useless, venting their sex starvation on servants or relatives . . . these practical, disillusioned modern women, in spite of serious lapses, are . . . in the end of greater use to their community and friends.[52]

Repression, rather than expression, was in the 1920s perceived as unlovely and immoral.

To be sure, however, there was disagreement about the usefulness of the young flapper who brought together in one figure all the hallmarks of modernity—new ideas of gender, sexuality, beauty, and entitlement and self-indulgence. The older generations despaired of these "lifestyle feminists" who, author Margaret Deland noted, had "learned only to say 'I can,' 'I will,' and 'I want,'—but not 'I ought.'"[53] In the words of Charlotte Perkins Gilman, by 1920 young women had "'totally repudiated their two tutelary deities' of past times, Duty and Decorum"; women's "advancement" was marked by "an unchecked indulgence in appetite and impulse . . . and a wholesale resistance to any restraint . . ."; their "freedom" consisted in "a somewhat flaunting adoption of ordinary vices and vulgarities."[54] Antismoking reformers and first-generation New Women were largely unconvinced that the flapper represented progress or liberation for women or society. But young women were more certain.

On college campuses across the nation, coeds demanded the right to smoke with the same self-assurance that they flaunted bare knees and bobbed hair. They faced criticism from parents and even from some peers, but ultimately won their point. Bryn Mawr set the precedent in

1925 when the all-female student body was granted the right to smoke on campus—and acknowledge in public what they had been doing clandestinely for years. The administration, alumnae, and students determined that smoking was "purely a question of taste, with no moral or ethical elements involved." Female students at Ohio State University won the same concession four years later. The Women's Student Council at Trinity (later Duke) University in Durham, North Carolina, enacted a rule against coeds smoking in 1924, but acknowledged that it was little more than a "pretty motion," passed to appease the South's provincial attitudes toward women but easily evaded. By 1931, the women on campus reversed the earlier rule and permitted smoking by women in the female dorms and in specified rooms on campus. In every case there was debate and opposition, but in many cases across the nation, campus policies on women and smoking changed to reflect the very real shift in custom and opinion among the younger generation. In the words of one Ohio State student, women "honestly enjoy[ed] the attendant physical sensations" of smoking—as well as dancing, dressing décolleté, and drinking—so why should they not?[55]

Young women bucked the double standard for male and female behavior and also abandoned, or at least demoted, the old notions of beauty and womanhood that had demanded from women an ubermorality and the suppression of their physicality, sensuality, and personal desires. Nor did they believe in the least that having done so compromised their identity as women or as good and decent people. The unfortunate fact for that Ohio State student was not that she and her friends had struck out on their own on this issue and were suffering the consequences in the court of public opinion. That was not the case. Rather, she regretted that the elders were "alarmed" and yet "refuse to conform their way of thinking to ours."[56] Journalist Marguerite Harrison likewise attested to the innocence of women's smoking as she asserted a "Sorority of Smoke on Wheels" and demanded smoking cars for women on trains.[57] Marie Manning's readers had years earlier argued that smoking provided for women the same relaxation and pleasure that it did for men, and claimed their right to such solace.[58]

Young women successfully revolted in the 1910s and especially in the 1920s against the "patent absurdities of Victorianism" that had denied them self-expression, evaded reality, and created a standard of petty morality that had nothing to do, they claimed, with true decency. "All the petty things to which you, a generation or two ahead of us, attach so much importance," young Regina Malone reassured readers of *The Forum*:

> are mere symbols of a revolt whose object is Freedom . . . and it is only in
> this light that they should be regarded. Beauty and idealism, the two eternal

heritages of Youth, are still alive. It is the form of expression which they
have assumed that has been mistaken for their death knell. Laugh it off, you
who are alarmed at this fabulous monster of Youth! Pay less attention to the
face signs of the revolt and more to the good being accomplished by it. . . .[59]

Young women recognized themselves as sensual as well as spiritual
beings and decried opposition to women's smoking on the grounds that
it was "the hall mark of the [disreputable, sexualized] half-world," and
"medieval."[60] Smoking retained the associations with pleasure and sensuality that had accrued to it in the nineteenth century when it was a
masculine endeavor, but no longer were those qualities off limits to
women.

In the last decades of the nineteenth century, then, and the first of the
twentieth, different groups and generations of New Women recast
social understandings of beauty and womanhood as they reshaped
their individual lives and opportunities. The emerging mass and consumer culture validated and influenced those New Women in their
overhaul of social identities.

Mass-circulation family and women's magazines were the products
and promoters of a consumer culture that inevitably reenforced,
reflected, influenced, and, yes, frequently exploited the demands of
the New Woman and her notions of beauty and self. The consumer culture offered women a curious mix of old and new ideas about their
roles and responsibilities to themselves and others. Cyrus Curtis inau-
gurated *The Ladies' Home Journal* in 1883 and, shortly after the turn of
the century, it became the first publication to garner more than one
million subscribers. Curtis and his editorial successors at *LHJ*, beginning with Edward Bok, asserted clearly that wife- and motherhood
ought to remain women's ultimate goal and responsibility; numerous
competitors followed suit. But early in the twentieth century the moral
component that had stiffened Victorian idealizations of womanhood
largely vanished from the editorials and advertising through which
these magazines spread their message.[61]

Wife- and motherhood remained woman's primary goals therein,
but by 1920 the proper performance of those roles no longer rested on
a woman's spiritual leadership or moral worth but on her consumption
of the appropriate goods. As Christine Frederick, consumer expert and
consultant/contributor to the *LHJ* put it, "consumer changes [were] the
very bricks out of which [early twentieth-century Americans were]
building [a] new kind of civilization." Manufacturers and advertisers of
everything from mops and mattresses to mascara connected their
products to women's success in their social roles. And women were in
a "working partnership" with those advertisers, having already made

up their minds to improve their own and their families' standards of living.[62] The good mother purchased the best household cleaners and the latest modern appliances, thereby securing her children from dirt and germs and providing herself more time away from household chores to devote to their welfare. The Association of Laundry Owners National encouraged women to use their services if they would be "a good wife in this modern age."

> Are you passing up enjoyable, stimulating, youth-bringing pleasures and pastimes because of this heavy burden? It is no wonder then that washday steals more of Youth and Beauty than the other six days can restore. . . . [But] if you will decide to *get the facts*; to see for yourself just what the modern laundry has to offer. In place of drudgery you are given a full day of freedom; happy hours for those pleasant pursuits . . . that make one a truly good wife . . . of the twentieth century husband.[63]

The good wife likewise invested in a variety of cosmetics and other goods meant to restore or enhance her beauty so that her husband would continue to find her appealing. The single woman presumably desired a husband and children, and should purchase and use those items that might aid in her quest to attract a man.

The use of cosmetics was at first resisted by the general population, even as the young wives and daughters of the middle class experimented with them. Even beauty culturists were initially interested in educating consumers in the methods and process of beauty rather than simply selling cosmetic preparations. By the early 1900s, though, the unobtrusive use of cold creams, powders, and even light rouges was becomingly increasingly routine among the urban middle class. *Harper's Bazar* endorsed and practically urged women's use of cosmetics because, an editor asserted, "no fair-minded person can behold a woman without realizing that God meant her to be attractive." Previously eschewed by most of the middle class as unnecessary at best and immoral at worst, the artificial enhancement of her appearance became woman's "inalienable prerogative" and a virtual obligation.[64]

Were these the type of advertisements likely to "validate and influence" young women in search of alternative standards? The "modern" consumer age *seemed* very conventional in its beliefs and messages about women then, insofar as it continued to place home and family at the center of women's lives. It hardly seems likely that the Gibson girl or flapper could have found justification for any kind of social rebellion. But in fact, as historian William Leach has argued, the ethic that lay behind the consumer culture and its physical expression and display had a transformative and emancipating impact on many women. The culture encouraged women to find and express themselves through the purchase of goods and to abandon self-denial as a guiding principle.[65] Leach argued particularly for the liberating effect of department stores on the women who worked there and the "mostly middle-class women" who were their patrons. I would like to suggest, too, that the New Women who are the subject of this essay located in advertisements a similar potential for liberation. To be sure, the advertisements were crafted to sell goods, and they did, but audiences constantly attach their own interpretation and meaning to what they see, hear, or read, and can easily subvert the message intended by the author of the cultural artifact. They attend not just to the advice and admonishment of experts and advertisers but to other cultural influences and especially their own social identities and ambitions. Then audience members, here consumers, can choose which portions of a message to adhere to, and which received ideas and images can and will be subverted and manipulated to justify new ideas or behavior within their specific context.[66]

Young women in the 1910s and twenties found that the modern consumer messages aided in the upset of old notions by presenting personal beauty as purely physical and making both beauty and womanly success purchasable. And the acceptance of cosmetics use was not the only departure by the popular press and its advertisers. Secondary messages embedded in ads for other products also promulgated new values. Consider, for example, the way in which Woodbury soap was sold to women as early as 1911: it was hygienic, cosmetic, *and* sexual. The J. Walter Thompson Advertising Agency created a campaign that touted Woodbury's as able to create "A Skin You Love to Touch." Granted, it directed women's attention to skin care for the sake of masculine attention. But it also recognized and even celebrated a certain sensuality in women that had been denied by Victorian rhetoric that emphasized women's sexual purity. This campaign created a sensation within the advertising world and among the public, yet ran in the *Ladies' Home Journal*, the most self-consciously wholesome of the women's mass-circulation magazines and one that ignored and even discouraged women's sensuality elsewhere in its pages.[67]

By the 1910s, when this campaign debuted, the public was by and large ready to accept the sexualization of "respectable" women in advertising for this familiarly feminine product. This "emotional" advertising, as the J. Walter Thompson Agency called it, encompassed women's heretofore unvoiced desires for sensual pleasure and fulfilment as well as their "inarticulate longings" for better housewares.[68] By the 1920s, women's sexuality was easily bound up with and exploited in advertisements for all sorts of products. The Fisher Company, for example, manufacturer of decidedly unsexy auto bodies, created arresting ads that featured not cars but the long, lithe, and lovely "Fisher Body Girl," the very model of the self-possessed modern woman. The fine text of the ads discussed the merits of Fisher craftsmanship and reputation among auto manufacturers, but in bold-faced type declared "95% Prefer 'Body by Fisher,'" and the image of the new modern woman unmistakably referenced sex, consumption, and the "New Woman."[69]

It is now conventional wisdom that the construction of women as sexual beings was a boon to advertisers. "Sex sells" is an old and well-respected truism. It is important to recognize, though, that advertisers did not force the issue. The acts and desires of Gibson girls, flappers, and other New Women contributed significantly to, if they did not in fact drive, the reconstruction of beauty and womanhood at the turn of the century to recognize, incorporate, and even privilege women's sexuality.

The case of cigarette advertising *vis-à-vis* women between 1880 and the 1930s demonstrates the cigarette manufacturers' desire on the whole to follow rather than initiate trends. For decades they struck a cautious balance that uncharacteristically sacrificed their desire for profit to their awe for the power of dominant public opinion. Thus, conscious of the determined opposition of antitobacco reformers to their product generally and the female smoker particularly, manufacturers and advertisers of cigarettes pointedly ignored the growing number of female smokers. Only in the late 1920s, when young Americans' new comprehension of beauty and womanhood was ascendant and women's cigarette habit an acknowledged and accepted fact, did lead-ing manufacturers finally make bold to advertise to them openly. Indeed, even in appeals to male smokers, cigarette manufacturers in the 1900s and 1910s exercised caution in employing the feminine image in their advertising, scarcely permitting women to appear in proximity of a cigarette; the public response in the 1880s and 1890s to some risqué trading cards had suggested to the industry the wisdom of respecting, not remaking, public opinion and mores.

Images of beautiful women had long been used, remember, to sell tobacco. The images employed before the late 1880s and 1890s were lithographs of "types" and "ideals" rather than actual women, and they generally observed the Victorian fiction of white women's passionless-ness by suppressing or displacing their sexuality. The woman repre-senting Virgin Leaf chewing tobacco was winsome, but not lewd or seductive. (Figure 3.3.) An image of Juno advertising a chewing tobacco of the same name was bare-breasted yet not in any way sexu-ally suggestive. Frances Willard lamented the prurient pictures of women available in cigar stores and saloons, knowing "that, if we were as self-respectful as we ought to be, [they] couldn't stay there over night," but since the cigar labels and window cards to which she

Figure 3.3. The modest figure embodied ideal womanhood in the late nineteenth century, and though the product was nowhere in evidence, was typical of many advertisements for plug and smoking tobacco. Courtesy of the Rare Book, Manuscript, and Special Collections Library, Duke University, Durham, North Carolina.

referred generally featured "exotic" (dark-skinned or "Eastern") women, they did not really threaten conceptions of American (read "white") womanhood and thus American civilization.[70]

"Buck" Duke's advertising for the newfangled cigarette broke the old rules about women and advertising, and drew more sustained criticism for its effect on public morals. In particular, Duke, founder of the American Tobacco Company, moved into new and controversial territory when he began offering trading cards with less-than-chaste photographs of lesser actresses and "sporting girls" as an inducement to buy his growing stock of cigarettes. Duke's innovation was not in the fact of such trading cards—other manufacturers (and Duke as well) produced collectible series featuring sports figures, military and political figures, birds, and flowers—but in their content. These photos left nothing to the imagination in their depictions of women décolleté and bare-armed, their legs covered only by tights. These daringly clad women bore little resemblance to the ideal of pure womanhood that "proper" Americans prized at the time, but were in fact white American women.[71]

Duke's bold trading cards challenged convention, but he apparently treated success as a virtue in its own right. If disreputable pictures of attractive, white, American women attracted more customers than they offended, then there was no sin. That, however, was an open question. Cigarettes gained in popularity throughout the latter years of the nineteenth century, but the product and its advertising sparked criticism and organized opposition.

The cards on which the images appeared served the practical function of a package insert to protect the cigarettes from crushing; they became collectors' items as well and a means of ensuring repeat business and brand loyalty. A worrisome question, however, was *who* collected them. Some observers within the tobacco industry—and, for that matter, within Duke's own company—suggested a move away from this mode of advertising. Buck's father, Washington Duke, expressed his concern and urged that another means of advertising be found that more closely conformed to contemporary sexual mores. He was, he wrote to his son:

> against circulating lascivious photographs with cigarettes, and have made my mind up to bring the matter to your attention in the interest of morallity [sic], and in the hope that you can invent a proper substitute for these pictures which will answer your requirements as an advertisement as well as an inducement to purchase. . . . I have always looked upon the distribution of this character of advertisement as wrong in its pernicious effects upon young man and womanhood, and . . . I am fully convinced that this mode of advertising will be used and greatly strengthen the arguments against cigarettes in the legislative halls of the States. . . .[72]

Writers at *Tobacco*, a tobacco retailers' trade journal, likewise chided Duke and other manufacturers for the use of those "lascivious photos." Presumably the journal approved an advertisement for Cross-Cut Cigarettes; the young woman at its center was sweetly coquettish rather than boldly available as she sat with her slippered feet demurely crossed and a forefinger just resting on her mouth. By contrast, the publication lavished praise on a lithograph series called "The World's Beauties." This latter series of collectibles was described as "chaste, beautiful, and deeply interesting" to a wide audience—unlike the actress pics, "which went principally to boys, men throwing them away without inspection."[73]

These friendly critics of the risqué cards sought to protect the future of the still-young industry by anticipating the response of the cigarette's foes. The Women's Christian Temperance Union (WCTU) noted at its 1895 convention that tobacco advertising, particularly that associated with cigarettes, was growing "more expensive and disgusting; the business [more] aggressive and persistent."[74] An antivice association in Boston moved against a "hawker [who] was selling upon the streets a very improper picture, an advertisement of a certain brand of cigarette."[75] These and other complainants charged that the cards challenged convention and morality, and threatened the souls and bodies of youth by luring them toward sexual vice as well as early use of and overindulgence in tobacco. The WCTU, an array of anticigarette leagues and associations, concerned parents, and schoolteachers petitioned localities, states, and even the United States Congress to outlaw the manufacture, advertising, sale, and distribution of cigarettes—and were rewarded with anticigarette legislation in over a dozen states and a drop in cigarette consumption in the last years of the nineteenth century.[76]

Duke's contentious advertising confirmed the association in the public mind of tobacco and women as objects of beauty and desire for men but in the 1880s and early 1890s was premature in its blatant uncoupling of feminine beauty from any pretense of domestic virtue or moral worth. Not only did the images offend Victorians' idealization of womanhood but, in their overtly prurient aspect, ran afoul, too, of Victorian notions of manly virtue, character, and self-restraint.

The heyday of trading cards passed around 1900, but the vogue for lovely women in cigarette advertising persisted, and the inclination to impute a sensual aspect to those women, be they "exotic" or "American," increased. Between 1900 and 1920, a fad for Turkish cigarettes dominated the tobacco industry. The packaging and advertising for these often featured lovely, veiled odalisques, supine and seemingly sexually available, and often (unlike earlier advertising) in close proximity to the tobacco product in question. Yet these images did not draw the same criticism that had greeted the sexy actress pictures of earlier decades. Opponents to the cigarette persisted, but the cultural ground was shifting beneath them in the 1910s.

Advertisements for Turkish brands were helped along, for example, by a widespread fascination with the Orient that existed in American, indeed Western, culture. The Western body of "knowledge" about the East, often as not, had little to do with the realities of Eastern life, but it remained remarkably constant, always associating "the East" with "luxurious ease," languor, extravagance, display, and (especially female) sexuality. The limited, stereotyped "knowledge" of orientalism promised release, self-realization, and better living to citizens of the West, even as it denigrated easterners and rationalized economic and political hegemony over the region.[77]

Orientalism pervaded virtually every aspect of early twentieth-century American culture but has the greatest significance here when considered in reference to the burgeoning consumer culture. In an era when more consumer goods were becoming available, images of a luxurious and ornamented East were used to sell all sorts of things—carpets, cars, clothing, *and* cigarettes—at home in the West. The consumer could think himself as rich as any pasha and his home as mysterious and delightful as any harem if it was decorated with Persian rugs, cloth of gold, and chinoiserie. "Mrs. Consumer," as Christine Frederick dubbed the American woman of the 1910s and twenties, purchased Shalimar and other "oriental" perfumes, decked herself out in turbans, slave bracelets, and other "Eastern"-inspired fashions and fancied herself one of the lovely, mysterious, and oh-so-enticing houris who captivated would-be pashas.[78]

The fascination with the Orient coincided with the ongoing redefinition of gender and beauty to provoke an unintended response on the part of women who viewed the advertising that proliferated for Turkish cigarettes in the first decades of the twentieth century. Omar, Turkish Trophies, and other brands took care to address a male audience in their advertising, but I suggest that those New Women who were working so hard to redefine their place in the world and the rules by which they would be guided found the meaning of Turkish cigarettes as suggested in ads appealing and compelling.

In the figure of the reclining Circassian beauty who graced advertising for Turkish Trophies and that of the pert houri who attended the jolly Omar pasha, as well as in the product that they sold, Gibson girls and flappers could locate freedoms and pleasures from which they were still formally excluded by the lingering restraints of Victorian society. (Figure 3.4.) The attire and posture of the women in the ads communicated the idea of physical freedom and comfort. Dress reform was a long time coming to Western women, but loose "tea dresses" had been worn by some since the late 1870s, and pantaloon gowns and the Eastern-inflected "lamp-shade tunic dress" enjoyed increasing popularity in the United States and Europe from the 1890s through the era of World War I. All of these presaged the end of corsets that is most often associated with the fashions of the 1920s. In the Circassian's possession of Turkish Trophies cigarettes American women may have seen someone who refused to deny herself personal enjoyment. This reading would thus make the act of a woman smoking a cigarette or adopting a relaxed style of dress seem a rational decision and a totem of liberation.[79] Engaging in some cultural cross-dressing allowed

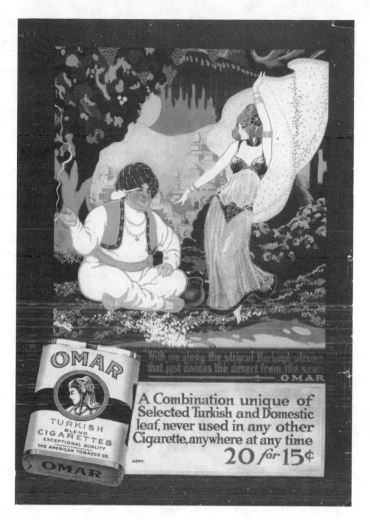

Figure 3.4. The fantastic "Eastern" setting of this American Tobacco advertisement for Omar cigarettes probably did not prevent America's emergent 'new' women from identifying with or envying the houri's physical freedom and teasing sensuality – qualities that marked the female figures used in many advertisements for Turkish and Turkish blend cigarettes in the 1910s. Courtesy of the Warshaw Collection, Archives Center, Smithsonian Institution, Washington, D.C.

American women to broaden the range of behavior that was acceptable within their society.[80]

Of course, it is difficult if not impossible to know precisely how any of these particular advertisements affected individuals' behavior, and much of the foregoing analysis is conjectural. Women were not part of the intended audience for Turkish Trophies or Omar advertisements in the 1900s and 1910s, yet I argue that women read themselves into the images to sanction their growing cigarette habit. Certainly their habit *was* increasing. Numbers are virtually impossible to come by, but the spate of articles reacting to women's smoking, the testimony of industry insiders, as well as a tremendous spike between 1910 and 1916 in the number of cigarettes consumed nationally support the claim that women responded to new opportunities in the 1910s and joined men once more in the enjoyment of tobacco in defiance of continued criticism and despite the fact that they were pointedly ignored by manufacturers and national advertisers.[81] The transformation of gender and consumer culture in which Gibson girls, coeds, flappers, and working women participated bore on the relationships or associations customarily assumed between men and women and all commodities, and changed them. Notably, this redefinition of roles and image permitted some women to reinterpret their relationship with that forbidden fruit of the marketplace, the cigarette.

Though the Turkish fad waned after 1918, the number of women smoking increased in the 1920s. By 1926 an observer in the advertising industry estimated that at least 40 percent of women between the ages of twenty and fifty smoked at least occasionally. They accounted for perhaps 15 percent of the tobacco consumed in the United States and spent at least $103,200,000 on their habit in 1925.[82] Though the reformers kept up the hue and cry, the ground on which they were arguing had shifted. Their young antagonists had succeeded in making smoking thoroughly compatible with womanly beauty.

The leaders of the cigarette industry seem to have been the last to realize this, though, and failed to compete openly for the female market until the late 1920s. Other advertisers had not only long noticed but discreetly catered to the female smoker. Macy's department store began carrying special costumes in 1913 for the chic female smoker, many of them incorporating an Eastern flair that was in keeping with the vogue for Turkish cigarettes. (Fashionable department stores and hotels in many cities had long before that moved to provide ladies' smoking rooms on their premises.) Manufacturers of smoking paraphernalia like cigarette cases and holders noted a dramatic increase in the demand for their goods after 1914 and attributed it solely to the rise in the number of female smokers. The trade journal *Tobacco* noted in 1920 that indeed cigarette smoking among women all over the United States was: "becoming as prevalent now as it is in Europe. . . . The young woman from Toledo or Kansas City is no longer shocked by the cigarette, but carries her own stock; in fact, she carries the carmine-tipped cigarettes so that the rouge will not spot the tip. And she also packs her cigarette holder in her vanity case."[83]

These up-to-date, fashion-conscious young women subscribed to the mantra of modern womanhood that emphasized personal pleasure, individualism, and independence; they also clearly concerned themselves with personal appearance and hygiene as they presented themselves to the world, and found various products available for their purchase that would ensure the latter as they pursued the former. Ads from early to mid-1920s for Pepsodent toothpaste promised to combat the smoke-stained film dimming those pearly white teeth that contributed so to personal beauty. LifeSavers made breath "sweet and pure" and were "gym-dandy after smoking."

The modern female smoker increasingly met with amiable tolerance and acceptance in the popular culture of the 1920s. *Life* magazine published a "Smokes Number" in 1920 that featured on its cover a jaunty young woman clearly versed in the arts of smoking, carrying matches in her purse, and willing to offer a friendly light to a male fellow traveler. A cartoon in the same issue made it clear that it wasn't just the single flapper who indulged a penchant for smoking: a young mother checking in on her sleeping son confiscates a pack of cigarettes that she finds in his room, not with words of horror or condemnation but happy in the realization that she can now replenish her own supply. "It's lucky I found them," she tells her visitor, "I haven't a single one left."[84] *Life's* 1926 "Commencement Number" featured "Our Sweet Girl Graduate" on the cover, complete with bobbed hair, rolled stockings, free-and-easy posture, and cigarette in hand. *Our Dancing Daughters* brought this flapper to life on celluloid in the character of Diana Medford. Full of sass, acutely aware of herself as a sensual and sexual individual, and a confirmed devotee of the cigarette (as well as other so-called vices condemned by her elders), Diana was the new ideal of American womanhood, pure, decent, full of promise, and an appropriate representative of her age. Her triumph in the film demonstrated the redefinition of womanly purity and beauty to encompass an acknowledgment of women's sexuality and formerly taboo behavior, and the ultimate twining of sex and cigarettes (her innocent but suggestive declaration to Ben of her "yearning . . . for . . . a cigarette!" is priceless). Joan Crawford rose to stardom with this film, and the apotheosis of the cigarette as a fit and even glamorous prop of the modern woman was complete.

Finally, as the 1920s turned to the 1930s and evidence of the woman smoker's cultural acceptance abounded, the "big three" of the early twentieth-century cigarette industry (American Tobacco, R. J. Reynolds, and Liggett & Myers) launched sustained campaigns to win the brand loyalty of female smokers. An editor for *Tobacco* made the novel suggestion in 1927 that the extreme caution being exercised by the industry *vis-à-vis* women was justified, lest women, given the encouragement of advertising, become the majority of cigarette smokers, and men forsake an effeminate product for a more masculine pipe or cigar.[85] A more likely explanation for manufacturers' standing back throughout most of the decade was their fear of a public backlash that might revive the failing efforts of antitobacco reformers in the state legislatures. Further, the leaders had watched smaller companies fail to capture the female market with specialty cigarettes that were meant to be especially feminine. Gold-tipped and scented brands failed to achieve anything approaching national appeal. As a general rule, they did not even try for such a thing, preferring to rely on small retailers with their existing female clientele rather than general and widely disseminated advertising.

Philip Morris was the first (then) small manufacturer to aim directly for the national female market when it launched its Marlboro brand late in 1924. Advertising for the new cigarette appeared in tony publications like *Bon Ton* and *Vogue* and made a refined but unmistakable appeal to their female readers. The Marlboro package itself was feminine—white with a royal crest under the brand name, and the company name "Philip Morris" overlaid the crest in florid script. Early advertisements pictured an obviously female hand holding a cigarette over copy reading "Mild as May." Subsequently campaigns featured women actually smoking, and the copy explained that the cigarette of choice would naturally be Marlboro since "Women–when they smoke at all–quickly develop discerning taste."

This elitist tone suggested the glamour of smoking but proved misguided as a means of approaching bold, active women who were claiming their rights to the same smoking (and other) pleasures enjoyed by men. Although *Advertising and Selling* praised the Marlboro campaigns of the twenties, the cigarette that was "Mild as May" failed to capture the essence or attention of the flappers who comprised such a significant proportion of the intended audience. In 1931, after nearly seven years of effort, Marlboro still had less than 1 percent of the cigarette market.[86]

Liggett & Myers moved cautiously in the "right" direction to attract female smokers in 1926. Its famous "Blow Some My Way" campaign marked the first effort to lure women to a leading national brand cigarette: Chesterfield. In fact, the campaign's appeal was oblique: none of the ads showed women smoking or even holding a cigarette. But the message was clear, suggestive, and in step with the sensibilities and desires of the modern woman. In tandem with the image of an attractive couple seated close in the moonlight, the woman's tag line "Blow Some My Way" both implied her equal enjoyment of cigarettes with men *and* linked women, sex, and cigarettes in a way that ads for other brands, many of them also peopled with women, did not.[87]

The advertising for Reynolds' Camel cigarettes, for example, frequently featured women throughout the late 1920s, but was slow to address the female smoker directly. Women appeared as men's comrades and confidantes, relaxed and elegant in their interactions, but the pleasure of smoking was, until late in 1928, reserved for men.

Gradually the advertising implied an invitation to women—by placing a cigarette pack next to her elbow on the dinner table or, more directly, by showing two men offering her a cigarette. Although the woman hesitated to accept the invitation throughout 1927 and most of 1928, Reynolds did, of course, cross the Rubicon to show women enjoying its product. An ad in a 1929 issue of *Modern Priscilla* showed a chicly attired woman seated at a desk catching up on her correspondence, an open pack of Camels helping her to strike "Just the Right Note." Other ads, showing women and men smoking while in evening clothes or as fashionable spectators at the races or clay court, described Camels as "To the Manner Born," and suggested that the same was true of the discerning men and women who smoked them.[88]

Camel advertising associated the brand with the New Woman of the 1920s and 1930s, but as a marker of her sophistication rather than her sexual identity, as in the Chesterfield ads of 1926. That striking campaign for Chesterfields, in fact, survived only briefly and did not capture the female market to vault Chesterfield to industry dominance. Early in the 1930s, though, Liggett & Myers' advertising for Chesterfield returned to the theme of woman's equality with men in matters of smoking and sexual pleasure in ads in which a well-dressed woman averred to her male companion that "I'm 'that way' about Chesterfields, too" or "I Like What You Like." (Figure 3.5) Does she mean cigarettes? Does she mean sex? The enduring slogan for Chesterfields simply promised the consumer, male or female, that "They Satisfy."

American Tobacco's Lucky Strike cigarettes, though, were the overwhelming choice of the modish and liberated woman of the 1920s. Though Liggett ads in the 1930s claimed that millions of women had found a "new smoking pleasure" and joined the ranks of satisfied Chesterfield smokers, many more switched and remained loyal to Lucky Strikes. American Tobacco's president, George Washington Hill, made Luckies' industry dominance his "main interest in life." In 1927, he determined that capturing the female market would ensure that dominance. Initially wary of potential backlash, Hill began slowly with testimonials from famous women who were beyond the criticism of pesky reformers. Alla Nazimova, for example, was not only exempted from the smoking taboo that was to govern American women, but, as an actress and a Russian émigré, was virtually expected to smoke. Amelia Earhart was likewise excused her cigarette habit as an American heroine who, succeeding in the male-dominated world of aviation, existed far outside the bounds that contained the lives of most women. These and other endorsements introduced the American public to famous and admired women who apparently enjoyed a good cigarette. They further purported to demonstrate Lucky Strike as the best

I'm "that way" about
Chesterfields, too—

the cigarette that's MILDER
the cigarette that TASTES BETTER

Figure 3.5. By the 1930s, advertisers recognized that many American women took the same pleasure in smoking that men did, and no longer held themselves at a distance from the female market. Image in author's collection.

cigarette to smoke—because "It's Toasted" and could calm nerves and eliminate throat irritation. The ads were interesting, but they did not speak directly to the average female smoker, and by the end of 1928 Hill knew it.[89]

In that year, Hill and American's advertising agency, Lord & Thomas, unveiled the most candid appeal yet made in advertising to the American woman. His famous "Reach for a Lucky Instead of a Sweet" campaign aimed directly at women striving for the thin, trim elegance highlighted in fashion, film, and flapperdom. His next move in the battle for female smokers was less obvious but undoubtedly a success in the long run. Edward Bernays, the so-called "father of public relations," orchestrated on Hill's behalf a "Torches of Freedom March" down New York's Fifth Avenue on Easter Sunday, 1929. The sight of roughly a dozen debutantes strolling the avenue ostentatiously puffing on their cigarettes created a sensation on the nation's front pages, but Bernays had worked so effectively that the stunt seemed not an advertisement but a validation of women's right to smoke and *any* manufacturer's right to recruit their brand loyalty. Hill struck the right chord in his advertising, and between 1925 and 1931 his company's profits more than doubled and Lucky Strike became the number one brand in America.[90]

The change in cigarette advertising at the turn of the 1920s to incorporate and address women as consumers was dramatic and profitable. But it was not made on the initiative of the tobacco companies. Women had transformed themselves and the standards by which they would live. They had created a space for themselves in which to indulge in a formerly forbidden behavior. They laid the groundwork for the American cigarette industry finally to advertise to women in the late 1920s. George Washington Hill and his peers did not set out to reconfigure public opinion so that they might recruit women to Lucky Strike, Chesterfield, and the rest; women themselves, in conjunction with the larger consumer culture, had liberated themselves from an old construct of gender and beauty that branded cigarettes and the cigarette-smoking woman immoral and unlovely, and had transformed an industry.

NOTES

1. Henry Ford, *The Case Against the Little White Slaver* (Detroit, MI: Henry Ford, 1916); John Bain and Carl Werner, *Cigarettes in Fact and Fancy* (Boston: H. M. Caldwell Co., 1906).

2. Consumer culture is most frequently read by scholars as co-opting the language of feminism and promising liberation to the female consumer, while the dominant message of the advertisements peddled women's primary role as that of wife and mother. See Rayna Rapp and Ellen Ross, "The 1920s: Feminism, Consumerism, and Political Backlash in the United States," in *Women in Culture and Politics: A Century of Change*, ed. J. Friedlander, et al. (Bloomington, IN: Indiana University Press, 1986); Roland Marchand, *Advertising the American Dream: Making Way for Modernity, 1920–1940* (Berkeley, CA: University of California Press, 1985); Nancy Cott, *The Modern Groundings of Feminism* (New Haven, CT: Yale University Press, 1987); Stuart Ewen, *Captains of Consciousness: Advertising and the Social Roots of Consumer Culture* (New York: McGraw Hill, 1976); Jennifer Scanlon, *Inarticulate Longings: The Ladies' Home Journal, Gender, and the Promises of Consumer Culture* (New York: Routledge, 1995). I am not disagreeing that the overall message of the ads of consumer culture was confining, but arguing that women may yet have been able to find justification for use of the forbidden cigarette by manipulating the secondary messages of the culture.

3. Jackson Lears importantly noted that a "favorable moral climate" was required for the firm and successful establishment of a consumer culture. He argued that there was between 1880 and 1930 a "shift from a Protestant ethos of salvation through self-denial toward a therapeutic ethos stressing self-realization in this world" that provided such a favorable moral climate. Lears's examination of the connection between changing social values, advertising, and America's redefinition as a consumer culture was an influential starting point for me here. I have, however, narrowed my focus to shifting definitions of a single quality—beauty—and how those competing and changing definitions of beauty, intimately connected to changing standards of womanhood, impacted the use of a particular consumer good—the cigarette. See T. J. Jackson Lears, "From Salvation to Self-Realization: Advertising and the Therapeutic Roots of Consumer Culture, 1880–1930," in

The Culture of Consumption: Critical Essays in American History, 1880–1980, ed. Richard Fox and T. J. J. Lears (New York: Pantheon Books, 1983), 1–38.

4. For the associations of smoking with prostitutes and other disreputable women, see, for example, Lois Banner, *American Beauty* (Chicago: University of Chicago Press, 1983), 76; Dolores Mitchell, "Images of Exotic Women in Turn-of-the-Century Tobacco Art," *Feminist Studies* 18/2 (Summer 1992): 327–343.

5. Ella Wheeler Wilcox, "The Woman Who Smokes," *New York Saturday Evening Journal*, (March 30, 1911).

6. Caroline Ticknor, "The Steel-Engraving Lady and the Gibson Girl," *Atlantic Monthly* (July 1901): 105–108.

7. Alfred Dunhill, *The Gentle Art of Smoking* (New York: G. P. Putnam's Sons, 1954): 127; no author, *The Smokers', Chewer's, and Snuff Taker's Companion, and Tobacconist's Own Book* (Philadelphia: Turner and Fisher, 1841), 21, 31, 36; Carl Werner, *Tobaccoland* (New York: Tobacco Leaf Publishing Company, 1922), 70.

8. As will be seen below, this notion of rivalry occasionally took a poetic and somewhat humorous form in the late nineteenth century. But it was an idea clearly and more seriously articulated by some clergy in the mid-nineteenth century who embarked on an antitobacco crusade and turned to women for support and assistance. See, for example, James Parton, *Smoking and Drinking* (Boston: Ticknor & Fields, 1868).

9. For revisions of stereotypical understandings of Victorians, and especially Victorian women, as prudish, sexually repressed, or neurotic, see Carl Degler, "What Ought to Be and What Was: Women's Sexuality in the Nineteenth Century," *American Historical Review* 79/5 (December 1974): 1467–1490; Christina Simmons, "Modern Sexuality and the Myth of Victorian Repression," in *Passion and Power: Sexuality in History*, ed. Christina Simmons and Kathy Peiss (Philadelphia: Temple University Press, 1989); Victoria Steele, *Fashion and Eroticism: Ideals of Feminine Beauty from the Victorian Era to the Jazz Age* (New York: Oxford University Press, 1985); and Karen Lystra, *Searching the Heart: Women, Men, and Romantic Love in Nineteenth-Century America* (New York: Oxford University Press, 1989).

10. J. M. Barrie, *My Lady Nicotine: A Study in Smoke* (Boston: Joseph Knight Company, 1896), 4 and *passim.*

11. *Atlantic Monthly* 100 (1917): 143–144.

12. Duke folders, Box 4, Tobacco Trade and Industry Section, Warshaw Collection of Americana, Archives Center, National Museum of American History, Smithsonian Institution, Washington, D. C. This poem is only one of many scattered throughout the Duke folders and the entire tobacco section of the Warshaw Collection. See also, Sylvestre Watkins, *The Pleasures of Smoking, as expressed by those poets, wits and tellers of tales who have drawn their inspiration from the fragrant weed* (New York: H. Schuman, 1948).

13. From a pamphlet issued by the cigar shop of the Hotel Lafayette in Philadelphia, John M. Campbell, "The Puff of Peace and Consolation" (Philadelphia: Louis Smith, n.d.), 7–8. In Miscellaneous folder, Box 20, Tobacco, Warshaw Collection.

14. See Dolores Mitchell, "Images of Exotic Women," 327–343.

15. For discussions of the moral underpinnings of the Victorian ideal of beauty—and the shifts away from this ideal—see Lois Banner, *American Beauty* (New York: Alfred A. Knopf, 1983), 12–13, 208, 264, and *passim*; Elizabeth Haiken, *Venus Envy: A History of Cosmetic Surgery* (Baltimore, MA: Johns Hopkins University Press, 1997), 23 and *passim*; Kathy Peiss, *Hope in a Jar: The Making of America's Beauty Culture* (New York: Metropolitan Books, 1998), 24–27 and *passim.*

16. Harry Thurston Peck, "Beauty," *The Cosmopolitan* 30 (December 1900): 181.

17. Cocroft is quoted in Kathy Peiss, "Making Faces: The Cosmetics Industry and the Cultural Construction of Gender, 1890–1930," in *Unequal Sisters: A Multicultural Reader in U.S. Women's History*, ed. Vicki Ruiz and Ellen Carol DuBois (New York: Routledge, 1994).

18. Harriet Hubbard Ayer, *Harriet Hubbard Ayer's Book: A Complete and Authentic Treatise on the Laws of Health and Beauty* (Springfield, MA: The King-Richardson Company, 1902): 40.

19. Robert Tomes, *Beauty: Its Attainment and Preservation* (New York: Butterick Publishing Company, 1890), 16–17.

20. Production of cigarettes increased 1400 percent between 1880 and 1920, and consumption kept pace so that by 1920 cigarettes represented 51 percent of all sales and internal revenues derived from tobacco. Charles Barney, *The Tobacco Industry* (New York: Charles D. Barney & Co., 1924): 21, 24.

21. The first crusade against Americans' tobacco use took shape in the 1840s and 1850s, an outgrowth of the Second Great Awakening and the contemporary temperance movement. No tangible successes are associated with this first effort—no statutes or marked decline in consumption—but it established many of the arguments that would be used in

the second crusade of the 1890s and 1900s. In particular, there was a clear concern for youth, a linkage to alcohol consumption, and an expectation of women's support of the cause.

22. See, for example, Lester C. Hubbard, *Tobacco and Its Bondage. By a Slave Who Became Free* (New York: Lester C. Hubbard & Co., 1900); Ford, *The Case Against the Little White Slaver*; *The Anti-Tobacco Gem* 9/5 and 9/6 (May and June, 1892).

23. *Anti-Tobacco Journal* 2 (1872): 51; *The Anti-Tobacco Gem* 9/10 (October 1892): 3. The *Gem* pointed as well to "The Dutch nation whose ships once swept the seas." Its citizens had "smoked till they [we]re contented" and had lost their spirit of enterprise and with it considerable economic influence.

24. See, for example, *The Anti-Tobacco Gem* 9/8 (August 1892): 3; "A Foolish Father and Foolish Son," *The Anti-Tobacco Crusader* 10 (July 1897).

25. Women's Christian Temperance Union, *Union Signal* (July 12, 1883): 6.

26. *Anti-Tobacco Journal* 2/3–5: 71–72.

27. "Anti-Smoking," Box 19, Tobacco, Warshaw Collection of Americana, Smithsonian Institution, Washington, D.C.

28. Hubbard, *Tobacco and Its Bondage*, 59.

29. *Ibid.*, vol. I, nos. 2–3.

30. Marie Manning, *Ladies Now and Then* (New York: E. P. Dutton and Co., 1944), 46 (italics mine). Marie Manning began publishing under the name "Beatrice Fairfax" in 1898 in the New York *Journal*.

31. They often adhered to the cautious practice of frequenting empty tobacco shops to avoid detection or claiming to be making purchases for their husbands. A New York retailer and contributor to the trade journal *Tobacco* (February 17, 1888) noted the popularity of snuff among women but noted that:

    the various pretexts under which they buy it are amusing. Some use it "for nervous headaches; some, because it preserves the teeth; some, because it sweetens the breath; others, simply because they like it." Ladies, apparently well-to-do, use it with the same eagerness as women who are not ladies. They usually wait their opportunity when the store is empty to get their regular supply. . . .

    See *Tobacco* (November 2, 16, and 30, 1894) for early observations and laments about "advanced" women who wanted to smoke and for accounts of the efforts of certain reformers, Mrs. F. H. Ingalls of the WCTU, for example, to stamp out cigarette use among men *and* women.

32. Clarence King, *Mountaineering in the Sierra Nevada* (Philadelphia: Lippincott, 1963 [1872]), 28, 96.

33. Havelock Ellis, *Studies in the Psychology of Sex,* vol. 1 (New York: Random House, 1942), 222–230, 245–251.

34. Harold Frederic, *The Damnation of Theron Ware*, ed. Everett Carter (Cambridge, MA: Belknap Press of Harvard University Press, 1960); Arthur B. Reeve, "The Murder Syndicate," in *The War Terror*, vol. 4 (New York: Harper & Brothers, 1915): 22–34; Helen Duncan Queen, "Change," *The Designer and The Woman's Magazine* (April 1926): 14, 71–76. See also Hugh Cockerell, "Tobacco and Victorian Literature," in *Ashes to Ashes: The History of Smoking and Health*, ed. Stephen Lock, Lois Reynolds, and E. M. Tansey (Amsterdam: Rodopi, 1998), 89–97.

35. *The Boy* 7/4 (April 1908): 7.

36. Lauretta E. Kress, M.D., "Tobacco Using Among Women," *Life and Health* (January 1916): 295–297.

37. Mrs. Carrie Flatter to President William Oxley Thompson, January 3, 1921, in the Ohio State University Archives, William Oxley Thompson Papers, (RG 3/e/34/37), "Ohio No-Tobacco League: Correspondence: 1920–1922."

38. See, for example, Mrs. F. L. Townsend, "Again, the Cigarette," *Union Signal* (June 20, 1912): 3; Mrs. E. B. Ingalls, "The Cigarette Evil," *Union Signal* (November 28, 1912): 14; Dr. L. J. Lenieux, "Canadian Government Studies," in *the Tobacco Source Book*, n.d., Women's Christian Temperance Union Archives, Evanston, Illinois; "Things I Know," *The Boy* (April 1908): 2.

39. *Union Signal* 3 (October 1, 1927): 595.

40. "The Pope's Appeal to Men to Reform Women's Dress," *Literary Digest* 72 (January 29, 1927): 27–28, 57–59.

41. *The Boy* 4/1 (April 15, 1903); *The Christian Citizen* 2/7 (March 1897); "The Pope's Appeal to Men to Reform Women's Dress," 27–28, 57–59; Harry Burke, "Women Cigarette Fiends," *Ladies' Home Journal* (June 1922): 19, 132; Mark Sullivan, *Our Times: The United States, 1900-1925*, vol. 3, *Pre-War America* (New York: Charles Scribner's Sons, 1930), 529–532; Harrison, "The Romance of Tobacco"; J. D. Hunting, "Women and Tobacco," *The*

National Review 14 (1899): 218–228; F. L. Townsend, "Again, the Cigarette," *Union Signal* (June 20, 1912).

42. Edgar Saltus, "The Mystery of Beauty," *The Cosmopolitan* 28 (December 1899): 138; Gertrude Lynch, "Racial and Ideal Types of Beauty," *The Cosmopolitan* 38 (December 1904): 229.
43. Christine Stansell, *City of Women* (Champaign/Urbana, IL: University of Illinois Press, 1984).
44. This story is well-told in Kathy Peiss, *Cheap Amusements* (Philadelphia, PA: Temple University Press, 1985).
45. Caroline Ticknor, "The Steel-Engraving Lady and the Gibson Girl," *Atlantic Monthly* 68 (July 1901): 105–108; Lynch, "Racial and Ideal Types of Beauty," 230; Martha Banta, *Imaging American Woman: Ideas and Ideals in Cultural History* (New York: Columbia University Press, 1987), 212–214.
46. Manning, *Ladies Now and Then*, 59.
47. Regina Malone, "The Fabulous Monster," *The Forum* (1926): 26–30.
48. Ellen Key, "The Woman of the Future," *The Independent* (October 31, 1907): 1043–1045.
49. Ellis, *Psychology of Sex*, ix.
50. Notices for books on sexology and sex education appeared in the *Saturday Evening Post* as early as 1908; the "Sex and Self" series advertised in *Life* in the 1920s. Manning, *Ladies Now and Then*, 190–191.
51. Royden, *Sex and Common Sense* (London: G. P. Putnam's Sons, 1922), 37.
52. Alyse Gregory, "The Changing Morality of Women," *The Current History Magazine* 19 (1923): 295–299.
53. Margaret Deland, "The Change in the Feminine Ideal," *Atlantic Monthly* 85 (March 1910): 290–302.
54. Charlotte Perkins Gilman, "Vanguard, Rearguard, and Mud-Guard," *The Century Magazine* 104 (1922): 348–353.
55. "Women and the Weed," *Literary Digest* 87 (December 19, 1925): 312; Ohio State *Lantern* (January 10, 1922); *Trinity Chronicle* (December 17, 1924, January 17, 1925); *Student Handbooks*, Duke University, 1932–1933. See also Paula Fass, *The Beautiful and the Damned: American Youth in the 1920s* (New York: Oxford University Press, 1977).
56. Ohio State *Lantern* (January 10, 1922).
57. Marguerite Harrison, "Sorority of Smoke on Wheels," *New York Times Book Review and Magazine* (July 2, 1922).
58. Manning, *Ladies Now and Then*, 47–8.
59. Regina Malone, "The Fabulous Monster."
60. Harrison, "Sorority of Smoke on Wheels."
61. See, for example, Jennifer Scanlon, *Inarticulate Longings: The Ladies' Home Journal, Gender, and the Promises of Consumer Culture* (New York: Routledge, 1995); Richard Ohmann, *Selling Culture: Magazines, Markets, and Class at the Turn of the Century* (London: Verso, 1996); Helen Damon-Moore, *Magazines for the Millions: Gender and Commerce in the Ladies' Home Journal and the Saturday Evening Post, 1880–1910* (Albany, NY: SUNY Press, 1994). Nancy Cott does not focus on the creation of the consumer culture as Scanlon and Ohmann do, but does discuss the commodification of womanhood in *The Grounding of Modern Feminism* (New Haven, CT: Yale University Press, 1987), 143–173. Kathy Peiss's latest work is all about the redefinition and commodification of beauty. Unlike Scanlon, however, she does not see men or the desire to please them prompting women's use of cosmetics. Peiss, *Hope in a Jar*, 176–177.
62. Christine Frederick, *Selling Mrs. Consumer* (New York: The Business Bourse, 1929), 29–31, 335.
63. *Better Homes and Gardens* (December 1929): 63, reproduced in Marchand, *Advertising the American Dream*, 174. See also, for example, Cott, *The Grounding of Modern Feminism*, 168–173; Scanlon, *Inarticulate Longings*, esp. 49–76; and Nancy Tomes, "Making the Modern Health Consumer: Some Reflections on the History of Advertising and Public Health," paper presented at American Association for the History of Medicine Annual Meeting, Toronto, Canada, May 1998.
64. George Harvey, "Reflections Concerning Women," *Harper's Bazar* 41 (March 1907): 297. For discussion of nineteenth-century attitudes toward cosmetics, see Peiss, "Making Faces"; Peiss, *Hope in a Jar*; and Banner, *American Beauty*.
65. William R. Leach, "Transformation in a Culture of Consumption: Women and Department Stores, 1890–1925," *Journal of American History* 71/3 (September 1984): 319–342.
66. For a concise demonstration of the ways in which audiences constantly redefine that which has been created for them (and for a useful discussion of some of the historiogra-

phy of this theory), see Margaret T. McFadden, "'America's Boy Friend Who Can't Get a Date': Gender, Race, and the Cultural Work of the Jack Benny Program, 1932–1946," *Journal of American History* 80/1 (June 1993): 113–134.

67. Scanlon, *Inarticulate Longings*, 207.
68. Edith Lewis, "The Emotional Quality in Advertisements," *J. Walter Thompson News Bulletin* 97 (April 1923): 11–14; Lois Ardery, "She Wants It But She Doesn't Know It—Yet," *J. Walter Thompson News Bulletin* 110 (December 1924): 18–21. Both in the J. Walter Thomspon Archives, Special Collections Library, Duke University, Durham, North Carolina.
69. *Saturday Evening Post* (November 24, 1928), 34 and (February 2, 1929), 30, reproduced in Marchand, *Advertising the American Dream*, 180, 104.
70. Frances Willard, *Glimpses of Fifty Years* (Chicago: Women's Temperance Publishing Association, 1889), 426–427.
71. Patrick Porter, "Advertising in the Early Cigarette Industry: W. Duke, Sons and Company of Durham," *North Carolina Historical Review* 48 (1971): 35; George S. Chappell, *Evil Through the Ages: An Outline of Indecency* (New York: Frederick Stokes Company, 1932). 286; Kluger, *Ashes to Ashes*, 20–26. See also tobacco advertising collections held by Special Collections, Perkins Library, Duke University, Durham, North Carolina; and the Valentine Museum, Richmond, Virginia.
72. Washington Duke to James Duke, October 17, 1894, Correspondence Series, Box 65, 1894 Letterbook, in Benjamin Duke Papers, Special Collections Library, Duke University.
73. *Tobacco* (January 20, 1888; February 20, 1888; April 20, 1888; May 4, 1888).
74. *Union Signal* (November 7, 1895).
75. Annual Report of the Watch and Ward Society for 1898–1899, quoted in Paul Boyer, *Purity in Print: The Vice-Society Movement and Book Censorship in America* (New York: Charles Scribner's Sons, 1968), 11.
76. Between 1896 and 1900, cigarette production and consumption dropped from 4,043,798,737 to 3,258,716,305 units. *The Tobacco Industry* 21. For a thorough examination of the anticigarette crusade and its legislative efforts, see Cassandra Tate, *Cigarette Wars: The Triumph of the Little White Slaver* (New York: Oxford University Press, 1999).
77. Most Western nations seem to have shared a cultural fascination with the Orient that surfaced at least as early as the eighteenth century and survived at least through the first quarter of the twentieth century. An article published in the middle of the nineteenth century nicely captured the Western reading of the Eastern culture and character. See "Orientalism," *The Knickerbocker* (June 1853): 479–496. The fascination with things oriental manifested itself profusely in nineteenth- and early twentieth-century American high and popular culture–in everything from architectural motifs to opera settings and novels. American architecture has always borrowed heavily from European style. In the nineteenth century, when the Europeans were borrowing from the Orient, so did the United States. Entertainment impresario Phineas Taylor Barnum's home Iranistan (completed 1848) was a Turkish-inspired confection of minarets, domes, and lacy ornament set on the shore in Fairfield, Connecticut. See Philip B. Kunhardt, et al., *P.T. Barnum, America's Greatest Showman* (New York: Alfred A. Knopf, 1995), 84–85. Rudolph Aronson, the "leading impresario of Viennese opera in America," wanted ordinary Americans to enjoy opera and other theater in extraordinary surroundings and built his Casino Theatre as a four-story Moorish palace. John Dizikes, *Opera in America: A Cultural History* (New Haven, CT: Yale University Press, 1993), 209. Richard Morris Hunt brought a more subdued rendition of Islamic architecture to the masses in his design for New York's Tweedy's department store. John Sweetman, *The Oriental Obsession: Islamic Inspiration in British and American Art and Architecture, 1500–1920* (Cambridge: Cambridge University Press, 1988), 237. Composers of opera continually relied on exotic settings and characters—usually drawn from orientalist stereotypes—to attract the public: Georges Bizet's *Carmen* (1878) had a beautiful and seductive gypsy trickster as the central character; Verdi's *Aida* (1871) was about an Ethiopian princess enslaved in Egypt; Meyerbeer's *L'Africaine* (1865) told the story of an African beauty who fell in love with European explorer Vasco da Gama; and Victor Herbert's light opera or operettas (all composed in the late 1890s or early 1900s) *The Ameer*, *The Idol's Eye*, and *The Tattooed Man* were set in Afghanistan, India, and Persia respectively. See Dizikes, *Opera in America* and June Ottenberg, *Opera Odyssey: Toward a History of Opera in Nineteenth-Century America* (Westport, CT: Greenwood Press, 1994). For brief discussions of the impact of orientalism on fashion and consumer culture, see Steele, *Fashion and Eroticism*, and James Laver, *Costume and Fashion: A Concise History* (New York: Thames and Hudson, 1982). In the field of fiction, see, for example, two best-sellers: Robert Hichens, *The Garden of Allah* (New York: Grosset and Dunlap, 1904) and E. M. Hull, *The Sheik* (New York: A. L. Burt

Company, 1921). In each of these novels, the desert of the East figures as a mecca of freedom and peace for discontented residents of the modernizing Western world. It also becomes the site of a woman's sexual awakening and realization of her full womanly and human potential. For literature on the hegemonic theory of orientalism, see Edward Said, *Orientalism* (New York: Vintage Books, 1979); Rana Kabbani, *Europe's Myths of Orient* (Bloomington: Indiana University Press, 1986); Reina Lewis, *Gendering Orientalism: Race, Femininity and Representation* (London: Routledge, 1996); and Malini Schueller, *U.S. Orientalisms: Race, Nation, and Gender in Literature, 1790–1890* (Ann Arbor: University of Michigan Press, 1998).

78. Victoria Steele quotes men and women of the 1910s and twenties—Cecil Beaton, Sonia Keppel, and Loelia, the Duchess of Winchester—as saying that women indeed fantasized about taking on the odalisque's persona. These individuals are admittedly English but, given the American public's fascination with "high society" figures and British society especially, it is plausible to suggest that some Americans engaged in the same fantasies. Steele, *Fashion and Eroticism*, 233.

79. See Gail Ching-Liang Low, "White Skins/Black Masks: The Pleasures and Politics of Imperialism" *New Formations* 9 (Winter 1989): 85, for a discussion of "totems."

80. See Low, "White Skins/Black Masks" and Sandra Gilbert, "Costumes of the Mind: Transvestism as Metaphor in Modern Literature," in *Writing and Sexual Difference*, ed. Elizabeth Abel (Chicago: University of Chicago Press, 1982), for discussions of the importance attached to costume and the ways in which costume and accessories could aid in the creation of one's public identity.

81. Between 1910 and 1913, cigarette production in the U.S. nearly doubled, from 8.6 billion to 15.6 billion. From 1913 to 1916, there was another increase of more than 50 percent, to 25.3 billion. Women were undoubtedly part of this increase although the industry had a hard time counting women since many of them did not, as men did, smoke on the street, where a lot of the informal counting and surveys took place. As one of those "counters" reported to *Tobacco* in 1920: "They [female smokers] are numerous, but the habit among them is not yet sufficiently sanctioned by society to embolden them [to smoke on the street]." Moreover, he went on: "women usually wear gloves and that prevents my scrutinizing their fingers for nicotine stains, which they usually prevent, anyway, by the use of cigarette holders. Then, of course, they do not have cigarette boxes sticking out of their pockets." But, he continued, women had, in recent years, "become less timid about going into shops and buying cigarettes." See *The Tobacco Industry; Tobacco* (July 29, 1920): 17.

82. Lin Bonner, "Why Cigarette Makers Don't Advertise to Women," *Advertising and Selling* 7 (October 20, 1926): 21, 46–47.

83. *Tobacco* (January 29, 1920): 32; (February 12, 1920): 32; Gerard S. Petrone, *Tobacco Advertising: The Great Seduction with Values* (Altglen, PA: Schiffer Publishing, 1996), 220.

84. *Life* (April 15, 1920): cover, 711.

85. "Cigarets and the Girl," *Tobacco* (August 4, 1927): 8.

86. Marlboro Collection, Smithsonian Institution; "Marlboro Makes a Direct Appeal," *Advertising and Selling* 8 (March 23, 1927): 25; Nancy Bowman, "Philip Morris," in *The Encyclopedia of Advertising* (Chicago: Fitzroy Dearborn Publishing, forthcoming).

87. Lin Bonner, "Why Cigarette Makers Don't Advertise to Women," *Advertising and Selling* 7 (October 20, 1926): 21ff; "Blow Some More My Way," *Printers' Ink* (April 14, 1932): 20.

88. *Modern Priscilla* (March 1929), reproduced in Jane Webb Smith, *Smoke Signals: Cigarettes, Advertising and the American Way of Life* (Chapel Hill, NC: University of North Carolina Press, 1990, for the Valentine Museum, Richmond, Virginia), frontispiece; *True Story* (January 1930): fourth cover, reproduced in Marchand, *Advertising the American Dream*, 197; Nannie Mae Tilley, *The R. J. Reynolds Tobacco Company* (Chapel Hill, NC: University of North Carolina Press, 1985), 340–342; *Tobacco* (March 3, 1927): 15, (July 5, 1928): 15, (August 8, 1929): 7, (September 5, 1929): 7.

89. *Tobacco* (June 7, 1928); *Atlantic Monthly* (October 1928).

90. Edward Bernays, *Biography of an Idea: Memoirs of Public Relations Counsel Edward L. Bernays* (New York: Simon and Schuster, 1965), 372–400; "Easter Sun Find the Past in Shadow at Modern Parade," *New York Times* (April 1, 1929); Nancy Bowman, "American Tobacco Company," *The Encyclopedia of Advertising* (Chicago: Fitzroy Dearborn Publishing, forthcoming).

Collars and Consumers

CHANGING IMAGES OF AMERICAN MANLINESS AND BUSINESS

CAROLE TURBIN

*T*he detachable collar, essential to men's dress from the 1840s to the 1920s, has faded from view, relegated to antique shops, costume museums, and old photographs. Yet it left a lasting legacy. In the 1900s, officials borrowed the name to designate new occupations, white-collar jobs, and later the white-collar class.[1] In 1907 Cluett, Peabody, and Co., Inc., a major collar manufacturer, made advertising history with its Arrow Man, the centerpiece of advertisements for Arrow Collars until 1931. Arrow Collars became synonymous with detachable collars and were preserved in American culture through a Cole Porter song, "You're the Top (You're an Arrow Collar)."[2] The Arrow Man, created by noted illustrator Joseph C. Leyendecker, was the Gibson girl's male equivalent and visual representation of the "new man." The history of the rise and decline of the Arrow Collar and Arrow Man is partly a story of links between business decisions and shifting consumer tastes and markets. How market changes were related to changing social structure and culture, most especially ideal images of manliness, in the twentieth century's volatile first decades is the subject of this essay.

COLLARS AND GENTLEMEN

Legend has it that the detachable collar was invented in 1827 by Hannah Lord Montague, wife of a businessman in Troy, New York, to solve a common household problem. Laundering, an arduous household task, had become more troublesome in the early nineteenth century when prosperous people began to view cleanliness of body and garments as intimately related to each other and to other social characteristics. Thus men like Orlando Montague expected to appear clean in public daily. Because collars were attached to shirts, their wives had to launder the shirt when only its collar was soiled. Hannah Montague wrote in a letter to relatives that the idea came to her "suddenly as if by inspiration" one day while she was preparing to do household laundry. She stopped work, reached for a pair of shears, and snipped the collar off a shirt. By "attaching a piece of white tape at either end and sewing the selvage," she made a detachable collar that could be washed, starched, and ironed separately from the shirt.

Hannah Montague's invention spawned an industry closely identified with Troy, still nicknamed "Collar City." Like other garment trades, collar-making began in households. In the 1840s entrepreneurs set up establishments employing hand and later machine stitchers, including Montague's enterprising husband and a partner. By the 1860s, Troy's shirt, collar, and cuff industry produced most of the nation's detachable collars, ranking seventh in capital investment of New York State's apparel industries, including New York City's vast clothing trades.[3]

Behind this story are wide-reaching social and economic changes; detachable collars were invented and became successful because of shifts in the ways prosperous people demonstrated respectability and affluence. Collars had long been linked to high status. In the eighteenth century and the first few decades of the nineteenth, U.S. working-class men, artisans, wage-earners, and many shopkeepers wore shirts without collars, adding a muffler for warmth; high-status men wore shirts with stiff fronts and attached collars, often with a cravat, ancestor of the twentieth century's necktie.[4] The first collar manufacturers found ready markets for detachable collars because the proportion of men who wore formal dress in public daily was increasing.[5] Consumerism is usually associated with women, but detachable collars were highly styled garments marketed to and often purchased by men for themselves in furnishing shops and men's sections of department stores.[6]

Hannah's husband Orlando Montague, prosperous merchant and manufacturer of women's fine shoes, was typical of new entrepreneurs in late eighteenth- and early nineteenth-century settings like Troy, towns or small cities whose economy was based on commerce or emerging industries. They represented an emerging capitalist class that dominated new commercial and industrial enterprises; men and women of this class sought to differentiate themselves from humble wage-earners, farmers, small shopkeepers, and artisans by identifying with old, elite families who maintained elegant homes, wore tasteful fashions, and exhibited polite behavior. These entrepreneurs transformed older, elite gentility into a new ethos of middle-class respectability that combined consumerism, taste for luxury goods,

cleanliness, and genteel manners, as well as the self-discipline and productivity central to economic success.[7] By signaling cleanliness and
taste, detachable collars marked strict boundaries fundamental to
Victorian life: social position, gender, age, and situations delineated by
space and time (morning, afternoon, workplace, evening, outdoors,
indoors, public and private school, and place of entertainment).

Most collars were constructed of linen, the fabric of choice for
respectable gentlemen and imitators, but some were highly starched
cotton and others, paper (stiffened with a muslin lining), celluloid, or
rubber.[8] The original "string collars" were awkward, high-standing
affairs constructed of two layers of linen slightly stiffened with starch
and supported by haircloth buckled at the back. They attached to shirts
by means of long, narrow bands of tape wound around the neck over
collar and shirt band and tied at the back to secure them in place. Until
the collar button's invention, even tightly tied collars would separate
from shirts.[9] Figure 4.1 shows a sample of the array of styles produced
by Troy's many collar manufacturers. Collars varied in height, width of
opening between points, stiffness, finishing (amount of gloss on the
side worn outward), characteristics of points (long, short, narrow,
square, or rounded), decoration (pleats or tucks), and fastenings.

Throughout the nineteenth century, standing collars of various
heights (such as Tresnal and Lerayn) were most popular for formal
wear. The highest styles were popular in the 1890s; Rimbert (Figure
4.1), for instance, was two and a quarter inches high. Informal
turnover collars, constructed like twentieth-century shirt collars (such
as Palgrave and Elatia), were more common in the first half of the
nineteenth century. Turned-outward collars such as Chatley and
Lebrun appeared in the second half. Some had turned-down tips or
side edges, later termed "wing collars," which also varied enormously.[10]

Detachable collars were key to appearance because of their relation to the body. Collars, like hats, drew attention to the head and
face.[11] The face, often perceived as representing an individual's "natural" state, is a major focus in social relations, especially formal interaction.[12] Faces took on new meaning in this period, as people became
familiar with photographs of prominent people and the possibilities
of managing appearance through makeup and lighting.[13] Collars
could detract from, flatter, or neutralize the look of features, skin
quality, and expression. Because collars firmly encircled the neck,
they constrained movements and the position of the head, neck, and
shoulders and encouraged the wearer to sit, stand, and walk in a particular manner.

Collars also created the appearance of bodily cleanliness because
they suggested but did not reveal what was hidden from view. Men's
outer garments—waistcoat (usually high-buttoned), and jacket (often

Figure 4.1. This page from Cluett's *Illustrated Catalogue* (1886) displays a sample of the hundreds of styles of collars manufactured by George B. Cluett, Bro., & Co. Photographs of detachable collars and advertisements for Arrow shirt collars and shirts are courtesy of the Rennsselaer County Historical Society, Troy, New York.

knee-length)—covered upper bodies; most collarless shirts were undergarments not meant for public display. No respectable man appeared in shirtsleeves when uncomfortable, but wore a jacket, waistcoat, and cravat in public during his entire workday. Parts of the body not hidden by outer garments were adorned with detachable, starched linen: a "bosom" concealed the shirtfront not covered by waistcoat, and collars and cuffs covered neck and wrists. The neck, strategic because it accumulated perspiration and airborne dirt, bordered the less-than-clean private body; most men did not bathe their bodies daily. Detachable collars simultaneously displayed outer personal qualities and represented the private body and inner garments. A soiled collar told tales of uncleanliness elsewhere.

Detachable collars also represented qualities key to the white, middle-class, male ideal. From the late eighteenth to late nineteenth century, there were several interrelated and overlapping masculine ideals; the image most closely related to economic achievement was not muscular but slender, refined, and even graceful. Manly strength was not rooted in a brawny physique but in economic or political authority; it resided in the entrepreneur, whether gentleman property holder, independent farmer, or owner of shop or factory, and in political leaders. Manly authority was also demonstrated through personal characteristics of self-discipline, restraint, and autonomy in private life, business, and politics. The names of collars themselves (for example, Hurworth, Chatley, Warville) evoked British gentlemen, associated with civilization and epitomized by British refinement, gentility, and political authority at home and abroad.[14]

Middle-class men's posture and gestures also conveyed authority. From at least the sixteenth to the early twentieth century in western Europe, a gentleman held his head upright, thrust his chest out, and drew in his stomach.[15] He gazed ahead, moved head and shoulders purposefully, and avoided bending or making abrupt movements. The downward gaze typified gestures of servants; "lolling," lowered shoulders and slouching, marked lowly laborers, farmers, and small tradesmen.[16] Detachable collars and other respectable middle-class men's fashions constructed the bodies of gentlemen. In the late nineteenth century, men's garments were less tightly fitted than early in the century, but trousers were narrow and suit coats had tucked-in waists; belts, replacing suspenders, helped flatten the waist. Tightly buttoned waistcoats held in the stomach and straightened the back.[17] At the peak of the popularity of high-standing collars in the 1890s, collars of high-ranking men (including many employers) prevented a downward gaze, differentiating them from clerks, whose low collars allowed movements required for writing.[18] To look downward, high-status men had to literally look down their noses.

Middle-class white men's manly attire contrasted with working-class men's daily occupational dress. Manual workers and shopkeepers wore overalls, loose work jackets, and work shirts with soft, attached, turned-down collars; these were dyed indigo to conceal stains and loosely fitted to allow upper movements necessary for physical labor without straining seams. Yet functional work clothes also had social meanings. Through occupational dress, working men displayed respectability and manhood rooted in pride in skill and success in a trade, muscularity, and physical prowess.[19] Astute observers could distinguish manual workers and shopkeepers from gentlemen because in their own milieu workingmen's movements, gestures, and posture were appropriate to their occupations and garments.

American middle-class manliness differed from the British model because it incorporated the contradictory double-edged ideology that simultaneously recognized the limitations of wage-earning yet celebrated opportunities for mobility. On the one hand, U.S. class divisions were deep. Prosperous Americans pitied white-collar employees, albeit middle-class, because they were dependent on wages. Many working-class men resented office men who imitated employers—the term "white-collar" originated in the 1880s as "white-collar stiffs," a skilled workers' term for clerks who put on airs because they were privileged to dress like employers.[20] Yet Americans believed that U.S. social distinctions should be fluid. Manly ideals were not entirely closed to enterprising, white, working-class men, because apprentices in skilled crafts could become master craftsmen and entrepreneurs. New entrepreneurs represented modified manliness based not on inherited property or acquired skill but on success in business, industry, or professionals.[21]

Many manual workers considered themselves respectable in the middle-class sense and emulated fashionable dress and demeanor in public, especially on Sundays. Detachable collars played a special role in working-class men's imitation of middle-class demeanor, because collars were less expensive than other accoutrements of middle-class status—jackets, trousers, waistcoat, coats, and fine linen that required careful laundering to maintain a clean, white appearance.[22] Until commercial laundries and indoor plumbing became common in the early twentieth century in urban areas, only the most prosperous families could afford servants necessary for daily washing, starching, and ironing white linen.[23] Detachable collars, originally signaling privilege, also required laundering, but a skilled worker who could afford a suit, coat, and shoes could purchase several collars and appear on Sundays as clean and respectable as a more privileged neighbor or employer.[24] In the U.S., unlike Europe, work clothes did not permanently define humble men's status.

THE ARROW COLLAR MAN AND SHIFTING IMAGES OF MANLINESS

The history of detachable collars' lasting legacy in American occupational structure and culture is interwoven with the history of Cluett, Peabody, and Co., a major collar maker from the 1850s whose Arrow line became synonymous with collars in the early twentieth century. In 1889 George B. Cluett, Bro., and Co merged with Coon and Co., which contributed a sales manager named Frederick Peabody and the little-known Arrow trademark. Nine years later Peabody became president of the firm, now Cluett, Peabody, and Co., and introduced a new line of Arrow collars.[25] Constructed of cotton, the new collar was not a radical departure but met older standards of formal attire while introducing characteristics that Cluett believed were more appealing and accessible to people of diverse backgrounds. Still, cotton, less costly and easier to care for than linen, was considered plebeian; other firms disdained the "debasement" of a high-status product, and retailers resisted because they doubted cotton collars would appeal to customers.[26]

In order to entice consumers and convince retailers to sell Arrow Collars, Peabody hired Charles M. Connolly, cartoonist, magazine writer, and editor of the Chicago men's apparel trade journal, *Haberdasher*, to be the firm's advertising manager. Connolly envisioned a model man shown wearing an Arrow Collar and commissioned Joseph Christian Leyendecker, whose illustrations appeared in the *Saturday Evening Post*, to create the Arrow Man. The Arrow Man's success exceeded Peabody's and Connolly's expectations. Gracing advertising copy from 1907 to 1931, the Arrow Collar Man became the Gibson girl's male equivalent and received fan mail from women, including marriage proposals, and gifts on Christmas and Valentine's Day.[27] Other manufacturers, for example, George P. Ide, and Co., produced attractive imitations, but Leyendecker's creation endures as a piece of the golden age of illustration.

The Arrow Man and Arrow collar represent significant changes in consumer markets related to a constellation of economic, cultural, and social developments. First, the Arrow Man captured the popular imagination because of Leyendecker's visually compelling compositions and images conveying idealized appearance. Manufacturers had been using advertising since the eighteenth century, but before the 1880s most relied on text with few illustrations. Aided by innovations in visual representation, especially photography and color lithography, at the turn of the century national corporations and large retailers began to reach consumers through advertising campaigns with high-quality illustrations designed to create the desire for goods and foster loyalty through brand-name recognition.

Pictorial advertising helped spawn mass-circulation newspapers and magazines of the 1890s and early 1900s. The Arrow collar advertising campaign was among the earliest to employ what was later termed a "soft sell," a restrained, refined message that did not display the collar alone but highlighted the social background and environment of those using the product.[28] (Figure 4.2.) Visual depiction of a product's user was as important as images of the products themselves and contributed to new ideals of appearance. As popular culture, films, photographs, and illustrations in mass-circulation magazines increasingly portrayed idealized images of individuals in the public eye, people became more aware of their own physical appearance.[29] Increasingly images in the mass media became models by which people, especially the middle classes, evaluated their own appearance.

At the same time, ideals of American manhood had changed. The demise of businesses during the severe depressions of the late nineteenth century, combined with increased consolidation and vertical and horizontal integration, convinced many middle-class families that older sources of male authority were less available to their sons. Corporate growth, the beginnings of separation of management from ownership, and scientific management produced more salaried positions. Many young, native-born, white men whose fathers had looked forward to steering their economic course as entrepreneurs became white-collar workers earning a salary or wages. Increasingly, a salaried employee did not carry the stigma of a failed man. Some middle-class

Figure 4.2. This advertisement (J. C. Leyendecker, 1913) pictures elegant men in Arrow collars and shorts enjoying an evening at the theater. Note the variety of collars and the man (far left) wearing new fashions of the early twentieth century, favored by youth.

families still pitied white-collar workers, but many salaried employees enjoyed new sources of authority in management and professional occupations; these did not require taking sole responsibility for a firm's risks as entrepreneurs but called for the ability to influence and work closely with others and, increasingly, for education.

As middle-class families perceived that male authority no longer rested on independence from wages and saw fewer distinctions between well-paid salaried employees and independent entrepreneurs, they abandoned the ideal of the autonomous, restrained, self-reliant, self-made man. Native-born, middle-class men's manliness was challenged in other ways: women's increased presence in public life, suffragists' stepped-up demands for political representation, immigrant men's increased control of local politics, and militant unions' efforts to control industry. The consumer culture's message of spending money and time to fulfill desires undermined older manly ideals of self-control, thrift, and restraint of emotions and sexuality.[30]

The new model for white, middle-class men was less class-specific than before and more firmly rooted in American culture rather than European patterns of gentility. Many white, middle-class men, worried that men's refinement and women reformers' challenges weakened men and the middle class, rejected European gentility as effeminate and "overcivilized." The appearance of class distinctions between men of different backgrounds declined as white, middle-class men began to perceive bodily strength and prowess as integral to male authority.

Carole Turbin

The "new" man conveyed his status not only through a confident demeanor that implied internal authoritative qualities but also by the outward appearance of physical strength. At the same time, some white, middle-class men participated in aspects of working-class manliness formerly viewed as crude and unrefined, such as boxing and other spectator sports; as these activities became more respectable, they became part of American consumer culture.[31] A new term, *masculinity,* conveyed the new more homogeneous image of American men. Historian Gail Bederman notes that nineteenth-century manliness referred to specific attributes of the manly man, while "masculine" was defined as inherent in all men, usually in contrast to feminine.[32]

The Arrow Collar Man, a visual representation of the new man, conveyed characteristics that revealed contradictions and complexities inherent in changing ideals of manliness.[33] The new man, like the Arrow Man's collar, was not entirely novel but a combination of the old ideal with newly emerging patterns. Class differences appeared to be less distinct in the early twentieth century, but they did not vanish. White, middle-class men continued to differentiate themselves from their working-class neighbors. The new man, educated and erudite, sought a cultured, middle-class version of physical strength rather than the brawniness of those who did physical labor; he favored the physical activities enjoyed by the respectable and affluent: golf, tennis, bicycling, motoring, hiking, and camping. Leyendecker's images captured these nuances.

The Arrow Man was not slightly built, like his nineteenth-century counterparts, but broad-shouldered with muscular hands. His features were well defined—high brow, chiseled nose, bow lips, and a large jaw with cleft chin. Yet his face was refined, and he wore elegant dress with ease and confidence. Although his gaze was that of a man with authority, direct and reserved, it was not forbidding but frank and often sensuous. In informal, intimate settings like that depicted in Figure 4.3, he had a relaxed, easeful posture that in another context might signify subordination. Yet the room, a library, is a cultured, middle-class setting, and one man reads a newspaper, a sign of concern with serious masculine matters. The Arrow Man's external appearance combined physical presence and virility with gentlemanly reserve, refinement, and authority; he was silent, cool, confident, and "where necessary, tough."[34]

The Arrow Man represented another new development—the mass production and systematic marketing of high-quality fashions to men of diverse backgrounds. In the mid- to late nineteenth century, when the manly ideal was modeled on the English or Continental gentleman, elite dress set the most visible trends, and custom tailors were undisputed arbiters of high fashion. Some tailors produced a few ready-made men's garments in addition to custom work, filling a growing demand for consumer goods. Ready-made menswear manufacturers produced utilitarian clothing for seamen, undergarments, shirts, and some formal attire, such as jackets and overcoats for farmers, shopkeepers, and others.[35] Most ready-made garments, marketed to the working and lower middle classes, were serviceable, inexpensive, and unvarying from one year to next.

When the ready-made garment industry "took off" in the last decades of the nineteenth century, menswear developed more rapidly, although the takeoff was driven by women's wear.[36] As the contracting system declined, many manufacturers produced ready-made garments in relatively large "inside shops" which incorporated most aspects of production—cutting, stitching, finishing—and gave producers more control over styling variations. Some menswear manufacturers began to compete more vigorously with the custom trade. They realized that unvarying staple goods were less profitable because they could not compete with other producers who offered different styles; moreover, the demand for quality stylish clothing was on the rise.

A trade journal claimed that the increase in "demand for better clothing" was not "sudden," "spasmodic," or confined to "a sector or . . . class of buyers," but "all embracing" and due to "well-matured conditions."[37] In order to produce more stylish and higher-quality garments, manufacturers employed designers who paid "scrupulously careful attention" to tailoring details, "as distinguished from merely clothesmaking. . . ."[38] As a result, manufacturers' products diverted "trade from the custom tailor to the clothier;[39] custom tailors' market share narrowed and many lost businesses or became contractors, a few retaining shops in major business districts. Dressmakers also disappeared, albeit more slowly than tailors, as manufacturers of ready-made women's garments copied Paris *haute couture* which emerged at the end of the nineteenth century.[40]

A trade journal described the enormous array of styles and fabrics of garments as "bewildering,"[41] but hindsight reveals more significance: the center of fashion trends was shifting. At first, some manufacturers produced quality fashions that imitated but lagged behind elite trends, but later they devised more sophisticated means of copying popular styles.[42] Because high-quality ready-made clothing imitated custom tailoring, middle- or working-class men could purchase garments resembling those of wealthy elites. But a more fundamental change was in the making. Manufacturers also began to create their own designs, and many did not originate in British or European elite styles but reflected popular American tastes.

Clothing retailers, too, actively influenced style and quality and, with manufacturers, used mass-circulation magazines to promote qual-

Figure 4.3. This 1910 advertisement (J. C. Leyendecker) pictures young, handsome men attired in more loose-fitted fashions in a cultured setting. Note the men's strong features, casual postures, and intense expressions.

ity fashions to men of diverse backgrounds; manufacturers utilized the new railway networks to distribute goods to retailers in regions that previously had limited access to consumer goods.[43] Wealthy gentlemen no longer led middle-class men's high-fashion trends, and custom tailors' position as fashion's arbiters waned.

Paradoxically, the ready-made clothing industry provided an enormous variation of styles for men of different clothing tastes and needs, and at the same time resulted in less clearly defined distinctions in the appearance of men of different backgrounds. As manly ideals became less class-based, white men of different classes began to resemble each other more closely in appearance. Some middle- and working-class men imitated elite styles, but custom tailors' reign waned and the center of men's fashion trends shifted away from a small, privileged group to more diffuse sources.

Distinctions in men's appearance blurred because the new fashions were part of emerging popular consumer culture, including idealized images of personal appearance in visual media and a more homogeneous male ideal. Arrow Collars were an ideal subject for an advertising campaign because they carried the complex and changing messages of men's fashions in the first decade of the twentieth century: the Arrow brand combined new perceptions of physicality with older characteristics of gentlemanly authority and refinement at the same time as it represented a promise inherent in both the detachable collar and mass marketing of consumer goods—that an elegant appearance and respectability were available to the ordinary man.

After World War I, Cluett, Peabody and other companies faced a crisis as the popularity of detachable collars waned, eclipsed by soft collars and attached-collar shirts. Shirts and collars had a new place in men's dress. The new fashions for looser, softer trousers and jackets with natural, unpadded shoulders were more comfortable. High-buttoned waistcoats (but not the vests) vanished, leaving shirtfronts visible. Detachable shirtfronts became outmoded and neckwear took new forms. Cravats narrowed, evolving into bow ties or neckties that highlighted shirtfronts and created a visible connection between shirtfront, neck, and face; the neck no longer appeared isolated from the lower body. Soft, unstarched cotton collars, cut low and shaped to fit the neck, were smaller than their stiff, starched counterparts; because shirtfronts were visible, no longer hidden by waistcoats, collars were less distinct from shirts and thus were a segment of a total image. Shirts became significant outer garments, a means to display taste, status, and affluence. They were often made from soft, varied fabrics such as linen or silk, and featured pale colors and patterns. Yet many men still wore detachable collars, and attached shirt collars were often white, their presence highlighted through color contrast.[44]

Increasingly, many workingmen wore the new fashions. Some manual workers wore shirts and ties to and from work, changing into work clothes at shops or adding overalls, apron, or a loose jacket to protect stylish clothing on the job.[45] Some employers substituted occupational dress evoking British gentry with informal American styles. An observer noted that some New York department stores replaced salesmen who wore "livery" and behaved like butlers with young men in white-collar attire. The new salesman was no longer "starched" and "apologetic" but met customers on an "equal footing."[46]

Not only did men of different backgrounds appear to look more like each other, but also the lines between informal and formal, public and private occasions blurred.[47] A newspaper article criticized wealthy men for dressing for a resort evening in "sports clothes" and chastised college boys for wearing "soft collar attached shirts with their tuxedos."[48] Another complained that men who wear "a four-piece sports suit" for "everything except dinner dress" economize on clothing expenses and "attain comfort that every man seems to be demanding." A few years previously, "a man would not have been allowed to wear a soft shirt while following his vocation. Everybody wore a bosom shirt and accepted this garment as a matter of course. Now nobody wears a bosom shirt and everybody wears soft shirts," and "a soft collar would not have been permitted in stores and offices but now everybody from the boss to the office boy" wore them.[49]

Informal styles, especially soft collars and attached-collar shirts, appealed especially to young men, to some employers' disgust. When managers of a large New York financial institution forbade employees to wear informal styles, young men protested. In April 1920, Chicago's University Club, consisting of 3,500 bankers, businessmen, and professionals, announced plans to "banish the collar button in favor of blue chambray shirts and attached collars." They formed a "Collar and Shirt Strike Committee" with a manifesto: "Wanted: Ten thousand slaves of collar button to rise and not only emancipate themselves from the despotic yoke, but to forswear the white starched collar and the silk, the linen, and pongee and all other costly shirts." The group invited others to don "soft shirts with attached collars" made of "material the cost of which does not exceed $2.50."[50]

The new 1920s fashions constructed the body differently; many young, white, middle-class men began to take on aspects of manual workers' physical movements. Critics characterized soft collars and loose clothes as "easeful garb" and "flaccid fashions" associated with postures and gestures, specifically slouchiness, unbecoming to men with authority. Loose clothes equaled slouchiness, which equaled lack of "backbone." "A man with a soft collar would have been regarded as a slouch a few years ago."[51] "[L]oose clothes" are appropriate for "loose occasions" but inappropriate at work. Men "who O.K. orders for goods and who punch mysterious buttons on their desks . . . may let down" for golf or poker but they have little "regard for slouchy men around their offices."[52] A 1920s memoir characterizes British officers' "open-necked jackets" as "warning" of the "imminent decline of the idea of Empire." New York City police officers became "weak and corrupt" when open-necked jackets replaced closed coat collars in the late 1920s and declined further when they were allowed to appear in shirtsleeves.[53]

For many writers of newspaper articles, the decline of masculine self-discipline, physical strength, and moral fortitude meant white, middle-class men's feminization. One suggested that starchless collars signaled men's weakness in face of forbidden and erotic temptations. The article, subtitled "spineless linen," likened "the boneless collar" to "a serpent hanging from a tree, always ready to tempt somebody." "[T]he starchless collar, matching the shirt, has apparently come to stay. It is forbidden fruit and therefore pungent to the palate."[54] A clothing merchant identified the new posture with feminine weakness. Men "have . . . become like untidy women" who prefer "ease and laxity of dress." For that writer, the clothing trade, especially tailors, were guardians of manly virtues and moral order. Men "need more starch; they have let down too much. . . . They need to be tailored more rigidly; braced up in other words." Men must be brought back to the "correct pose" through education. First, "their backbones need stiffening." The clothing trade can "take the public in hand and prescribe" calisthenics "that will get the patient back on his feet."[55]

As soft collars began outselling the old-fashioned stiff variety, manufacturers created new soft-collar styles. The most successful were designed for multiple occasions, in keeping with the decline of strict distinctions between various types of formal and informal settings. Cluett, Peabody designated their Outing Collar (1911) for leisure and active wear. But Earl and Wilson's 1919 catalogue describes soft collars as "more than Sports' Collars" because they are "recognized as correct for daily business wear. . . ."[56] The Phillips-Jones Corporation's semisoft Van Heusen (1921) had stiff collars' appeal without soft collars' disadvantages. Curved to fit the neck comfortably, its flexible, webbed fabric was not "sloppy" and retained shape, finish, and size after washing, even in a basin at home. It was so popular that at first demand outstripped supply.[57]

Despite these innovations, collar companies' sales fell. After a peak of more than $32 million in 1920, Cluett, Peabody's sales dropped to $25,700,000 in 1921 and $23,600,000 in 1922. In 1923 Cluett, Peabody attempted to recover by producing semisoft collars, the Aratex and Service lines, which lacked the Van Heusen's curved shape but were similar enough to result in lengthy litigation over patent rights with Phillips-Jones. Despite having to pay royalties for each semisoft collar sold, Cluett, Peabody's net sales rose briefly, to a little over $28 million.

Although the nation overall recovered from the economic recession of 1921, collar companies' sales continued to decline and worsened during the Great Depression. In 1925 Cluett, Peabody's net sales totaled less than $25 million and in 1927 plummeted to $21 million. Edgar H. Betts, the firm's president (former president of Coon and Co.) decided to use sales of inexpensive shirts, now a substantial part of the firm's production, to support the fading collar business because he believed detachable collars would return to fashion.[58]

The company did not climb out of its financial hole until a new president, Chesley Robert Palmer, decided that the future lay not in detachable collars but in quality shirts. In 1929, when Palmer was appointed, Cluett, Peabody was the world's largest collar company, but almost half its sales were in shirts, about 20 percent of which were sold to department stores that applied a private label. In 1931 Palmer retired the Arrow Collar Man, decreased production of private-label shirts sold to department stores, and launched an advertising campaign to identify the famous Arrow label with quality shirts. By 1936 the firm was the second largest producer and seller of shirts and one of five companies (among 800 makers) that sold prelabeled shirts. In 1935, the invention of Sanforizing (which prevented shrinkage from laundering) made Cluett, Peabody one of the nation's foremost manufacturers of men's quality shirts.[59]

Why was Cluett, Peabody slow to realize that detachable collars were gone forever? The firm did not lack business acumen: over the years it had utilized new techniques, incorporated processes formerly the purview of independent enterprises (such as laundering), formed trade associations to counter labor unions' demands, and reconfigured through mergers.[60] Nor was the company unaware of marketing and retailing developments and the increased significance of personal appearance. Along with other businessmen, collar manufacturers became more competitive, devising strategies to attract customers such as lowering prices. Style names such as Aratex and Service evoked American cultural values about technology and serviceability rather than British gentility. In addition to advertising widely, manufacturers designed pamphlets advising retailers on organizing selling space and customers on appearance.

A 1920 pamphlet advised owners to display collars as low-cost items to entice customers into shops offering more expensive wares and urged retailers to provide dressing rooms to encourage customers to consider carefully a garment's enhancement of appearance. Other brochures prescribed collars for diverse occasions and instructed men of various facial types on which collars would enhance features.[61]

Cluett, Peabody's managers had the vision to create the Arrow Man because the "new man" was part of their social and cultural milieu, but they did not recognize broader changes underlying the detachable collar's demise. Changes in laundering and household technology in the early twentieth century made Hannah Montague's invention less relevant. Home laundering became easier and commercial laundering more widespread. Many middle-class people, especially in urban areas, had indoor plumbing, including hot water for bathing and laundering, and electricity. Washing machines, available since the late nineteenth century, were more sophisticated; machines run by electricity replaced hand-cranked models. The cleaning products industry developed and marketed granulated soaps and other washing agents designed for machine use. Most people did some home laundering, but commercial laundries offered a variety of services, ranging from "finished wash—washing, starching, drying, and expertly ironing all garments and household linen—to "damp wash," affordable for many working-class families.[62] For middle- and working-class women who could afford such amenities, washing an entire shirt was less costly and almost as easy as laundering only the collar, whether soft or starched.

Also, by the 1920s the economy and occupational structure had changed, and with it, white-collar work and perceptions of detachable collars. On the one hand, the nation's middle class was expanding, and social and spatial boundaries were blurred. Despite economic depressions in the twentieth century's early decades and deep divisions and continued poverty, especially for many African Americans, Southern whites, and recent immigrants, a larger proportion of Americans than before could purchase garments and other consumer goods enjoyed by the middle class. More people from families lacking access to capital could achieve middle-class status and prosperity, and the security of many male manual workers increased through powerful unions. White-collar jobs were on the increase due to continued changes in business structure and strategies, and many working-class men still sought white-collar work that required education and carried the mark of a middle-class life.[63]

On the other hand, the middle class was overall a less privileged group; white-collar jobs, occupations that contributed to the appearance of increased social homogeneity, were changing for the worse. The fortunes of many white-collar workers declined, especially clerical workers, many of whom were women; most did not have industrial workers' advantage of strong unions. White-collar earnings rose just after World War I, but real wages lagged behind inflation and fell in relation to industrial workers' earnings. Ileen DeVault points out that white-collar work offered opportunities to women, but women's presence decreased the status of salaried white-collar men, who were now even further from the goal of becoming entrepreneurs.[64]

Collar manufacturers, themselves part of the nation's elite, were slow to recognize new configurations of social distinctions. Most large clothing companies were relative newcomers who set up business in the 1890s, unlike collar companies founded in the 1860s or earlier, when custom tailors set menswear standards. Founding entrepreneurs who owned and managed collar firms probably retained custom tailors' presumptions that markets for stylish menswear were respectable gentlemen or their imitators. In 1921 E. H. Cluett, a spokesman for the firm, revealed to laundry owners (who shared collar manufacturers' hope for the starched collar's revival) that Cluett, Peabody preferred to produce stiff collars for gentlemen. "[T]he soft collar is different because it can be manufactured by anyone anywhere who has a needle. . . . We prefer making starched collars because it is more of an art." "[W]e have always thought that the starched collar was the collar of a gentleman," but "I do not mean . . . that the man who wears a soft collar is not a gentleman." Nevertheless, he was glad that one of New York's "large financial institutions" has "forbidden . . . employees to wear the soft collar."[65] A 1920 advertisement for an Arrow collar named Prince that pictured a figure evoking British nobility carrying a sign that read "The Prince of Arrows" suggests that the firm persisted in assuming that white, middle-class men sought to emulate the appearance of English and Continental elites.

Collar manufacturers did not realize that customers' tastes had shifted partly because of a new social divide—generation. Young, white, middle-class men who preferred comfortable, brightly colored, serviceable garments differed culturally from their fathers. In the eyes of youth, formal, dark-colored, constraining dress was stodgy and conservative. World War I veterans, especially, perceived their bodies differently from older relatives. They had become accustomed to looser, serviceable garments, enjoyed sports, and many took seriously campaigns advocating health, diet, and exercise.[66] Young men especially complained about detachable collars' discomfort, now legitimated by physicians whose articles appeared in mass-circulation magazines. Echoing criticisms of women's corsets, physicians claimed that stiff collars were unhealthy and detracted from appearance. In 1924 a physician noted that hard, tight collars caused gestures that irritated observers and could injure the wearer. Men often shifted points of pressure "upon the neck or throat" by pulling "the neck through the collar" or twisting "it from side to side . . . to side." Tight collars constricted blood vessels, prevented proper breathing, interfered with such internal organs as the thyroid and lymph glands, and might cause headaches that warn of "pending rupture of a blood vessel in the brain" resulting in "paralysis." Pressure on "cervical glands and lymphatics" that "guard against infection" could result in "tonsilitus, sore throat, laryngitus, coughs. . . . " In growing boys, ". . . pressure at a vital point may stunt development."[67]

Not only were the new white-collar workers younger and relatively less affluent, but detachable collars had become more expensive to buy and maintain. The cost of commercial laundering increased in the 1920s and home washing machine prices fell.[68] Stiff linen collars, previously comparatively inexpensive, now seemed costly compared to simply constructed cotton collars that could be laundered at home, even without a washing machine. Many new white-collar workers had to stretch limited budgets to purchase sufficient supplies of the older generation's elaborately constructed collars, and they could not afford commercial starching and expert ironing. E. H. Cluett conceded that if he were "a man of small means," he "would . . . wear the soft collar rather than pay 60 cents a dozen for laundering."[69]

In an effort to understand shifting styles and markets in the 1920s, Cluett, Peabody's managers clipped and pasted in scrapbooks newspaper articles that disapproved of the new menswear fashions that changed middle-class men's appearance at work and play. In this period of flux in menswear and proliferation of styles, Cluett, Peabody's managers saw only short-term implications—that men's public appearance increasingly lacked visible signs of social distinctions. High-status men appeared in attire previously reserved for informal occasions or for workingmen and adopted a looser, more relaxed posture that some critics of the new fashions identified with feminine weakness. Cluett, Peabody failed to see that the detachable collar was no longer associated with privileged businessmen and ideal, white, middle-class manhood. Men of different backgrounds wore similar attire in public; attached-collar shirts, along with ties and hats, highlighted the face and displayed taste and affluence. White-collar attire had become public rather than occupational dress.

Changes in consumer tastes and markets for detachable collars reflected not only fluctuations within the fashion system and entrepreneurs' decisions but social transformations that changed the meanings of specific garments and dress in general. Detachable collars were especially significant because middle-class men used collars and other extensions of inner garments as props in self-presentation in order to create the appearance of a laundered shirt and washed body, and thus cleanliness, refinement, and respectability. Collars embodied within a single small garment complex but crucial contradictions in American ideologies about class-based manliness. Manual work denoted inferior, subservient social position, but enterprising wage-earners could become autonomous employers; work clothes did not permanently define humble men. In the early twentieth century, the shift from stiff to soft collars, along with the rise of the ready-made garment industry and other fashion changes, contributed to a convergence in the physical appearance of middle-class and working men. This convergence matched new class-based ideologies of manliness; earning a salary no longer signaled failure, and the manly ideal was largely American, not based on British elites. The Arrow Collar Man, an idealized image of the new masculinity, appeared in mass-circulation publications aimed at the expanded middle class but was likely observed by many more humble Americans as well. By the 1920s, consumerism was emerging, and many Americans resolved the contradiction between deep social divisions and the ideology of opportunity by acquiring material possessions. The Arrow Man, depicted in glamorous, luxurious settings, embodied in a single compelling image the resolution of social contradictions that persisted beneath the increased similarity in the appearance of men of different backgrounds.

ACKNOWLEDGMENTS

I owe thanks to those who commented on this paper: Mary H. Blewett, Christine Bose, Nancy Breen, Elspeth Brown, Sally Clarke, Myra Marx Ferree, Laura Frader, Evelyn Nakano Glenn, Alice Kessler-Harris, Kathy Peiss, Frances Rothstein, Philip Scranton, and Wilbur R. Miller. Special thanks to the staff of the Rensselaer County Historical Society, especially Kathryn Sheehan, my guide to the Cluett Collection.

1. The term *white-collar* was first used in the 1900s in discussions about determining "criteria . . . used to steer pupils into . . . diverse schools or curricula." The terms used were "abstract-minded class," "hand-minded class," "mechanical-minded pursuits," and "white collar jobs." Jurgen Kocka, *White Collar Workers in America, 1890–1940: A Social-Political History in International Perspective* (Beverly Hills, CA: Sage, 1980), 113–114. The term blue-collared worker stems from manual workers' indigo-dyed work clothes. It was first used in the mid-twentieth-century U.S. to distinguish industrial from white-collar workers. *Oxford English Dictionary*, vol. II (Oxford: Oxford University Press, 1989), 324.

2. Premiered in 1934 in the Broadway show, "Anything Goes." (www.coleporter.org).

3. Carole Turbin, *Working Women of Collar City. Gender, Class, and Community in Troy, New York, 1864–86* (Urbana, IL: University of Illionois Press, 1992), chap. 1 (quote on p. 20). Also see Rutherford Hayner, *Troy and Rensselaer County, New York,* (New York: Lewis Historical Publishing Co., 1925), 662; and Samuel Hopkins Adams, "Grandfather and the Montague Collar," *The New Yorker,* reprinted by The Arrow Company, 1950.

4. O. E. Schoeffler and William Gale, *Esquire's Encyclopedia of Twentieth Century Men's Fashions* (New York: McGraw Hill, 1973), 229–231; Doriece Colle, *Collars, Stocks, and Cravats: A History and Costume Dating Guide to Civilian Men's Neckpieces, 1655–1900* (Emmaus, PA: Rodale Press, 1972), 75–184. Christobel Williams-Mitchell, *Dressed for the Job: The Story of Occupational Costume* (New York: Blandford, 1982), 102–103, notes that manual workers wore mufflers or neckerchiefs with colored shirts. British workingmen continued to wear collarless shirts with mufflers well into the twentieth century.

5. Turbin, *Working Women,* 26–29. Mary P. Ryan, *Cradle of the Middle Class: The Family in Oneida County, New York, 1790–1865* (New York: Cambridge University Press, 1981).

6. Susan Porter Benson, *Counter Cultures: Saleswomen, Managers, and Customers in American Department Stores, 1890–1940* (Urbana, IL: University of Illinois Press, 1988).

7. Richard Bushman, *The Refinement of America: Persons, Houses, Cities* (New York: Vintage Books, 1993), 7–9; Wendy Gamber, *The Female Economy: The Millinery and Dressmaking Trades 1860–1930* (Urbana, IL: University of Illinois Press, 1997), 10–11; Grant McCracken, *Culture and Consumption: New Approaches to the Symbolic Character of Consumer Goods and Activities* (Bloomington, IN: Indiana University Press, 1990), chap. 1.

8. Claudia B. Kidwell and Margaret C. Christman, *Suiting Everyone: The Democratization of Clothing in America* (Washington, DC: Smithsonian, 1974), 121; *Clothing Gazette* (January 1900): 20.

9. Turbin, *Working Women,* chap. 1.

10. Colle, *Collars, Stocks, and Cravats,* 11–28, 189–192; Schoeffler and Gale, *Esquire's Encyclopedia,* 198–199; Arthur James Weise, *The City of Troy and Its Vicinity* (Troy, NY: E. Green, 1886), 271–73; Horace Greeley, et al., *Great Industries of the United States,* (Hartford, CT: J. B. Burrand Hyde, 1873), 607–617, 1144–1148.

11. Susan I. Lewis, "Beyond Horatio Alger: Breaking Through Gendered Assumptions about Business 'Success' in Mid-Nineteenth-Century America," *Business and Economic History* 24:1 (Fall 1995): 97–105.

12. Judith L. Goldstein, "The Female Aesthetic Community," *Poetics Today* 14:1 (Spring 1993), 143–163, views makeup as "dress" for the face, a second skin through which women represent inner selves by manipulating outer appearance.

13. Kathy Peiss, *Hope in a Jar: The Making of America's Beauty Culture* (New York: Metropolitan Books, 1998), 48–50.

14. Gail Bederman, *Manliness and Civilization: A Cultural History of Gender and Race in the United States, 1880–1917* (Chicago: University of Chicago Press, 1995), chap. 1, 60–67; E. Anthony Rotundo, "Learning about Manhood Gender Ideals and the Middle-Class Family in Nineteenth-Century America," in *Manliness and Morality: Middle Class Masculinity in Britain and America, 1800–1940,* ed. J. A. Mangan and James Walvin (New York: St. Martin's Press, 1987), 35–51.

15. Herman Roodenburg, "How to Sit, Stand or Walk: Towards a Historical Anthropology of Dutch Paintings and Prints," in *Looking at Seventeenth Century Dutch Art,* ed. Wayne Franits (New York: Cambridge University Press, 1997).

16. Phillippe Perrot, *Fashioning the Bourgeoisie: A History of Clothing in the Nineteenth Century* (Princeton, NJ: Princeton University Press, 1994), 136–137; Bushman, *Refinement,* 66–69. By the late eighteenth century in the U.S., high-ranking men avoided stiff and awkward movements of imitators of higher ranks by standing erect while appearing graceful and at ease with themselves and others. Illustrations in advertisements and catalogues depict well-dressed men posed with weight on one foot, arms bent gracefully, perhaps with hat, cane, or small book in hand, head turned slightly to one side. *The 1902 Edition of The*

Sears Roebuck Catalogue (NY: Bounty Books, 1969), 1122–1123; *Montgomery Ward & Co. Catalogue and Buyers' Guide*, No. 57, Spring and Summer 1895 (NY: Bounty Books, 1969), 266–268.

17. Bushman, *Refinement*, 65; Perrot, *Fashioning*, 136.
18. Williams-Mitchell, *Dressed for the Job*, 102–103, explains the significance of collars of different heights.
19. Elliott J. Gorn, *The Manly Art: Bare Knuckle Prizefighting in America* (Ithaca, NY: Cornell University Press, 1986), 132–133; David Montgomery, "Workers' Control of Machine Production in the Nineteenth Century," *Labor History*, 17 (Fall 1976): 485–509; Ava Baron, "Acquiring Manly Competence: The Demise of Apprenticeship and the Remasculinization of Printers' Work," in Mark C. Carnes and Clyde Griffen, eds., *Meanings for Manhood: Constructions of Masculinity in Victorian America* (Chicago: University of Chicago Press, 1990), 152–163; Mary H. Blewett, "Manhood and the Market: The Politics of Gender and Class among the Textile Workers of Fall River, Massachusetts, 1870–1880," in *Work Engendered* ed. Ava Baron, (Ithaca, NY: Cornell University Press, 1991), 92–113.
20. Kocka, *White Collar Workers*, p. 86, notes that in 1888 a Plumbers' Union member complained about cooperating with the Retail Clerks' International Protective Association: "What do you expect to do with these white collar stiffs? ...[A] $15 a week collar and cuff clerk thinks he's far superior to a $25 a week blouse and overall mechanic."
21. Michael Kimmel, *Manhood in America: A Cultural History* (New York: Free Press, 1995), 16–19, 26–27.
22. Kidwell and Christman, *Suiting Everyone*, 121.
23. Ruth Schwartz Cowan, "The 'Industrial Revolution' in the Home: Household Technology and Social Change in the Twentieth Century," in *Material Culture Studies in America*, ed. Thomas J. Schlereth (Nashville, TN: American Association for State and Local History, 1982), 222–236.
24. Kidwell and Christman, *Suiting Everyone*, 21; John F. Kasson, *Rudeness and Civility: Manners in Nineteenth Century Urban America* (New York: Hill and Wang, 1990), especially chaps. 1 and 2.
25. The firm originated as a partnership formed in 1851 by Maullin and Blanchard, later joined by George Cluett, who formed his own company in 1863. Until the collar business declined after World War I, Cluett, Peabody, and Co., Inc., was the "top U.S. manufacturer" of detachable collars. "Cluett, Peabody," *Fortune Magazine* (February, 1937): 113–127; "Arrow Advertising: A Study in Consistency," *Tide: The Newsmagazine for Advertising Executives* (April 13, 1951): 44–46.
26. James Morske, "And It All Began with One Woman," and Ken Johnson, "Personal Investments: J. C. Leyendecker and the Arrow Collar Man," in "The Arrow Man: Collar City Chic," a brochure for an exhibition at Russell Sage College Gallery, Troy, New York, September 1–October 10, 1987.
27. Morske and Johnson, "The Arrow Man"; "Cluett, Peabody," *Fortune*, 119–120; "Arrow Advertising: A Study in Consistency," *Tide: The Newsmagazine for Advertising Executives*, (April 13, 1951): 44–46.
28. Christopher Breward, *The Culture of Fashion: A New History of Fashionable Dress* (Manchester: Manchester University Press, 1995), 130; William Leach, "Strategists of Display and the Production of Desire," in Simon J. Bronner, ed., *Consuming Visions: Accumulation and Display of Goods in America, 1880–1920* (New York: W. W. Norton, 1989), 99–132; William Leach, *Land of Desire: Merchants, Power, and the Rise of a New American Culture* (New York: Pantheon, 1993), 42–50; Stephen Fox, "The Origins of American Advertising: The Age of Lasker," *Adweek*, (June 1984): 26.
29. Breward, *Culture of Fashion*, 182–184; Peiss, *Hope in a Jar*, 45–50.
30. Bederman, *Manliness and Civilization*, 12–41. Kimmel, *Manhood in America*, Chapter 4.
31. Roy Rosenzweig, *Eight Hours for What We Will: Workers and Leisure in an Industrial City, 1870–1920* (Cambridge: Cambridge University Press, 1983), Gorn, *Manly Art*, 132–133; Montgomery, "Workers' Control," 485–509; Baron, "Acquiring Manly Competence," Carnes and Griffen, *Meanings for Manhood*, 152–63; Blewett, "Manhood and the Market," 92– 113.
32. Bederman, *Manliness and Civilization*, 17–20.
33. For discussion of complexities of middle-class manliness depicted in visual images, see Eric Segal, "Norman Rockwell and the Fashioning of American Masculinity," *Art Bulletin* 77 (1996)4 633–646, and Michael J. Murphy, "Arrow's Eros?: Homoeroticism and J.C. Lyendecker's Arrow Collar Man," unpublished paper, Fall 1999.
34. On the Arrow Man's appearance, see Murphy, "Arrow's Eros?," "Cluett, Peabody," *Fortune*, 120. Quote is from "The Arrow Man." See Erving Goffman, *Gender Advertisements* (New York: Harper and Row, 1979), 40–42, on deference and physical movements.
35. Philip Scranton, "The Transition from Custom to Ready-to-Wear Clothing in Philadelphia,

1890–1930," *Textile History* 25 (1994: 2) 243– 73; Kidwell and Christman, *Suiting Everyone*, 53–63; Nancy L. Green, *Ready-to-Wear, Ready-to-Work: A Century of Industry and Immigrants in Paris and New York* (Durham, NC: Duke University Press, 1997), 23, 27, 47.
36. Green, *Ready-to-Wear*, 40–43.
37. *Clothing Gazette* (July 1901).
38. *Clothing Gazette* (November 1901): 29–38; The June, 1901 issue of *Clothing Gazette*, p. 30, added: "Shoulders, collars, pockets, lapels, no feature, however trifling, has escaped the designers, practiced eye, and many . . . are genuinely artistic."
39. *Clothing Gazette*, (January 1901): 20.
40. Scranton, "Transition," 246–258; Green, *Ready-to-Wear*, 39. When manufacturers marketed ready-made dresses, dressmaking took different forms as women used standardized patterns to sew garments or become dressmakers. Gamber, *Female Economy*, chap. 5, 127–156, 216.
41. *Clothing Gazette* (June 1901): 30.
42. The *Clothing Gazette* (January 1901): 20 claimed that because ready-made styles no longer lag "one or two years behind" custom models, differences between them are "almost unnoticeable."
43. Green, *Ready-to-Wear*, 27, 66–67, notes that U.S. women's fashion began reflecting American tastes in the early twentieth century. The *Clothing Gazette* remarked (May 1901, p. 31): "Manufacturers recognize this season, more than ever, that the retailer has well-defined notions of his own as to style. . . .
44. Kidwell and Christman, *Suiting Everyone*, 161–163; Schoeffler and Gale, *Esquire's Encyclopedia*, 7–8, 76.
45. Kidwell and Christman, *Suiting Everyone*, 130–132.
46. "Salesmen with Starched Collar is Losing Caste," *New York News Record* (February 20, 1924).
47. See Richard Sennett, *The Fall of Public Man* (New York: Knopf, 1976), for analysis of shifts in personal and public life.
48. "Van Zandy Scores Recent Decline in Dress Ethics," *New York News Record*, (October 11, 1922).
49. *New York News Record* (September 29, 1922).
50. "E.H. Cluett's declaration," *New York News Record* (November 17, 1921); "Chicago Plans Strike to Doom Collar Button," *New York Sun* (April 26, 1920).
51. *New York News Record*, (September 29, 1922).
52. "Smart Dresser Readily Passes for Smart Man; if Rich You'd Get, until it Hurts, Watch Your Ties, Likewise Your Shirt," *New York News Record*, (August 25, 1923).
53. Luigi Bazini, *Memories of Mistresses: Recollections from a Life* (New York: Collier Books, 1986.), 248–250.
54. "Spineless Linen," *New York News Record* (May 27, 1924).
55. "Men Need More Starch," *New York News Record* (September 29, 1922).
56. "Cluett, Peabody and Co.'s Style Book," 1909, "Barker Brand Linen and Madras Collars" (1913–1914), and style books of Earl and Wilson (1918, 1919) and George P. Ide, Co., Inc. (undated), in Cluett Collection, Rensselaer County Historical Society, Troy, NY.
57. "Cluett, Peabody," *Fortune*, 122; Max Phillips, "An Unusual Layout Simplifies a Complicated Advertising Story: How the Van Heusen Checkerboard Came into Being," *Printers' Ink: A Journal for Advertising* 125:9 (November 1923): 33–36; "New Era Seen in Introduction of Flexible Collar," *New York News Record* (October 27, 1921).
58. See annual reports for Cluett, Peabody, & Co., Inc., 1917–1933, Rensselaer County History Society, Cluett Collection; also, "Cluett, Peabody," *Fortune*, 113, 122.
59. "Cluett, Peabody," *Fortune*, 114–116.
60. Turbin, *Working Women of Collar City*.
61. "New era seen in introduction of flexible collar," *New York News Record*, (October 28, 1921); "Collar Manufacturers Requested to Cut Down Prices: State retailers' association to Ask Collar Houses to help Stores Sell at .25 center—Condemn Clothing Reductions," *New York News Record*, (April 28, 1920); "Collar Prices Slide Down to Former Level," *New York News Record*, (May 1, 1920); "Cluett, Peabody and Co., Inc. Announce New Style Collar," *New York News Record* (October 28, 1921). "Collars as Money Makers" and other pamphlets are in the Cluett Collection, Rensselaer County History Society, Troy, NY.
62. Susan Strasser, *Never Done* (New York: Pantheon, 1982), 110–24.
63. C. Wright Mills, *White Collar: The American Middle Classes* (New York, 1956) and Kocka, *White Collar Workers*. For the new middle class, see Richard Hyman and Robert Price, eds., *The New Working Class? White Collar Workers and their Organizations* (New York: Prometheus Books, 1983), especially Anthony Giddens, "The Growth of the 'New Middle Class,'" 98–101.

64. Kocka, *White Collar Workers*, chap. 1, 156–8, 166–7; Ileen A. DeVault, *Sons and Daughters of Labor: Class and Clerical Work in Turn-of-the-Century Pittsburg* (Ithaca, NY: Cornell University Press, 1990), 172–178, notes that because women and men white-collar workers were sex segregated, men could disassociate themselves from women coworkers and confirm identification with men.
65. "E.H. Cluett's Declaration that Soft Collar Vogue Is on Wane Brings Joy to Laundresses," New York *News Record* (November 17, 1921).
66. Schoeffler and Gale, *Esquire's Encyclopedia*, 125.
67. "Question of collar comfort crops up once more with warmer Weather—Doctor gives views on 'Soft or Starched,'" N.Y. *News Record*, (May 21 1924).
68. Strasser, *Never Done*, 120, explains that commercial laundries remained local, decentralized, and technologically backward while washing machine manufacturers utilized new technology, transportation networks, and marketing and retailing strategies.
69. "E. H. Cluett's Declaration that Soft Collar Vogue Is on Wane Brings Joy to Laundresses," New York *News Record* (November 17, 1921).

"Fighting the Corsetless Evil"

SHAPING CORSETS AND CULTURE, 1900–1930

JILL FIELDS

During the nineteenth century virtually all freeborn women in the United States wore corsets. Yet from mid-century onward the purpose and meaning of the corset generated heated debate among physicians, ministers, couturiers, feminist dress reformers, health and hygiene activists, and advocates of tight lacing. Their lengthy argument suggests that keeping women in corsets was an ongoing project.

In the early twentieth century these corset debates intensified. Turn-of-the-century corset styles became even more constricting, and so protests against their use gained ground. In addition, young women in the 1910s began to reject the Victorian moral sensibilities—and the fashions inspired by them—which symbolically and literally restricted women's mobility in both private and public spheres. Women's claims to wagework, to academic and physical education, to public protest over access to suffrage and birth control, and to pleasurable leisure activities such as dancing at tango parties all brought daily corset wearing into question. Arguments supporting corset use changed as a result. And, though most women continued to wear corsets, demands for more comfort in clothing and the rising appeal of "modernity" as a sales tool changed their shape.

G. B. Pulfer, treasurer and general manager of the Kalamazoo Corset Company, explained in the trade journal *Corsets & Lingerie* why women wore corsets in 1921:

> Fear! Fear of ill health, fear of sagging bodies, fear of lost figure, fear of shiftless appearance in the nicest of clothing, fear of sallow complexion. Fear sends them to the corsetiere, trembling; the same corsetiere from whom they fled mockingly a couple of years back, at the beck of a mad style authority

who decreed "zat ze body must be free of ze restrictions, in order zat ze new styles shall hang so freely."[1]

Pulfer addressed these comments to the journal's national readership of corset manufacturers, retailers, department store buyers, and saleswomen. His article was one of a series addressing industry concerns about women's continued consent to wearing corsets and was part of an intensive coordinated effort by manufacturers to revitalize and revamp procorset argumentation. Thus Pulfer's article also addressed the fear of corset manufacturers. Their fear, which exploded on the panicked pages of *Corsets & Lingerie* throughout the early 1920s, was of losing control over how and when women changed the way they dressed.[2] (See Figure 5.1.)

Scholarship on nineteenth-century women's history and dress explores the power of corsets to regulate women's behavior as well as to signify women's subordinate status. Studies by Helene Roberts, David Kunzle, Lois Banner, and Valerie Steele demonstrate the well-established and lasting iconic power of the corset as a conveyor of social meaning. As these scholars disagree about just what that meaning was for female corset wearers as well as for corset defenders and opponents of both sexes, their studies also make abundantly clear that the corset became a locus for a number of competing significations. To move beyond previous corset controversies, we thus need to ask not only how dressing practices function as structures of domination or as resources of resistance, but also how these functions are instituted and why these practices generate both contested and contradictory meanings. These questions address not only the history of the corset as a pervasive and persistent article of women's clothing, but also the history of how the corset's meanings affected women's lives as they struggled to alter the shape of femininity and gender relations.[3]

Building upon earlier studies, this essay picks up the chronology with the turn-of-the-century period, when use of the rigid nineteenth-century corset declined, and continues through the first decades of the twentieth century, when challenges to the corset intensified. Significantly, this time frame also encompasses an era of heightened agitation for women's political, sexual, economic, and social equality. Yet we also know that achievements in one period do not prevent backlashes in succeeding decades. Analysis of how the commercialized practice and ideology of corsetry worked in significant ways to shape the way women viewed, imagined, and experienced their own bodies can help us understand both the persistence and reshaping of problematic gender structures and identities.

Fashions in dress are particularly useful for analyzing culture as contested terrain because a central defining element of fashion is

Figure 5.1. Whose fear sends her "to the corsetiere, trembling?" A 1921 Kalamazoo corset. (*Women's & Infants' Furnisher*, January 1921).

change. Controlling the direction of this change is difficult, not only because of the fashion industry's perpetual dependence upon innovation but also because of the simple fact that everyone wears clothes. As a result, the apparatus that monitors dressing practices, evident in written and unwritten dress codes and their enforcement by myriads of "fashion police," is widely dispersed. The accepted power of clothing to express identity in such categories as gender, personality, sexual preference, class, and social status heightens the stakes for how fashion changes take place and take shape. Fashion, both a system of signification and a set of regulatory practices, is thus an arena of social struggle over meaning.[4]

Corset manufacturers' coordinated response to women's new widespread defiance of older fashion standards, a response that enlisted corset saleswomen to deploy their merchandising campaign against the "corsetless evil," emphasized youthful standards of beauty, developed scientific discourse that viewed the female body as inherently flawed, and connected ideologies of racial purity, national security, and heterosexual privilege to corset use. Examining the marketing strategies developed and disseminated to keep women in corsets, as well as the oppositional practices that these strategies sought to corral, reveals how the corset's instrumentality changed in the twentieth century. Nineteenth-century efforts to keep women corseted drew upon, legitimated, and constructed particular notions about femininity, propriety, and the female body. In the twentieth century, corset discourses also incorporated ideas about race, nation, and the importance of science and modernity to everyday life. The meanings corsetry impressed upon women's bodies thus shifted with industrialization, as women's fears of aging, imperfect, inferior, unfashionable, and unscientific bodies replaced earlier fears of moral turpitude and questionable respectability. And most significantly, industrialists' fear of diminishing profits played and preyed upon the long-standing fear of unrestrained women.

After 1900 corsets got progressively longer on the hips, and the top of the corset moved down the torso toward the waistline. The popularity of the uncomfortable S-curve corsets favored by Gibson girls of this era, which threw the bust forward and the buttocks back, declined after 1905 with wider use of straight-front corsets. The S-curve blunted the athleticism and mobility of the Gibson girl, and the obvious manipulation of the body necessary to create the S-curve silhouette was an easy target for anticorset agitation which defended the "natural" body. However, the necessity of wearing a corset was also vigorously defended throughout this period and, once the straight-front corsets succeeded the S-curve corsets, anatomical reasons were stressed as the basis for the corset's necessity.[5]

Havelock Ellis was among the experts cited in the popular press who claimed that female humans required corseting because the evolution from "horizontality to verticality" was more difficult for females than for males. "Woman might be physiologically truer to herself," Havelock Ellis insisted, "if she went always on all fours. It is because the fall of the viscera in woman when she imitated man by standing erect induced such profound physiological displacements . . . that the corset is morphologically essential."[6] A supporting argument claimed that recent archaeological finds in Crete and Greece, in addition to the discovery of cave paintings in Spain and France, proved that women had cinched their waists for the past 40,000 years due to anatomical necessity. Thus corseting continued to be an evolutionary requirement. The extent to which present concerns colored the interpretation of ancient representations may be seen in the detection in cave paintings of the "debutante slouch," a hunched posture popularized by young women in the 1910s.[7]

Straight-front corsets continued to be quite long over the thighs in order to conform the body to the slimmer line of skirts. (Figure 5.2.) These longer corsets could be extremely confining, as wearing one actually made it difficult to bend the legs enough to sit down. The binding of the legs persisted with the notorious "hobble skirt" introduced in 1908, which had an extremely narrow hemline around the ankles that inhibited walking. French couturier Paul Poiret related his claim to invention of the hobble skirt to another claim, that of successfully waging "war upon [the corset]." Poiret stated in his autobiography, "Like all great revolutions, that one had been made in the name of Liberty—to give free play to the abdomen: it was equally in the name of Liberty that I proclaimed the fall of the corset. . . . Yes, I freed the bust but I shackled the legs."[8]

Women in the United States did not toss away their corsets en masse after Poiret's introduction of dresses designed to be worn without corsets. Achieving the fashionable line actually still required most women to be corseted. In fact, Poiret's corsetless fashions were in part an appropriation of design ideas from the cultural fringe that he marketed to the middle class. Since the nineteenth century, the idea of abandoning the corset had been floating in the margins of feminist dress reform and of esthetic and communitarian movements. In addition, turn-of-the-century health and hygiene movements, as well as the availability of bicycles, encouraged active play for adult urban dwellers. Furthermore, growing numbers of women experienced the benefits of organized sports in women's colleges. Women's access to sports and physical exercise in this period heightened their desire for less restrictive garments and prompted the development and marketing of sports corsets made of lighter and more flexible materials. Embedded in sports corsets was thus a measure of give and take between women's demands for greater comfort and freedom of movement and manufacturers' needs for profits from continued corset sales.[9] (Figure 5.3.)

By 1914 another popular phenomenon, the tango, also affected active American women's corset use. Women began removing their stiff corsets at parties in order to dance, and corset manufacturers responded once again by marketing dance corsets. But, like the flapper herself, who appeared in the mid-1910s but would not gain mainstream attention if not cause outright alarm until the next decade, corsetless-

Figure 5.2. The long corset of the 1910s. (*Women's & Infants' Furnisher*, January 1910).

Figure 5.3. Sports corsets "give freedom to the body." (*Women's & Infants' Furnisher*, April 1918).

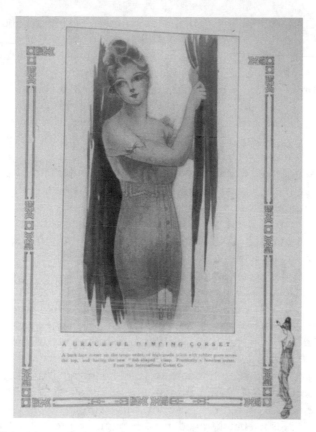

Figure 5.4. "A back-lace corset on the tango order . . ." (*Women's & Infants' Furnisher*, February 1921).

ness remained a situational phenomenon practiced by a daring minor-ity of mostly young and slim women at this time. Yet while *Vogue* con-ceded in 1914 that "the mode of the corsetless figure is an established one—for a season, at least," it also noted that "the point has been reached where women do not have to be dictated to, as formerly, in the matter of corsets." Rather than doing away with corsets entirely, *Vogue* argued that since many corset models were now available, "the present mode is not a uniform one. . . . A year ago where one or two corsets would answer, it is now not a luxury, but a necessity, to have a greater number, and each of a different sort." Thus corset manufacturers' deci-sion to supply women with lighter and more flexible corsets was not mere concession but also a means to increase the total number of corsets sold. Nonetheless, increasing the number of corset styles avail-able also created a situation in which a monolithic fashionability began to dissolve, and women's power to determine their own shape within fashionability expanded.[10] (Figure 5.4.)

Vogue duly noted the dangers of women's expanded power in a 1917 article entitled "Woman Decides to Support Herself." Giving sportswomen the credit for the initial blow toward "undermining the power of fashion" while also castigating her "absurd willingness to support her figure without external aid," *Vogue* then proceeds to analyze "the fatal mistake of couturiers" that caused this turn of events. Couturiers, *Vogue* explains, did not foresee the ramifications of their recent designs based on the so-called "natural figure." Significantly, shaping a woman's body into the "natural figure" required looser corsets than those worn previously. When couturiers attempted to reimpose a more constricted waist, "the unexpected, the unprecedented, happened. Women refused to wear them; they actually did that unheard-of thing." Eventually, according to *Vogue*, fashionable women and couturiers reached a compromise—waists would be taken in, but not much.[11]

Women's desires for self-sufficiency, alluded to in the article's title, were not, of course, limited to the sphere of dress. Agitation for suffrage and birth control was in full swing by 1917, including daily picketing in front of the White House until the passage of women's suffrage in 1919. In addition, once World War I ended, some of the mid-1910s subcultural trends hit the mainstream. Shorter skirt lengths, which resulted in the shocking appearance of women's bare legs, became a focus of controversy. While ministers admonished from the pulpits, college deans instituted dress codes, and women formed short skirt defense leagues, debates raged in the popular press over what was seen as either the new immodesty or the new freedom in women's dress and behavior.[12]

Debates regarding the redefinition of women's propriety took place in a context of uncertainty during postwar reconstruction. In 1919, an unprecedented four million workers participated in over 3,000 strikes to consolidate wartime gains and achieve further improvements in working conditions. Employers characterized this labor unrest as unduly influenced by the Bolshevik revolution, and saw both as merely the first stage in the undoing of the current world order. In 1920 the Department of Justice responded to this fear by arresting thousands of radicals and deporting hundreds of immigrants to quell opposition. Known as the Red Scare, this state suppression of dissent disrupted many lives and raised troubling questions about the government's role in maintaining power at the expense of constitutional freedoms.[13]

The construction of corsetlessness as a dangerous evil drew upon similar moral language employed in the domestic suppression of radicalism. Corsetlessness had, after all, been long identified with radical feminist and utopian movements. Confusion also persisted about which postwar changes were American and modern, and which foreign and menacing. New York City resident Mildred Rosenstein, for example, whose lifelong anticommunism probably began in those years, was called a Bolshevik by her brother when she bobbed her waist-length hair in the late 1910s. As late as 1925 a report on corset manufacturer's efforts to "reestablish a vogue for their wares" related the current posing of the "query, are corsets only another obsolete tradition to be cast aside?" to "the unchartered freedom of the Bolshevist figure."[14]

Trade journals were an industry mechanism for disseminating procorset argumentation. In 1921, *Corsets & Lingerie* identified corsetlessness as a dangerous and evil fad. According to subsequent trade accounts, this fad began after the end of World War I. However, as we have seen, corsetlessness had been a twentieth-century "look" since Poiret's introduction of corsetless dresses in 1908. *Vogue* magazine acknowledged this fashion trend in a 1914 procorset article entitled "Corseting the Corsetless Figure." That same year *Corsets & Lingerie* noted "the popularity . . . of the corsetless figure," and a 1915 ad for foundations advertised its product on a similar basis. Yet six years later, this trade journal expressed a decided panic about corsetlessness. Moreover, it continued to refer to the specter of the evil corsetless fad throughout the 1920s.[15]

In his 1921 *Corsets & Lingerie* article, "Fighting the Corsetless Evil," G. B. Pulfer described industry strategies working to stifle corsetlessness:

> The same publicity media which spread this first corsetless fad story . . . is now being utilized to spread the story of danger, the warning that has aroused our sane women to righteous fear, the warning that's sending them back to the corset shop . . . in droves. . . . When it was announced that no corset shall now be the rule, it was expected that the American corset manufacturer and the merchant would gasp, then bow their heads in gentle and piteous submission to the commands of the Parisian boulevardier. But did they? They did not. . . . The publicity campaign that sprang into life immediately could not have been more ably managed if it had been under one directing general. . . . The corset manufacturers have flooded the trade with literature and advice on how to spread the true story of the corsetless fad. The newspapers have helped considerably.[16]

Pulfer concludes by exhorting readers to "keep your literature going out Mr. Corset Maker; keep your customers informed, Mr. Dealer."

Trade journal articles, such as "Evils of the No-Corset Fad," "Flappers Are Responsible for Corsetless Craze," and "Eminent Surgeons Endorse the Corset," indicted corsetlessness as a threatening menace. Reasons given included dissipation of muscular strength, injury to internal organs, corruption of standards of beauty, damage to moral fiber, contamination of race pride and purity, and destruction of American sovereignty. Some of these contentions, particularly the medical and hygienic, had been articulated previously as part of nineteenth-century debates about the corset. Other claims, such as the patriotic and racial, were more recent concerns.[17]

The identification and explication of corsetlessness as an evil fad served not only to bolster support among those whose livelihoods depended upon the continuing use of the corset, but also armed the industry with the weapon of ideology. As G. B. Pulfer quite openly pointed out, this ideology could then be further disseminated in a range of tactical discourses, from public advertisements in mass-circulation print media to private conversations with women customers in the intimacy of corset fitting rooms. This deployment of procorset ideologies, culled from the discourses of professionalized medicine, the eugenics movement, and Victorian constructions of femininity, and their circulation through mass media and the marketplace reveal how manufacturers constructed the corset as an instrument of cultural hegemony.

Extreme assertions in the trade journals about the wide-ranging detrimental effects of corsetlessness convey the panic manufacturers felt about the potential for women to stop wearing corsets. Panic is also revealed by many contradictory statements that at one moment express relief over the fad's demise, at the next moment state the continuing need to exhort against it, and end by bemoaning the fad's ongoing effect on sales and profits. In addition, panic can be sensed in confused comments regarding manufacturers' continuing ability to manipulate women's fickle fashion sensibilities. Moreover, the sensibilities expressed in the trade journal articles seem to emanate more from emotion than fact, because the authors never produce any concrete data to support their anxious fears about declining corset sales. As one popular magazine put it, "Naturally these groups of elders are in a panic—'Are corsets doomed?'"[18]

The postwar economic depression of 1920 to 1922 also contributed to the climate of anxiety. The clothing industry was one of the first to decline, in April 1920. Prior to this time, production had finally reestablished levels close to those in force before the 1914 to 1915 depression. In other words, 1919, a year of "general prosperity and expansion" in the industry, was followed by yet another slump. The lowest level of employment reached in the garment industry occurred in June 1921, and was 35 percent below June 1914 levels. Figures for the underwear industry, which did not include corsets, show a dramatic 50 percent drop in sales between 1920 and 1921. Profitability in that sector of the trade returned in 1922, though sales remained below 1920 levels for several years.[19]

Census statistics for the corset industry, however, indicate insignificant change in the value of products manufactured between 1919 and 1921, and a 3.2 percent increase between 1921 and 1923. Therefore, there is no evidence to substantiate a frightening drop in corset sales, especially considering the depression in the garment industry and in the U.S. economy generally. In fact, the corset industry managed very ably through this short but sharp economic decline. Thus the corset panic looms even larger as a strictly ideological phenomenon, spawned by wider circumstances of social transition and economic upheaval.[20]

The three tactical strategies of the corset panic articles—denial, attack, and incorporation—utilized assertions drawn from medicine, politics, and the culture of beauty and fashion, but not economics. Corset manufacturers and department store buyers, often the authors of these articles, drew on proscriptive discourses to infuse corset use with ideologies of domination. As a result, corset manufacturers as well as the dominating classes as a whole benefited because these discourses circulated in new ways, including the further commodified probing of female flesh. The successful imposition of dominant ideologies via the corset thus worked to reinscribe women's subordination generally. Corset manufacturers' panic about losing control over their female market would be eased by invoking and thus reenforcing broader structures of control.

Denial of the fad's existence worked as a strategy to mitigate the fears of people in the trade. It also reproduced the deflating idea that corsetlessness was not popular and therefore not fashionable. In a July 1921 interview entitled "Corsets Still In Vogue," Miss O'Neill, a department store corset buyer, states that "while the fad for the corsetless effect is still raging, it is more a matter of 'effect' than of actuality." Manufacturers accommodated modern sensibilities by offering the new, lighter, and more flexible girdle to women as the up-to-date alternative to the corset. Though girdles were initially considered appropriate only for smaller women, the Elastowear Manufacturing Company opened up the girdle market by producing Elasto girdles for "stout women." Trade journals also discussed the importance of renaming corsets as girdles in order to shake off passé connotations. In addition, the older corset itself was cited as the cause of current figure problems that required newer corsets and girdles for correction.[21] (Figure 5.5.)

Assigning blame for the instigation and spread of the corsetless fad was, however, problematic for manufacturers. Laying the blame on Paris had its appeal, but was also double-edged. Ultimately this argument undermined manufacturers' desires to keep women under the sway of elite style makers as much as possible. The idea of a top-down

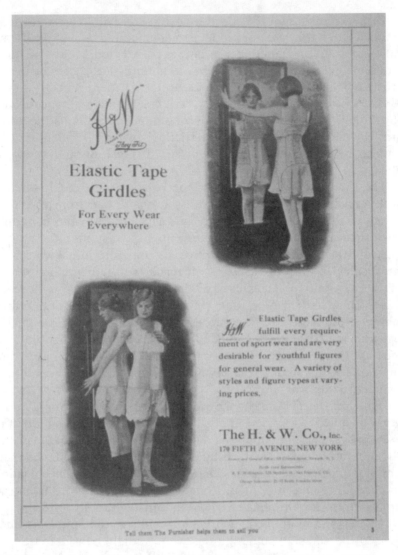

Figure 5.5. Renaming corsets as girdles. (*Women's & Infants' Furnisher*, May 1921).

fashion regime appealed to manufacturers because it provided a more controlled progression of fashion changes. Breaking down the importance of Paris as arbiter of fashionability could be dangerous.

One way out of this dilemma can be seen in an article from August 1921 entitled "Parisian Women Wear Corsets." This article claimed within one paragraph that Parisian women had gone without corsets in past years, that the idea circulating in the United States in 1920 that these women weren't wearing corsets was erroneous, that the corsetless trend in France existed but was exaggerated in the American press, and that in any event, all French women, including couturier mannequins, were wearing corsets once again. Three months later an article entitled "Paris on the Corset Question" reasserted Parisian hegemony:

> The question of corsets or no corsets as raised by the recent styles put forward by the foremost Parisian couturiers is being answered by Parisian couturiers in a characteristically Parisian fashion. The new corsets are more like the corsetless figure than the corsetless figure itself. . . . That is Parisian cleverness all over. They have made a figure more natural than the natural figure and far more beautiful. . . . [22]

American women's distinctiveness provided a basis for other arguments regarding nationality. In a curious *Corset and Underwear Review* article called "The American Woman and Her Corset," columnist Gertrude Nickerson claimed that American women must wear restrictive garments because she:

> has no definite type. We are a composite race of women . . . [who] must acknowledge our mixed blood and, while we are very proud of it, let us not forget just what it means where our figure is concerned. As we develop and approach maturity some "wayback" foreign grandmother, or several at once, may and most likely will make her hereditary attack upon us. . . . We now realize that we have indeed a handicap which we must accept as a result of our mixed races. We can understand now why the real American woman requires her corset or confining foundation for figure training more than her sisters overseas. [23]

Sisters closer to home unfortunately bore the brunt of racial argumentation. Mr. Leonard Florsheim, Corset and Brassiere Association Vice-President and head of Kabo Corset Company, constructed the specter of the "grotesque" Indian squaw to safely position white, middle-class American women between overly sophisticated French women and uncivilized Native American women. In his November 1921 *Corsets & Lingerie* interview, entitled "The Evils of the No-Corset Fad," Florsheim first preyed upon fears of corsetlessness as a cause of premature aging and a thickened waistline before launching into his racial attack:

> The Indian girls are known for shapely body lines in their youth, despite the fact that they never get a chance to enjoy the protection of corset or brassiere. They grow and develop "wildly." But at the age when they acquire the sobriquet of squaw, what a transformation! Squaws, especially those who have become mothers, are well known for their grotesque bodies. Nature has given them in youth well developed, shapely lines, muscles that withstand the first score and ten, but then nature changes her course and begins to add weight

that gradually rounds out and converts form into the well known "mattress-tied-in-the-middle" proportions.[24]

Florsheim's depiction allowed white women to both identify with and reject the impact of "nature" upon Native American women.

Dutch surgeon Dr. Jan Schoemaker broadened the scope of racial concerns in an interview printed the following month:

> Firmly-muscled women are vital, charming, full of that potential race force which must be coined into American supremacy among men tomorrow. But we are not trying to breed Amazons, nor are we trying to raise a race of Oriental dancers. Your corsetless girl has naturally to fall into one class or the other. The moment you begin to get too much of the Amazon variation, you begin to get fuzzy upper-lips with them, and a frothy type of male, a sort of listless love-bird, sufficiently spineless to be able to mate and marry the domineering female of the Amazon type.[25]

According to the doctor, corsetlessness promoted dangerous transformations in male as well as female character and anatomy with disastrous consequences for the white American "race" and its global prospects in the political and economic realignments of the postwar era.

The homophobic hint about "fuzzy upper-lips" was further embellished by Dr. Schoemaker in his discussion of the exercise regime required in order to maintain muscular health without the use of a corset:

> There is in Holland a Mrs. Dr. Mensendieck who undertakes this sort of work for women who have ambitions in that direction. She compels them to go through their exercises absolutely nude, and on each individual of a class . . . she keeps her eye. When a certain set of muscles sag down, as of course they will, she cries out at the woman, 'Keep that stomach in. Hold up there in the rear.' And so on.[26]

The liberation promised by renunciation of the corset thus produced a new sort of subjugation. The required submission to bodily discipline entailed submission as well to the critical and intrusive gaze of a harsh and clearly unfeminine female authority.

Schoemaker expounded further on the dangers of women's claims to new forms of authority in spheres outside of fashion and health. While the doctor conceded that women of a certain natural build may go without corsets, he disparaged these active and politically engaged New Women as failures at being either men or women:

> [T]he woman with a tight-muscled tense abdominal wall, flat hips, mannish chest, is usually to be pitied. She is unfortunate. If she has been produced and admired in quantities in England . . . it is not because the English are producing any healthier race, but because the number of biological mistakes among females are [sic] increasing.

He also linked this type of woman to feminists who favor corsetlessness: "There is a certain strident type of woman publican abroad in the land today who welcomes any move toward freedom appearing to register new approximation to sex equality." However, the race will survive such women because "women who imitate men are not the kind that Nature selects to mother the next generation." Connecting corsetlessness with a dismissive portrayal of radical politics and ideas about racial degeneracy, Schoemaker attacks all three in an effort to stifle women's desires to control their bodies and their destinies in the postsuffrage era.[27]

In November 1922 the Royal Worcester Corset Company announced the "retreat to the perfect figure," a figure that could be created only with the aid of a corset. Census figures do indicate an increase in corset manufacturers' profits for the following year. However, in what is perhaps a measure of their lingering anxiety, the trade journals continued to proclaim the end of corsetlessness throughout the decade. The "renaissance of the corset" and a decline in popularity of the corsetless figure was noted as late as 1930, while Lily of France president Joel Alexander assured buyers of the long-awaited return of "real corsets" in January 1935.[28] (Figure 5.6.)

A 1921 series of articles on specialized fitting procedures discussed the importance of corseting young girls because they were the "future mothers of our race." When this time arrived maternity corsets would protect not only her health, but also her child's. Utilizing the strategy of incorporation, the new 1920s emphasis on the science and art of corset fitting acknowledged past discomfort but laid the blame on the fit, not on the corset itself. The science of corset fitting, often taught at special sessions organized by corset companies, particularly identified a young girl's first experience in the corset shop as critically important in making her into a lifelong corset customer.[29]

The discursive linking of corsets with "science" dated back to the nineteenth century, with the use of medicinal arguments for corset promotion, and for combating the health claims of opponents to corset use. Nineteenth-century doctors such as brothers I. De Ver and Lucius C. Warner, founders of the Warner Brothers Company in Bridgeport, Connecticut, named their late-1870s designs the Sanitary Corset and the Health Corset to stress their healthful benefits. In the 1920s manufacturers' reliance on scientific arguments intensified as they expanded marketing strategies from the focus on corset design to include corset fitting.[30]

Corset fitting became a part of corset selling and marketing after the introduction of the straight-front corset, which needed "to be fitted in nearly every case." This resulted in the installation of corset fitting rooms within most corset departments. Modart Corset Company

Figure 5.6. The Royal Worcester Corset Company declares an end to the "corsetless period," but frames this change as a "retreat" for women. (*Corsets and Lingerie*, November 1922).

Supervisor of Instruction Bertha A. Strickler's 1925 publication, "The Principles of Scientific Corset Fitting," explained that recent changes in corsetry compelled a greater level of specialized training for corset fitters. The past practice of buying corsets over the counter was possible when corsets served the singular purpose of suppressing the waist. She claimed that fitting contemporary corsetry required more than waist measurement because "today corsets are scientifically designed and must be scientifically fitted." However, an earlier account provided an alternative viewpoint, explaining that "these advantages are not alto-gether new in the modern corset except in so far as they are now uni-versal whereas they were formerly restricted to the made-to-order corset or the ready-made one of exhorbitant price." The wide avail-ability of ready-to-wear corsets through their mass production and marketing changed the nature of their consumption considerably.[31]

Recasting corset fitting as a science in the 1920s relied on the wide-spread knowledge and faith in the practices of scientific management. The transformation of industrial work in the early twentieth century through implementation of the concepts of efficiency and rationaliza-tion as well as the turn to technology for problem-solving promoted deskilling of workers and thus loss of an important basis of their power in the workplace. Utilizing the ideologies of scientific management, corset manufacturers transformed the consumption experiences of saleswomen and their customers when they bought, sold, and wore corsets. While this strategy sought to keep women customers bound in corsets, it did, at least temporarily, give corset saleswomen a measure of new status and prestige. However, women's bodies were literally the vehicle for the successful shifting of scientific management ideologies from the workplace to the marketplace and the home.[32]

Many of the major corset manufacturers sponsored special courses in "scientific corsetry," "scientific reduction," or "scientific corset fitting." The courses took place most often in New York City, where many corset companies' showrooms and factories were located, though companies also sponsored courses in regional commercial centers such as Chicago, Dallas, or Atlanta. These courses offered a new way for companies to dis-tinguish their product from others on the market. In addition, the courses demonstrated a company's seriousness regarding women's med-ical health and their reliance on scientific methods to ensure it.[33]

Some corset school curricula especially stressed the importance of medical knowledge for corset fitting. The International School of Scientific Corsetry, sponsored by the International Corset Company, included the subjects of anatomy and medical fitting in its 1921 cur-riculum, which also covered modern merchandising, retail advertising, and "scientific salesmanship." Kleinart's School of Scientific Reduction employed Dr. Harriet Von Buren Peckham in 1925 to explain in a series of lectures "the proper way to reduce every part of the body, together with practical suggestions for fitting every type of figure." For the latter part of the course, Dr. Peckham was "assisted by expert fitters, compe-tent models and an experienced sales woman." Attendees would also have the opportunity to "fit the reducers on a live model."[34] (Figure 5.7.)

The Modart Company's course included a section on "The Anatomical Requirements of a Corset," which explained a medical con-dition called "ptosis." Modart claimed that most women suffered from

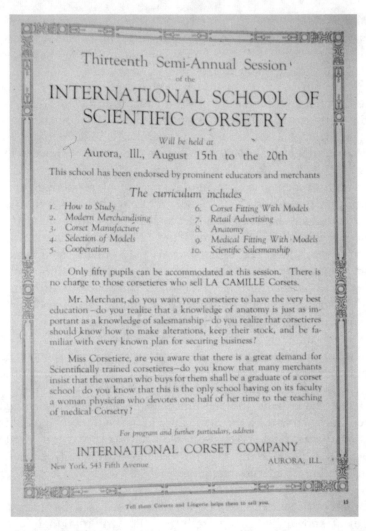

Figure 5.7. The International Corset Company directly addressed "Mr. Merchant" and "Miss Corsetiere" to engage them in a profitable discourse of "scientific corsetry." (*Corsets and Lingerie*, July 1921).

ptosis, "a loss in muscles of the power to contract." However, while improperly fitted corsets caused ptosis, properly fitted corsets were needed to arrest its development. Ptosis was particularly associated with the stress of "modern city life to which women are not yet adjusted. . . . Constipation, debility, headaches, backaches, sallow complexion, appendicitis, general weakness are some of the ailments associated with this condition."[35]

Department store retailers nationwide became persuaded of the value of sending their employees to corset fitting schools as evidence surfaced regarding the profit margins of corset departments. In 1917 *Women's Wear Daily* credited the presence of trained corsetieres in department stores with increasing the sales of higher priced and thus more profitable corsets. Trained corsetieres also inhibited the number of returns, and the need for alterations—the bane of retailers. Moreover, corset departments from the 1920s through the 1940s usually had the highest profit margins of all departments within a store.[36]

The Warner Brothers Company noted the profitability of corset departments in a 1921 trade journal advertisement, citing a National Retail Dry Goods Association report. Warner's then argued that merchants would see even better profits if they carried fewer corset lines. It's seven-point plan for improvements in retail profit-making also included the admonition to "educate your salesgirls that they can ably assist the customer in her selection. It is the worst possible mistake to sell a woman a corset that is not designed for her figure."[37]

Corset schools primarily served to educate retailers and saleswomen on the finer points of selling their particular brand. With the proliferation of types and styles of corsets by the early 1920s, many major companies produced several lines of corsets for some variation of "stout," "average," and "slender" figure types.[38] These figure types might be further complicated by additional styles for bodies heavier on the top or the bottom, for those long- or short-waisted, or by maternity and postsurgical styles. Companies also had different style lines based on price. As *Good Housekeeping* noted: "Nowadays a single corset company will have almost one hundred models, each one made up in a variety of sizes." Retail buyers and saleswomen thus needed to know quite a bit about how each company's products were organized in order to determine which corset would best fit each customer. Companies were dependent upon saleswomen's successful mastering of this information to sell their products. Warner Brothers, for example, sent out pamphlets in 1921 to corset departments throughout the United States to explain their figure type classifications and the corsets designed for each type, with the expectation that having an illustrated guide on hand would direct saleswomen to show and to sell Warner's corsets. *Corsets & Lingerie* also endorsed collaboration between manufacturers and retailers in a 1925 editorial, stating that: "the lines which were going best were the lines in which the manufacturer cooperated with the store in teaching the girls how to sell corsets."[39]

Corset companies' creation of figure types classification schemes also bolstered their claims to scientific validation of their products and to the need for professional fitters. Each company's classification scheme corresponded to the corsets that they produced to fit each type. Selling retail buyers on a figure classification scheme was thus a means of selling retailers on their line of corsets as well. Thus these different schemes did not usually concur on the "scientific" classifications of women's bodies. Gossard's early twentieth-century chart defined nine figure types, Warner's 1921 classification had eight, and Berlei's 1926 study of Australian women found five.[40]

Figure typing schemes allowed corset companies to standardize product lines and formed an organizing principle for merchandising. In 1929, the Bon Ton company explained that its chart of nine figure types, entitled "What Figure Type Are You?" forms: "the basis of our entire merchandising plan . . . and makes possible for the first time real scientific control of fit, balanced model stocks, smaller inventories, fast turnover and more sustained profits." Yet an unstated but critical element of this plan was persuading women to identify with the figure types presented. Once a woman identified herself in terms of "her" type, she would be more easily sold on the corset deemed appropriate, if not necessary, for her body.[41]

Commercial classification of figure types intensified both the notion of the "problem figure," and the identification of "figure faults." Previously, corsets constructed the hourglass figure of the late nineteenth century by remolding women's bodies into a general curved shape with a nipped-in waistline. Dress design and strap-on garments such as bustles provided additional shaping. Twentieth-century outerwear was less elaborate and constructed by fewer layers of clothing. Foundation garments assumed the entire burden of molding the body into the fashionable silhouette. The identification of figure faults thus came about as women's bodies became more publicly visible.

The greater public presence and freedom in body display and movement achieved by women in the 1920s were attenuated by this reformulated and internalized emphasis on female imperfection. Marketing corsets on their ability to solve "figure faults" meant that the identification of faults assumed greater importance as a persuasive means of guiding women into corsets that resolved their defects. Corset saleswomen, for example, were instructed to first identify a customer's figure type and then her particular figure problems. However, it was not necessarily considered good form to point out figure flaws to customers. One saleswoman's guide suggested that: "the salesgirls should be cautioned never to point out figure faults to a customer. If she had a roll at the waistline and a long girdle is selected to minimize this, the salesgirl should not say, 'That terrible roll will not look as bad with this corset.' Instead she should remark, 'What a lovely, smooth waistline this girdle gives you. Your silhouette looks so well in it.'" Another guide admonished: "Never tell the stout customer she is stout. Emphasize the fact that she has good proportions. . . . Remember you are selling the joy of possession as well as comfort and fit."[42]

Figure classification schemes and the identification of figure faults objectified and commodified women's bodies in new ways. Manufacturers and retailers colluded in subjecting women's bodies to the scrutiny and discipline of scientific rationalization. Corset saleswomen were on the front lines of enacting the regulation of women's bodies through corsetry, and implemented corset discourses to sell corsets. Ethel Allen, Supervisor of Instruction at the Kabo School of Corsetry, acknowledged this function, stating that: "with every sale by an expert corsetiere goes the all-important and invaluable message to her customer of the proper selection of a model and the proper method of adjustment. They get the many "dos and don'ts" of our profession, and the assurance that a properly fitted corset can be a thing of beauty, of comfort and of great self-respect."[43]

The relationship between corset saleswomen and customers both worked against and assisted the rationalization process. Exposing intimate figure problems to a corsetiere and granting her the probing access to the body required for measurement created a special relationship between customer and corsetiere. As Women's Wear Daily noted: "A corset fitter gets much closer to her customers than the average salesperson can. Customers talk much more freely to their corset fitters than they do the girl who sells gloves, and they are willing to confide, in a manner of speaking, to the fitter, because usually the corset fitter has her own clientele, who insist on coming to that particular fitter each time they purchase a new corset." Charlotte Drebing, a corset buyer for the Crosby Brothers Mercantile Company of Kansas, agreed: "Corset customers . . . are the most appreciative people in the world. Because a good foundation garment can do such a vital job for a woman, she is eternally grateful to anyone who helps her find one— and that's why any service you can give her is worth while."[44]

A corsetiere especially benefited from customers with identifiable figure faults, as women's desires for rectification promoted dependence upon the corset fitter's expertise. Ethel Allen, referring to the problematic full-proportioned figure type, knew "no other class of customers who are more appreciative and loyal," while the top-heavy figure type "is willing to pay almost any price for a garment which will give her comfort and at the same time give her the easy graceful figure she so much desires." The top-heavy figure "will not only give to the corsetiere her patronage but will become a loyal booster among all her friends and acquaintances." Another sales manual noted that "the larger woman knows she is difficult to fit, and is willing to pay more than the slender woman. Juniors and slender women can buy garments any place at any price, but the larger woman, when correctly fitted, is everlastingly grateful and becomes a loyal repeat customer." Large women customers also augmented job prospects for large women as corsetieres, as "Mrs. Larger Woman feels more comfortable when a larger woman fits her." This customer also provided a source of job satisfaction. "Larger women are important to your business because properly corseted she looks 'smart' and gives you the feeling of having accomplished something."[45]

The relationship between corsetiere and customer was not without tension. One guide for saleswomen noted that "the worst faux pas of all is to say: 'I wear this girdle myself for my own roll'. No woman wants to be identified in any way with the salesgirl.'"[46] However, Ethel Allen avoided the potential for a subservient relationship to customers inherent in the shopping encounter by positing an alternative metaphor:

> As corsetieres we must never lose sight of the fact that we stand in the relation of a hostess to our guest, the customer, while she is in our shop or department. Were we serving afternoon coffee and one of our guests refused coffee we would immediately say, "Let me make you a cup of tea." Even so with our business guests. If they are prejudiced against either front-laced or back-laced corsets, show them first what you consider correct. Call their attention to the corrective points of the garment for their particular needs. Then if you cannot convince them that your judgement is correct, without argument simply give them what they want and give with it a sweet smile and willing service.[47]

The professionalization of corset fitting through specialized training and the assumption of the title "corsetiere" also bolstered these saleswomen's status with both customers and department store managers. Corset schools thus served to enhance manufacturers' promotional needs, retailers' profit margins, and corset saleswomen's power as workers while also heightening the presence of "scientific" epistemologies and the processes of specialization in women's daily lives. Corset fitting manuals, usually written by experienced corsetieres employed as teachers in corset schools, consistently stressed the professional aspects of this work. Positioning the corsetiere as "physician to her customer's body," a role encouraged by instruction in anatomy and the work of fitting maternity and postoperative corsets, encouraged the construction of the corsetiere as professional. Jean Gordon, author of *The Good Corsetiere,* published by the Strouse, Adler Company, explained: "When one is ill, the patient wants the family doctor who comes to the beside with a friendly, gracious attitude. . . . When a customer enters the corset department with a sick figure, she too, wants kindness."[48]

Another strategy for professionalization characterized corset fitting as an art: "A new salesgirl must be taught to consider her job as one of beautifying women. Instead of working with cosmetics she works with garments. Instead of beautifying the face and head she must improve the entire body of her customer. It is in some cases a tall order. She may be called upon to achieve the impossible. But whatever she can accomplish helps to increase beauty and in this respect is a work of art." Ethel Allen noted that women seek "the services of a thoroughly competent and trained professional corsetiere, one who understands all the alluring intricacies of the human form divine."[49]

Figure types classification included the bodies of girls and younger women in the category of problem figures. However, their figures were actually more of a problem for manufacturers because the "young girl figure," described as slim and "undeveloped," did not conform to usual descriptions of figure types that required corseting. The 1920s corset panic heightened manufacturers' attention to the young-girl figure not only because younger women were most likely to achieve the corset-less look without a corset, but also because the fashionable 1920s sil-houette was based on the young-girl figure. By targeting the young-girl figure and convincing women that this figure required a corset, manu-facturers thereby convinced all women concerned with fashionability that corsets remained a necessity.[50]

The special corsets developed for the young-girl figure were part of the growing specialization for the youthful market (termed "junior" by the late 1920s) taking place in the garment industry generally to increase sales. Corset manufacturers were especially interested in exploiting the growing distinction between clothing for younger and older women because "the junior customer has no set habits or buying tendencies which must be overcome" and thus seemed "to be a new hope for the corset industry." Lucien T. Warner noted "the necessity of courting this trade, for upon the younger generation of women the future of the corset industry depends. . . ."[51]

Manufacturers still maintained concerns that younger women in the 1920s might never wear corsets if they did not undergo the initia-tion into corset wearing that women had in previous generations. They looked closely at the circumstances of a young girl's first corset fitting in order to find ways of luring young women to a corsetiere. Once at a corset fitting, a young woman, and perhaps her mother, could also be drawn into corset discourses that worked to convince her of a lifelong need of corsetry: "Even the young girls who have never before ven-tured into a corset department find a new delight in looking at the attractive garments, and convincing sales talk . . . soon brings them into the fitting rooms." Concerns regarding the initiation into corsetry persisted into the 1940s, when *Corsets & Brassiere* advised: "It may take urging to get her into her first girdle, but your efforts will be rewarded as she blossoms into a model customer. . . . It's up to you to win her confidence and build her into a life-long customer."[52]

Since the early twentieth century, the "college girl" had been identified as a customer with special needs based on age and lifestyle
rather than on figure type *per se*. The college-girl category also
included the white-collar worker, or "business girl," whose corset needs
presumably differed from older women who did not work outside the
home. A 1910 advertisement for H. & W. Sheathlyne Corset Waists,
aimed toward college girls, noted that: "by encouraging deep breathing,
it quickly develops the chest and bust." In 1915 Wanamaker's, a large
department store, created the first special corset fitting room for young
women who wore "misses" sizes. The *Women's and Infants Furnisher*
felt that this innovation was "one of the most striking that has come
out in some time," especially because of the "undeveloped possibilities" of "catering particularly to young girls."

> One of the principle reasons that very few retail stores have the business
> that should come to them in misses' corsets is the failure of stores to take
> into consideration the natural reticence of girls to enter into any discussion
> of the individual corset problems with matrons and dowagers about. By pro-
> viding a special demonstration and fitting room for misses, it is safe to say
> that any store so doing will reap the benefit of an immediate appreciation of
> this delicacy. And, since appreciation expresses itself in terms of dollars and
> cents, it can hardly be other than a profitable investment.[53]

Manufacturers did indeed develop this profitable concept, and by
1929 *Corsets & Brassieres* included a monthly "Junior Department" in
each issue. Juniors were girls between twelve and eighteen years of
age, and the column often dealt with the special care required for their
commercial rite of passage. "Each child is fitted as her individual need
requires and for this work there are special fitters trained to care for
the children. . . . The younger girls do not like being disrobed and fitted, but now that the new silhouette is so apparent even the 12–year-
olds are offering much less resistance."[54]

Miss Mildred Tucker, head of a corset department in Denver, discussed the importance of "tactfulness" in dealing with the "little girls
and even college girls [who] are not quite used to the return of youth
to corsets, which the new Princess line in dress styles has necessitated." She explained that: "tact . . . usually consists of compliments
and direct conversation to the child." Another column noted: "Buyers
who are wise will put their best foot forward to encourage and capture
this class of customers." By March 1930, Lucien T. Warner reported
that: "a large number of smaller sizes are being called for by the
younger girl."[55]

In July 1930, the Corset and Brassiere Manufacturers Association
laid plans for the first National Junior Corset Week to take place the following September.[56] This was a specialized version of the previously

held National Corset Week, a coordinated national advertising campaign by merchants, retailers, and trade journals to boost corset sales. The need for a such a cooperative effort was explained by *Corsets & Lingerie* in a 1924 editorial:

> Why A Week? . . . most people found out they could do a lot in a week if they all started to talk at once and talked long enough and loud enough. . . . If the corset industry wants to put corsets on every woman and keep them there; all they've got to do is talk a language that most American women understand—English. Talk to each age-group of women about their particular corset problems and if the industry is smart, and economical as well, they'll also get about 10,000 merchants to do a lot of talking for them. . . . "[57]

The editorial also encouraged manufacturers to imitate other branches of the garment industry in their use of "the principle" of style. Style played an especially important role in the younger market, as the editorial noted: "If corsets were as crazy as some of the shoes we see, the flapper would buy a pair of corsets with every new dress."[58]

The National Junior Corset Week's purpose was clear: "Insistent propaganda has really aroused an interest on the part of the young girl, and buyers realizing that they have succeeded in luring the girl into the department are tireless in these efforts to keep her interest." Lauding the junior department at Gimbels Department Store in New York City, *Corsets & Brassieres* reported that: "every possible kind of restraining garment that is manufactured for the young figure is found here . . . made to appeal to the eye of the discriminating youngster. . . . There are many girls, not only the debutantes and society girls but even working girls who are willing to pay for better class merchandise, just as these girls have always been fastidious in the matter of their lingerie." The month following the Junior Week, *Corsets & Brassieres* reported: "increased sales among the younger women in all the larger retail centers. Girls who never before wore a foundation garment came in to buy some type of fashion-forming garment and college girls stocked up generously for the season's needs." Three years later, the trade journal stated that "nearly all the stores now have special sections in their corset departments devoted to garments for the young figure."[59]

Making lighter and more flexible girdles in junior sizes was one means of keeping young women in foundation garments. These were available in increasing numbers as the means of producing elastic stretch fabrics improved. In the 1910s elastic insets in corsets provided an early form of augmenting flexibility. The number of elastic and rubber sections utilized in corsets increased into the 1920s. However, the primarily elastic girdles available in 1921 were still considered a novelty item. Several years later, when the youth appeal of elastic girdles was more apparent, manufacturers' and retailers' resistance to them ended. By 1924 elastic step-in girdles were sold in corset departments nationwide.[60]

As use of elastic girdles spread, novelty status transferred to rubber reducing corsets, an extremely popular phenomenon for several years. One of the most well-known brands sold nationally was the Madame X. These controversial all-rubber corsets were marketed on their ability not only to slim the wearer's appearance, but also to achieve actual weight loss. Manufacturers and retail buyers debated the staying power of rubber girdles on the market, but acknowledged that their presence raised the price of foundations generally. The ability to sell great quantities of the more expensive rubber corsets let manufacturers and retailers know that women were willing to pay more for corsets.[61]

The decline of the "boyish form" silhouette in the late 1920s and the return to the "womanly" figure in the 1930s meant a strong market for corsetry, even during the worst years of the Depression. The industry had responded on many fronts to the 1920s threat of the corsetless look. Profitability continued as the foundation market broadened to include young girls, juniors, and college coeds, as well as the numerous figure types of older women. Identifying a variety of types allowed manufacturers to produce and retailers to market corsets aimed at particular groups of women. This strategy of segmentation also produced and marketed new understandings of the female body, which personalized and intensified the presence of scientific discourse in women's intimate everyday life.

The new perceptions about the female body that the industry deployed also encouraged most women to accept identification in terms of flaws and faults and to thus construct their subjectivity in terms of self-negation. However, the industry was unable completely to dismiss women's desires for greater comfort and freedom of movement. While the corsetless fad did not free women from the obligation to be corseted, some women were able at least to wear the more flexible and lightweight stretch girdles. Yet the popularity of even the light pantie girdle worn extensively in the 1930s did not mitigate continuing widespread use of more binding foundations. "All-in-one" garments, for example, which first appeared in the 1920s, firmly shaped and controlled the entire torso from bust to hips.

The well-organized corset industry continued to benefit from their persistent interventions in fashion changes and the construction of women's desires for "ideal figures." They reaped the results when the waistline was once again accentuated in the 1930s, but at this point were too close to the corset panic years to rest on their laurels. Their ongoing machinations received even greater rewards after the end of

World War II, when fashionable corsetry returned with pinching vengeance and fetishized glory in new structured forms such as waist cinchers or "waspies" that supported the popular—and contested—New Look of 1947.[62]

Corsets' fading fashionability and their replacement by the new restrictive girdles in this period occurred within a process of contestation and negotiation among women who purchased and wore these garments, manufacturers and retailers who produced and sold them, and fashion experts such as department store saleswomen and fashion writers. As moral imperatives that controlled women's fashions declined, women sought and in some measure achieved greater freedom of choice and mobility in dress. However, fashion industrialists worked hard to maintain control over the shape of women's bodies and over women's fashion choices. Drawing on modernist ideologies, they countered claims about the damaging health effects of corset use by repositioning corsets within contemporary scientific discourses, and refuted young women's rejection of corsets as old-fashioned by designing lighter and more flexible foundation garments and marketing them as contemporary girdles. Making use of existing fashion institutions, including popular magazines, trade journals, and department stores, and creating new ones, such as corset-fitting schools, corset manufacturers and retailers actively interceded in influencing fashion change. Women's demands for more comfortable attire and their demonstrated willingness to defy conventional notions of feminine propriety prompted manufacturers' organized opposition to the "corsetless fad," and the subsequent development of policing strategies aimed at women of all ages. Their efforts sustained the importance of figure-shaping garments as essential elements in women's wardrobes. While wearing these garments would no longer be a measure of a woman's moral propriety, they could attest to her knowledge of modern techniques of constructing a fashionable body and the importance she gave to maintaining an up-to-date appearance. Women's "spontaneous consent" to wearing these garments was an ongoing and contested process that served fashion industry needs for continual purchase. Innovations in dress that supported women's desires for comfort would continue because industrialists sought not to end women's desires for fashion change, but to contain them.

Throughout the early twentieth century and in succeeding decades, the high profit margins of departments selling corsets, girdles, and other foundation garments in stores nationwide provide one measure of the success of marketing strategies mounted by manufacturers and retailers. American women's continuing preoccupation with conforming to particular notions of beauty in regard to body size and shape serves as another. The late twentieth-century interest in diet drugs and programs, willingness to undergo liposuction surgery to reduce and reshape the female abdomen and hips, and the strong sales of "body shapers," the current term for flexible foundation garments, all demonstrate that women's struggles getting in and out of corsets have not entirely ended, for the meaning of these various methods of reshaping female bodies is not restricted to their immediate physical effect. As Michel Foucault notes, "the endlessly repeated play of dominations . . . is fixed, throughout its history, in rituals, in meticulous procedures that impose rights and obligations. It establishes marks of its power and engraves memories on things and even within bodies."[63] Imbuing 1920s corsetry with essentialist notions about flawed female bodies, racial hierarchies, nationalist imperatives, dubious sexual identities, and suspect political standpoints inscribed dominant ideologies upon women's bodies. Persuasive because of their power in other spheres, these particular mediations of women's relationship with their own bodies long outlasted the corsets and girdles worn in the early decades of the twentieth century.

ACKNOWLEDGMENTS

I wish to thank scholars Lois Banner, Adrienne Hood, Ruth Linden, Tania Modleski, Steve Ross, Peter Stearns, and the anonymous reader of the *Journal of Social History* for their thoughtful comments and helpful suggestions on earlier versions of this essay. I also would like to acknowledge the support I received for my research on this topic from the Veronika Gervers Research Fellowship in Textile and Costume History at the Royal Ontario Museum, and the Stella Blum Research Grant awarded by the Costume Society of America.

NOTES

1. G. B. Pulfer, "Fighting the Corsetless Evil," *Corsets & Lingerie* (November 1921): 30.
2. Examples of trade journal articles sparked by panic regarding corsetlessness include "The Evils of the No-Corset Fad," *Corsets & Lingerie* (November 1921): 24–25; "Flappers Are Responsible for the Corsetless Craze," *Corsets & Lingerie* (November 1922): 33; "Eminent Surgeons Endorse the Corset," *Corsets & Lingerie* (December 1921): 32–35.
3. Helene E. Roberts, "The Exquisite Slave: The Role of Clothes in the Making of the Victorian Woman," *Signs: Journal of Women in Culture and Society* (Spring 1977): 564–569; David Kunzle, "Dress Reform as Antifeminism: A Response to Helene E. Roberts's 'The Exquisite Slave: The Role of Clothes in the Making of the Victorian Woman,'" *Signs* (Spring 1977): 570–579; Helene Roberts, "Reply to David Kunzle's 'Dress Reform as Antifeminism: A Response to Helene E. Roberts's' 'The Exquisite Slave,'" *Signs* (Winter 1977): 518–519; Joanna Russ, "Comment on Helene Roberts 'The Exquisite Slave: The Role of Clothes in the Making of the Victorian Woman,' and David Kunzle's 'Dress Reform as Antifeminism,'" *Signs* (Winter 1977), 520–521; David Kunzle, *Fashion and Fetishism: A Social History of the Corset, Tight-Lacing and Other Forms of Body-Sculpture in the West* (New Jersey: Rowman and Littlefield, 1982); Lois Banner, *American Beauty* (Chicago: University of Chicago Press, 1983); Valerie Steele, *Fashion and Eroticism: Ideals of Feminine Beauty from the Victorian Era to the Jazz Age* (New York: Oxford University Press, 1985).
4. The concept of cultural hegemony is integral to analysis of culture as contested terrain. As the meaning of hegemony is also contested, see Antonio Gramsci, *Selections from the Prison Notebooks*, trans. Quintin Hoare and Geoffrey Nowell Smith (New York:

International Publishers, 1971), esp. 12; and Raymond Williams, *Marxism and Literature* (Oxford: Oxford University Press, 1977), 110 for interpretations that inform the analysis presented here. See also more recent debates among cultural historians, such as T. Jackson Lears, "The Concept of Cultural Hegemony: Problems and Possibilities," *The American Historical Review* (June 1985): 567–593; and George Lipsitz, "The Struggle for Hegemony," *The Journal of American History* (June 1988): 146–150. In regard to culture and clothing, costume historians generally and feminist critics particularly have long understood the power of fashion to regulate and signify. However, the sensibility expressed here regarding fashion as a regulatory practice draws upon Michel Foucault, *The History of Sexuality, Volume 1: An Introduction*, trans. Robert Hurley (New York: Vintage Books 1978), and also upon Judith Butler's analysis of Foucault in *Gender Trouble: Feminism and the Subversion of Identity* (New York: Routledge, 1990). This article is in some sense a response to Butler's call for a "critical inquiry that traces the regulatory practices within which bodily contours are constructed [that] constitutes precisely the genealogy of "the body" in its discreteness that might further radicalize Foucault's theory," p. 133. For semiotic analysis of fashion as a system of signification, see Roland Barthes, *The Fashion System*, trans. Matthew Ward and Richard Howard (New York: Hill and Wang, 1983). For an excellent discussion of many of the major twentieth-century works of fashion history and theory, see Fred Davis, *Fashion, Culture and Identity* (Chicago: The University of Chicago Press, 1992).

5. Elizabeth Ewing, *Dress and Undress: A History of Women's Underwear* (New York: Drama Book Specialists, 1978), 110–113.

6. Havelock Ellis, "An Anatomical Vindication of the Straight Front Corset," *Current Literature* (February 1910): 172–174.

7. "How Prehistoric Woman Solved the Problem of Her Waist Line," *Current Opinion* (March 1914): 201–202.

8. Paul Poiret, *My First 50 Years* (London: V. Gollancz, 1931), 72–73.

9. Ewing, *Dress and Undress*, 89–91, 93, 108–110; C. Willett and Phillis Cunnington, *The History of Underclothes* (London: Faber and Faber, 1981, 1951), 87,114, 125–126; Norah Waugh, *Corsets and Crinolines* (London: B.T. Batsford, Ltd, 1954), 87. See Peter Wollen, "Out of the Past: Fashion/Orientalism/The Body," in his *Raiding the Icebox: Reflections on Twentieth-Century Culture* (Bloomington, IN: Indiana University Press, 1993), 1–34, regarding the influence of both the Russian Ballet and the rational dress movement upon Poiret's designs. Fashion layouts and advertisements, such as "New Low Bust Flexible Model" and "New Supple Figure Corsets," *Women's and Infants' Furnisher* (January 1914): 42–43, and "The Athletic Girl's Experience," Bon Ton Corset advertisement, *Vogue* (May 1914): 93, displayed the more flexible and sports corsets.

10. Ewing, *Dress and Undress*, 120; Mitchel Gray and Mary Kennedy, *The Lingerie Book* (New York: St. Martin's Press, 1980) 15; "A Graceful Dancing Corset," *Women's and Infants' Furnisher* (February 1914): 31. Banner, *American Beauty*, 176, offers evidence regarding the emergence of the flapper in the mid-1910s; "Where Efficiency and Economy Meet," *Vogue* (April 1914): 54–55; "Corseting the Corsetless Figure," *Vogue* (January 1914): 58.

11. "Woman Decides to Support Herself," *Vogue* (August 1917): 67, 80.

12. See Eleanor Flexner, *Century of Struggle: The Woman's Rights Movement in the United States* (Cambridge: Harvard University Press, 1959, 1975); and Linda Gordon, *Woman's Body, Woman's Right: A Social History of Birth Control in America* (New York: Penguin, 1977), regarding the suffrage and birth control movements respectively. The *New York Times* reported extensively on the fashion debates. For example, see August 30, 1922, p. 17, regarding the skirt length controversy; see January 17, 1919, p. 5; February 16, 1921, p. 15; February 17, 1921, p. 6; May 22, 1919, p. 9; May 23, 1921, p. 15; June 15, 1921, p. 7, and June 21, 1921, p. 19, regarding modesty and morality; and February 26, 1922, p. 12, regarding college dress codes.

13. Howard Zinn, *A People's History of the United States* (New York: Harper Collins, 1980), 366–372.

14. My grandmother, Mildred Rosenstein Schwartz (born 1902), has on many occasions provided me with historical data drawn from her life experience; "The Renaissance of the C-rs-t", *The Independent* (July 25, 1925): 88.

15. *Corsets & Lingerie* first identified corsetlessness as dangerous in "Buyers Against Corsetless Fad: New York Department Store Buyers All Against Fad and Say It Is on the Wane," *Corsets & Lingerie* (September 1921): 27, 29. The first assertion that it was also evil can be found in "The Evils of the No-Corset Fad," *Corsets & Lingerie* (November 1921): 24–25. *Corsets & Lingerie* (January 1924): 31, and *Women's Wear Daily* (September 24, 1924): 28, identify the fad's beginning date. Nicole Thornton, *Poiret* (New York: Rizzoli International Publications, 1979), 1; Paul Poiret, *My First Fifty Years* (London: Victor

Gollancz Ltd., 1931), 72–73; Julian Robinson, *Body Packaging: A Guide to Human Sexual Display* (Los Angeles: Elysium Growth Press, 1988), 78; "Corseting the Corsetless Figure," *Vogue* (January 1, 1914): 58; "Tango Popularizes Corsetless Figure," *Women's and Infants' Furnisher* (January, 1914): 68; Anderman Form Company advertisement, *Women's and Infants' Furnisher* (February, 1915): 20. *The Women's and Infants' Furnisher* first published in 1895, changed its name to *Corsets & Lingerie* in July, 1921, and then again to *Corsets & Brassieres* in March, 1926. Its publication continues today under the name *Intimate Fashion News*.

16. G. B. Pulfer, "Fighting the Corsetless Evil," *Corsets & Lingerie* (November 1921): 30.
17. "The Evils of the No-Corset Fad," *Corsets & Lingerie* (November 1921): 24–25; "Flappers Are Responsible for the Corsetless Craze," *Corsets & Lingerie* (November 1922): 33; "Eminent Surgeons Endorse the Corset," *Corsets & Lingerie* (December 1921): 32–35.
18. "Woman's Friend, the Corset, *Literary Digest* (November 5, 1921): 20.
19. "The Depression of 1920–1922 in the Women's Clothing Industry," Research Department, International Ladies Garment Workers Union (ILGWU). Report included with letter from Mitchell to Dubinsky, May 11, 1945. ILGWU Collection, Labor-Management Documentation Center, Cornell University, David Dubinsky Box 160, Folder 2B. "Table 1—Corsets and Allied Garments—Summary for the United States: 1899–1929," 1930 Census of Manufacturers, M1930.2, p. 385; *Profits of Underwear Manufacturers, 1918–1942: A Survey Made for Underwear Institute*, Research & Statistical Division (New York: Dun & Bradstreet, Inc., 1943); Joseph Swanson and Samuel Williamson, "Estimates of National Product and Income for the United States Economy, 1919–1941," *Explorations in Economic History* (Fall 1972): 53–74. I am grateful to Kathleen Barrett for providing the latter citation and sharing her expertise in business history with me.
20. 1930 Census of Manufacturers, p. 385; "The Corset," *Fortune* (March 1938): 95–99ff.
21. "Corsets Still in Vogue," *Corsets & Lingerie* (July 1921): 37, 52; "New Novelties for Fall," *Corsets & Lingerie* (August 1921): 32. "Elastic Girdles and Novelties," first appeared as a "new department" in *Corsets & Lingerie* (June 1922): 43. *Corsets & Lingerie* (October 1922): 4. A discussion of the girdle as merely a new name for the corset appears in *Corsets & Lingerie* (April 1924): 32. *Corset and Underwear Review* (December 1924): 89, blames the older corset for figure problems.
22. "Parisian Women Wear Corsets," *Corsets & Lingerie* (August 1921): 31; "Paris on the Corset Question," *Corsets & Lingerie* (December, 1921): 25–26.
23. Gertrude L. Nickerson, "The American Woman and Her Corset," *Corset and Underwear Review* (November 1924): 83–84.
24. "The Evils of the No-Corset Fad," *Corsets & Lingerie* (November 1921): 24–25.
25. "Eminent Surgeons Endorse the Corset," *Corsets & Lingerie* (December 1921): 32–35.
26. *Ibid.*
27. *Ibid.* See Steven J. Ross, "Struggles For the Screen: Workers, Radicals and the Political Uses of Silent Film," *American Historical Review* 96 (April 1991): 333–368, for more on the mocking of radical women as failed men in a variety of popular media.
28. Royal Worcester Corset Company advertisement, *Corsets & Lingerie* (November 1922): 7; 1930 Manufacturers Census, p. 385; Helen Walser, "The Renaissance of the Corset," *Corsets & Brassieres* (February 1930): 55; "Corset Show Big Help," *Corsets & Brassieres* (December 1930): 33; "Joel Alexander Looks at 1935," *Corsets & Brassieres* (January 1935): 45.
29. Ethel Allen, "Corset Fitting the Young Girl Figure," *Women's and Infants' Furnisher* (April 1921): 28; Ethel Allen, "Corset Fitting the Top-Heavy Figure," *Women's and Infants' Furnisher* (May 1921): 28; Ethel Allen, "Corset Fitting the Curved Back Figure," *Women's and Infants' Furnisher* (June 1921): 32; Ethel Allen, "Corset Fitting the Full Proportioned Figure," *Corsets & Lingerie* (July 1921): 34; Ethel Allen, "Corset Fitting the Thigh Figure," *Corsets & Lingerie* (August 1921): 30; Ethel Allen, "Corset Fitting the Maternity Figure," *Corsets & Lingerie* (September 1921): 34. In 1921, Ethel Allen was the Supervisor of Instruction at the Kabo School of Corsetry.
30. *Corsets & Lingerie* (January 1921): 64.
31. *Women's & Infants' Furnisher* (January 1921): 44; "Corsets of Distinct Types," *Women's and Infants' Furnisher* (September 1906): 35.
32. For other sources on the movement of scientific rationalization into the domestic sphere, see Dolores Hayden, *The Grand Domestic Revolution: A History of Feminist Designs for American Homes, Neighborhoods, and Cities* (Cambridge, MA: MIT Press, 1981); and Ruth Schwartz Cowan, *More Work for Mother: The Ironies of Household Technology from the Open Hearth to the Microwave* (London: Free Association Books, 1989).
33. *Corsets & Lingerie* (July 1921): 15; (January 1925): 23; *The Principles of Scientific Corset Fitting* (New York: Modart, 1925); *Women's and Infants' Furnisher* (March 1921): 49; *Corsets & Brassieres* (July 1928): 41.

34. *Corsets & Lingerie* (January 1925): 23.

35. *The Principles of Scientific Corset Fitting*, 12; "Woman's Friend, The Corset," *Literary Digest* (November 5, 1921): 20; Modart's employment of ptosis to sell corsets was similar to other discoveries of medicalized conditions for advertising purposes in the 1920s, such as Listerine's promotion of halitosis. See Stephen Fox, *The Mirror Makers: A History of American Advertising and Its Creators* (New York: William Morrow, 1984), 97–98, and Roland Marchand, *Advertising the American Dream: Making Way for Modernity, 1920 to 1940* (Berkeley, CA: University of California Press, 1985), 18–20, 218–219.

36. "The Corset Stock Is One of the Safest of All the Stocks in the Dry Goods Store," *Women's and Infants' Furnisher*, 1896, quoted in their twenty-fifth anniversary issue (January 1921): 61; "Corset Departments Lead in Store Profits!" Warner Brothers ad, *Corsets & Brassieres* (January 1933): 3; *Corsets & Brassieres* (February 1938): 25; *Corset Preview: The Bulletin of the National Retail Dry Goods Association* (July 1941): 13; *Corset & Underwear Review Sales Training Manual Issue* (August 1942): 122; "Corset Selling Is An Art," *Corsets & Brassieres* (February 1946): 34.

37. *Women's and Infants' Furnisher* (April 1921): 2. Gossard also encouraged the reduction in the number of lines each department carried. Its 1921 analysis of the current economic depression suggested that the problem of "stock liquidation" could be resolved by carrying complete lines by fewer companies. The point of view expressed by Warner's and Gossard obviously favored larger companies that widely advertised their products. *Women's and Infant's Furnisher* (January 1921): 3.

38. These are the category names used by Modart Corset Company in *The Principles of Scientific Corset Fitting*.

39. "How to Choose the Right Corset," *Good Housekeeping* (September 1921): 52–53; "Modern Styles Do Not Cater to One Type of Silhouette But to Several," *Corsets & Brassieres* (May 1933): 26–27; *Corsets & Lingerie* (January 1921): 43; "A Matter of Opinion," *Corsets & Lingerie* (February 1925): 35.

40. Ewing, *Dress and Undress*, 136; *Corsets & Lingerie* (July 1921): 43; Ewing, 137.

41. "A Significant New Development in Modern Merchandising," Bon Ton Corsets advertisement, *Corsets & Brassieres* (February 1929): 14.

42. "Curriculum For the Corset Salesgirl," *Corsets & Brassieres* (July 1941): 34–35; *Corset & Underwear Review*, Sales Training Manual (August 1942): 26–27.

43. Ethel Allen, "Corseting the Curved Back Figure," *Women's and Infant's Furnisher* (June 1921): 32.

44. *Women's Wear Daily* (May 19, 1917): 15; (November 14, 1940): 31.

45. Ethel Allen, "Corset-Fitting the Full Proportioned Figure," *Women's and Infant's Furnisher* (July 1921): 30; Ethel Allen, "Corset-Fitting the Top-Heavy Figure," *Women's and Infant's Furnisher* (May 1921): 28; *Corset & Underwear Review*, Sales Training Manual (August 1942); *ibid.*

46. "Curriculum For the Corset Salesgirl," *Corsets & Brassieres* (July 1941): 34–35. For a fuller discussion on the tensions between department store saleswomen, customers, and managers, see Susan Porter Benson, *Counter Cultures: Saleswomen, Managers and Customers in American Department Stores, 1890–1940* (Chicago: University of Illinois Press, 1986).

47. Ethel Allen, "Corseting the Curved Back Figure," *Women's and Infants' Furnisher* (June 1921): 32.

48. *Women's & Infants' Furnisher* (April 1918): 38; Gordon, *Woman's Body*, 9.

49. "Training the New Salesgirl," *Corsets & Brassieres* (September 1946): 48–49; Allen, *Women's and Infants' Furnisher* (June 1921): 32. Regarding corset selling as an art see *Women's & Infants' Furnisher* (May 1925): 27; and "Corset Selling Is an Art," *Corsets & Brassieres* (February 1946): 34.

50. Ethel Allen, "Corset Fitting the Young Girl Figure, *Women's and Infants' Furnisher* (April 1921): 28; *Corsets & Brassieres* (January 1933): 35.

51. "New Interest in Junior Garments," *Corsets & Brassieres* (January 1929): 28; "Warner Opening Well Attended," *Corsets & Brassieres* (March 1930): 41.

52. The retailer B. Altman & Company, for example, focused on this commercial rite of passage in its advertisements that announced "that a young girls' first corset is an important event." *Women's Wear Daily* (April 2, 1931); *Women's Wear Daily* (April 30, 1931): sec. 2, 4; *Corsets & Brassieres* (August, 1946): 16.

53. *Women's and Infants' Furnisher* (February 1915): 49.

54. "The Junior Department," *Corsets & Brassieres* (April 1930): 34–35.

55. "The Junior Corset Department," *Corsets & Brassieres* (January 1930): 41; "A Prosperous Outlook—Corset Buyers and Manufacturers Are All Very Optimistic," *Corsets & Brassieres* (February 1930): 25; *Corsets & Brassieres* (March 1930): 41.

56. *Corsets & Brassieres* (July 1930): 43; (October 1930): 27.

57. *Corsets & Lingerie* (January 1924): 31–32.
58. This point is also made in *Corsets & Brassieres* (January 1933): 35.
59. "Junior Week Arouses Interest," *Corsets & Brassieres* (July 1930): 43; "Junior Corset Week a Success," *Corsets & Brassieres* (October 1930): 27; *Corsets & Brassieres* (January 1933): 35.
60. *Corsets & Lingerie* (September 1921), n.p.; (October 1922): 34; (July 1921): 37; (June 1922): 43; *Women's and Infants' Furnisher* (January 1914): 39; *Corsets & Lingerie* (April 1924): 29; *Women's Wear Daily* (September 3, 1924): 32.
61. *Corsets & Lingerie* (June 1924): 49; *Women's Wear Daily* (September 3, 1924): 32; (September 24, 1924): 28; *Corsets & Lingerie* (February 1925): 9; "What Others Say About Rubber Goods," *Corsets & Lingerie* (February 1925): 40–41; "Do Corsets Further Femininity?" *Corsets & Lingerie* (April 1925): 29.
62. For more on the New Look from 1947 to 1952, see "Return of the Repressed (Waist)," chapter 7 of Jill Fields, *The Production of Glamour: A Social History of Intimate Apparel, 1909–1952* (Berkeley, CA: University of California Press, forthcoming).
63. Michel Foucault, *Language, Counter-Memory, Practice: Selected Essays and Interviews*, ed. Donald F. Bouchard (Ithaca, NY: Cornell University Press, 1977), 150.

Part 2

BUSINESS AND WORK

A Depression-Proof Business Strategy

THE CALIFORNIA PERFUME COMPANY'S MOTIVATIONAL LITERATURE

KATINA L. MANKO

E arly in the Great Depression, in 1930, more than 25,000 women throughout the nation looked to Avon products to supplement their income. Selling door-to-door, they generated more than $2,500,000 in annual sales. Three years later, following a concerted effort by the company to increase the size of the sales force, the representative corps had increased by 20 percent to 30,000, and sales climbed with it. As one California Perfume Company report stated in 1931, "when most firms were glad to make two thirds of the profits they enjoyed the year before, our sales were *greater* than the previous year."[1] The trend continued and Avon remained remarkably profitable throughout the Depression, posting sales increases of 10 to 15 percent every single year between 1930 and 1938. "Seemingly depressions have little ill effect on [our] business, for which we are indeed thankful. People can hardly believe us when we say we are doing more business this year than last, and that last year was a good year," David H. McConnell, Avon's president, wrote in 1933. When the stock market crashed in 1929, he calmly explained, the California Perfume Company (CPC), as Avon was known then, was more than forty years old and had already survived three depressions. CPC's unique distribution methods, its handpicked traveling and sales force, the high quality of the line of products, and the "general morale of the whole CPC family—these reasons explain why we go ahead when other concerns cease to grow or fail completely."[2]

This essay explores the California Perfume Company's business strategy during the Depression and argues that the company's unique market niche in rural America, its devotion to selling a business opportunity to women, and its strong commitment to maintaining its door-to-door sales and service strategy not only helped CPC survive the Depression, but made its prosperity possible. The first half of this essay focuses on CPC's business structure and key strategies that the company employed to meet the economic crisis, including recruiting methods, sales management, product and market development, plus advertising, which for all intents and purposes had not existed before 1936. Ironically, some of the company's most important strategies, including the introduction of the Avon brand cosmetics and skin-care line in 1929, the targeting of urban markets in 1935, and the development of a national advertising campaign in 1936, had been conceived and developed much earlier in the company's history. The Depression, therefore, did not stimulate institutional innovation but instead actually reinforced CPC's traditional approach to managing its workforce.

The second half of this study explores the role of motivational literature, which CPC used to teach its scattered female workforce to manage their direct-selling businesses. Motivational literature was an essential component of the California Perfume Company's strategy. Using an evangelical style, company literature assured women that a career in direct selling would provide the power to create and control their own wealth. Company leaders promised to democratize business and to support equality, opportunity, and fairness, while defending the role of an ethical business in an economically depressed society. CPC's motivational literature appealed to durable American values supporting ideals of work and ownership, and built a relationship with its representatives that reflected a peculiar combination of paternalism, compassion, self-help, and economic self-interest—a mind-set that characterized CPC's and, indeed, the entire direct-selling industry's management style throughout the Depression.

Several myths inform common explanations for why Avon survived the 1930s, but none holds up to close scrutiny. At first glance, the direct-sales formula alone might explain Avon's success. Indeed, the entire direct-selling industry, which overall employed more than a quarter million men and women nationwide each year during the 1930s, seemed surprisingly "Depression proof." Even CPC thought of itself as such: "We are convinced that the right company, with the right products, with the right selling representatives, can develop a depression-proof business," wrote W. J. Alley, CPC's secretary and treasurer, in 1933.[3] Direct sales had that reputation. Like CPC, Fuller Brush (founded in 1911) posted sales increases throughout the 1930s. Starting with a $5 million total for 1930, Fuller increased sales by a million dollars each year until 1938.[4] Sears split off *Encyclopaedia Britannica* in 1933, turning it into a direct-selling company offering just one product.[5] Stanley Home Products, founded in 1929 by former stereopticon salesman and Fuller Brush Company executive Frank Stanley Beveridge, also became a very successful direct-selling company during the Depression.[6] Yet many direct-selling companies went out of business during the Depression. According to one report presented to the National Association of Direct Selling Companies, more than one third of the more than 6,000 companies in business before the Depression folded, and for many of the same reasons as other businesses: improper management, insufficient finances, and manufacturing products that had lost their markets.[7]

Still, many traditional retailers and manufacturers fell into the trap of thinking that direct sales could be a way out of the crisis. The simplicity of direct sales appealed to them. On the surface it appeared to involve merely distributing samples, catalogs, and order books, and offering a straight 30 percent or 40 percent commission; representatives who did not sell product did not get paid and therefore cost the company very little in terms of salaries, office space, and labor costs. Similarly, recruiting seemed just a matter of finding people who had lost their jobs or who needed a source of quick cash, for direct selling did not require special skills or previous sales experience. Yet they were wrong, and direct-sales distribution did not neatly translate into a lifeline for traditional business.

Managing a direct-sales company defied the logic of traditional firms, and few had CPC's experience to draw on. Traditional producers and retailers, operating under a mistaken impression that direct-sales provided a low-overhead, low-maintenance distribution option, found that maintaining a direct-sales force required unusually high expenses, especially in shipping and recruiting. Moreover, it only worked for certain types of products. Companies had to create items small enough that individual representatives could deliver them, such as cosmetics and vacuums, for example, rather than refrigerators or difficult-to-install products. Direct sales also required higher distribution costs, for companies shipped to representatives only the products they ordered, no matter how small the request, unlike retail marketers, who received products in bulk. Furthermore, individual agents earned higher commissions (generally 30 to 40 percent of the product's retail price) than the wholesale-retail margins available to retail stores. Crucially, most representatives received their products on credit—generally, representatives took orders from customers, received the products from the company, collected payments on delivery, and then paid the wholesale invoice. Not surprisingly, companies that extended credit to thousands of representatives lost money, as representatives could not reliably collect from customers during the Depression. Other companies invested in maintaining credit and collection departments, which also added to costs.[8] Record-keeping for thousands of representatives, rather than a few hundred marketers, plus funding new equipment, samples, and warehousing, all became new overhead expenses borne by the manufacturer.

Traditional firms found that recruiting expenses drained away profits. Unlike CPC, which employed a traveling force to recruit women on a face-to-face basis, some companies cut corners by recruiting through newspaper advertisements or direct-mail inquiries. Under this system, prospective contractors received information and samples through the mail and never met a company official. Such companies found it difficult, if not impossible, to check for suitability or references. Several experienced direct-sales firms also tried this method, but most found that after the Depression it made more sense to maintain branch offices with salaried managers who recruited, trained, and managed sales on the local level. Local branch managers alleviated credit issues by providing training and encouragement to representatives and teaching them how to collect payments from customers, thus benefiting both the representative and the company.[9]

Direct selling, therefore, was not necessarily a viable solution for dealing with the Depression. Management and recruiting techniques, necessary for maintaining a direct-sales representative staff, could not easily be incorporated into an inexperienced firm's existing structure, and even direct-selling companies found it difficult to survive. A second explanation, that the popularity of inexpensive color cosmetics drove Avon's success, is also unsatisfactory.

AVON COSMETICS

CPC's success went hand in hand with increased sales of beauty products market-wide during the Depression. During the first third of the twentieth century, the beauty industry as a whole experienced stunning increases in both the types of products manufactured and in overall sales, and it is therefore also tempting to explain Avon's success during the Depression by pointing to the growing trend in color cosmetics during that era.[10] On closer examination, however, that argument proves simplistic. The company's strongest base came from its toiletries and skin-care lines, not from sales of color cosmetics. Before the 1940s Avon lagged behind beauty industry leaders; women did not look to Avon for variety or for indulging in the latest trend product. Indeed, the company sold more basic toiletries, such as toothpaste, shampoo, and soap, than it did cosmetics. In the 1920s, the California Perfume Company had carried an extensive line of toiletries and skin-care products, but only a very limited line of color cosmetics, including tinted face powders and rouges. CPC introduced its first lipstick in 1917 as part of the Daphne fragrance line, and sold it in shades Light and Dark, but despite the growing popularity of these products, CPC did not expand its color cosmetics line, or even its lipstick line, the most popular of all color categories, until after World War II.[11]

CPC's product designers did watch beauty industry trends closely, however. The foundation of the beauty trade, skin-care products—soaps, astringents, moisturizers, massage creams, bleaching creams, and night masks—became popular among American urban and rural women alike early in the century. In the 1920s, many companies had organized skin-care products into "systems," which celebrities and "scientific" and beauty experts endorsed.[12] In 1928, CPC followed suit, and launched its own celebrity-endorsed skin-care system under the name of Gertrude Recordon.[13] Unfortunately, it failed after just one year.

In 1929, a second family line of cosmetics heralded better results: Avon.[14] The first "Avon" brand color cosmetics product, a face powder and lipstick compact in a blue-and-silver package design, appeared in catalogs just in time for Christmas.[15] By 1934, CPC had repositioned most of its line of cleansers, toners, massage creams, and moisturizers under the new Avon brand family line. The California Perfume Company seemed poised to succeed, if only because it had developed the right product at the right time. In this context, its profitability during the 1930s is not surprising, for while not entirely Depression-proof products, both color cosmetics and skin-care categories remained strong sellers industrywide throughout the 1930s. "Women who went without new clothes," Kathy Peiss noted, "could still afford to indulge in a new lipstick," and Avon's, available in an expanded color line, which now included Light, Medium, Dark, and Vivid (also known as orange) with coordinating rouges, sold for fifty-two cents.[16]

Still, cosmetics was a volatile trade, and many companies experienced only short bursts of success. Several firms, such as Tangee and Armand, did not survive the 1930s. As Peiss noted, only three cosmetics companies, Max Factor, Maybelline, and Revlon (founded in 1908, 1914, and 1932 respectively) prospered through and after the Depression.[17] Furthermore, Avon came late to an established color cosmetics market in the 1930s. Its color line appeared remarkably limited in comparison to other companies', carrying fewer categories of products—lipstick, rouge, tinted face powders, cake mascara, and nail enamel—and a conservative color palette. Instead of cosmetics, CPC's most successful sales products consisted of skin care and toiletries, such as soaps, toothpaste, shampoo, and shaving creams, and home-use items such as baking products, flavoring extracts, and household cleaners. Therefore not just its lipsticks, skin-care goods, and perfumes but also its extensive line of toiletries and household products carried CPC sales throughout the Depression.

This diversification is even more important given that CPC developed its market niche in rural America. Before and during the Depression, Avon representatives sold cosmetics and toiletries to a population underserved by modern retail establishments. In 1929, more than 80 percent of the Avon sales force lived in towns with populations fewer than 2,500, more than two thirds of which lay west of the Mississippi River. While women in these small communities may have had access to general stores and catalog merchants, they lived well beyond the reach of the department stores and retail chains popular in Northeastern cities. Part of McConnell's sales strategy was the claim that his creams and lotions were fresher than those available at country stores, whose inventory frequently turned rancid or became worn and hence unsuitable to give as gifts. By the 1920s, however, despite the increasing availability of cosmetics through drugstores and mail-order catalogs, as Peiss has argued, rural women remained much more reluctant than their city sisters to purchase and use color cosmetics.[18] Farm women's use of cosmetics increased throughout the 1930s, but until then, products more controversial than lipstick or rouge held little appeal.[19] Rural women did welcome, however, the toiletries and household staples that CPC representatives sold. Overall, McConnell's firm embodied two basic concepts: distributing products from company representatives directly to consumers in their homes and providing women independent earning opportunities.

Rural American towns' most important resource, for McConnell, was their vast pool of women, particularly married women, whom he deemed ideally suited to become the backbone of his sales force. McConnell had purposely targeted rural women both as purveyors and as consumers of his company's products. "When Mr. McConnell started out selling from door to door," a CPC editor wrote in 1933, "he noticed that women thrown upon their own resources had only three means of livelihood if they were not trained as nurses or teachers . . . running boarding houses, sewing, or clerking from 12 to 18 hours a day. They [sic] did not provide a decent living. It occurred to him that women could do what he was doing. The CPC is the result."[20] As CPC approached its fiftieth anniversary, McConnell enjoyed telling his company's history, and one thing is certain: that between the time he first wrote its history in 1905, and 1937, the year he retired from CPC leadership, McConnell transformed his vision of the company's early years and embellished his dedication to helping women earn an income.

Although no master file of representatives survives, according to published sources, internal newsletters, and correspondence, men historically represented less than five percent of the CPC sales force. By contrast, males constituted over 90 percent of direct-sales agents nationally.[21] As a result of the efforts of CPC's traveling agents who sought out women fitting a specific demographic—married and needing money—the company secured an overwhelmingly female sales force.

Although it is impossible to pinpoint why McConnell chose to recruit women—whether he intended to do so when he started his company or if this approach was a by-product of a recruiting tradition over which he did not have control—women constituted more than 95 percent of the CPC sales force, 6,500 strong in 1900, 20,000 by 1920. Of that 95 percent, more than 85 percent carried the title "Mrs.," a trend that continued through to the 1990s. Indeed, by the post–World War II era, women represented at least 98 percent of the Avon sales force, and married women predominated. Throughout its history, CPC's dedication to recruiting a married, female sales force stands out. In the 1930s, when women accounted for less than 22 percent of the U.S. labor force overall and less than 12% percent of married women participated in paid work, CPC's roster stands in marked contrast to traditional industry.[22]

Married women fulfilled important social and public relations functions in McConnell's business scheme. He made a conscious effort to distinguish his company and representatives, and his direct-to-the-home selling methods, from commercial peddlers because he needed to appeal to rural consumers who remained suspicious of traveling salesmen. "One thing we want you to bear in mind distinctly," he told his recruiters in the 1899 traveling agent's manual, "[is] that this is not peddling or anything of that kind. . . ."[23] At the turn of the century, traveling salesmen had a reputation as hucksters.[24] Their products were deemed unreliable, if not completely bogus, and their service fleeting, for many travelers worked routes that brought them into towns but once or twice a year, leaving few opportunities for follow-up sales, no chance for service, and no avenue for buyers to express complaints. CPC's recruiting and sales manuals explicitly spoke to issues of women's reliability and respectability in the trade. McConnell believed that married women commanded more respect as sales agents, symbolized stability, and were more visible in their communities. More important, their social networks could be exploited for selling purposes, especially regarding repeat sales.

McConnell also hoped that women's reputations and networks would help him avoid some real legal issues. Several communities throughout the United States had protested against traveling salesmen, and many towns passed local ordinances banning unsolicited sales. In a Supreme Court decision known as the Green River Ordinance, towns could ban unsolicited salesmen outright, which led to the creation of

Figure 6.1. Cover of the Avon Sales Representative's business manual, 1933. (Hagley Museum and Library, Avon archives)

crafty techniques even among legitimate companies. Fuller Brush, for example, claimed its salesmen only left its catalog with a housewife on his first visit, and on the second only wanted to pick it up—but if in the course of conversation the lady of the house mentioned she would like to order a few items, well all the better. Local intolerance of traveling salesmen continued through the 1920s and 1930s, and CPC representatives and recruiters wrote many stories in sales manuals and journals detailing how they dealt with signs on doors of homes, train stations, and post offices saying "solicitation not welcome." McConnell believed that by hiring women who built customer bases on preexisting kin, friendship, and community networks, few, if any, complaints or lawsuits would be lodged against his company.[25]

McConnell's advice to his traveling agents (his recruiting staff) also suggests that he knew that the women he sought to recruit had few other viable work options. "Inquire for widow ladies," he wrote. "Or ambitious married ladies, or ladies with sickly (or lazy) husbands, for maiden ladies, . . . teachers who are not teaching, stenographers, clerks or nurses who are out of employment."[26] McConnell hoped that his agents would be available to handle the trade four to six hours a day. Most would not, although they welcomed the opportunity to earn some extra cash. CPC in no way asked representatives to make choices between work and family or paid employment and domesticity, and McConnell never suggested that women would give up their domestic responsibilities in order to canvass their neighborhoods and take orders. Although recruiting literature did emphasize that women needed to learn to budget their time, McConnell encouraged them to combine their home and family duties with their business. "Arrange your home affairs so as to give as much of your time as you possibly can to this work. You cannot expect to succeed at anything unless you give it thought and give it energy."[27] Children and home frequently appeared in recruiting and sales management literature as women's incentives for working. The company encouraged women to set goals—new clothes, new furniture, and children's education all figured prominently—and to envision their business supplying the means for obtaining them.

During the Depression, CPC literature inflated the traditional explanation for hiring women, but the message essentially remained the same. McConnell's idea, as an *Outlook* editor explained in 1931, was:

> to offer an opportunity to make money to women to whom many other avenues of earning were closed—women with families, who lived away from industrial centers, who had no previous training . . . women who wished to be independent and in control of their own actions and time, [who] were eager to grasp the chance to practically enter business for themselves in a protected territory and without investing any capital.[28]

At a time when business, labor, and society in general urged women to leave the workforce, CPC provided an opportunity for them to become involved in business as independent contractors.

In his more heady moments, McConnell encouraged women to make selling their full-time occupation, yet he knew that they would not. McConnell recognized that most women stayed with the company for only a few months and produced less than $100 of business before "retiring." Throughout the 1910s and twenties, turnover rates among the representative staff were very high, often approaching 90 to 100 percent every year. Sales statistics and representative sales force information for the 1930s has not survived, but several accounts suggest that annual turnover averaged 200 to 400 percent in the worst years of the Depression. Spectacular as those numbers sound, an average "good" year can help illustrate the CPC recruiters' task and the scope of problems CPC confronted on a yearly basis.

According to tenure and sales reports of the New York office, which organized more than 12,000 representatives (see Table 6.1), of the total number of representatives on file on December 31, 1928, nearly 60 percent were "new," meaning that they had been appointed that year. The remaining 40 percent had been appointed in previous years.

According to this report, of the women who had stayed with the company for more than one year, 72 percent would not stay more than two years. However, of the group who had stayed with the company for two years, some 40 percent would be likely to stay for more than three years. In other words, a solid core of experienced representatives who received enough benefits from their association with California

Table 6.1

Tenure-rate Analysis of 12,370 Contracts on File in the New York office on December 31, 1928 [29]

Date of Appointment	Number	Percentage of Workforce 12/31/28
1928	7,375	59.6
1927	1,542	12.4
1924–1926	2,147	17.4
1923 or before	1,306	10.6
Total	12,370	100.0

Table 6.2

Total Annual Business of 12,370 Contracts on File in the New York office on December 31, 1928 [30]

Annual Order Values	Number	Percentage of Workforce 12/31/28
Under $10	2648	21.4
$10–$249	9075	73.4
$249–$499	555	4.5
$500+	92	0.7
[$1,000+]	[13]	[.01]

Perfume Company to continue on a long-term basis balanced the larger percentage of short-term representatives.

Individually, most representatives were not very prolific. (See Table 6.2) According to a sales report analysis for the same group in 1928, the vast majority of women garnered less than $250 a year in sales. Despite the company's encouragement to pull together orders of $100 or more a month, which would have given representatives $40 a month in commissions, only a tiny minority achieved that. Most stunning, however, is the percentage of women who produced less than $10 in wholesale orders a year: 21 percent, fully one fifth of all representatives sold barely enough to cover the cost of recruiting them.

Moreover, a representative's sales performance related directly to her length of tenure. According to an analysis of Sales Representative Prize winners in the New York office in 1922, fewer than 5 percent of "new" representatives earned sales prizes awarded to any representative who sent in orders of $30 or more.[31] Other analyses of sales trends within New York, Kansas City, and Canadian divisions from 1918 to 1927 showed similar results. Orders totaling $30 or more accounted for only one third of all orders received (ranging from 20.8 percent in the Kansas City division in 1927 to 54.8 percent in the New York division in 1920). The average order nationwide over a ten-year period was $26 (ranging from $21.14 in the Canadian division in 1927 to $32.35 in the New York division in 1920). Average order size was an important indicator for CPC analysts. In all its literature, CPC encouraged representatives to submit orders of $30 or more; as an incentive, these representatives earned free shipping of their orders. However, as the reports make clear, barely one third of representatives reached this threshold, thereby saving CPC significant overhead expenses by making less-than-diligent representatives pay shipping costs for the smallest—and the vast majority—of orders. As a result, CPC paid shipping charges on only 35 percent of the orders it received.

Despite the problems of high turnover and low individual sales, McConnell had learned to manage his company so that he could profit from even the smallest sale. Building a broad sales base gave him the leeway to profitably retain those women with low total sales who consistently submitted orders. CPC's mastery of the direct-selling format, in place for more than forty years when the worst of the Depression hit, gave the company a distinct competitive advantage.

DEVELOPING CITY MARKETS AND A NATIONAL ADVERTISING CAMPAIGN

In 1926, when the leader's son, David McConnell Jr., joined CPC's executive ranks, top managers started to think seriously about how to improve sales in cities, by which they meant locales with populations of more than 5,000. Recruiting in large cities had always posed problems for CPC traveling supervisors. McConnell and his managers identified three characteristics of city and urban districts that made creating a market difficult: the relative impersonality of city residents, the difficulty in defining territories for representatives to work, and competition with other employers for women's part-time labor. Representatives in cities seemed reluctant, apparently, to develop a regular trade among their neighbors. Perhaps the size of districts overwhelmed them, or perhaps they found CPC instructions to "canvass every home" unmanageable. Moreover, since CPC could not draw more distinct territories in city neighborhoods than in rural regions, representatives and business in cities floundered.

Until the 1930s, CPC managers had never thought through the unique problems and challenges of city markets, nor did they have a sense of differentiation among types or sizes of cities. Sales manuals essentially recommended that cities be treated as oversized small towns and did little to adapt their approach to recruiting and training representatives or merchandizing products. "There are two ways of working Sales Districts of five thousand up to a million population," the 1924 guidebook stated: direct inquiry or by advertising in daily papers.[32] CPC recommended that traveling agents find a local person to describe various sections of the city so that she could divide into districts that would each comprise some "good population." Then she could either start knocking on doors to look for prospects, or place an advertisement and rent a reply box with the local paper. Success varied by agent and city.

Race factored into how CPC and its agents judged the efficacy of city markets—a town of 3,000 might need two workers, if they would only work part-time, whereas "a town of 20,000 might have nearly [a large] colored or foreign population, when three or four [representatives] would be sufficient."[33] In both rural towns and urban districts, CPC did not "approve of the appointment of a colored Representative" but tried to allow for exceptions. "[T]here is sometimes a good colored section in that town where a nice business could be done, if a *reliable* colored Representative could be appointed."[34] When agents appointed blacks, they restricted sales to black sections of towns and required that cash accompany all orders, eliminating the credit options available to whites. But regardless of whether CPC representatives were white or black, home office managers could not understand why city representatives seemed more reluctant to sell, less willing to knock on the doors of strangers, and less productive overall. Women's networks seemed more disorganized and unproductive in cities than in towns.

McConnell Jr. tried to tackle these problems in the late 1920s, and in 1935 organized three initial test markets in Houston, San Antonio, and Wichita, "because they were very much like country towns." As one executive recalled, "[i]n Texas the problem wasn't getting in [the door], it was getting [back] out[;] they wanted you to have cake and coffee."[35] CPC authorized eleven city sales offices in Texas, Kansas, Nebraska, Oklahoma, and Minnesota in 1936; twenty-three more opened in 1937, all in states west of the Mississippi River.[36] Not only did CPC executives believe that the character of Midwestern and Western towns made them more conducive to the direct selling approach, but Wayne Hicklin and Russel Rooks, executives at the Kansas City branch office (which handled all sales west of the Mississippi), promoted the city sales offices faster than did the managers in New York. Although the new city sales offices would eventually come to dominate the Avon sales system, in the 1930s the sporadic sales they generated barely covered their high start-up costs. During the Depression, therefore, city markets had almost no impact on CPC's overall profit or income.[37]

It seems surprising that CPC waited so long to develop urban markets. In the context of the entire direct-selling industry, as in the cosmetics industry, CPC lagged behind the times. The vast majority of direct-sales companies, including Fuller Brush, Stanley Home Products, and Real Silk Hosiery, sold almost exclusively in urban areas. Fuller Brush, for example, which began in a city market, hired permanent managers to recruit, train, and monitor their local sales representatives.[38] (Within the direct-sales industry this is known as "branch office" management.) CPC on the other hand, sent recruiters, or traveling agents, to small towns throughout the nation to recruit women to sell products on commission (a system known as "home office" management.) Once a woman had signed her contract, it was unlikely that she would ever see another representative from the company again. Instead, CPC provided a constant stream of instruction manuals, product literature, and personalized letters explaining new products, suggesting sales pitches, and offering motivation. A complex Kardex filing system recorded every order, sales report, and bit of correspondence to track each representative's progress.[39] Supervising a workforce through the mail presented distinct problems, however, for CPC ultimately had no control over how independent agents represented the company or whether or not they even worked.

CPC managers were reluctant to market in cities in part because of competition from department stores and other retail outlets. Put simply, Avon brand products and services did not stand out in urban areas. Potential customers, increasingly aware of brand-name goods, did not recognize the Avon name and, just as important, did not know where to find the products. Meeting these problems, which did not seem as noticeable in rural districts, required a reorganization of representative recruitment and training strategies, as well as a new conception of selling territories and markets.

Avon (as the company was officially known after 1937) made its most serious efforts to work through these issues during World War II. However, the company's first attempt to create a brand-name awareness came with a newly designed, continuous, national advertising campaign in the mid-1930s. CPC/Avon's first mass-circulation advertisement, designed by the Monroe Dreher advertising firm, appeared in *Good Housekeeping* in November 1936. It featured a two-page stylized drawing of Avon cosmetics and a text insert explaining where consumers could purchase them. Later advertisements featured explanations of the sales procedure and invited magazine readers to welcome Avon callers. Nevertheless, when McConnell Jr. announced the first advertising campaign, several executives remained unconvinced of its usefulness. "National advertising was hard to sell," Wayne Hicklin recalled, "but Mr. McConnell Jr. and Mr. Ewald insisted it would be good. Many of us in the branches thought that was the most peculiar thing; how would that help us? It didn't help right then, but the cumulative effect over four or five years was very evident."[40]

Radio advertising also helped to create a brand-name awareness and boost sales. Lela Eastman, a CPC traveling agent since 1924 and the first city sales office manager in Pasadena, California, believed that changing the name from California Perfume Company to Avon made an enormous difference. She quickly realized advertising advantages. The Avon brand name was new to both city markets and the entire country in the early 1930s. By 1935, CPC substituted Avon for its company name in most of its literature and catalogs. Eastman had just opened the Pasadena sales office and took it upon herself to spread the word about the "new" company. "I was told that they changed the name from California Perfume Company to Avon," Eastman recalled, "because [during the Depression] when the girls would go to the doors saying they represented the California Perfume Company the people would say, my dear, we can't afford food. We can't afford perfumes. So . . . you'd say Avon and people didn't know what you were talking about."[41] Radio advertising seemed like a logical next step to Eastman:

> So I decided that if I could put the word Avon in their mind, it would happen
> just like that and it happened almost in the twinkling of an eye. People in
> the home were listening to the radio and the man came on and with a nice
> voice telling about Avon, telling about their credentials, and that a lovely
> lady would call at their home to show them the merchandise. And after he
> would tell them that she would have a little gift for them. And it went over
> big. Many girls would tell me that they would knock on the door and say
> that they were the Avon representative and the people would say come in, I
> just heard your ad over the radio. . . . [42]

Despite the differences in executive's and local managers like Eastman's assessment of the efficacy of mass advertising, few saw it as something the company needed to pull it through the Depression, which is not to say that Avon managers were hardly unconcerned about the Depression and did nothing new. Most chose a more conservative approach, such as establishing higher recruiting goals, which in turn resulted in a larger representative staff so that sales grew proportionally, rather than dedicating money to city branch offices and national advertising, despite the success of those strategies for other companies. Such programs would not have served the majority of Avon representatives who continued to work in rural districts, despite the company's forays into cities. Increasing the number of agents' appointments, however, changed only the degree of Avon's business, and did not symbolize a fundamental shift in company strategy.

Higher recruiting goals resulted in a larger representative staff. Eventually the base number of contracts on file leveled out at about 25,000 from 1933 to 1937. Sales grew from just under $2.8 million in 1929 to $3.6 million in 1933, then nearly doubled to $6.5 million by 1939. Given the higher turnover rates of the Depression era, this meant that recruiters had to appoint between 25,000 and 30,000 new women every year just to maintain an average of 25,000 active representatives. Clearly, CPC's ability to compensate for high turnover and low individual sales saved the company during the 1930s, when annual turnover rates skyrocketed. Although Avon had to step up the pace of recruitment during the Depression, managing a temporary, part-time, and low-earning sales force did not present any fundamental challenges to its existing system.

Continued sales increases in the mid- and late 1930s, in light of the stable number of representatives, resulted from two merchandising strategies. John Ewald, then CPC's general manager and later Avon's third president, instituted various plans to encourage women to make more sales. Traditionally, CPC had required that representatives submit an order, preferably of $30 or more, every month. Ewald thought that representatives took too much time canvassing their territory and believed that he could increase the number of orders by shortening the selling cycle from four weeks to three weeks. This maneuver would increase the number of orders from a steady worker to eighteen per year, rather than twelve. The new mind game managers played with representatives essentially became a speedup.

Initially, McConnell was not easily convinced. "It wasn't easy to sell the home office," Hicklin said, "though Kansas City was a lot of little young upstarts. Eventually the home office was sold and overnight that was put into effect."[43] CPC adopted Ewald's scheme with very little fanfare in August 1932. The company informed recruiters of the new plan just days before they told representatives: "I am sure you will be mighty enthusiastic over the new 20 day sales campaign. . . ." Kansas City manager O. F. Blatter wrote to his traveling agents, "we are expecting, because of this, that it will stimulate quicker interest in the minds of our Sales Representatives resulting in a greater volume of business for the period indicated."[44] In the representatives' newsletter, *Avon Outlook*, John Ewald introduced the new campaign format along with a special "20-day sales campaign" to sell Avon Ariel and Vernafleur face powders, regularly 75 cents each, at two for $1.00.[45] The three-week selling campaign and the new "two for a dollar sale" showed instant results, as the number and size of representatives' orders rose dramatically. "We had just as big orders in three weeks as we had in a month," Hicklin said.[46] The phenomenal success of the shorter sales campaign taught CPC executives that representatives willingly followed instructions or "suggestions," which managers could use to control how a representative conducted her "business."

Not all of Ewald's plans, however, proved successful, and one failure in particular may have had more impact on the way the entire CPC management team approached the 1930s than any other. In 1932, Ewald had convinced McConnell Sr. to test out a new system for paying representatives a fixed monthly salary of $15 per month for agreeing to work full time. McConnell Sr. reluctantly agreed. Within a matter of just three months, the plan proved an utter failure. According to Wayne Hicklin, then the Western division sales manager, guaranteeing salary under absentee management could not work. "When you've got people out there the best thing to do is give 'em an incentive where if they work they make money," he said. Under such circumstances the independent contractor relationship was more sensible than a traditional one that included fixed salaries: "We have to sell them on what they should do. . . . We're challenged, we have all these people, we've got to keep selling and getting them to do things they don't think they can do."[47] McConnell, Ewald, and many others learned that fixed salaries proved to be an incentive for unsupervised representatives not to work, and they never tried it again.

Avon managers opted not to follow the trend of increasing corporate control of its sales staff. Placing workers on salary and promising them benefits was most effective only in controlled environments. The failed salary plan also exposed how business strategies worked within structures that reflected assumptions about gender. Fuller Brush had also tried a similar project (and although the records are not clear, Avon may have hired Fuller Brush managers to try converting its system.)[48] However, the Fuller Brush system differed significantly from Avon's in that Fuller Brush men worked full-time, unlike Avon Ladies, who worked part-time. Even though Fuller Brush men's tenure rates were also short, like the Avon representatives', they put in more hours each week.[49] Avon's managers accepted that Avon representatives treated their sales business as providing a supplementary rather than a primary source of income. Ultimately, the collapse of Ewald's salary plan reinforced the traditional CPC strategy. Radical changes to a proven system seemed unjustifiable in the midst of an economic crisis. Selling representatives on their jobs, however, as Hicklin suggested, resulted in a unique and effective method for increasing sales: motivation.

MOTIVATIONAL LITERATURE—A STRATEGY FOR EMOTIONAL CONTROL

Following Ewald's attempt to increase performance by paying representatives a fixed salary, CPC/Avon managers recommitted themselves to energizing representatives with emotional techniques, building their emotional and moral awareness and highlighting each representative's commitment to the company.[50] Motivational literature became key to CPC's strategy for it served instructional purposes and conveyed a sense of business ownership and responsibility. CPC encouraged women to set goals for themselves—a logical consequence of not being able to assign them specific tasks or enforce strict objectives. The technique placed responsibility for the success of the business directly in the hands of representatives, but without a formal, bureaucratic connection between women and the company, CPC took an enormous risk, for CPC had no system for overseeing a representative's activity. Not only did the CPC representative work without supervision, but also the company set remarkably low sales quotas for her to maintain an active contract status. For example, CPC sent letters of inquiry after a representative had not submitted an order for three months, and did not threaten to replace her until about six months had gone by, in part because the company did not have enough recruiters available to reassign territories. Indeed, unlike commercial salesmen, who maintained client lists and reported to supervisors, a CPC representative's clients and day-to-day performance were not monitored.

Motivational literature served to train representatives for their jobs but also pressed attention to their work habits. The representative's job required a degree of self-confidence that even a socially active woman found daunting. It necessitated that she knock on the doors of strangers and ask for a sale, facing rejection from two of every five households she approached. Most women simply gave up, as the low annual sales figures suggest. Without on-site supervision to help women through the first few difficult days, CPC lost many representatives to a simple lack of interest in the work or fear of rejection.[51] These circumstances, unique to the direct-sales industry, drove CPC's use of motivational literature as a business strategy. Managers believed that each woman needed to feel a part of the larger organization and cultivate her awareness and belief that her success depended on her own aptitude, ingenuity, and willingness to work. During the Depression, CPC's optimism seemed strangely out of place in the context of both national economic disaster and its own corporate history of high turnover and low individual sales. The inefficiency and irrational nature of CPC's system went hand in hand with the emotional, inefficient technique of distributing motivational literature and success stories to create direct selling's most visible, consistent, impossible-to-measure, and ultimately effective means of "irrational management."

CPC's motivational literature professed a democratic spirit. It emphasized that a woman should work virtuously and act responsibly for herself, her career, her family, community, and the company itself. Editors relied on women to write and ultimately define the Oz-like promise of CPC business opportunities. Not only did CPC's message hold cultural appeal, but in the world of direct selling the success ethic was also more than a rhetorical trope—it was a central organizing feature of CPC business strategy. American business rarely applied positive thinking, goal setting, and evangelical spirit—characteristics of modern management, progressive ideology, and religious philosophy—so directly to rural women. CPC literature directly spoke to women's emotions, appealing to their commitment to family and their social position not only as wives and mothers but as women living in the context of a rural, agrarian polity, as women who had a long tradition of combining outside work with household management. Women, CPC said, had to take responsibility for their neighborhoods' and the nation's economic security by entering business. To a nation whose vivid progressive imagination still held tightly to the moral strength of the individual's entrepreneurial power and social responsibility, and to tens of thousands of that nation's women, Avon's message resonated with particular urgency.[52]

McConnell and his managers held that all women paid in direct proportion to their productivity had the same potential to earn and prosper, regardless of experience or social background. Emphasizing the independent nature of agency work, Avon writers always described a woman's association with the company as a result of a well-thought-out, independent, and progressive choice, and made the representative's success or failure a direct corollary of her time and effort. According to McConnell, positive thinking generated the individual's economic success. In the *Outlook* and all company correspondence, he reminded his representatives that despite the Depression, rewards were limitless to those who wanted to work. "Pessimists are whimpering over the unemployment situation," McConnell wrote in a

1931 editorial, "people are out of work, they say, and cannot find jobs." This confused him, for on his desk next to the reports on national unemployment were several sales reports for orders of more than $100 each: "Instead of being turned from doors," one representative wrote, "I am called back." "The enterprise and will to work, reflected in the splendid sales of thousands of our Representatives, gives me faith that prosperity is not far away," McConnell wrote. "Women—the ones you meet on your sales trips—still do 80 percent of the spending. . . . It is your responsibility to give them the opportunity to secure your merchandise. . . . When people get into the buying habit again, the wheels of industry will turn at full speed and there will be work for all."[53]

Outlook editors employed a variety of rhetorical strategies for making their motivational messages more powerful. Most significantly, they encouraged women to write their personal stories and strategies for success. Assigning authorship to ideas about success and ownership and rhetoric that linked representatives' responsibility to their communities belied the fact that negotiations between individual representatives and Avon took place between two very unequal parties. Managers, therefore, in order to foster representatives' trust, continually assured them of the corporation's paternalistic goodwill, a technique that allowed representatives to speak both for themselves and the company in the literature.

Representatives' voices had always played a very conspicuous role in Avon's publications. CPC used women's stories to teach lessons about the free-enterprise system and to emphasize the potential of the individual to succeed despite any limit set before her, establishing a business vernacular that supported a political and economic vision of social democracy.[54] Avon featured personal stories from representatives in its earliest newsletters and manuals as a way to prove to women that no obstacle could justify why they stopped selling, or serve as an excuse for why they were not earning money and improving their character. Many women claimed to have benefited physically, psychologically, and financially from Avon's positive outlook: "From a physical viewpoint I can say my work has been of more benefit to me than all the money I have ever spent," Mrs. Charles McNutt wrote from Oklahoma. "I sincerely believe that most ills are caused by a mental state of mind. I find that my work creates a diversion of thought, that in no way can be associated with the ordinary ills of today. . . ."[55]

Stories from other women who suffered from sickness, the death of a spouse, bankruptcy or debt and who had learned to turn hardships into incentives pervaded Avon literature. "[Avon] has helped me financially, but most of all it kept me from doing a lot of worrying," wrote Mrs. Fred Them of Indiana. "For instance, three years ago I lost one of my babies and could not stand to be at home." She went to work for

Figure 6.2. The Avon Single Rouge Compact in a thin blue and silver case sold for fifty two cents and was offered in four shades: light, medium, dark, and vivid. (Hagley Museum and Library, Avon archives, catalogs, 1935)

CPC: "It did not take me long to get started and I have had such wonderful results." Another representative, Mrs. Cora Coffin of Massachusetts, wrote that she had started Avon work when she was "on the verge of a nervous breakdown." "I began to regain my health from the start. . . . My three children were young . . . and my husband being an ordinary working man, he was unable to meet all the expenses. So I always dressed the children from my earnings," she wrote.[56] According to these women, their fresh sense of power and possibility came from their new business acumen. "These women have *learned their own value*. . . . They plan to get what they want," General Manager John Ewald wrote in his 1931 editorial, "Success Is Not An Accident."[57]

Overall, the direct-selling industry seemed to have thrived on morality tales, particularly those written by representatives who had overcome hardships. "Before I took up this work . . . I was a widow alone, no one to depend on and living in fear all the time," wrote Hattie McGoovan of Oklahoma. "Since I have been with the Company I have paid off $1,500 of debts left me by the ex-husband five years before, have a comfortable place to live, am living well and enjoying life to the fullest extent, for to be really happy one must be serving our fellow beings and building and making progress, which I am doing every day with the aid of the California Perfume Company."

Avon had featured exotic stories from representatives in its earliest newsletters. In the 1920s CPC had featured a woman in Alaska who used sled dogs and Eskimo guides to deliver her soaps to customers in the frozen tundra. In the January 1931 *Outlook,* under the heading "You Can't Keep a Good Representative Down," representative Miss Susie Robinson received praise for selling Avon merchandise from her hospital bed following an operation. She had booked more than $15 in orders from nurses, doctors, janitors, and even other patients, and used the money to help pay her hospital bill. "There are not many people who would think of turning their ills to such good account," the *Outlook* editor commented.[58]

Thousands of women like McGoovan and Robinson shared their experiences, and in each instance Avon singled out business opportunity as a catalyst for their success. These success stories "are taken from our records as an inspiration to you, to have the things these women have—new clothes, nice homes, paid up doctors bills, comforts for aged ones, [and] education for the younger generation," the *Outlook* editor wrote. "When you join the ranks of the [Avon] organization, your future success is in your hands. . . . How you capitalize on it depends on your own efforts."[59] Positive thinking and hard work became the simple and obvious solutions to any problem, including the Depression. As general manager John Ewald wrote, "Those who use Hard Luck as an alibi for lack of effort, and prefer to bemoan their hard lot rather than cure it, are the victims of their own lack of foresight."[60]

In its most insidious form, Avon literature even suggested that business could become a substitute for social networks. "Sometimes a Representative will start out with the traditions of an older age. She will decide to make a few social calls. She will take her sales portfolio along, hoping to pick up a little business as she goes," one editorial titled "Our Work is the Test of Our Value" began.

> But if she is the forward-looking, up-to-date type, she soon drops this attitude for that of the new age. She goes out to WORK—like her progressive sisters everywhere. She finds her social life as she goes. For in her portfolio she carries the key to every woman's confidence and friendlines—the desire to appear at one's best before the world.[61]

At Avon, however, beauty culture went beyond personal application of red rouges and vivid lipstick; it was colored green with economic incentives for those selected as "ambassadors of beauty" in their neighborhoods.

Ironically, the chorus of women's voices that reaffirmed CPC's business strategy, and its moral and emotional support of independent business owners, provided the ammunition CPC needed when the government's regulation of business threatened the CPC's business contract. Singing the praises of CPC—its business characterized by fairness, unlimited potential, and quality—CPC women enthusiastically supported the continuation of a business contract that afforded them no security or benefits beyond their commissions.

INDEPENDENT CONTRACTOR REGULATION, 1936

While CPC continued to profit during the 1930s as tens of thousands of women tried their hands at hawking Avon products door-to-door through the nation, the federal government undertook to alleviate the Depression in part by regulating business. During the second New Deal, programs such as Social Security and the National Recovery Administration mandated that businesses restrict workers' hours, guarantee minimum hourly wages, and pay income taxes. If these laws were to apply to the direct-selling industry, the consequences could have been devastating. In its representative literature, CPC had always supported Roosevelt's efforts. It was easy to boost the NRA in the 1933 to 1934 period, as it required little from CPC other than lip service (CPC placed NRA stickers on recruiting literature packets and catalogs), but the threat of regulation by the Social Security Administration and the NRA presented an impracticable situation. The National Association of Direct Selling Companies (NADSC), an umbrella trade organization (CPC was a founding member in 1910), lobbied the government to exempt it from laws designed to regulate industry.

The NADSC fought hard against the changes imposed by the federal government to regulate business during the Depression and successfully appealed to the Federal Trade Commission in 1936 to classify direct-sales representatives as "independent contractors."[62] The unsupervised nature of representative work, the NADSC argued, made it impossible for companies like CPC to monitor employees' hours and the quality of their work, factors which did not affect how the company had previously regulated or rewarded representatives, who only had to meet minimum order quotas. Ultimately, the Federal Trade Commission's independent-contractor ruling exempted direct-selling companies from paying representatives' social security taxes and from adhering to minimum wage requirements. However, it also carried legal restrictions on what direct-selling companies could and could not do regarding their representatives. Thereafter companies could neither "hire" nor "fire" representatives, nor could they restrict representatives' selling activities either by establishing protected territories or enforcing product pricing (other laws prevented representatives from charging more than published prices, but representatives could reduce prices). Moreover, direct-sales employers could not require representatives to submit documentation of their business activities beyond the paperwork required for processing orders. But, as with many New Deal initiatives, the federal government could not provide the mechanisms needed to enforce its new law, and CPC/Avon did not feel the full impact of the 1936 decision until several decades later, when the federal government established regulatory committees to monitor the direct-selling industry.

Meanwhile, by 1936, CPC managers could rely heavily on their company's fifty–year-long experience in managing its sizeable sales force. McConnell was a leader in the industry, and his company represented the model of how to build a successful direct-selling organization. McConnell's system worked; CPC clearly filled a need for customers and distributors alike. Given his perfected motivational techniques, even a lackadaisical sales representative could profit the company so long as overhead was kept low enough, whereas the costs to transform the independent sales force into a mass of "employees" would have been overwhelming. Therefore, while the contractor rulings of 1936 would become significant in the longer view of Avon's and the direct-selling industry's history, they made little impact on the organization and management style of the California Perfume Company at the time. CPC remained devoted to treating its distributors as independent business owners and was as likely to use the phrase "Now you are in business for yourself" in 1940 as in 1920.[63]

CONCLUSION

In the early years of the Depression, Avon had touted direct selling as a vehicle for developing women's agency to alleviate a national crisis. As the decade wore on, however, its need to emphasize women's role in business as a necessary and valuable component in helping the country to survive became more subdued, until by 1936 the firm dropped all references to the economic crisis. Avon practically ignored the Depression, at least in terms of its business strategy, and instead placed a heavy emphasis on sales techniques, service skill development, product information, and beauty how-to advice. Structural changes within the organization coincided with this shift in emphasis. A new group of managers took control of Avon—the patriarchal head, David McConnell Sr., died in 1937, leaving his son and heir in charge. That year also marked the opening of city markets. It is also safe to say that by 1938, as the Depression was lessening in its strength, Avon knew that it had survived, and its managers no longer felt compelled to focus on the long-running crisis.

Ironically, we can look at Avon in the 1930s and not confront the Depression, which ultimately had little long-term effect on the company. The economic crisis certainly increased the degree and intensity of Avon's message to representatives, providing fodder for the "conquer and overcome" theme in the motivational literature; the myth of the "self-made [wo]man" became more exaggerated and embellished as a result. Yet organizationally, the most important changes at Avon between 1929 and 1936 had been planned before the economic crisis took its full toll. Development of the color cosmetics line, late in the broader context of the beauty industry, began at Avon only in 1928. The reorganization of city markets, a priority in the late 1920s, remained untested before 1935 and had little or no effect on Avon's bottom line until World War II. Even the first national advertising campaign did not seriously affect Avon's management or sales, at least not to the extent that it could explain Avon's success during the Depression. In fact, CPC never used national advertising before the 1930s, a practice that in Peiss's analysis drove the popularity of cosmetics in the 1920s, and many within the firm seriously questioned its value when it was proposed in 1936.[64] Ultimately, Avon's success came without the benefit of either national advertising or urban markets, its sales garnered instead by way of face-to-face transactions in parlors and kitchens between individual women in rural America.

There were a few spur-of-the-moment decisions in the early 1930s that had long-term consequences—for example, General Manager John Ewald's decision in 1932 to change the selling campaign from four weeks to three weeks while simultaneously offering product specials— a two-for-a-dollar sale on face powder, for example. These did boost sales in 1932 and taught managers a valuable lesson about creating sales incentives for customers and representatives. However, the major changes of the 1930s, planned earlier, reflected the leadership of the founder's son, David McConnell Jr., who took over the company in 1927. Two keys, then, underwrote Avon's success in the 1930s: its ideological and managerial commitment to, and mastery of, direct sales, and its unique market niche in rural America.

ACKNOWLEDGMENTS

Special thanks to the Hagley Museum and Library, which manages the Avon Products, Incorporated manuscript and archive. Unless otherwise noted, all primary source citations of Avon literature are from Hagley accession 2155. Avon's published and bound volumes are cited by title and date. Avon's correspondence, reports, and other information are noted by series, box, and folder.

NOTES

1. Quotation from "45 Years of Steady Growth: Do You Really Know What the Great CPC-Avon Organization Represents?" *Avon Outlook* (February 1931): 2.
2. "The CPC Business is Better Than Ever on Our Forty-Seventh Anniversary," *Avon Outlook* (May 6, 1933): 2.
3. W. J. Alley, "Evidence . . . A Depression-Proof Business," *Avon Outlook* (January 2, 1933): 2.

4. See Alfred Fuller, *A Foot in the Door: The Life Appraisal of the Original Fuller Brush Man as Told to Hartzell Spence* (New York: McGraw-Hill, 1960), 172.

5. On Encyclopaedia Britannica, see Herman Kogan, *The Great EB: The Story of the "Encyclopaedia Britannica"* (Chicago: University of Chicago Press, 1958).

6. On Beveridge's training with Fuller Brush, see Fuller, *A Foot in the Door*, 133–134. On Beveridge's direct-selling company, Stanley Home Products, see his company history: Joan Marcus, *To Better Your Best: Stanley Home Products, The First 50 Years* (Westfield, MA: Stanley, Inc., 1981).

7. "Direct Selling Takes a New Direction: NADSC—1910 and After," unpublished manuscript in Direct Selling Association archives, Washington DC, n.d. Report closely follows style, language and format in Avon archives on report to NADSC by Norman Chadwick, 1963. See also Nicole Biggart, *Charismatic Capitalism* (Chicago: University of Chicago Press, 1989), 32.

8. On direct-sales expense-management issues, see Victor P. Buell, "Door-to-Door Selling," *Harvard Business Review* 32 (May-June 1954) 113–123.

9. On post-Depression direct-selling company management style, see Biggart, *Charismatic Capitalism*, 32.

10. On popularity of cosmetics in the 1920s, see Kathy Peiss, *Hope in a Jar* (New York: Metropolitan Books, 1998) chap. 4, 96–133.

11. Daphne fragrance lipstick appeared in the 1917 Color Plate Catalog.

12. Peiss, *Hope in a Jar*, 73–74.

13. Color Plate Catalog, 1928. Anna J. Figsbee, an accounts manager who began her CPC career in 1902, described the Recordon line as a prestige product (Figsbee, "My Company and Me," unpublished bound manuscript, Series 8, Box 125).

14. The very first product to carry the name Avon was a powdered general cleanser, called Avon Maid, featuring a cartoon image of a girl or woman with a handkerchief tied around her head and wielding a dust rag. One year later CPC launched Avon—the cosmetics brand—with a letter to representatives on special letterhead, portentously claiming "The Dawn of a New Era."

15. See Color Plate Catalog, 1929.

16. Peiss, *Hope in a Jar*, 196. Avon's trade catalogs, 1932, 1936.

17. Peiss, *Hope in a Jar*, 103.

18. For availability of products in rural areas, see Peiss, *Hope in a Jar*, 169–170. "It was not until the end of the 1930s that farm women's use of cosmetics approximated that of urban dwellers," 170.

19. See Peiss, *Hope in a Jar*, 97–133.

20. "The CPC Business Is Better Than Ever on Our Forty-Seventh Anniversary" *Avon Outlook* (May 6, 1933): 2.

21. According to Biggart, women represented fewer than 10 percent of all direct sales representatives. Susan Strasser found similar results in commercial sales forces, (*Charismatic Capitalism*, 186). where women represented less than 5 percent of traveling agents. (See n23.)

22. On married women in the labor force, see Alba Edwards, *Comparative Occupation Statistics for the United States, 1870-1940*, U.S. Department of Commerce, 16th census of the United States: 1940 (Washington DC: U.S. GPO, 1943); Janet Hooks, *Women's Occupations through Seven Decades*, U.S. Dept. of Labor, Women's Bureau Bulletin No. 218 (Washington DC: U.S. GPO, 1947); Alice Kessler-Harris, *Out to Work*. (New York: Oxford University Press, 1982); Lynn Weiner, *From Working Girl to Working Mother: The Female Labor Force in the United States, 1820–1980* (Chapel Hill: UNC Press, 1985); Leslie Woodcock Tentler, *Wage Earning Women: Industrial Work and Family in the United States, 1900–1930* (New York: Oxford University Press, 1979).

23. "Manual of Instruction for depot managers," 1899. (Series 3, Box 113)

24. On the seedy reputation of traveling salesmen throughout history, see Karen Halttunen, *Confidence Men and Painted Women: A Study of Middle-Class Culture in America, 1830–1870* (New Haven, CT: Yale University Press, 1982), esp. 198–210; Timothy B. Spears, *100 Years on the Road: The Traveling Salesman in American Culture* (New Haven: Yale University Press, 1995). Susan Strasser, "The Smile that Pays," in *The Mythmaking Frame of Mind: Social Imagination and American Culture*, eds. James Gilbert, Amy Gilman, Donald M. Scott, and Joan W. Scott (Wadsworth, CA: Belmont, 1993).

25. In 1904, the city of King, CA (Monterey County) filed a lawsuit against CPC for a local representative. McConnell and CPC won its right to solicit for sales. On the 1922 Green River Ordinance, see Biggart, *Charismatic Capitalism*, 32. On Fuller Brush approach techniques, see Fuller, *A Foot in the Door*, 55. Informal complaints were lodged against recruiters, however, not against the representatives who did the actual selling. In this regard, McConnell's

tactics worked. On community resistance to direct-sales agents, see Biggart, chap. 2. Local merchants and Chambers of Commerce sponsored legislation that required distributors to purchase business licenses. The Agent's Credit Association, formed in 1910 by ten firms, including the California Perfume Company, and later known as the National Association of Direct Selling Companies with 91 members—both distributors and suppliers in 1925—fought these laws. "In 1927 the NADSC general counsel opposed 164 state and local ordinances and reported 'killing 111 of these bills.'" (Biggart, 32, 183 27) See also *Report and Minutes of the 1927 Annual Convention* (Winona, MN: NADSC, 1927) 4.

26. From "Instructions for General Agents" (1915) "Information" 4, CPC.

27. McConnell's Scrapbook, New York "California Perfume Company" May 1, 1899, Series 3, Box 114.

28. "45 Years of Steady Growth," *Avon Outlook* (February 1931): 2.

29. "Tenure-rate analysis of 12,370 contracts on file in the New York office on December 31, 1928" (Series 3, Box 113, Representatives/Sales Statistics, 1902–1928). The New York sales office did not include Pennsylvania, which had its own office. Tenure rates varied from year to year: another recruiting report shows that the New York office appointed 10,816 women as representatives in 1927, of which (according to the 1928 statistics) only 1,542 (14 percent) were still working at the end of 1928. (Series 3, Box 113).

30. "Total Annual Business of 12,370 contracts on file in the New York office on December 31, 1928" (Series 3, Box 113).

31. In Ohio, for example, of the fifty-one representatives who earned prizes in 1922 for submitting orders of $30 or more, only three were "new." Overall, Eastern Division representatives earned 186 prizes (twenty nine by beginners); Western Division representatives earned 159 prizes (fifteen by beginners); and the Southern Division representatives earned 143 prizes (ten by beginners). Company analysts later found a strong correlation between length of tenure and annual business. According to sales data from the postwar era, representatives who had worked for more than one year submitted substantially larger individual orders and accumulated higher levels of annual business than representatives on contract for less than one year. In the post–World War II era, Avon's managers recognized the significance of this and improved training and motivation techniques in order to help new recruits earn greater sales, but more important, improved incentive plans and motivation that spoke to the needs of the "older" representatives with two or more years of experience who generated the bulk of sales.

32. *Handbook for District Supervisors*, "Working Large Cities," (California Perfume Company, 1924): 45.

33. *Ibid*. Italics in original.

34. *Ibid.*, 15. Italics in original.

35. October 1965 interview with Wayne Hicklin, President of Avon Products.

36. Schedule of City Sales Offices, opened during the period December 15, 1935 to February 10, 1941" (Series 5, Box 122, Sales System/Field Organization/City Sales, 1935–1941). CPC organized sales offices in Boston and Philadelphia in 1938 but waited until after 1940 to organize most of the northeast corridor. It did not even attempt to organize New York City until the 1950s.

37. In 1938, the earliest year for which city sales statistics are available, Avon had organized 4,038 representatives (of 30,000 active representatives) in fifty-four city sales offices nationwide. City sales representatives generated nearly $800,000 in sales. (Series 7, Box 124). Operating costs for city offices totaled nearly $140,000, or 17.5 percent of sales, the highest margin in company history. See "City Sales Total Busines and Cost" in "Aveon Round Table: Check of Facts and Figures" management conference, 1943, 30.

38. See Biggart, 32.

39. On managing representatives with the Kardex system, see Katina Manko, "Ding Dong! Avon Calling!: Gender and Business of Door-to-Door Selling, 1886–1962" Chapter 1 "'Now You Are In Business For Yourself'" dissertation in progress, Department of History, University of Delaware. On Kardex system, see Joanne Yates, *Control Through Communication: The Rise of System in American Management* (Baltimore: Johns Hopkins, 1989), ch. 2.

40. Hicklin interview transcript, 6.

41. Eastman interview, 1972, 38–39.

42. Eastman interview, 1972, 38–39.

43. Hicklin interview transcript, 5.

44. "Our Daily Chats," July 25, 1932, bound volume.

45. *Avon Outlook*, August 1 to August 23, 1932.

46. Hicklin interview transcript, 5.

47. On the employee relationship and the failed salary plan, see Hicklin interview transcript, 1964, quotes from 1–2.

48. See Hicklin interview transcript, 1964, 6.
49. On Fuller Brush's expectations for their salesmen, see "The Fuller Recruiter's and Trainer's Manual" (Hartford: Fuller Brush Company, 1928) and "Making Good, and Making Money" recruiting pamphlet (Hartford: Fuller Brush Company, 1937) copies in author's possession, courtesy of the Fuller Brush Company. See also Friedman, Walter A., "The Peddler's Progress: Salesmanship, Science, and Magic, 1880 to 1940 (Direct Marketing, John H. Patterson, Henry B. Hyde, Alfred Fuller)," unpublished PhD dissertation, Columbia University, 1996. Biggart places Beveridge's start in 1932: *Charismatic Capitalism*, 33.
50. Nicole Biggart's *Charismatic Capitalism* studies emotional control and motivation through the lens of sociology and Weberian theory. Her study analyzes multilevel marketing companies, including A.L. Williams Life Insurance, Amway, and Mary Kay, from about 1970 to 1980. She argues that direct-selling organizations fundamentally differ from firms in both their social relations and managerial strategy. Direct-selling businesses, in response to their use of independent contractors to distribute products, rely on alternative, emotional management devices that bind individuals morally and emotionally to the institution. As a result, direct-selling companies do not necessarily follow rational decision-making but, Biggart argues, an alternative, emotional logic can in certain circumstances be more economically advantageous than strict rational, dispassionate judgments. Direct-sales managers create an alternative form of enterprise in order to better control their distributors. (See Biggart, 1–19.)
51. In 1940, Avon asked local city sales office managers to survey women who had discontinued their Avon contracts. Whereas less than 1 percent cited their husband's objection to their working, fully one-third said they had lost interest or "didn't like" the work. (Series 7, Box 124, Conferences/Reports).
52. The classic analyses of the self-made man literature include: Irvin G. Wyllie, *The Self-Made Man in America: The Myth of Rags to Riches* (New Brunswick: Rutgers University Press, 1954); John G. Cawelti, *Apostles of the Self-Made Man* (Chicago: University of Chicago Press, 1965); and Richard Weiss, *The American Myth of Success: From Horatio Alger to Norman Vincent Peale* (New York: Basic Books, 1969).
53. "Our President Writes a Stirring Appeal on Helping Unemployment Through Capitalizing the CPC Opportunity" *Avon Outlook* (May 1931): 3.
54. See Marchand, *Creating the Corporate Soul* (Berkeley, CA: University of California Press, 1998).
55. "No Finer Tribute Could Be Paid Mr. McConnell, Our President," Representative letters on his seventy-sixth birthday, 1934.
56. *Ibid.*
57. "Success Is Not an Accident," *Avon Outlook* (August 1931): 2.
58. "Will You Help Bring Back Prosperity," *Avon Outlook* (January 1931): 6.
59. "45 Years of Steady Growth," *Avon Outlook* (February 1931): 2.
60. "Success Is Not an Accident," *Avon Outlook* (August 1931): 2.
61. "Our Work Is the Test of Our Value" *Avon Outlook* (September 1931): 2.
62. See Biggart, 40–41.
63. CPC did not inform representatives of their new status. According to Biggart, federal attempts to challenge the "status laws" were modest during the 1940s. Not until 1968 did the IRS begin vigorously to challenge the law and propose to have distributors declared employees. It lost its bid, however, and the Tax Equity and Fiscal Responsibility Act of 1982 defined distributors as independent contractors for federal tax purposes. Many direct-sales companies use the "status laws" in their recruiting, pointing out that contractors can qualify for tax-deductible business expenses. (See *Charismatic Capitalism*, 185 n49.)
64. Peiss, *Hope in a Jar*, 97–134.

"I Had My Own Business . . . So I Didn't Have to Worry"

BEAUTY SALONS, BEAUTY CULTURISTS, AND THE POLITICS OF AFRICAN-AMERICAN FEMALE ENTREPRENEURSHIP

TIFFANY MELISSA GILL

*I*n 1939, after interviewing various beauty operators and clients in Harlem for the Works Progress Administration (WPA), Vivian Morris boldly proclaimed at the end of her analysis: "INTERESTING PLACES—THESE BEAUTY SHOPS."[1] Unfortunately, sixty years later, very little scholarship has merged business history with the ever-expanding field of African-American women's history. In either literature, the existence of these uniquely autonomous black female worlds of beauty shops within black communities goes practically unnoticed. To that end, this essay seeks to fill a historiographic void by exploring the formation and evolution of a thriving industry based on black female beauty, specifically hair care, created primarily by black women and controlled by black female entrepreneurs for most of the twentieth century. By examining the work of beauty culturists in what has been called the "golden age of black business" (1900 to 1930) as well as the more politically based entrepreneurship of those I call "beauty activists" (1930 to 1960), this essay will demonstrate the role the hair care industry played in the development and redefinition of beauty culture, entrepreneurship, and social action in the lives of African-American women.[2]

BEAUTY CULTURISTS IN THE "GOLDEN AGE OF BLACK BUSINESS"

The creation of the National Negro Business League (NNBL) by Booker T. Washington in many ways marked the genesis of the "golden age of black business." During his travels throughout the country in the late nineteenth century, Washington explained that he was "continually coming in contact" with a great number of "successful business men and women of the Negro race." This observation led him to "believe that

the time had come for bringing together the leading and most successful colored men and women in the country who were engaged in business." These men and women, who met in Boston, Massachusetts, in
August 1900, represented one of the earliest gatherings of black business people and ushered in changes that impacted not only this small
yet burgeoning business community, but black America in general.[3]

Prior to the Civil War, both enslaved and free black men and
women owned a few small business ventures. Juliet E. K. Walker
explains that African-American slaves operated as both "intrepre-
neurs," those who had some authority in managing their owner's business affairs, and entrepreneurs, those who hired out their services and
established enterprises that they owned outright.[4] She further argues
that free blacks formed what should be considered capitalist enterprises in a multitude of venues. Based on the mutual aid and benevolent associations of free blacks in the seventeenth and eighteenth
centuries, nineteenth-century antebellum free blacks entered business
as jewelers, merchants, steamboat owners, restaurateurs, grocers, real
estate speculators, barbers, and hairdressers.[5]

From the onset of freedom until the turn of the century, most
blacks engaged in entrepreneurship that was an extension of the activities of blacks in slavery—ventures based on performing tasks that
whites did not wish to do.[6] According to St. Clair Drake and Horace
Cayton in their seminal study of Chicago, these "colored businessmen
did not serve an exclusively Negro market [but] served a white clientele."[7] However, as the nineteenth century drew to a close with the
early stages of what would eventually become the Great Migration to
northern and urban areas, the number of black businesses increased,
coupled with a simultaneous decline in the number of whites as clients
and customers.[8] Booker T. Washington's NNBL was born in this
moment of transition.

Washington was not the only black leader who desired to unite and
organize the black business community. W. E. B. DuBois, often
depicted as Washington's rival in all matters pertaining to black leadership and civil rights, called for black men to engage in business.[9] As
director of the Fourth Atlanta Conference in 1899, entitled "The Negro
in Business," DuBois proclaimed the need for blacks to create an economic infrastructure, and called for an "organization in every town and
hamlet where colored people dwell, of Negro Business Men's Leagues"
and the eventual creation of "state and national organizations."[10]
Ironically, just two years later, it was Washington who brought this
dream to fruition when he formed the NNBL.

Despite the fact that leaders like Du Bois and Washington generally
described business as an honorable pursuit for the men of the race,
black women in general, and beauty culturists in particular, were at

the forefront not only of the NNBL, but of the black business community at large.[11] According to the minutes of the NNBL's first meeting, the business success of the race was made synonymous with restoring the manhood of the race. Gilbert C. Harris delivered a speech entitled "Work in Hair," and admitted that he had "to do some business to be a man and be recognized among men," even if that meant entering into a profession that would eventually become female-dominated.[12] Equating manhood and business pervaded the first meeting; only one woman was even allowed to address the convention. While most of the male orators spoke directly about the business enterprises they were involved in, the only female speaker, Mrs. Alberta Moore-Smith, theorized concerning "Women's Development in Business" in a monologue very much in line with the views of the men in attendance:

> To the minds of many there is a new woman but in actuality she does not exist. Theories have been put forth to show that she is new, but the only satisfactory evidence or conclusion agreed upon is that she is simply progressing; her natural tendencies having not changed one iota . . . on the contrary, with all the knowledge gained from free and unconventional education she takes her place in society as a faithful friend, in the business world as a judicious counselor, and in the home as a loving wife and queen.[13]

Mrs. Moore-Smith's comments did little to challenge the placement of men at the center of the black business community. While she made no direct reference to restoring black manhood through involvement in business, she clearly did not see the black woman as upsetting black male leadership in business but as "taking her place" in a supportive role.

Just one year later at the Chicago convention, Alberta Moore-Smith gave a more demanding, albeit strangely titled speech, "Negro Women's Business Clubs: A Factor in the Solution of the Vexed Problem," where she tempered a pride in women's accomplishments with a sense of racial duty and declared:

> Negro women's business clubs do not desire to be known only by their names, but by their good works and the influence they exert in encouraging our women in opening establishments of their own, no matter how small the start may be. This is one of their main objectives, and no power on earth is strong enough to deter them from their purpose, for they are well on the high-road to success. They will also inevitably enlarge the education of women and assist them in the formation of opinions concerning the mooted questions of the day in which men are deeply interested.[14]

Perhaps Moore-Smith was more assertive on behalf of her gender at this convention because she was no longer the lone female voice. She was joined by Mrs. E. Lewis of Chicago, who spoke on "Hair Dressing," and Mrs. Dora A. Miller of Brooklyn, who discussed the organizing activities and accomplishments of "Some Eastern Business Women." In fact, Miller's comments on the role of black women in business went even further than Moore-Smith's. "In the East as in other sections of the country, Negro women," Miller proclaimed, "are taking a firm grasp of business principles and in the struggle for capital are proving themselves the equal of men." Further demonstrating her point, Miller gave a list of successful businesswomen in New York City who were instrumental in organizing the Colored Women's Business Club of New York in 1900. [15]

Still, women's roles in the early years of the convention, for the most part, were limited to speeches where women attempted to justify their place in a male-dominated business community—that is, until 1912. At this particular convention, held in Chicago, Madam C. J. Walker demanded time to speak on the lack of respect given to beauty culturists in particular and independent black female entrepreneurs in general, and in the process changed the NNBL's opinion of black female entrepreneurs. By 1912, Madam Walker (formerly Sara Breedlove) had already amassed a small fortune manufacturing beauty products and teaching her hair-care system. While Walker did not invent the straightening comb, as legend would suggest, she was by 1912 prominent in the black beauty industry, with her incorporated company grossing over $100,000 a year.[16] The first member of her family born free, Walker worked her way out of the Louisiana cotton fields, migrated north, and toiled as a washerwoman as late as 1905. With $1.50, a young child, and a divine revelation, Walker began her hair-care empire. After two unsuccessful marriages—one that failed in part because of her former husband's desire to control her business—Madam C. J. eventually emerged in total control of the Walker Company.

Correspondence between Booker T. Washington and Madam Walker demonstrates that they clashed often—usually over whether or not Walker's beauty methods should be placed in the Tuskeegee Institute's curriculum and whether she could sell her hair products on the school's grounds. Washington usually objected on the grounds that beauty culture was not a worthwhile profession for his female students to pursue. [17] However, their most public clash occurred at the 1912 NNBL convention, when Walker was snubbed by Washington and not given an opportunity to speak. This was even more of an affront since a male beauty manufacturer, Anthony Overton, founder of the Overton Hygenic Manufacturing Company of Chicago—a company that sold, among other goods, cosmetics (Overton's High Brown Face Powder) and hair-care products (High Brown Shampoo Soap and Pressing Oil)—received the utmost respect.[18]

When George Knox, publisher of the Indianapolis newspaper *The Freeman,* asked the "convention for a few minutes of its time to hear a remarkable woman. She is Madam Walker, the manufacturer of hair goods and preparations," Washington ignored Knox, and instead recognized a male Texas banker as speaker. After the banker's long lecture and Washington's favorable response, Walker rose to her feet and began an impromptu passionate speech that described her rise from a washerwoman to an established businesswoman. She also questioned the lack of respect given to those in the beauty business—particularly the female entrepreneurs. "I have made it possible," Walker proudly announced when she finally reached the podium, "for many colored women to abandon the washtub for a more pleasant and profitable occupation." She went on to add: "the girls and women of our race must not be afraid to take hold of business endeavors and . . . wring success out of a number of business opportunities that lie at their very doors." [19]

So many of the conference participants were moved by Walker's speech—including Washington himself—that at the convention one year later, Washington took pleasure in introducing Walker as "one of the most progressive and successful businesswomen of our race." Walker then gave another inspirational speech on the personal entrepreneurial progress and that of the race, after which Washington added, "You [Walker] talk about what the men are doing in a business way. Why, if we don't watch out, the women will excel us!" [20] In fact, by 1915, Walker's female-dominated profession was so respected that the NNBL chose the "Beauty Parlor Business" as a major theme of its Sixteenth Annual Convention. Madam C. J. Walker's involvement demonstrates that black female entrepreneurs were at the forefront of the creation and evolution of the NNBL and that they understood that economic issues were important to the uplift of the race. [21]

Studying black female beauty entrepreneurs in the golden age of black business not only compels a revision of black women's roles in the early formation of the black business community, but also a reconsideration of the very nature of black female organizing. Specifically, it demonstrates that ignoring the economic components of racial uplift greatly obscures much of what black women thought was important in the late nineteenth and early twentieth centuries. While a plethora of books and articles have focused on the black female club movement and the racial uplift programs they were involved in, few scholars have attempted to understand their economic- or business-driven activism. [22] In fact, many beauty culturists were clubwomen actively involved in social reform. Tullia Brown Hamilton's dissertation provides biographical profiles of 108 women who were leaders in the National Association of Colored Women (NACW) from 1896 to 1920. Of the women profiled, 73 percent worked outside the home. Of these who worked outside the home, five women, Ezella Mathis Carter, Patricia Garland, Annie Turnbo Malone Pope, Maude Reynolds, and Madam C. J. Walker—were involved in the hair-care industry at some point in their lives. Examining the life of one of these women who was both an active clubwoman and a beautician will illustrate how her occupation as a beauty culturist and her activism complemented and even reinforced one another.

Ezella Mathis Carter was both the consummate clubwoman and an entrepreneur. Her life provides insight into how these seemingly incongruous worlds of business and social reform intersected one another. Her 1935 biography, written by Kathryn Johnson (who actually accompanied her on her journeys), sheds light on this historically obscure yet accomplished woman. While Johnson was more concerned with illuminating Carter's heroics than with providing the details that historians crave, the reader does manage to learn some aspects of Madam Carter's life. For example, Ezella Mathis was born in Girard, Alabama, and her family moved to Atlanta when she was one month old. Later in life, Carter earned money by teaching and eventually attended Spelman Seminary, where she specialized in "Teachers' Professional and Missionary Training Courses."[23] She graduated from Spelman in 1907 and subsequently went on to teach at Kowaliga Academic Institute, a school several miles from Booker T. Washington's Tuskegee Institute.

Mathis's marriage in September 1909 to Mr. Carter (Johnson does not give any more information concerning her husband) "naturally changed her career." Shortly thereafter, she migrated to Chicago and studied to become a beauty culturist at the Enterprise Institute. Upon graduating, Carter received a certificate conferring the title of Madam, and opened up her own beauty shop where she taught the "art of hairdressing." Like the famous Madam C. J. Walker, Carter "experimented with various oils for the hair, and was finally successful in compounding her own hair preparations," which her biographer mentions were still in demand at the time the book was published in 1935.

Madam Carter merged the entrepreneurial with the philanthropic, a custom that beauty operators would adhere to throughout the twentieth century. Carter engaged in a door-to-door sales approach, entering black women's homes and teaching them how to care for their hair. She consciously sought out not only well-to-do women with disposable incomes, but poor ones as well:

> With her hair preparations, Mme. Carter began traveling and introducing them to the public and placing them on the market. She went back to her native Southland and into the far reaches of the rural sections, where she

introduced her oils and taught the native backwoods woman, as well as the city woman, how to cultivate her hair, keep the scalp clean and healthful, and make the hair, which had been made harsh and brittle by exposure to the hot scorching, southern sun, soft and straight enough to be handled with ease.[24]

Hair care and straightening were not linked to attaining whiteness but to cultivating healthy hair that had been damaged by the sun—an approach that would have resonated with women who spent a great deal of time outdoors doing harsh agricultural work. Madam Carter did more than sell products; she understood what she was doing as racial uplift work. Biographer Kathryn Johnson explains:

> She would go into the cabins, which probably had no more than two or three rooms; there she would heat water on the open fireplace, and with what conveniences she could find, shampoo the hair; then with infinite patience, apply the pressing oil; the straightening comb and the presser, and at the end of an hour and half or perhaps, two hours, she would be talking to the woman, giving her a lesson on how to improve her condition and her neighborhood.[25]

Madam Carter seized the opportunity offered by entering black women's homes under the nonthreatening guise of selling beauty products, and used it to do race work. However, this aspect of racial uplift has not been addressed in the many books on the black woman's club movement.

The strategy used by Madam Carter, namely, meeting the needs of and administering to the poor within their homes, was a staple strategy of clubwomen in the early decades of the twentieth century. As a part of what they termed the "good" homes project, clubwomen targeted poor black women in their homes. Mary Church Terrell, the first president of the NACW, explained in a 1902 essay that it was only through the home: "that a people can become really good and great. More homes, better homes, purer homes is the text upon which sermons have and will be preached."[26] Other clubwomen echoed the importance of the black household. "The Negro home," Josephine Bruce said, "is rapidly assuming the position designated for it. It is distinctly becoming the center of social and intellectual life; it is building up strength and righteousness in its sons and daughters, and equipping them for the inevitable battles of life which grow out of the struggle for existence."[27] Paula Giddings accurately sums up what the home represented to black female reformers: "for these black women, the home was not so much a refuge from the outside world as a bulwark to secure one's passage through it."[28]

Madam Carter clearly understood that the home was not only the site in which she could advance herself entrepreneurially but a place where she could act as a social reformer and establish herself as a true race woman. The NACW took notice of her abilities and named her the chair of the organization's Business Section.[29] In addition, she also sponsored clubs on the local level. After training other women in the beauty trade and in their role as racial uplifters, Madam Carter gathered her sales agents into "Life Boat clubs," appropriately named since the clubs "were designed to save the people in the sections where [the agent] traveled."[30] These clubs were educational, industrial, and benevolent in nature. They collected dues, distributed money to those who were ill, and in the event of death, provided funeral expenses. These Life Boat clubs were eventually incorporated under the laws of the State of Illinois and even became affiliated as an associate member of the National Council of Negro Women (NCNW). In 1927, the club expanded its mission and established a center for rural girls.

Carter's death in 1934 did not go unnoticed, as she was fondly remembered by Florence Read, President of Spelman College, and R. R. Moton, President of Tuskeegee Institute, and eulogized by Gwendolyn Brooks in a poem entitled "A Chicago High School Girl."[31] Still, despite all of Madam Carter's accomplishments she has fallen into historical obscurity, and when she is remembered at all, it is for her work as a clubwoman and not for her entrepreneurial savvy. Carter is such a historical enigma, perhaps, because she did not fit neatly into categories. She was at once the consummate twentieth-century clubwoman, claiming moral and intellectual superiority over the women she wished to help, a role that an elite black woman was expected to fulfill. Yet she was also an astute businesswoman who studied Business Management at the LaSalle Extension University and traveled extensively teaching sales agents her system. More important, she exploited an underserved consumer—the rural black woman. These two ventures, beauty work and race work, while intelligently synergized by Carter, had a very complicated relationship in the early twentieth century. Although many clubwomen supported black women as entrepreneurs, some found the beauty business problematic and harmful to black women. In other words, beauty culturists not only had to establish themselves within a male-dominated black business community that was often less than welcoming, but also had to try and gain acceptance from many black elite clubwomen who felt threatened by their success.

Nannie Helen Burroughs, a clubwoman who founded the National Training School for Girls and Women to prepare and professionalize domestic workers, boldly and repeatedly expressed her disdain for the beauty industry as a whole, and asked: "What does this wholesale bleaching of the face and straightening of hair indicate? From our viewpoint, it simply means that the women who practice it wish that they had white faces and straight hair."[32] However, most of the successful and established black female beauty manufacturers, such as Madam C. J. Walker and Annie Turnbo Malone, refused to sell skin-bleaching products and insisted that their hair systems were more about hair care, good grooming, and enhancing the beauty of black women, rather than hair-straightening and emulating white women. In fact, Noliwe Rooks explains that: "Walker did not argue that there was nothing wrong with African American women straightening their hair; she flat out denied that hair straightening was what she had to offer."[33] In an examination of the advertisements of black-owned beauty manufacturers, Rooks finds that hairdressing was linked to racial uplift and an improvement in status. Black female beauty entrepreneurs, through their advertisements, emphasized cultivating, as opposed to creating, the beauty of black women that had been hidden due to poor health and historical and social denigration. For example, Rooks argues that white manufacturers of beauty products in the antebellum period were "driven primarily by popular ideas about race" that presented black women as "'suffering' from an African heritage and searching for the 'cure' that whiteness can offer."[34] On the other hand, in the advertisements of African-American entrepreneurs, women were urged to strive for healthy hair. One advertisement declared that a particular treatment would: "cultivate, beautify and grow a person's hair, so long as there is no physical ailment which will prevent it."[35] These black female manufacturers understood beauty work to be as much race work as the social programs of Nannie Helen Burroughs, Mary Church Terrell, and the other women of the NACW— even if it was not always regarded that way.

Although many beauty culturists joined the NACW, they understood that the manner in which they approached racial uplift set them apart from many clubwomen. To that end, beauty culturists organized on their behalf. Among the most influential organizations were those formed by Madam Walker, namely the Madam C. J. Walker Hair Culturists Union of America, founded in Philadelphia in 1917, and the National Negro Cosmetic Manufacturers Association, also founded in 1917. Darlene Clark Hine says of Walker's Hair Culturists Union:

> The national conventions honored and granted cash prizes to the clubs and
> individuals that had the largest number of agents, the greatest sales volume,
> and the most outstanding record of benevolent work. The conventions
> cemented a sense of community, promoted professionalism, and enabled
> black women to engage in political discussions even though they could not
> yet vote. The politicization of black beauty culturists was quickly
> manifested.[36]

These organizations also had very practical functions pertaining specifically to the beauty industry. The charter of the National Negro Cosmetic Manufacturers Association stated that its founder members had formed the association in order to better protect themselves against the "dishonest and illegitimate" manufacturers of hair goods and to "promote the spirit of business reciprocity among ourselves, to encourage the development of Race enterprises and acquaint the public with the superior claims of high class goods. . . ."[37] Similarly, in 1919 a group of beauticians formed the National Beauty Culturists League (NBCL), which soon was the first predominately female organization to become a part of the NNBL in 1921 and the largest organization in the black beauty industry. The organizers saw a need for beauticians to "encourage constant improvements as good citizens by participating in civic and community work, [to] seek legislation beneficial to the beauty profession" and "to promote the general welfare and raise the public image of those engaged in the beauty culture field."[38]

For the NBCL, raising the public image of beauty culturists was paramount. Even though most beauty culturists did not become as wealthy as Madam Walker, professionally they considered their status to be among the best women of the race. In many ways, the beauty industry compromised the position of elite blacks whose uplift ideology and belief in the rule of the Talented Tenth became increasingly irrelevant to the lives of many blacks as the century progressed. By the late 1920s, black female organizations like the NACW faced a decline in popularity and in power.[39] However, the female presence in the beauty industry and the organizational power they created lasted much longer and had a much wider appeal than any of the "woman's era" clubs. Indeed, as elite blacks began losing their prominence in the black community and were unable to hold rank based on color, education, and the financial security that such advantages afforded them, the hair-care industry and, to a large extent, beauty parlors became sites where tensions over class, color, and status were exacerbated. Although Madam C.J. Walker died in 1919, the fact that a dark-skinned, uneducated former laundress could not only make a fortune in this industry but in the process empower thousands of other women to believe that they could be considered the best women of the race posed a threat to elite black women.

Alice Dunbar-Nelson, poet and clubwoman, publicly and privately voiced her discomfort with the opportunities and attitudes of black beauty culturists. Kevin Gaines's examination of Dunbar-Nelson's life, as well as her posthumously published diary and writings, further illuminates the contradictory life of a woman who was quite conscious of issues of color, status, and class. In a 1928 *Washington Eagle* article, Dunbar-Nelson complained that: "women [working] in beauty parlors drag their social ambitions into their commercial life. A woman or girl from a class which they feel is superior socially to their own gets short shrift, poor service, and insulting discrimination."[40]

Gaines notes that women were more vulnerable to distinctions made over issues of class and color, and makes a fascinating assessment of Dunbar-Nelson's encounter in the beauty salons, arguing that "the beauty parlor . . . is revealed here as a site of class conflict among black women."[41] The perceived disrespect by beauty operators was such a problem for Alice Dunbar-Nelson that three years later, this self-proclaimed race woman stopped patronizing black-owned salons altogether. She recounted in her diary:

> I had made engagement to have waved at a beauty parlor at Ninth and King [Wilmington, Delaware]. Didn't know whether I'd "get by" [not be challenged because of race], but evidentially did. Nice wave. Nice place. Nice girls. Beauty problem solved.[42]

In other words, the beauty salon provided a space where black women of different classes and hues congregated and often conflicted. Relationships between and among customers, as well as those between beautician and client, could foster a sense of community or exacerbate existing tensions.

Harlem in the first three decades of the century was at the center of the most volatile issues confronting the black community—namely, class and gender conflict and ideas about politics and leadership. This stretch of blocks in New York City also housed many black beauty salons, and "among the persons of wealth and social influence in Harlem were the community's great beauticians."[43] In 1911, a black woman named Madam J. L. Crawford, originally from Virginia and educated at the New York School of Chiropody and Dermatology, opened one of Harlem's first beauty shops. Despite her training in the medical field, Crawford decided that the business world offered her the greatest possibilities. Starting in 1901, Crawford worked as an "itinerant hairdresser" in the Mt. Vernon section of New York for a white and black clientele. There, she also began manufacturing cosmetics, hair pomades, wigs, and toupees. By 1908, Madam Crawford owned and operated a beauty shop at 341 West 59th Street in Midtown Manhattan that exclusively served black customers. According to a report on "Negro Beauty Parlors in New York" compiled by the WPA in 1936, Crawford's combination dry goods store and beauty parlor "was the first Negro establishment of its kind in New York City."[44]

Few in those early years would have predicted the success achieved by Crawford and the other black female beauticians who would follow in her footsteps. Harlem, in fact, became such a thriving place for the black beauty industry that Madam C.J. Walker decided to settle there in 1914. Already a woman of considerable wealth by this time, Walker, along with her daughter A'Leila, who would become one of the leading figures in the social life of blacks during the Harlem Renaissance, established not only a beauty parlor in Harlem, but also Leila College, the Walker Company's beauty school.[45]

One of the first graduates of Leila College was Lucille Green. Described as a light woman of medium height and build with a head of short cropped hair, Green was born Lucille Campbell in Christianburg, Virginia in 1883. She attended Howard University, where she studied to become a schoolteacher and met and married Joseph Green, who died shortly after the couple moved to New York City. Lucille Green gave up schoolteaching upon the death of her husband and enrolled in Leila Beauty College. After graduating, Green "not only started her own salon on 135th Street, but also became a close friend of Madam Walker and a member of the 'society' that grew up around her in Harlem."[46] It was during her trips back and forth to her hair salon on 135th Street and Lenox Avenue (which just happened to be down the corridor from Ernest Welcome, who in 1914 was the head of the Brotherhood of Labor), that Ms. Green caught the attention of twenty-five-year-old Asa Philip Randolph. Randolph's biographer Jervis Anderson describes their subsequent courtship as "brief and unspec-tacular," stating that Philip took Lucille to stage shows, movies, and of course political lectures. Anderson also explains that Mr. Randolph was not very fond of parties or dances, and that when Lucille invited him to Madam Walker's soirees, he declined and said that he did not have time to waste on "fly-by-night people."[47]

However, even if A. Philip Randolph did not claim to be impressed with Madam Walker's parties and her cohort of "successful speculators of recent vintage, community clubwomen, new urban professionals, and other parvenu varieties," he certainly learned to respect the lucra-tiveness of the hair-care industry.[48] In fact, it was the marriage of the "socialist and the socialite" in 1914 that made A. Philip Randolph's career and political activism possible. The new Mrs. Randolph joined the socialist party shortly after the marriage, and as a couple they com-mitted themselves to political activism.

"I had a good wife. She carried us," A. Philip Randolph says of Lucille's financial backing of his socialist newspaper *The Messenger.* Lucille Randolph distributed the paper from her salon and periodically used her earnings to pay its debts. In 1919, the Justice Department described *The Messenger* as "by long odds the most dangerous of all the Negro publications," and when eulogizing Mrs. Randolph, a columnist for the *New York Post* later wrote:

> Lucille Greene Randolph seems entitled to the honor of being called the one
> time second most dangerous Negro in America. The title would certainly
> have once been official if the agents of the U.S. Justice Department had had

the initiative and wit to intercept her postal money orders which helped support A.Philip Randolph's subversive activities.[49]

When A. Philip Randolph was asked to organize the Brotherhood of Sleeping Car Porters (BSCP) in 1925, he discussed the job with Lucille, who enthusiastically supported his decision to assist the then-fledgling union. Her financial support became even more crucial while her husband held this post, since Philip did not receive a regular salary from the organization until 1936.[50] She also persuaded her friend and colleague, A'Leila Walker (heir to the hair-care empire), to donate money to the BSCP, as well as organized other Walker salon operators to contribute money and prizes for the beauty contests that the Brotherhood held.

Mrs. Randolph's support of her husband was not only financial but social as well. Through her contacts, he met wealthy African Americans and prominent left-wing whites who added prestige to his political pursuits. She was also the one to introduce Philip to Chandler Owen—the person with whom he partnered at the Brotherhood.[51] Clearly Lucille's relationship to her husband is an important area to study, but her accomplishment as a hairdresser and salon owner in Harlem should be explored in its own right. Jervis Anderson explains:

> Lucille became one of the more accomplished and sought after of the Walker students. Her customers ranged from the black elite in Harlem to well-to-do crinkly haired whites from "downtown." And one day a week she traveled out to the fashionable Marlborough Blenheim Hotel in Atlantic City, to serve a similar white clientele. Her prices seem to have been high, and brought her a considerable income.[52]

However, Anderson argues that as Philip's reputation as a "wild-eyed radical" spread, Lucille's business declined, and by the 1930s she was no longer successful. On the other hand, in her dissertation on beauty culture, Gwendolyn Keita Robinson argues that: "nationalism, radicalism, and high classed life styles were often fused in those days. . . . Lucille, though a socialite, ran for the New York City Board of Alderman on the Socialist Party ticket in the 1930s, while at the same time, maintaining her beauty salon, without suffering any apparent pangs of contradiction."[53]

In fact, Lucille Randolph's business problems in the 1930s probably derived less from her husband's reputation and more from the fact that the beauty industry, like most businesses, suffered during the Great Depression; in other words, the Depression brought the golden age of black business to an end.[54] Labor historian Jacqueline Jones argues that during the Depression a personal beauty regimen had become too expensive for many black working women and that beauty operators were forced to lower their prices and even barter their services for food and clothing.[55] A study of employment conditions of black- and white-owned beauty shops in four cities published by the U.S. Department of Labor in 1935 determined that:

> Wage reductions and lessened work opportunities in the last few years, resulting in curtailed purchasing power of the Negro Worker, have had a marked effect in reducing the number and activities of Negro shops. Hair pressing, previously indulged by many Negroes, especially by domestic workers, had by 1934 become a luxury to large numbers, even though prices in many shops had been materially reduced.[56]

In 1938, the periodical *Opportunity* published a piece by Le Roy Jeffries, entitled "The Decay of the Beauty Parlor Industry in Harlem," where he described a dismal picture for black female beauticians. Jeffries explained that from February to June 1936 he made an "intensive survey of the conditions of beauty parlors in the Harlem area." Based on these findings, he felt qualified to declare that: "the road to fortune which was once open to beauty culture workers in the Harlem area has definitely curved into a dead end."[57] He further noted that the New York State Department of Labor recently became interested in the plight of the black female beautician, and demonstrated that not only were most of the beauty operators in Harlem unlicensed but they also were not benefiting from the legislative enactments that came as a result of the New Deal:

> They are without workman's compensation, therefore may not be compensated for accidents incurred during the course of their employment; they are without the protective covering of unemployment insurance designed to offer some income for periods of unemployment; they will not be included among those who are guaranteed a minimum wage.[58]

Despite the reality Jeffries described, there remained a great deal of optimism surrounding the black beauty industry, primarily because beauty operators fared better financially than their sisters employed as agricultural workers and domestics, whose already dubious financial stability the Depression worsened.[59] For example, Sara Spencer Washington, founder of the Apex Beauty System, urged black women to enroll in her beauty school and "plan for [their] future by learning a depression-proof business."[60] Similarly, the inability of black women to pay for hair-care services did not mean that beauty parlors lost their presence as a gathering place for black women. Elizabeth Cardozo Barker, the founder of the extremely successful Cardozo Sisters Beauty Shop in Washington, D.C., recalled that during the Great Depression, in the establishment where she first learned hair work, customers would come and sit in the beauty parlor "for hours, sometimes. They'd play cards; sometimes they'd gossip . . . they just came expecting to sit."[61] In addition, the beauty industry, with its practice of door-to-door sales, hairstyling in one's home, and even styling in a salon became an integral part of black women's development of a leisure culture that was in many ways dependent upon traditional modes of black female gathering.

Historian Kathy Peiss describes these shifts in the black beauty industry and adds that during the Depression there was also a noticeable change in the marketing strategies of beauty manufacturers, as well as in the political nature of their beauty work. Before the 1930s in the periodicals produced by black hair-care companies: "beauty columns ran alongside stories on politics and notable African Americans; by the mid-thirties, these had disappeared, replaced by articles on romance, marriage, and the psychological effects of beautifying." Advertisements also began centering black women's identity on achieving beauty to attract men as opposed to enhancing beauty for self-worth.[62]

In other words, Peiss argues that the "commercial images" portrayed by the beauty business during this period were much more depoliticized than previously, even though she acknowledges that beauty salons as sites involved themselves in civic matters and "endured as vibrant sources of economic, social and even political strength in black communities."[63] Her elucidation of this shift is compelling; however, in addition to illuminating the way the manufacturing and commercial components of the beauty industry moved away from politics, I posit that it is important to examine the significance of beauty parlors as "political outposts" and hair-care workers as beauty activists.[64] In the post-Depression era, black beauticians were once again at the forefront of expanding the very nature of business and the role of an entrepreneur. The beauty activists who came of age in this era inherited the political and philanthropic traditions of Madams Walker and Carter but modified them to meet the changing needs of their communities. In fact, for beauticians such as Rose Morgan, Ella Mae Martin, and Bernice Robinson, the hair-care industry in the post-Depression era represented endless possibilities, both entrepreneurial and political.

THE EMERGENCE OF THE BEAUTY ACTIVIST

The issue of state licensing, unimportant in the earlier decades, was one that was foremost in the minds of beauty culturists across the country in the 1930s and 1940s. Despite the fact that the New Deal era signaled the entrance of social legislation designed to protect workers from the perils of unfair labor practices, black women's work in the beauty industry, like their work in domestic labor and agriculture, remained unprotected for many years. Still, beauticians, both salon owners and employees, understood that their industry should benefit from government protection and representation on labor boards as well. Once beauty culturists realized that the government was not immediately willing to assist them in their profession, they relied upon a strategy that had served them well in the past—they organized on their own behalf. The National Beauty Culturists' League (NBCL) by the 1940s began pushing for better state regulation of beauty culture and "spearheaded the fight to eliminate segregation because of race on boards of beauty control, state beauty inspectors, and examiners."[65]

New York, with its precedent of poor conditions in beauty salons, waited until the late 1940s to address the inequities in the beauty industry. In 1947, the New York State Department of Labor convened the Beauty Service Minimum Wage Board to make recommendations to the Industrial Commissioner. Not only was this board groundbreaking in its attempt to examine the beauty industry thoroughly, but it also included "the first Negro beauty shop owner to hold membership on a New York State Wage Board." This board member was Rose Morgan, who in 1947 was one of the three employer members of the Wage Board. According to the report, Morgan's nomination: "for a place on the Wage Board, whose recommendations will affect the interests of some 12,500 workers in the industry throughout the state, was sponsored by the Manhattan Beauty Shop Owners Association of which she is a member." Rose Morgan's life, both personal and professional, offers insights into the role of beauty culturists from the 1930s to the 1960s.[66]

Rose Morgan was an entrepreneur and philanthropist who likely would have been forgotten had the Schomburg Center for Research in Black Culture not decided to conduct a videotaped interview of her in 1988. James Briggs Murray interviewed an elderly but elegant Morgan at the Rose Morgan House of Beauty, 251 Adam Clayton Powell Boulevard in Harlem. Ironically, the perfectly coifed, sophisticated, elderly woman with the conservative mauve suit on the videotape was once incorrectly referred to by a magazine as a "plain Jane from Shelby, Mississippi." Morgan admitted that she had come a long way and was not embarrassed by her humble beginnings. Morgan was born in Edwards, Mississippi in 1912, moved to Shelby with her family when she was two years old, and remained there until she was six. In the interview, Morgan spoke fondly of her early years in Mississippi, where her father rented land on a cotton plantation and where the family— including her eight siblings—worked as sharecroppers. When Morgan was six years old, her family migrated north to Chicago, where her father embarked on a career in the hotel business.

Morgan admired her father's business initiative and says that he inspired her to begin her first informal business; she made and sold cut paper flowers door-to-door at the age of ten. At the age of twelve Morgan began experimenting with the profession that would ultimately bring her success—hairdressing—and began pressing hair informally for small wages. During this taped interview over fifty years later, Morgan admitted that she "never wanted to do anything but hair." Still, like most black women in that era, she was forced to drop out of school at sixteen to enter the workforce, and took a job shaking sheets in a laundry. The work was difficult, and young Rose knew immediately that this was not the path she wanted her life to take. She then decided to do hair full-time and began working in a salon as an apprentice while also styling hair out of her home.

In 1930, Morgan enrolled in Marcy's Beauty Academy to learn the scientific aspects of hair care in order to take the Illinois state board exams. She began meeting "theater people" and eventually ended up doing actress and singer Ethel Walter's hair at the Capitol Theater. A friend and fellow manicurist then suggested that Morgan come to New York City and pursue her cosmetology career there.

Harlem's "Sugar Hill" community of black elites proved to be the source of Morgan's success, and she remained there for over four decades. By 1946, after a failed partnership with Emmeta Hurley, sister of the owners of the Cardozo Sisters House of Beauty in Washington, D.C., and a performer in the Ziegfeld Follies, Morgan became co-owner of the Rose-Meta House of Beauty, Inc. with Olivia Clarke. The salon boasted a clientele of luminaries such as dancer Katherine Dunham and Eslanda Robeson, the wife of Paul Robeson. Billed by *Ebony* magazine as the "biggest Negro beauty parlor in the world," the salon was located in a five-story brownstone at 148th Street and St. Nicholas Avenue, complete with twenty hair operators, three licensed masseurs, a registered nurse, and a full-service cafeteria.[67] In 1955, Morgan withdrew from managing this salon and built a $225,000 enterprise with a surprisingly interracial staff of 80 beauty operators, complete with a children's department, a hat and clothes designer, a charm school, and a cosmetic and accessory counter. A young customer summed it up best when she said, "this place is the end. Under one roof it has everything a woman needs to get re-styled, upholstered and reconditioned."[68]

When asked if communication and information was shared in her salons, Rose Morgan explained that her "girls" were not allowed to talk to customers beyond hair issues. She did not want her salon to be a "gossipy place." Still, while Morgan did not want the public sphere to enter her salon, she engaged in many public and philanthropic activities. She had a strong presence on the NYS Labor Board, was instrumental in raising the minimum wage for beauticians to $16 to $25 per week, and continued to lobby on the state level thereafter. In addition,

Morgan worked on behalf of Nelson Rockefeller, Robert Kennedy, and Congressman Charles Rangel, and received an honorary degree from Shaw University for her many years of service to the black community.[69]

Other contemporaries of Morgan—especially those in the South—were much more controversial in using their positions as beauticians within their communities as well as the use of their salons as public spaces. On an organizational level, they made a bold entrance into the public sphere as well. In 1952, the activities of the NBCL even captured the attention of the National Association for the Advancement of Colored People's (NAACP) executive secretary Walter White, who joined the organization for a pilgrimage to the grave of Madam C. J. Walker. Five years later, in 1957, the guest of honor at their annual convention was Dr. Martin Luther King. The leadership of the NBCL also initiated a voting campaign that year, commanding the members to make use of their right to vote:

> We have a distinguished right, as American citizens. Make use of our right to vote. Don't be denied of these rights. . . . You have seen Southern Senators in their last ditch fight to defeat President Eisenhower's Civil Rights Legislation. They have attacked bitterly every bill that would tend to free people of color in our shops and schools and we should interest ourselves enough to see to it that every customer, every student that goes in and out of our doors, are taking an active part in their city, state, and national government.[70]

The then-president of the NBCL was Katie Whickham, who, as civil rights activist Ella Baker announced in a 1959 newsletter of the Southern Christian Leadership Conference (SCLC), was elected as the first female staff officer of SCLC:

> We believe that Mrs. Whickham will bring new strength to our efforts. The National Beauty Culturists's League, Inc., of which she is president, has strong local and state units throughout the South and voter registration is a major emphasis to its program.[71]

In other words, while the activism of beauticians, both through their powerful national organization and through their strong presence on the local level, might be lost on historians of the modern Civil Rights movement, it was plainly evident to their contemporaries, who were aware of the strategic power of beauticians as "bridge leaders" in their communities.[72]

Many beauty culturists heeded the call of the NBCL and continued this activism in their local communities. Those living in the South were especially active even though they must have been aware that the appeal broadcast by the NBCL was directed more at Northern beauticians who at least had the opportunity to vote. Instead, beauticians in the Jim Crow South had to deal with more immediate concerns surrounding the right to vote. Ella Martin, president of the Georgia State Beauty Culturists' League from 1946–1968, explains the situation in Atlanta:

> We would encourage the people. Some beauty shops we would use for the people to register to vote, to get them interested in voting and get them registered, and after getting them registered, to try our best to get them to go the polls, educate them to go to the polls to vote.[73]

Martin's words show the extent to which beauticians were involved in political activism and thereby transformed their salons into the sole entrepreneurial and institutional spaces in the black community that were within the control and under the leadership of black women.

The life of Bernice Robinson demonstrates that beauty work was not only a key economic skill but a politically valuable one as well. Born in Charleston, South Carolina, in February 1914, the child of a bricklayer and a homemaker/seamstress, Robinson was raised to be self-reliant and specifically taught to avoid dependence on the white community. After completing high school (where she studied cooking, sewing, laundering, and piano), she, like many Southern blacks in the first three decades of the twentieth century, migrated north to New York City. There she lived with her sister and worked in the garment industry. However, according to Robinson, she was found it necessary to return periodically to South Carolina and work as a domestic, for employment in the garment industry was not steady.[74]

In her estimation, Robinson finally followed the advice of her parents to become economically self-sufficient by entering beauty school and becoming a beautician in the service of black women. With a friend in 1937, she opened a beauty shop in Harlem on 145th Street between Convent and Amsterdam Avenues. Robinson originally worked there part-time on the weekends but had so many customers after just three weeks that she then became a full-time beautician, often working eighteen hours a day. Still, once World War II began and government jobs slowly began opening up to black women, Bernice followed her sister to Philadelphia, passed the civil service exam, and secured a job with the Philadelphia Signal Corps. However, she later returned to New York, where she again passed a civil service exam and worked for the Internal Revenue Service and the Veterans Administration. In 1947, Robinson moved back to Charleston, planning to stay for only a few days to care for her ailing parents but actually remaining there until the 1990s.[75]

Harsh segregation, voter discrimination, and poor employment prospects caused Robinson to become disappointed with Charleston and fueled her subsequent political involvement. After being repeatedly rejected for government jobs despite passing the civil service exam yet again in South Carolina and having extensive experience in New York and Philadelphia, she turned to the profession that had previously served her well, beauty work.

By 1952, Robinson had become involved with the NAACP while engaged in beauty work out of her home. Robinson admits: "It got to the point where we were working so hard getting people to register to vote that I would leave people under the dryer to take others down to the registration office to get them registered." In addition, Robinson was also instrumental in the growth of the NAACP's Charleston chapter. She encouraged her customers to join the organization, recognizing that her position as a beautician gave her freedom to engage in political activities that many other blacks did not have. Robinson explained:

> I didn't have to worry about losing my job or anything because I wasn't a schoolteacher or a caseworker with the Department of Social Services or connected with anything I might be fired from. I had my own business, supplied by black supply houses, so I didn't have to worry. [76]

Her Charleston beauty shop became a "center for all sorts of subversive activity where many of her customers had their membership and any mail from the NAACP sent."[77]

Robinson had firsthand knowledge of the peril of joining the NAACP when one was dependent upon whites for one's employment. In 1955, her first cousin Septima Clark lost her job as a public schoolteacher simply because she refused to renounce her membership in the NAACP. After her dismissal, Myles Horton, the founder of the Highlander Folk School based in Tennessee, approached Clark to direct a workshop to enlighten middle-class blacks about the work being done at Highlander. Myles Horton had opened the Highlander School in 1932 with the intention of educating "rural and industrial leaders for a new social order."[78] After two decades working primarily in the labor movement, in 1953 the Highlander staff launched a series of workshops that focused on community desegregation. In 1957, with the assistance of Septima Clark, a Citizenship School project developed on the South Carolina Sea Islands. The primary goal was to teach black adults to read and write to prepare them to register to vote. Clark immediately thought of her cousin Bernice to run the first school that was established on Johns Island.[79]

When asked to become the first teacher for Highlander's citizenship education program in the South Carolina Sea Islands, Robinson was surprised, for she had neither experience as a teacher nor a college education. This did not present a problem for Highlander's leadership—their main concern was that the islanders would have a teacher they could trust and who would respect them. Myles Horton articulated the strategic importance of beauticians to the success of his program and explained in his autobiography why he chose Robinson:

> Bernice was a black beautician. Compared to white beauticians, black beauticians had status in their own community. They had a higher-than-average education and, because they owned their own business, didn't depend upon whites for their incomes. We needed to build around black people who could stand up against white opposition, so black beauticians were very important.[80]

On January 7, 1957, Robinson stood before her first class on Johns Island and quickly developed teaching methods that were so successful that by February of the next year, all of the voting-age adults with at least five months of classes were able to read the required paragraph in the state constitution and sign their names in order to receive their voter registration certificates. Horton acknowledged that more than anyone, Robinson "developed the methods used by the Citizenship Schools.[81]

Robinson was not the only beautician involved in the Highlander Citizenship schools. Witnessing the success of the Johns Island school, hairdresser Marylee Davis of North Charleston asked for help in starting a school on Wadmalaw Island and offered her beauty parlor as a meeting place for adult literacy classes.[82] Horton began to realize that many of the people most involved with Highlander were beauticians, and began running workshops specifically to enhance their leadership skills. While most people thought he was gathering them for vocational purposes, Horton explained:

> They thought that I was bringing these beauticians together to talk about straightening hair or whatever the hell they do, [but] I was just using them because they were community leaders and they were independent. . . . We used beauticians' shops all over the South to distribute Highlander literature on integration.[83]

In many ways, Myles Horton's statement illuminates the key issues surrounding the unique ways beauty culturists throughout the twentieth century merged business with racial uplift and politics. He understood that members of their communities perceived them as community leaders and that their complicated status and class position placed them in an ideal situation for cultivating leadership. Beauty culturists, for the most part, were highly regarded in their communities and strove to be among the best women of the race. However, because of segregation and their indebtedness to the black community for a client base, beauty culturists were never removed from their respective communities. However, that is not to say that beauty parlors were homogenous utopias. Alice Dunbar-Nelson's experience is a reminder of the ways beauty salons policed race, class, color, and respectability.

Secondly, Horton's observations also point to the independence that black female beauticians had relative to other blacks—especially black women—whose occupations were usually under the watchful eyes of whites. Throughout the years this study treats, black women primarily worked as domestics, doing work that was often isolating and constantly supervised, clearly not offering a site to organize collective resistance. Even black professional women such as schoolteachers within segregated school systems faced constraints due to their dependence upon white-run school boards and city councils. Beauticians worked within black female-owned establishments, supplied by black manufacturers, patronized by black female clients, within segregated communities.

While Horton appreciated the work of beauticians in providing leadership, he was perhaps most thankful that these women had access to "free spaces."[84] In fact, he utilized beauty salons as black-owned institutional spaces, similar to the black church. However, what is even more compelling about these spaces is that they were often hidden and even subversive. Even beauty culturists like Ezella Mathis Carter and the many Walker sales agents who used door-to-door sales created a hidden space within the home where they could engage in racial uplift work.

In many ways, like Myles Horton, this essay confirms that the hair-care industry in general and the black beauty parlor in particular should be examined as an important, albeit unique, institution in the black community, a space that was at once public and private, where the matrix of beauty, business, and politics allowed black women actively to confront the issues of their day. This journey through the first six decades of the twentieth century, with beauty culturists as our guides, provides a telling example of the need for historians to examine hidden spaces in order to unearth the ways black women created a political voice for themselves and their communities. Willie Coleman wrote in a 1983 poem that "beauty shops could have been / a hell-of-a-place to / ferment a . . . . revolution."[85] As the beauty culturists in this essay demonstrate, they were.

ACKNOWLEDGMENTS

I would like to thank the members of David Levering Lewis's African American History Seminar (Spring 1998) for their assistance in the earliest stages of this essay. Also, versions of this paper were delivered at the Rutgers Center for Historical Analysis Black Atlantic: Race, Gender, and Nation Project and the Hagley Museum and Library's Beauty and Business Conference in the Spring of 1999. I especially wish to thank Kathy Peiss and Philip Scranton for their comments and suggestions.

NOTES

1. Works Progress Administration, "Harlem Beauty Shops," *American Life Histories Manuscripts from the Federal Writers' Project, 1936–1940*; http://lcweb2.loc.gov/ammem/wpaintro/wpahome September 20, 1999.

2. For a discussion of the "golden age of black business," see Juliet E. K. Walker, *The History of Black Business in America: Capitalism, Race, Entrepreneurship* (New York: Twayne, 1998), 182–224. Walker explains: "In African American business history, the period from 1900 to 1930 marked the first of three waves in the rise of black corporate America. This was the golden age of black business, which saw the emergence of leading black capitalists who achieved millionaire status and established million-dollar enterprises. Their wealth reflected their success within a black economy, which developed in response to the nation's rise of two worlds of race" (182–183).

3. Booker T. Washington, *The Negro in Business* (1907; New York: Johnson Reprint Corp., 1970), 268.

4. Walker, *The History of Black Business in America*, 52–53.

5. For example, the autobiography of Eliza Potter, *A Hairdresser's Experience in the High Life* (1859; New York: Arno Press, 1988) tells the story of a mulatto who arrived in Cincinnati in 1840 and became a hairdresser for the wealthy white population.

6. For information on the antebellum and Reconstruction black business community, see Juliet E. K. Walker, *The History of Black Business in America*; and Ronald Bailey, ed. *Black Business Enterprises: Historical and Contemporary Perspectives* (New York: Basic Books, 1971).

7. St. Clair Drake and Horace Cayton, *Black Metropolis: A Study of Negro Life in a Northern City* (New York: Harcourt, Brace and Co., 1945).

8. Bailey, *Black Business Enterprises*, 6.

9. For more information on the Washington/ DuBois differences of opinions see Louis Harlan, *Booker T. Washington: The Making of a Leader* (New York: Oxford University Press, 1972); and David Levering Lewis, *W.E.B. Du Bois: Biography of a Race 1868–1919* (New York: Henry Holt, 1993)

10. DuBois, quoted in Lewis, *W.E.B. DuBois*, 220.

11. For a more detailed discussion of the masculine construction of business, see Wendy Gamber, "A Gendered Enterprise: Placing Nineteenth Century Businesswomen in History" *Business History Review* 72 (Summer 1998): 188–218; and Kathy Peiss, "Vital Industry and Women's Ventures: Conceptualizing Gender in Twentieth Century Business History," *Business History Review* 72 (Summer 1998): 219–241.

12. Gilbert C. Harris, "Work in Hair," Minutes of the National Negro Business League, First Annual Convention, Boston, 1900, p. 77.

13. Alberta Moore Smith, "Women's Development in Business," Minutes of the National Negro Business League, First Annual Convention, Boston, 1900, p. 132.

14. Alberta Moore Smith, "Negro Women's Business Clubs: A Factor in the Solution of the Vexed Problem," Minutes of the National Negro Business League, Second Annual Convention, Chicago 1901, p. 62.

15. Dora Miller, "Some Eastern Business Women," Minutes of the National Negro Business League, Second Annual Convention, Chicago, 1901, pp. 58–59.

16. Although Madam Walker was believed to be the first female self-made millionaire, Juliet E. K. Walker argues that Annie Minerva Turnbo Malone (1859–1957), a black manufacturer of hair products under the name Poro and Madam Walker's chief competitor, was in fact America's first female millionaire. Madam Walker was Malone's former employee and is rumored to have taken Malone's system and modified it for the Walker Company; see Walker, *The History of Black Business in America*, 208.

17. Madam C. J. Walker to Booker T. Washington, December 2, 1911, p. 384, and Booker T. Washington to Madam C.J. Walker, 6 December 1911, p.398 in *The Booker T. Washington Papers*, ed. Louis Harlan (Urbana, IL: University of Illinois Press, 1975). It is also worth noting that Washington continued to deny Walker's products a place in Tuskeegee's curriculum until his death.

18. An account of Walker's experience at the 1912 convention is recounted in A'Leila Bundles's young adult biography, *Madam C. J. Walker* (New York: Chelsea House, 1994), 11–13. Bundles, who has been extremely generous to me with her time and knowledge, is also at work on a full-length biography of Madam Walker and her daughter A'Leila.

19. Bundles, *Madam C. J. Walker*, 13.

20. Ibid. 17.

21. For more information on the life and activism of Madam C. J. Walker, see A'Leila Bundles's biography (n18), along with Darlene Clark Hine, "Booker T. Washington and Madam C. J. Walker," in his *Speak Truth to Power: Black Professional Class in United States*

History (Brooklyn, New York: Carlson, 1996), 95–104; Leroy Davis, "Madam C. J. Walker: A Woman of Her Time," in *The African Experience in Community Development: The Continuing Struggle in Africa and the Americas,* vol. 2, ed. Edward W. Crosby, Leroy Davis, and Anne Adams Graves (Needham Heights, MA: Ginn Press, 1980), 37–60; and Kathy Peiss, *Hope in a Jar: The Making of America's Beauty Culture* (New York: Metropolitan Books, 1998).

22. The past decade has yielded many exceptional works on black clubwomen, most notably Evelyn Brooks Higginbotham , *Righteous Discontent: The National Black Baptist Women's Convention* (Cambridge, MA: Harvard University Press, 1994); Stephanie Shaw, *What a Woman Ought to Be and to Do: Black Professional Women Workers During the Jim Crow Era* (Chicago: University of Chicago Press, 1995); and Deborah Gray White, *Too Heavy a Load: Black Women in Defense of Themselves* (New York: W. W. Norton, 1998). Unfortunately, none of these works pays very much attention to economic activism. One notable exception is an article by Darlene Clark Hine, "The Housewives League of Detroit: Black Women and Economic Nationalism," in *Visible Women,* ed. Nancy Hewitt and Suzanne Lebsock (Urbana, IL: University of Illinois Press, 1993), 223–241.

23. Kathryn Johnson, *What a Spelman Graduate Accomplished: Ezella Mathis Carter—A Biography and An Appeal* (Chicago: Pyramid, 1935), 12.

24. Ibid., 14.

25. Ibid.

26. Terrell is quoted in Paula Giddings, *When and Where I Enter: The Impact of Black Women on Race and Sex in America* (New York: William Morrow, 1984), 99. Originally from Mary Church Terrell, "What Role Is the Educated Negro Woman to Play in the Uplifting of Her Race?" *Twentieth Century Negro Literature,* ed. D. W. Culp, (Naperville, IL: J. L. Nichols, 1902), 175.

27. Bruce is quoted in Giddings, *When and Where I Enter,* 100. Originally from Josephine Bruce, "What Has Education Done for Colored Women," *The Voice of the Negro* (July 1905): 296.

28. Giddings, *When and Where I Enter,* 100.

29. Johnson, *What a Spelman Graduate Accomplished,* 23.

30. Ibid., 32.

31. Ibid., 76–77.

32. Nannie Helen Burroughs, "Not Color But Character," *The Voice of the Negro* (July 1904).

33. Noliwe Rooks, *Hair Raising: Beauty, Culture, and African American Women* (New Brunswick, NJ: Rutgers University Press, 1996), 64.

34. Ibid., 26.

35. Madam T. D. Perkins advertisement quoted in Rooks, *Hair Raising,* 43.

36. Hine, "Booker T. Washington and Madam C. J. Walker," 102–103.

37. Ibid., 104.

38. Vernice Mark, *The National Beauty Culturists' League History, 1919–1994* (Detroit: Harlo Printing Co., 1994), 18–19.

39. For the decline of the NACW, see Deborah Gray White's *Too Heavy A Load.* Also, Tera Hunter, in *To 'Joy My Freedom': Southern Black Women's Lives and Labors After the Civil War* (Cambridge, MA: Harvard University Press, 1997), describes how blues music and dance halls operated as an expression of working-class freedom in direct opposition to the aims of middle-class reformers and undermined their authority.

40. Gloria Hull, ed., *The Works of Alice Dunbar-Nelson, Volume 2* (New York: Oxford University Press, 1984), 227.

41. Kevin Gaines, *Uplifting the Race: Black Leadership, Politics, and Culture in the Twentieth Century* (Chapel Hill, NC: University of North Carolina Press, 1996), 220–221.

42. Gloria Hull, ed. *Give Us Each Day: The Diary of Alice Dunbar-Nelson* (New York: W. W. Norton, 1984), 420. Parenthetical explanations are a part of the text.

43. Jervis Anderson, *This Was Harlem, 1900–1950* (New York: Farrar Straus Giroux, 1981), 94.

44. Works Progress Administration, "Harlem Beauty Shops."

45. For more information on A'Leila Walker, see David Levering Lewis, *When Harlem Was in Vogue* (New York: 1979), and A'Leila Bundles's forthcoming biography.

46. Jervis Anderson, *A. Philip Randolph: A Biographical Portrait* (New York: Vintage, 1972), 70.

47. Ibid., 72.

48. Ibid..

49. William Dufty, quoted in Melinda Chateauvert, *Marching Together: Women of the Brotherhood of Sleeping Car Porters* (Urbana, IL: University of Illinois Press, 1998), 8.

50. Chateauvert, *Marching Together,* 8.

51. Anderson, *A. Philip Randolph,* 73.

52. Ibid., 70.

53. Gwendolyn Keita Robinson, "Class, Race, and Gender: A Transcultural Theoretical and Sociohistorical Analysis of Cosmetic Institutions and Practices to 1920," Ph.D. diss., University of Illinois at Chicago, 1984, 395 .

54. Juliet E. K. Walker, in *The History of Black Business in America,* does admit that the hair-care industry was one of the few black business enterprises that did at least survive the Great Depression. However, she acknowledges that the industry did experience some changes.

55. Jacqueline Jones, *Labor of Love, Labor of Sorrow: Black Women, Work, and the Family From Slavery to the Present* (New York: Basic Books, 1985), 214–215.

56. Ethel Erickson, *Employment Conditions in Beauty Shops: A Study of Four Cities,* U.S. Department of Labor, Bulletin of the Women's Bureau No.133, (Washington, DC: U.S. Government Printing Office, 1935), 37.

57. LeRoy Jeffries, "The Decay of the Beauty Parlor Industry in Harlem," *Opportunity: Journal of Negro Life* 15 (January 1938): 49.

58. Ibid..

59. For more information on the wages of black agricultural workers and domestic workers in the New Deal era, see Theresa Amott and Julie Matthaei, *Race, Gender, and Work: A Multicultural Economic History of Women in the United States* (Boston: South End Press, 1991).

60. Quoted in Kathy Peiss, *Hope in a Jar,* 237.

61. Elizabeth Cardozo Barker, quoted in Peiss, *Hope in a Jar,* 237.

62. Peiss, *Hope in a Jar,* 237.

63. Ibid., 114.

64. The notion of black beauty parlors as "political outposts" comes from Elliot Wigginton, *Refuse to Stand Silently By: An Oral History of Grassroots Social Activism in America, 1921–1964* (New York: Doubleday, 1991).

65. Vernice Mark, *The National Beauty Culturists' League History,* 19.

66. State of New York Department of Labor, "Beauty Service Minimum Wage Board, 1947."

67. "House of Beauty: Rose Meta Salon Is Biggest Negro Beauty Parlor in World" *Ebony* (May 1946).

68. "Harlem's New House of Beauty," *Ebony* (June 1955).

69. Rose Morgan, April 21, 1988, videotaped interview, Schomburg Center for Research in Black Culture, New York.

70. Mark, *The National Beauty Culturists' League History,* 40.

71. Ella Baker, quoted in Belinda Robnett, *How Long? How Long? African American Women in the Struggle for Civil Rights* (New York: Oxford University Press, 1997), 93.

72. Belinda Robnett, *How Long? How Long?* 20, defines the term *bridge leaders* as those activists—usually women—who:

> sometimes initiate organizations, do the groundwork, and when this is true, are more visible before an organization is formalized. They operate in the movement's or organization's free spaces, thus making connections that cannot be made by formal leaders. They employ a one-on-one interactive style of leadership for mobilization and recruitment. They have greater leadership mobility in nonhierarchical structures and institutions.

73. Clifford Kuhn, Harlon Joye, and E. Bernard West, eds. "Interview with Ella Martin," in *Living Atlanta: An Oral History of the City, 1914–1948* (Athens, GA: University of Georgia Press, 1990), 110.

74. Elliot Wigginton, ed. "Interview with Bernice Robinson," in *Refuse to Stand Silently By.*

75. Information on Robinson's life was derived from Wigginton, *Refuse to Stand Silently By;* Donna Langston, " The Women of Highlander," and Oldendorf, Sandra, "The South Carolina Sea Island Citizenship Schools, 1957–1961," in *Women in the Civil Rights Movement: Trailblazers and Torchbearers, 1941–1965* ed. Vicki L. Crawford, Jacqueline Anne Rouse, and Barbara Woods, (Bloomington, IN: Indiana University Press, 1993).

76. Wigginton, *Refuse to Stand Silently By,* 246.

77. Ibid., 247.

78. John Glen, *Highlander: No Ordinary School* (2nd ed., Knoxville, TN: University of Tennessee Press, 1996), 2.

79. For more information on the life of Septima Clark, see Septima Clark, *Echo in My Soul* (New York: Dutton, 1962); and Cynthia Stokes Brown, *Ready from Within: Septima Clark and the Civil Rights Movement* (Navarro, CA: Wild Trees Press,1986).

80. Myles Horton, *The Long Haul: An Autobiography* (New York: Doubleday, 1990),102.

81. Ibid., 105.

82. Glen, *Highlander,* 197.

83. Aldon Morris's interview with Myles Horton in *The Origins of the Civil Rights Movement: Black Communities Organizing for Change* (New York: Free Press, 1984) 145.

84. Sara Evans and Harry Boyte define "free spaces" as the "settings between private lives and large-scale institutions where ordinary citizens can act with dignity, independence, and vision," in Sara M. Evans and Harry C. Boyte, *Free Spaces: The Sources of Democratic Change in America* (New York: Harper and Row, 1986),17. I must thank Rhonda Mawhood Lee for interpreting the use of beauty parlors in the Jim Crow South as free spaces in her unpublished paper, "Tales to Curl Your Hair: African American Beauty Parlors in Jim Crow Durham," Seminar Paper, Duke University, 1995.

85. Willi Coleman, "Among the Things Which Use-to-Be," in *Home Girls: A Black Feminist Anthology* ed. Barbara Smith (New York: Kitchen Table—Women of Color Press, 1983), 222.

"At the Curve Exchange"

POSTWAR BEAUTY CULTURE AND WORKING
WOMEN AT MAIDENFORM

VICKI HOWARD

*I*n the March 1948 issue of Maidenform's company newsletter, the Pin-Up Girl of the month reported that "one of her greatest interests is beauty culture."[1] She was referring here to the "personal cultivation of beauty" through the development of skills such as hairdressing, cosmetic application, and fashion sense. According to the reporter for *The Maiden Forum*, the Pin-Up for March knew and used "all the feminine arts in achieving a lovely appearance." The glamorous photo (Figure 8.1) prominently placed in the Maidenform company newsletter attests to the fact. Sporting bare shoulders and rhinestone jewelry, well-coiffed hair, and a flawlessly made-up face, she was "sophisticated in appearance." With just a hint of a smile, her eyes averted from the camera's gaze, she posed as if for a publicity shot for her current Hollywood movie. Mary Smietanek, the March Pin-Up Girl, was an operator in Department 3A at the Bayonne, New Jersey, Maidenform plant. She was "fond of dancing and attending movies," but noted that "she's actually a 'domestic type,' and while she is not engaged, she hoped some day to 'meet the right man and settle down.'"[2] Mary Smietanek's expressed interest in the specific skills and activities tied to the act of beautifying was part of a larger feminized work culture that revolved around fashion, cosmetics, and hairstyling, as well as company-sponsored pinup and beauty contests, and weddings.

Beauty culture shaped the work experiences of women factory operatives and office staff at Maidenform in complex and often contradictory ways. Work culture, as Susan Porter Benson has defined it, is the "ideology and practice with which workers stake out a relatively autonomous sphere of action on the job." Out of this work culture comes both an adaptation and resistance to working conditions.[3] At

Pin-Up For March

Mary Smietanek, our Pin-up Girl for this month, has no difficulty in maintaining that Powers model look so evident in her photograph. One of her greatest interests is beauty culture, and she knows and uses all the feminine arts in achieving a lovely appearance. She often chooses clothes in shades of green which emphasize the color of her large blue-green eyes, and are a nice complement to her medium blond hair. Her coiffures are the envy of her friends— and Mary says that she rarely goes to a beauty parlor to have her hair "done," since she is particularly adept at hair-dressing.

MARY SMIETANEK   *Photo by Norton*

Born in Dupont, Pa., just twenty years ago on the ninth of this month, Mary has lived in Bayonne the greater part of her life. She started to work at Maiden Form in a part-time job while still in high school. Upon her graduation, Mary became a full-time operator, and is currently employed in Department 3A, where her supervisors are proud not only of her selection as a Pin-Up Girl, but of her consistently good work.

Mary is fond of dancing and attending movies. She also does a great deal of embroidery work and various other handcrafts. Sophisticated in appearance, she says that she's actually a "domestic type," and while she is not engaged, she hopes some day to "meet the right man and settle down."

What're you waiting for, boys?

Figure 8.1. Mary Smietanek, Pin-Up for March, 1948. The Company newsletter, the *Maiden Forum*, featured a monthly Pin-Up Contest for employees. Contestants typically described their romantic interests, hobbies, and career aspirations. Courtesy Maidenform Collection, Archives Center, NMAH, Smithsonian Institution, Washington, D.C.

Maidenform, beauty culture was work culture. As such, it went beyond acts of beautifying and the business of beauty to include a range of female rituals and activities. Shopping for clothing or items of personal adornment with coworkers, discussing details of wedding preparations and bridal fashions, showing off an engagement ring or wedding photographs at work were all ways that women at Maidenform participated in beauty culture and upheld its gender norms. Employees endorsed Maidenform's commercial beauty culture by participating in company-sponsored events. In the process of producing and consuming workplace beauty culture at Maidenform, women from a wide range of class and ethnic backgrounds participated in the dominant gender ideal fostered by their employer. At the same time, however, their work culture remained rooted in their own class and ethnic identities. This paper will examine the ways in which working women at Maidenform used commercial beauty culture to negotiate these divergent identities.

As part of the larger consumer culture that increasingly shaped work and leisure, commercial beauty culture has played a vital role in fostering sociability among working women. Historians have explored the role consumerism played in defining the work culture of a wide range of women, from department store sales clerks and factory workers, to waitresses and telephone operators. In the early twentieth century, participation in consumer culture did not necessarily preclude radicalism. In many cases, a shared interest in fashion, cosmetics, and hairstyles and in new commercial leisure activities led working-class women to form bonds that helped them to survive the often difficult and tedious conditions of their jobs, to unionize, and to strike. In the first decade of the century, striking shirtwaist workers used clothing to fashion oppositional political identities.

This often radical female work culture grew out of the shared experiences and interests of young unmarried women. Industrialization and urbanization had transformed the economic and social role of these women. Increasingly, young unmarried women moved to the city to find work, or became "breadwinning daughters" living at home and contributing to the household. Many young, unmarried, immigrant women viewed their workplace as a source of female-centered social life. In the early twentieth century, for example, work culture in the factory operated as a school that introduced Jewish immigrant women to American notions of romance and marriage and to Americanized forms of leisure and consumption. These interests, in which beauty culture played a central role, fueled ambitions and fostered workplace militancy by facilitating ties between workers.[4]

During the 1940s and 1950s, beauty culture continued to play a role in fostering sociability at work and forming bonds between women at the Maidenform company. The historical context for this aspect of work culture, however, had changed. Major shifts in the makeup of the workforce and the ideological changes that accompanied these changes transformed the meaning of women's participation in commercial beauty culture. Part of a long-term trend in women's increased workforce participation, married white women were wage-earners in greater numbers than ever before. Overall, wives earned wages in 21.6 percent of families in 1950. By 1960, this had increased to 30.5 percent. In the 1950s, wage labor was a central part of these women's lives, as some chose to continue working after marriage or to return to work after their youngest child began school.[5]

Rising postwar marriage rates also affected work culture. After the war, the age of first marriage for women declined to an unprecedented low. The relative postwar prosperity, the return from World War II, G.I. benefits, and a new celebration of the nuclear family led to an increase in marriages. These new families led the suburbanization movement of the late 1940s and 1950s, as large numbers of white, working-class families moved out of the city centers and into new suburbs such as Levittown.[6] Many single or married women at Maidenform worked toward building a family and home. These demographic and geographic shifts altered the context of workplace beauty culture. Whether single or married, women who worked would have taken part in regular bridal showers and attended numerous weddings of fellow employees. During this period, even the custom of collecting money to buy a coworker a wedding gift became a subject of humor.[7]

These broad changes shaped the ideological context of postwar beauty culture. Marriage was considered an interesting subject by Americans in the 1950s. College courses, women's magazines, and a range of experts addressed the topic. Postwar commercial beauty culture was increasingly depoliticized and was no longer the same source of workplace radicalism as it had been in the early twentieth century. Experts advised married women who worked to preserve their femininity and told single women that their primary goal was to find a husband. Commercial beauty culture did not reflect the fact that many women had to shoulder the double burden of their duties at work and home. Magazines told women to look glamorous for their husbands and not to let their work interfere with their domestic role or compete with their husband's role as provider.[8] Acts of beautifying, consumption of fashion, and other expressions of beauty culture would have been performed in the name of these postwar ideals. Work culture became steeped in the cult of marriage.

The value and meaning of beauty culture has been the subject of much debate among feminists and scholars.[9] Many have seen beauty culture as antithetical to feminism. From nineteenth-century dress reformers who bravely wore bloomers to 1960s protesters at Miss America beauty pageants, commercially produced notions of femininity and beauty have been contested.[10] Recently, feminist scholars have moved away from the anti–beauty culture view, calling for a more complex interpretation of beauty culture. According to this position, beauty pageants are not simply events that exploit women, or erase ethnic identity. Similarly, fashion also had the power to subvert authority and challenge dominant class, gender, and racial ideologies.[11] Lois Banner argued that the pursuit of beauty, fashion, and dress bound together women of different classes, ethnicities, and regions. Notions of fashionability and beauty often did not come from elites but rose out of working-class and immigrant culture. For example, actresses, who were not usually of the elite, had an immense influence on fashions in the nineteenth century. Elite control of fashion, moreover, was challenged by working-class factory women. Kathy Peiss defined beauty culture as: "a system of meaning that helped women navigate the changing conditions of modern social experience." For women, she argued, it became a "culture of shared meanings and rituals." Central to both Banner's and Peiss's understanding of beauty culture is the notion that the pursuit of a fashionable appearance has not wholly oppressed or victimized women.[12]

In the postwar years, new interpretations of femininity that acknowledged women's sexuality shaped the way advertisers addressed consumers; they celebrated female sexual allure and desire, positing them as key attributes of "the normal female psyche." While advertisers had acknowledged female sexuality in the past, they contained it safely in the story of romance and marriage.[13] Earlier Maidenform advertisements made appeals to "fashion" or ideas of "natural uplift," while those run during the war emphasized "scientific" support and protection.[14] Maidenform's national "I Dreamed" campaign, which ran from 1949 through 1969, reflected the new trends in advertising's representation of female sexuality. Advertisements pictured models, clothed from the waist down and wearing only a brassiere on top, doing very public things in their dreams, such as directing traffic or shopping. Each ad was accompanied by the phrase, "I Dreamed," and a brief description of the activity performed in a Maidenform bra.[15] The campaign's appeal thus derived from its successful transformation of the private into the public. Brassieres and other foundation garments manufactured by Maidenform were not meant to be seen by others. The ads drew attention to the disjuncture created by this mixture of outer clothing and exposed undergarments.

The Maidenform company founded the modern brassiere manufacturing industry. In the early twentieth century, the foundation garment industry was largely limited to the manufacture of corsets. At Enid's Frocks, a small New York dress shop in the early 1920s, Ida Rosenthal and Enid Bissett had begun producing simple brassieres to be worn with their dresses. The popularity of these support garments led Enid Bissett, Ida Rosenthal, and her husband, William, to incorporate in 1923. Throughout the 1930s their business grew. During World War II they continued to manufacture brassieres, receiving priorities in materials after convincing the War Department that women in defense industries needed brassieres for work.[16] In the 1950s, Maidenform had factories in Morristown, Bayonne, and Perth Amboy, New Jersey, as well as in Clarksburg, Huntington, and Princeton, West Virginia. Manufacturing contractors were also used in Union City, New Jersey, and in Puerto

Rico. Overall, Maidenform employed a total of 3,200 people in the mid-1950s and sold its products to over 20,000 retail outlets in the United States and abroad. By 1950, the reported volume of Maidenform sales was $14 million and continued to grow substantially over the next ten years.[17] By 1960, the firm sold 10 percent of all U.S. brassieres, its success being popularly attributed to the "I Dreamed" advertising campaign.[18]

The "I Dreamed" campaign became a part of popular culture. The company actively sought to bring the campaign into the public eye. Over a twenty-year period, Maidenform ran over one hundred Dream ads. Department store buyers and members of the press were invited to witness the unveiling of new themes at what were called Fashion "Dream" Shows. Contests were held to elicit new themes from the public.[19] Maidenform bras also entered people's homes through television commercials. The first company to market intimate apparel on television, Maidenform showed women working on construction sites or performing in orchestra pits wearing their Maidenform bras. Even Maidenform employees took the ad campaign home with them. For example, in 1955, the niece of an employee was photographed at home dressing up like a bride. The newsletter caption beneath the photograph read "I Dreamed I Was a Bride in My Maidenform Bra."[20]

Maidenform's national "I Dreamed" campaign linked the company with contemporary definitions of New Look glamour and femininity. Foundation garments followed the silhouettes promoted by the fashion industry. Brassieres and girdles like those produced by Maidenform were necessary for the sweetheart silhouette popularized by such Hollywood actresses as Elizabeth Taylor. In particular, the Chansonette line, with its conical construction and circular stitched cups, would have supported the form-fitting New Look styles introduced by Christian Dior in 1947. The New Look called for rounded shoulders, full busts, and narrow waists above wide hips created by a voluminous long-hemmed skirt. Women's natural shape did not conform to the exaggerated outline of the New Look and required the use of restrictive undergarments, what Maureen Turim has called "a form of gilded bondage."[21] Brassieres with names like the Tric-O-Lastic, the Twice Over, the Semi-Accentuate, the Hold-Tite, and the Gree-Shen attempted to make women's bodies conform to the era's fashionable hourglass figure through uplifting structures and padding.

As fashion historians have demonstrated, however, feminine and masculine ideals in clothing are social constructions that change over time. Garments such as corsets and girdles, which might seem uncomfortable in one historical moment, elicited different feelings in another time. In 1957, for example, some women preferred the more restrictive long-line Maidenform brassieres because they "like(d) the feeling of complete control" and the posture support it provided.[22]

The "I Dreamed" campaign reveals the complexity of gender ideology in the 1950s. The campaign was built around the idea of women taking on new, "feminine" identities in their Maidenform bra. These identities did not reflect the popular stereotype of the 1950s white woman as a suburban, middle-class mother and housewife. Rather, they seemed more akin to other popular images of women at that time, like the pinup or the Hollywood sex goddess. Ads sought to be risqué in their representation of sexuality through the half-clothed female body. These identities challenged notions of middle-class decorum and restraint. At the same time, their message mirrored that given by mainstream women's magazines in the 1950s advising married women to play the role of "glamour girl" for their husbands.[23]

The "model" Maidenform woman was white and middle class, without visible ethnic identification. Ethnicity was marked only if it appealed to notions of the exotic "Other." In the 1950 ad "I Dreamed I Was a Toreador," for example, a dark-haired model flirted with danger, wearing flaming red satin pants and a matching cape, which she held open as if awaiting the approach of the bull. (Figure 8.2) Many ads depicted models dreaming of doing things in their bras that associated them with aristocracy and high culture. A woman could transcend her class position and "live like a Queen." Imagined as works of art, a woman could become Venus de Milo.[24] She might dream she "went to the theatre" carrying her program in a gloved hand, or that she was "a social butterfly" wearing *haute couture* styles against an opulent background. Generally, these advertisements operated outside the realm of everyday life. ("I Dreamed I Brushed My Teeth in My Maidenform Bra" would not likely sell.) Ads depicted women escaping private middle-class life and gaining public notoriety by joining the circus or taking a screen test for the movies. To have shock appeal, the assumed identities had to be unusual. Thus in a Maidenform bra a woman might enter fantasy worlds as mermaids and medieval maidens, or against a background of misty castles she might find herself "enchanted."

Women in Maidenform ads appear as objects of consumption, but often in roles that challenged dominant gender ideology. On the one hand, as Barbara Coleman has shown, some denigrated women's abilities: the 1955 ad, "I Dreamed I Went back to School," portrayed a model sitting on top of a desk wearing her Maidenform bra, with a copy of *Vogue* and a notebook open on her lap with the figures $2 + 2 = 5$ written on it. On the other hand, the women portrayed in the "I Dreamed" advertising campaign break out of the domestic sphere, even engaging in activities understood as "masculine." Ads pictured half-clothed models at work in nontraditional occupations. Wearing their Maidenform brassieres, they became cowboys, railroad engineers, firefighters, and editors.

Figure 8.2. "I Dreamed I was a Toreador in my Maidenform Bra," 1950. The "I Dreamed" advertising campaign imagined women in non-traditional occupations or engaged in unusual activities while dressed in their Maidenform bra. Courtesy of Maidenform Collection, Archives Center, NMAH, Smithsonian Institution, Washington, D.C.

Coleman criticized these particular ads for their condescending parody of "women's unrealistic occupational aspirations." For example, a 1951 ad entitled "I Dreamed I Was a Lady Editor" depicted a disorganized-looking woman with two telephones. However, a later version of the editor theme, "I Dreamed I Was a Lady Editor in my Maidenform Girdle," depicted a women without any signs that she was "unsuited" for her dream career choice, except for the fact that she appeared clad only in her undergarments.[25] The occupation-oriented Maidenform ads reflected advertisers' recognition of changes in the makeup of the workforce. As more and more married women entered the workforce in this decade, a popular interest in working women and "working couples" developed. Magazines such as *Seventeen* (1944) and *Charm* (1950) sought advertising dollars by highlighting the economic role played by teenage girls and working women. Employing a slogan popularized during the war, advertisers increasingly recognized the "womanpower" of their earnings.[26] Maidenform ads were directed at those who wore foundation garments, many of whom would have been working women.

Just as the "I Dreamed" campaign attempted to make brassieres glamorous, Maidenform also tried to shape its company image by promoting commercial beauty culture. Factory production of the Maidenform brassiere was decidedly not glamorous work. When Maidenform first began, each operator worked on a complete garment. As the company grew beyond its initial size of ten employees and four sewing machines, however, it shifted to section work. Workers at Maidenform were members of the International Ladies Garment Workers Union (ILGWU), an organization with radical roots. In 1937, when Maidenform adopted a modified piecework system, the switchover took months of negotiation with the ILGWU. The union required that no layoffs would result and that no worker would make less under the new system. During the 1940s and 1950s, management-labor relations were not always friendly. In 1941, employees went on a strike at the Bayonne plant that ended after they were granted pay raises. In 1955, employees in New Jersey engaged in work stoppages and were charged with violating the collective bargaining agreement between Maidenform and the ILGWU.[27] Employees may have embraced commercial beauty, but they remained class-conscious.

Perhaps *The Maiden Forum*, which started in 1944, was an attempt to foster good relations between management and labor by constructing a visible "family" of employees who participated in company-sponsored events. *The Maiden Forum*, a newsletter "published by and for the employees," promoted this commercial beauty culture. Reporters for *The Maiden Forum* gathered news from their departments and then wrote it up for publication, often in a tongue-in-cheek style. Like earlier company newsletters, *The Maiden Forum* tried to foster a workplace culture revolving around company-sponsored sports teams, social events, and programs.[28] Beauty contests and features like the Pin-Up of the month may have been held to promote company loyalty and strengthen worker morale as well.

Maidenform fostered an interest in beauty culture by sponsoring a range of beauty competitions. These contests appeared to be a source of pride or at least of amusement among employees. Different plants held "Miss Maidenform" contests at which the plant manager would crown the queen chosen from among the local women employees. "Atlantic City (had) nothing on Maiden Form when it (came) to Beauty Contests," according to *The Maiden Forum*. More informal versions of

Figure 8.3. "Pulchritude Parade," 1946. Male managers, department heads, and ILGWU officials promoted employee participation in a host of company-sponsored beauty contests. Maidenform Collection, Archives Center, NMAH, Smithsonian Institution, Washington, D.C.

these Miss Maidenform beauty contests also took place. Department 2A staged a "Pulchritude Parade" in its cafeteria after Department Manager Betty Lipman had noticed that "there (were) so many pretty girls on (her) floor." (Figure 8.3) According to a *Maiden Forum* reporter, the idea for the contest "spread like wildfire" and brought about the "enthusiastic cooperation on the part of every member of the Department," although the name Pulchritude Parade suggests an element of parody was involved. The contest judges—men chosen "by the girls"—consisted of various managers, department heads, and interestingly, ILGWU officials. Winners received a pair of nylons, after the head of the designing department, Mr. Silvani, "took their measurements." The Master of

Ceremonies, who was an ILGWU Assistant Chairman, suggested that "the easiest way to pick the winners is by having each girl walk into the cutting room and then we can judge by the length of the whistles." Unlike the rest of the plant, the cutting department was male-dominated, as was typical in the garment industry.[29] Nevertheless, married women were among the winners, reflecting the shifts in the workforce that took place during World War II and in the postwar period.

Beauty contests and fashion shows were part of a feminized work culture, and Maidenform had a vested interest in fashion. Beauty pageants must have seemed a normal part of working life at a company that featured glamour and female sexuality in its advertising. These contests took place in the context of widespread promotion of beauty culture in places where women worked. Fashion shows, which also elevated physical beauty and female participation in beauty culture, took place in a range of industries. Telephone operators, waitresses, and department store employees all competed in beauty contests sponsored by their company or union. Women's entry into nontraditional occupations during the war brought beauty shops and lunch-hour Victory Fashion Shows into previously male-dominated workplaces such as Lockheed Aircraft. Companies supported commercial beauty culture and dominant gender ideals to foster loyalty and morale in the workplace. Working-class women, however, could also make these gender ideals work to their own advantage. The society connections of fashion show goers and the industry's elite associations could be turned on their head by working-class women, as Dorothy Sue Cobble has shown in her depiction of striking San Francisco hotel workers who parodied a Junior League fashion show being staged in their hotel during a 1941 strike.[30]

The company newsletter also encouraged beauty culture among its employees through its monthly Pin-Up contest. Chosen and interviewed by the plant employees who worked on their own time as editorial staff of *The Maiden Forum,* the characterization of each Pin-Up's appearance, personality, and interests can be seen as a fairly accurate index at least of how that individual wanted to be seen by others. It would have been in *The Maiden Forum*'s own interest to publish articles and news the employees wanted to read. Reporters such as Rita Kasper, an operator in 3A, interviewed prospective Pin-Ups and gathered information about them. The personal information chosen to accompany these Pin-Ups was consistent: generally, write-ups gave the honoree's occupation, education, hobbies, interests, age, personal qualities, and physical appearance, even though a photograph always accompanied it. With only a couple of exceptions, the Maidenform Pin-Ups were women, although one operator winkingly stated she would "like to have a pin-up boy every month." A handful of men were featured, as if in response to this request. Being a male Pin-Up, however, did not mean that men participated in beauty culture at Maidenform. While men might be described a handsome or as available bachelors, they also appeared in other roles. Reporter Dominick De Stefano, for example, was pictured with his daughters as the typical "American Father."[31]

The glamorous studio photographs of Maidenform women selected as Pin-Up of the Month reflected their adaptation of the commercial beauty ideals popularized by wartime pinups like Betty Grable, Rita Hayworth, and Lena Horne. Pin-Up Mary Hurley used these ideas as a model for her own personal style. She was described as "the personification of the office employees you see featured in magazines like *Vogue, Glamour, Charm*. Although she dresses simply, she always looks as though she had just stepped out of a fashion bandbox." Pin-Ups at Maidenform may have followed this commercial model, but Pin-Up discourse could also draw on working-class culture and ethnic identities. Robert Westbrook has demonstrated how ordinary American women constructed their own images in photographs sent to sweethearts overseas, using the poses and conventions of the pinup, such as the bathing suit, sweater, high heels, and the "coy 'come on' smile." Participating in the pinup trend did not necessarily mean a loss of ethnic identity. Pinups might use the publicity they received to validate ethnicity, as did Dolores Quinn, who was "proud of her Irish background," and was engaged to a "six-foot Irishman." [32]

Following fashion and maintaining a well-groomed appearance were ways one signaled both class and gender identification. Pin-Ups were drawn from a wide range of departments, and included men and women, blacks and whites, office workers and factory operators. Women of varying backgrounds adopted the pinup style, appearing well-groomed and fashionable, with a few exceptions. One case, which broke from the typical glamour head shot or cheesecake pose was Pin-Up Helen Miskura of the designing department. (Figure 8.4.) She appeared in two contrasting photographs, one that overturned beauty standards and one that conformed to the ideal of a well-groomed woman. In a photograph taken during the war, she adopted a comic pose in her uncle's "war working clothes." Wearing work pants, holding a pipe in her mouth, with her hair unstyled and covered by a hat, she cross-dressed, altering her class and gender identity. Helen Miskura's position in the designing department may have given her a middle-class identity and thus allowed her to transgress gender norms in this public way. Paired with this transgressive image taken "on a dare" was a more acceptable image—"the 'real' Helen," according to *The Maiden Forum* reporter. The "real" Helen was "a slender grey-eyed blonde" who "adorns the Designing Department."[33] The "real" Helen showed no signs of labor in her dress, except that spent achieving a fashionable appearance.

Vicki Howard

Our June Pin-Up

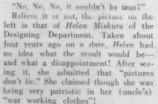

"No, No, No, it couldn't be true!" Believe it or not, the picture on the left is that of *Helen Miskura* of the Designing Department. Taken about four years ago on a dare, *Helen* had no idea what the result would be— and what a disappointment! After seeing it, she admitted that "pictures don't lie." She claimed though she was being very patriotic in her (uncle's) "war working clothes"!

As we glance at the other picture we notice the "real" *Helen*. A slender, grey-eyed blonde, *Helen* adorns the Designing Department. With Maiden Form for three years, *Helen* assists with the cutting and fitting of patterns. She also serves as the very capable reporter of fifth floor news for THE FORUM. Attractive, friendly, co-operative, *Helen* has a keen sense of humor to boot (Note: picture on left).

Figure 8.4. Helen Miskura, "Our June Pin-Up," 1946. Beauty culture could be a complex interplay of resistance and accommodation. Occasionally, employees mocked commercial beauty culture at Maidenform. Courtesy of Maidenform Collection, Archives Center, NMAH, Smithsonian Institution, Washington, D.C.

Maidenform may have fostered an interest in fashion and beauty through its advertisements, beauty contests, and Pin-Up features in the company newsletter, but women embraced them on their own terms as well. Throughout the twentieth century, commercial beauty culture has offered women the opportunity for economic independence. The pursuit of a fashionable appearance could be a hobby, but many also had hopes of turning it into a career. The women at Maidenform were skilled seamstresses. Sewing might have been an attempt to save money, but women also listed it as one of their pleasures. For example, Mary Kosakowski enjoyed "turning out her own clothes on the sewing machine at home." Some, like Mildred Sgambato and Helen Fetch, had aspirations to become designers and commercial artists.[34] Beauty culture and fashion could fuel dreams of success.

The monthly company newsletter reflected employees' interest in beauty culture. Reporters were people like Josephine Buonauito, an operator in 2A, who would have had to find time at work to record details of employee vacations, suntans, engagements, marriages, births, deaths, the purchase of a new car or home, or any number of matters that appeared regularly in department news sections. The questions reporters asked and the information employees volunteered can reasonably be interpreted as representative of their interests and values. Buonauito was interested in beauty culture herself, her specialty being "tricky and attractive hair-dos" with which she was willing to help others. When employees at Maidenform were surveyed on what articles they wanted to see in their newsletter, gender differences arose. Two men interviewed on this subject gave different requests: one mechanic asked for a gossip column, another asked for softball tips. Women asked for more employee news, fashion and homemakers' columns, gossip columns, and the "latest" on styles. The newsletter frequently published fashion and beauty tips. Work-related articles in the company newsletter repeatedly linked women employees to beauty culture by praising their fashion sense or their skill at arranging hair. Even articles on employee promotions highlighted this interest. For example, after announcing Rose Aloi's promotion to supervisory staff and praising her quality of work, a personal note was added that described how she spent most of her "off-the-job-time" in "setting hair and rattling her brains to think up new and different hair styles."[35]

As reflected in these pages, romance and not career ambitions or work concerns dominated these women's lives. Weddings and marriage were likely close at hand to the young women selected to represent Maidenform in the company newsletter as Pin-Up of the Month. Details of how a Pin-Up met her husband were described in detail. Even photographs taken for the contest bore an uncanny resemblance to bridal portraits published in the company magazine. While occasionally married, the Pin-Ups were most likely dating, engaged, or just hopeful. Information on their "dream man" or their unavailability was noted in humorous detail. Fiancés were described as replacing outside interests. Pin-Ups appeared to view romance, courtship, and marriage through the frame of beauty culture. Identifying one married Pin-Up, Alice Gryczkowski, the reporter noted, "Of course, such a pretty young lady could not remain single and it is Mrs. . . ." [36]

Employee courtships, proposals, engagements, bridal showers, weddings, and honeymoons were a central part of workplace beauty culture. Each of these rituals or activities called for a woman to dress to look her best. Each required the act of making up or beautifying. Women joked about dreaming of receiving "a diamond engagement ring while in (their) Maidenform Bra." Engagements, often accompanied by photographs of the bride-to-be or the couple, appeared in almost every issue and were deemed worthy of feature articles. In one, a reporter interviewed engaged or married female employees about how they got a man "to pop the question." Describing how she married a coworker, Joan Fedors reported: "And then there's the old story of 'he chased me until I finally caught him.'" According to the newsletter reporter, when Joan had been introduced to Joe Fedors she immediately decided she would marry him: "Persistence and a certain amount of feminine strategy soon paid off as working together led to lunch together—and their first Saturday night date. Joan proved to be a fast worker for eight months after their first date, the chase was over and they became Mr. and Mrs."[37] This "feminine strategy" surely involved some use of beauty culture.

Women's interest in weddings brought them together in many ways that would have strengthened bonds within and between different departments. The preparation for a wedding and its celebration often brought coworkers together on the shop floor and during leisure time. The details of weddings were a frequent topic of discussion at work and typically revolved around various aspects of beauty culture. When the daughter of a Maidenform employee married, the bride's picture might be published, along with details of the mother-of-the-bride's dress. On the job, employees shared the wedding photographs of daughters and discussed details of a coworker's wedding gown or a bridesmaid's costume, reception, and honeymoon destination. One department reporter noted the following: "Subjects of discussions around here were the gowns worn by our lovely brides, Gloria Maietta and Nellie Zuchowski (real 'woman talk')."

Women who worked together became friends, often serving as maid of honor or bridesmaid at each other's weddings. For example, when Florence Irving of the Morristown plant married Corporal Herbert White, Genevieve Habstock, a clipper at Maidenform, was her maid of honor. A wedding or birth was cause for a social occasion at work. Brides and pregnant women were both honored with corsages, showers, and cake during the workday and after hours at local restaurants and at one another's homes. Showers were sometimes attended by more than one department, and even by past Maidenformers who had left after marriage or after having children. When Tessie Czachur married, the reporter wrote, "Everybody loves a wedding . . . but it's of particular interest when one of our Maiden Formers takes the big step." Weddings and bridal showers could be a place where old and current employees reunited.[38] Since many women continued working at Maidenform after marriage, a wedding served to foster rather than sever work relations.

Beauty culture may also have bridged ethnic differences among Maidenform employees. While the model Maidenform woman of the advertising campaign was white and generally of undetermined ethnicity, the labor force at Maidenform's main Northeast plants in the late 1940s and 1950s included Italians, Russians, Poles, and African Americans, among others.[39] Some employees were first-generation immigrants, like Rae Sette, who came with her family from Italy as a baby in the 1930s. Several employees featured in the company newsletter were G.I. brides from Europe. Most employees, however, were second- and third-generation Americans descended from the great European immigration of the early twentieth century. Ethnic identity became part of workplace beauty culture through employee weddings. For example, the Irish customs at the 1959 wedding of Kathleen Hardy and Edward Coyle, who had met at a social gathering of an Irish organization, were the subject of a full-page feature in *The Maiden Forum*.[40] Employees learned about different ethnic customs by attending the weddings of coworkers or reading about them in the company newsletter. Beauty culture operated as a shared set of values and interests among these women.

Even the ILGWU participated in Maidenform beauty culture. Two years before the "I Dreamed" campaign, the ILGWU's Maryland-Virginia District Manager, Angela Bambace, wrote the assistant general manager at Maidenform that her staff had been commenting on the new brassieres. According to her, they were "all anxious to try them— and thereby attain that 'new look.'" From 1944 through the 1950s, every Christmas the ILGWU Maryland-Virginia district office staff members sent a list of their brassiere sizes and choice of style to the Bayonne, New Jersey plant. The office staff, as well as the district manager, enjoyed receiving these brassieres as gifts from Maidenform. Often, the Maidenform office sent reminders to the ILGWU office, asking for their bra sizes. Maidenform also sent questionnaires for the "girls to answer after they (had) worn the new brassiere for a little while." According to the secretary at the district office, the staff liked them and recommended them to their friends. The female staffers at the ILGWU office and the male management at Maidenform treated the custom with a degree of mock seriousness. In 1952, the ILGWU office sent them a "gem" to be used as potential advertising copy. Sent along with their list of sizes, this "gem" appeared as an office memo: "There's a Maidenform bra for every type figur' / We have them all—small, LARGE and BIGGER! / Our cups runneth over from A's until Z's / We challenge your wares to fit all of theeze."[41]

Women like the ILGWU office workers may have brought Maidenform products home with them and they may have attempted to shape their own bodies into the ideal Maidenform woman reflected in the "I Dreamed" campaign, but they also used beauty culture—a gendered "system of meaning"—to suit themselves. When negotiating over gifts of brassieres from management to the union office staff, the district manager did not fail to uphold the bread-and-butter interests of the ILGWU. In a letter to the chief industrial engineer at the central Bayonne plant, for example, Angela Bambace criticized Maidenform for delaying unionization of the Clarksburg plant, conveyed the Princeton plant's dissatisfaction with working a whole day on Saturday, and in the same breath, reminded the plant official of his promise of two brassieres for her staff.[42] ILGWU office workers and Maidenform employees alike subscribed to the ideals of female beauty and fashion perpetuated by Maidenform, yet also used them to their own ends.

As the humorous exchange of letters between the ILGWU and Maidenform management demonstrated, a shared language of gender could serve as a bridge between those with competing interests. From one perspective, Maidenform management's soliciting of ILGWU office staff members' measurements and their annual gift of brassieres to these union women could be construed as condescending, even sexist. When Maidenform's Chief Industrial Engineer William Woltz wrote to the ILGWU district manager that two size 44 brassieres she had requested were "obviously" not for her and instead sent on "three of a more appropriate size" determined from his memory of her, he may have offended the ILGWU official. Humor about women's bra sizes and the underlying belief that women are primarily interested in fashion and physical appearance stemmed from a gender-based system of unequal relations between men and women. The ILGWU office staff's participation in this gendered discourse, however, shows how class and gender interests overlapped in complex and often contradictory ways. The district manager chose to participate in the Maidenform tradition and over the years encouraged the practice.[43] She likely understood that such gifts could smooth the path for more important exchanges between the company and the union.

Maidenform employees' relationship to the commercial beauty culture fostered by the company was similarly complex. While beauty culture was a means of forging solidarity among those who worked at Maidenform, its gender norms and beauty standards were not swallowed whole. From the pages of the company newsletter it appears that employees may have viewed company beauty culture with some skepticism or at least with a sense of humor. Reporters giving department news might satirize women's obsession with beauty culture. For example, one department reporter pointedly described an "informal beauty contest limited to one contestant," in which the winner, Sophie Worosilo, was also "the judge of the 'contest.'" Employees found different ways to mock the company product. Playing Pinning the Donkey at an office party, Grace Romeo watched a blindfolded Kurt Metzger pin a brassiere on a drawing of a life-sized Maidenform woman. Department headings drawn for the company newsletter, such as "Making Ends Meet," pictured curvaceous women straining to do up their brassieres in the back. One department news heading, "At the Curve Exchange," showed a conscious understanding that on one level, Maidenform commodified the female body.[44] Mocking Maidenform brassieres ultimately did nothing to challenge the unequal relationship between men and women or between employer and employee. At the same time, noticing new hairdos, sharing styling tips, and laughing at beauty foibles were ways for women workers to find a common ground. This common ground, however, explicitly validated heterosexuality and marriage, uniting those women whose lives embodied the dominant gender ideology while implicitly excluding those who did not conform.

At Maidenform, the cultural production of femininity took place in several contexts. On the one hand, Maidenform marketing and company culture promoted a vision of femininity that narrowly defined women's identity. Through advertising, the company newsletter, beauty contests, Pin-Up of the Month competitions, and of course, the ultrafeminine form made possible by its brassieres and girdles, Maidenform contributed to postwar notions of glamour and beauty. On the other hand, the ambiguous message of the "I Dreamed" advertising campaign and the complex gender negotiations that took place between the ILGWU, Maidenform management, and female employees lend support to revisionist interpretations of the postwar era that have complicated the stereotype of domestic femininity.[45]

Maidenform promoted the idea that being a successful woman meant being attractive. In many ways, however, women in the beauty culture industry challenged the hard dichotomy outlined in fashion and consumer culture historiography—the question of whether fashions, cosmetics, commercially produced notions of beauty, and jobs that help (re)produce this "system of meaning" ultimately empowered or disempowered women. Beauty culture at Maidenform provided a language through which women articulated social relations among themselves. Sharing an interest in fashion, hairstyling, and weddings, women formed bonds on the shop floor. These practices engendered meaning in their lives, and provided them with hopes of economic mobility through careers in commercial beauty culture or through marriage. Maidenform Pin-Ups reflected the ethnic, racial, and class diversity embedded in American beauty culture during this period. Women like Mary Smietanek participated in its making and claimed the right to be glamorous.

Vicki Howard

ACKNOWLEDGMENTS

Thanks to Kathy Peiss for her helpful comments and suggestions. I would also like to acknowledge the readings given to earlier versions of this paper by Leilah Danielson, Janet Davis, Sean Kelley, Margaret Marsh, Jeffrey Meikle, and Christine Williams. Thanks also to Mimi Minnick and Jennifer Snyder for their help with the Maidenform Collection.

NOTES

1. "At the Curve Exchange" is the heading for one department's news in *The Maiden Forum* (August-September, 1946): 4, Series 4: Publications, 1931–1997, Subseries B: *Maiden-Forum* Newsletters 1944–1995, Maidenform Collection, Archives Center, National Museum of American History, Smithsonian Institution, Washington DC. (hereafter, MC)
2. "Pin-Up for March," *The Maiden Forum* (March 1948): 3.
3. Susan Porter Benson, *Counter Cultures: Saleswomen, Managers, and Customers in American Department Stores, 1890–1940* (Urbana, IL: University of Illinois Press, 1986), 228.
4. Susan Porter Benson, *Counter Cultures*; Dorothy Sue Cobble, *Dishing It Out: Waitresses and Their Unions in the Twentieth Century* (Urbana, IL: University of Illinois Press, 1991); Susan Glenn, *Daughters of the Shtetl: Life and Labor in the Immigrant Generation* (Ithaca, NY: Cornell University Press, 1990), 79, 145, 157–166; Stephen Norwood, *Labor's Flaming Youth: Telephone Operators and Worker Militancy, 1878–1923* (Urbana, IL: University of Illinois Press, 1990), 110–112; Kathy Peiss, *Cheap Amusements: Working Women and Leisure in Turn-of-the-Century New York* (Philadelphia: Temple University Press,1986); Nan Enstad, *Ladies of Labor, Girls of Adventure: Working Women, Popular Culture, and Labor Politics at the Turn of the Twentieth Century* (New York: Columbia University Press, 1999).
5. Alice Kessler-Harris, *Out to Work: A History of Wage-Earning Women in the United States* (New York: Oxford University Press, 1982), 273–274, 301–302.
6. For a discussion of social and demographic changes in the 1940s, see Susan Hartmann, *The Home Front and Beyond: American Women in the 1940s* (Boston: Twayne, 1982). For a discussion of the 1950s, see Elaine Tyler May, *Homeward Bound: American Families in the Cold War Era* (New York: Basic Books, 1988); Stephanie Coontz, *The Way We Never Were: American Families and the Nostalgia Trap* (New York: Basic Books, 1992), 24. For a history of the suburbs, see Kenneth T. Jackson, *Crabgrass Frontier: The Suburbanization of the United States* (New York: Oxford University Press, 1985).
7. *Jantzen Yarns*, February 1955, 19, Box 5, 1946–1955, Jantzen Knitting Mills Collection, Archives Center, National Museum of American History, Smithsonian Institution, Washington DC.
8. John Modell *Into One's Own: From Youth to Adulthood in the United States, 1920–1975* (Berkeley, CA: University of California Press, 1989), 284. Also, see Betty Friedan, *The Feminine Mystique* (New York: W. W. Norton, 1963), chap. 1; Elaine Tyler May, *Homeward Bound*, 65, 82, 119; Susan Hartmann, *The Home Front*, 164–165; "You Can't Have a Career and Be a Good Wife," *Ladies' Home Journal* (January 1944), in *Women's Magazines, 1940–1960: Gender Roles and the Popular Press*, ed. Nancy A. Walker (Boston: St. Martin's Press, 1998), 71–75; Jennifer Colton, "Why I Quit Working," *Good Housekeeping* (September 1951), in ibid., 82–85; "The Married Woman Goes Back to Work," *Woman's Home Companion* (October 1956), in ibid., 87–96.
9. For an overview of this debate, see Jane Gaines, "Introduction: Fabricating the Female Body," in *Fabrications: Costume and the Female Body*, ed. Jane Gaines and Charlotte Herzog (New York: Routledge, 1990), 1–27; Also, see Victoria de Grazia, "Changing Consumption Regimes: Introduction," in *The Sex of Things: Gender and Consumption in Historical Perspective*, ed. Victoria de Grazia with Ellen Furlough (Berkeley, CA: University of California Press, 1996), 7: Recent studies of women workers have examined their double role as consumers and producers. See Nan Enstad, "Fashioning Political Identities: Cultural Studies and the Historical Construction of Political Subjects," *American Quarterly* 50 (December 1998): 745–782; Wendy Gamber, *The Female Economy: The Millinery and Dressmaking Trades, 1860–1930* (Urbana, IL: University of Illinois Press, 1997).
10. Ellen Carol DuBois, *Feminism and Suffrage: the Emergence of an Independent Women's Movement in America, 1848–1869* (Ithaca, NY: Cornell University Press, 1978); Naomi Wolf, *The Beauty Myth* (New York: William Morrow, 1991); Susan Bordo, *Unbearable Weight: Feminism, Western Culture and the Body* (Berkeley, CA: University of California Press, 1993);

Well-known primary sources offering critiques of fashion and commercial beauty standards include Simone de Beauvoir, *The Second Sex*, trans. H.M. Parshley (New York: Knopf, 1953); 529, and Betty Friedan, *The Feminine Mystique*, 17, 65.

11. Judy Tzu-Chun Wu, "'Loveliest Daughter of Our Ancient Cathay!': Representations of Ethnic and Gender Identity in the Miss Chinatown U.S.A. Beauty Pageant," *Journal of Social History* 31 (Fall 1997): 6–9, 11, reprinted in this volume. See Nan Enstad, "Fashioning Political Identities," 745–782; Christine Stansell, *City of Women: Sex and Class in New York, 1789-1860* (Urbana, IL: University of Illinois Press, 1987); Susan Porter Benson, *Counter Cultures*; Kathy Peiss, *Cheap Amusements*.

12. Lois W. Banner, *American Beauty* (Chicago: University of Chicago Press, 1983), 3, 29, 70, 74–75, 86–87; Kathy Peiss, *Hope in a Jar: The Making of America's Beauty Culture* (New York: Metropolitan Books, 1998), 6, 61– 62, 261–262.

13. Kathy Peiss notes this shift in her discussion of the Fire and Ice Revlon lipstick advertising campaign in *Hope in a Jar* (248–251); According to Lois Banner, the "I Dreamed" campaign was one example of how advertising in the 1950s was becoming more sexual and exhibitionistic. Lois Banner, *American Beauty*, 273. For histories of advertising, see Roland Marchand, *Advertising the American Dream: Making Way for Modernity, 1920-1940* (Berkeley, CA: University of California Press, 1985); Jackson Lears, *Fables of Abundance: A Cultural History of Advertising in America* (New York: Basic Books, 1994).

14. "Brassieres . . . A Vital Necessity to Women at Work," 1943, Box 69, Series 6: Advertising, Subseries A: Advertisements, 1929–1996; Henry Lee, "Maidenform's J. A. Coleman," *Madison Avenue* (November, ca. 1960): 54, Box 2, Series 2: News Articles, 1941–1997, Subseries A: News Articles re Family, 1950–1997, M.C.

15. All Dream theme ads discussed hereafter are found in Box 22, 64, 69, Series 6: Advertising, Subseries A: Advertisements, 1929–1996, MC. (Collection being processed. Box numbers are tentative).

16. "The Story of Maidenform Inc., Where Life Begins at Forty," Newsclipping, n.p., ca. 1962, Box 2, Series 2: News Articles, 1941–1997, Subseries C: News Articles re Company, 1950–1997; "Maidenform's Mrs. R," reprint from *Fortune* (July 1950), n.p., Box 64, Series 2: News Articles, 1941–1997, Subseries C: News Articles re Company, 1950–1997; "Ida Rosenthal," *Maidenform News* (1987), Box 1, Series 1: Company History, 1922–1990; "Application to War Manpower Commission to Declare Business Essential: Original Exhibits Supplementary Brief" [8503-1], 1943–1944, Box 51, Series 9: World War II Activities, 1941–1946, Subseries B: Government Relations, 1942–1945, MC. Maidenform also manufactured silk parachutes for the war effort, and developed a homing pigeon vest that allowed paratroopers to carry the birds with them for military intelligence purposes.

17. In 1954, the Bayonne New Jersey plant, which was the design and manufacturing control center, employed 1,300 men and women. "Quality is not a sometime thing," *Women's Wear Daily*, (June 3, 1954), n.p., Box 2, Series 2: News Articles, 1941–1997, Subseries C: News Articles re Company, 1950–1997; "Keeping the Nation in Good Shape," Newsclipping ca. 1955, Box 2, Series 2: News Articles, 1941–1997, Subseries C: News Articles re Company, 1950–1997."The Story of Maidenform Inc." ca. 1962, MC.

18. The campaign was run by the William Weintraub Agency, which became Norman, Craig & Kummel. "'I Dreamed I was a Tycoon in my . . .' Ida Rosenthal," *Time* (October 24, 1960): 92, Box 2, Series 2: News Articles, 1941–1997, Subseries A: News Articles re Family 1950–1997, MC.

19. Barbara J. Coleman, "Maidenform(ed): Images of American Women in the 1950s," *Genders 21: Forming and Reforming Identity*, ed. Carol Siegel and Ann Kibbey (New York: N. P. 1995), 7; "Buyers, Press Representatives Witness Fashion 'Dream' Show at Hotel Pierre," *The Maiden Forum* (January 1951): 1; "I Dreamed" Contest, 1956, Box 68, Series 5: Sales and Marketing, 1929–1997, Subseries J, MC.

20. "Maidenform Campaign Seeks Rebirth: New Ads Key Part of Chapter 11 Reorganization Plan," *Advertising Age* (February 1, 1999): 8; "I Dreamed I Was a Bride in My Maidenform Bra," *The Maiden Forum* (February 1955): 10.

21. "Rosenthal's Influence on Industry Enduring," Newsclipping, 1958, Box 2, Series 2: News Articles, 1941–1997, Subseries A: News Articles re Family, 1950–1997, MC. Barbara Coleman also discusses Maidenform's connection with the New Look style in "Maidenform(ed)," 6; Susan M. Hartmann, *The Home Front*, 203; Maureen Turim, "Designing Women: the Emergence of the New Sweetheart Line," in *Fabrications: Costume and the Female Body*, ed. Jane Gaines and Charlotte Herzog (New York: Routledge, 1990), 212–228, 285.

22. "Keeping the Nation in Good Shape," ca. 1955. For a list of styles, see "Uplifting," *The New Yorker* (September 21, 1993), 34–35; for a discussion of the social construction of fashionable shapes, see *Men and Women: Dressing the Part*, ed. Claudia Brush Kidwell and Valerie

Steele (Washington, DC: Smithsonian, 1989); Anne Hollander, *Sex and Suits* (New York: Knopf, 1995); For a psychological interpretation of corsets, see Valerie Steele, *Fashion and Eroticism: Ideals of Feminine Beauty from the Victorian Era to the Jazz Age* (New York: Oxford University Press, 1985), 3; "Corsets Ready for Chemise: Modified Bra Shapes to Lead," reprint from *Women's Wear Daily* (November 21, 1957), Box 2, Series 2: News Articles, 1941–1997, Subseries C: News Articles re Company, 1948–1970, MC.

23. Susan M. Hartmann, *The Home Front*; 199. Robert B. Westbrook, "'I Want a Girl, Just Like the Girl that Married Harry James': American Women and the Problem of Political Obligation in World War II," *American Quarterly* 42 (December 1990): 587–614; Transcript: Interview with Kitty D'Alessio, August 8, 1990, Box 1, Series 1: Company History 1922–1990, MC; Thomas Hine, *Populuxe* (New York: Knopf, 1986), 30–31.

24. "I Dreamed I Was a Toreador," 1951, Box 69, Series 6: Advertising, Subseries A: Advertisements 1929–1996, MC; also, see "I Dreamed I Was a Work of Art," cited in Coleman, "Maidenform(ed)," 20.

25. Coleman, "Maidenform(ed)," 18–21, 5, 15–24. Coleman cites these advertisements as superficially appearing to be a response to the increase in wage-earning women, but ultimately dismisses this interpretation; "I Dreamed I Was a Lady Editor," Box 69, Series 6: Advertising, Subseries A: Advertisements 1929–1996, MC.

26. Sylvia F. Porter, "We are a Nation of Working Wives," *New York Post* (May 2, 1950), Estelle Ellis Collection, Archives Center, National Museum of American History, Smithsonian Institution, Washington DC; Kessler-Harris, *Out to Work*, 300–303: For a discussion of the Office of War Information "Womanpower Campaign," see Melissa Dabakis, "Gendered Labor: Norman Rockwell's Rosie the Riveter and the Discourses of Wartime Womanhood," in *Gender and American History Since 1890*, ed. Barbara Melosh (New York: Routledge, 1993), 190–191; Kessler-Harris, *Out to Work*, 276.

27. "The Story of Maidenform Inc.," ca. 1962; "Maidenform's Mrs. R." The 1,100 Bayonne employees were given raises of $1.50 to $2 a week. "Pay Rise Ends Bayonne Strike," *New York Times* (November 5, 1941): 46; Court Transcripts: Bayonne, NJ, 1955, Box 53, Series 10: Labor Relations, 1937–1990, MC.

28. Lizabeth Cohen, *Making a New Deal: Industrial Workers in Chicago, 1919–1939* (Cambridge: Cambridge University Press, 1990), 164, 179.

29. Maidenform plants in West Virginia also demonstrated a support for beauty culture. "Clarksburg," *The Maiden Forum* (June 1953): 8; Photograph of Shirley Bishop, Miss Maidenform 1954, Princeton Plant, *The Maiden Forum* (December 1953), n.p.; "Department 2A Produces Pulchritude Parade," *The Maiden Forum* (October 1946): 1; Gamber, *The Female Economy*, 125, 220–222.

30. Norwood, *Labor's Flaming Youth*, 14–15; Cobble, *Dishing It Out*, 127; "The Wedding Party from Our Spring Fashion Show," *Store Chat* (March 1949), back cover, Strawbridge & Clothier Collection, Hagley Museum and Library, Wilmington; Sherna Berger Gluck, *Rosie the Riveter Revisited: Women, the War and Social Change* (New York: Penguin, 1988), 11; "Department 2A Produces Pulchritude Parade," *The Maiden Forum* (October 1946): 1; Cobble, *Dishing it Out*, photograph and caption between p. 111 and p. 115.

31. "Reporter Profile," *The Maiden Forum* (June-July 1950): 7; "Inquiring Reporter," *The Maiden Forum* (April 1950): 9; "Pin-Up for June," *The Maiden Forum* (June-July 1950): 6. Also, see John Haraksin, "Pin-Up for January," *The Maiden Forum* (January 1952): 5.

32. "Pin-Up for October," *The Maiden Forum* (September 1950): 7; Westbrook argued that wartime pinups constructed women as "objects of obligation"—in other words, something to fight for. He also noted the differences between pinups with erotic appeal, like Rita Hayworth (Margarita Cansino), and those with working-class girl-next door appeal, like Betty Grable. Westbrook, "Political Obligation," 605–606, 589, 596–604; "Pin-Up for October," *The Maiden Forum* (November 1947): 4.

33. "Our June Pin-Up," *The Maiden Forum* (June 1946): 2.

34. Peiss, *Hope in a Jar*; "Pin-Up for January," *The Maiden Forum* (January 1949): 3; "Staff Profiles," *The Maiden Forum* (December 1944): 4.

35. *The Maiden Forum* (June-July 1955): 9; "Reporter Profile," *The Maiden Forum* (April 1950): 9; Some expressed different interests. For example, office employee Bernice Samuel asked for "personal reactions to movies, plays, current events." "Inquiring Reporter," *The Maiden Forum* (April 1950): 9; "For Women and (Peeping Toms)," *The Maiden Forum* (July 1946): 3; "You Can Change Your Face," *The Maiden Forum* (September 1950): 11; "Best Foot Forward," *The Maiden Forum* (August-September 1953): 8; "Rose Aloi Promoted," *The Maiden Forum* (February 1950): 9.

36. "Our Pin-Up for March," *The Maiden Forum* (March 1946). 2, "Belles and Beaux," "Pin-Up for January," *The Maiden Forum* (January 1944): 3; "Pin-Up for April," *The Maiden Forum* (April 1949): 2; For example, Irene Ostapko's "athletic interests [were] gradually being displaced

by her interest in Edward Bajor, her fiance," and her "dreams of that little white cottage." "And what could be more interesting," queried the reporter. "Pin-Up for May," *The Maiden Forum* (May 1949): n.p.; "Pin-Up for November," *The Maiden Forum* (November 1951): 6.

37. An entire issue featuring photos of Maidenform brides on its cover was devoted to such articles. *The Maiden Forum* (June 1953); "Engagements," *The Maiden Forum* (January 1951): 4; "Inquiring Reporter," *The Maiden Forum* (April 1950): 5; "Inquiring Reporter Visits Morristown," *The Maiden Forum* (December 1953): 4; "On the Job Romance," *The Maiden Forum* (February 1955): 5; *The Maiden Forum* (February 1955): 5–6.

38. *The Maiden Forum* (May 1947): 2; *The Maiden Forum* (September 1954): 6; *The Maiden Forum* (December 1951): 9; *The Maiden Forum* (June-July 1955): n.p.; For the period 1/1/46 to 1/1/60, of the 309 marriages of female employees at Maidenform plants recounted with any detail, forty-nine brides were known to continue work after their wedding, while five were known to stop working after their wedding. This figure is based on statements to that effect taken from their wedding announcements. Many others appeared to continue working (for example, their showers were held at work, and there was no mention of their leaving), but only those whose status could be confirmed were included in this calculation.

39. Some historians of consumption have seen mass culture uniting workers and bridging ethnic differences, while others have described it as flattening ethnic distinctions or destroying class consciousness. Cohen, *Making a New Deal;* Ronald Edsforth, *Class Conflict and Cultural Consensus: The Making of a Mass Consumer Society in Flint Michigan* (New Brunswick, NJ: Rutgers University Press, 1987); For a discussion of white ethnicity, see David Roediger, "Whiteness and Ethnicity in the History of 'White Ethnics' in the United States," in *Towards the Abolition of Whiteness* (London: Verso, 1994); David Roediger, *The Wages of Whiteness: Race and the Making of the American Working Class* (London: Verso, 1991).

40. "Pin-Up for August," *The Maiden Forum* (August 1947): 3; "Pin-Up for October," *The Maiden Forum* (October 1946): 2; "Girl of the Month," *The Maiden Forum* (February 1951): 9. Elfrieda Shukert and Barbara Scibetta, *War Brides of World War II* (New York: Penguin, 1988); "Maidenform's Mrs. R.," *The Maiden Forum* (June 1959): 7.

41. Angela Bambace to Ellis Rosenthal, December 5, 1947, ILGWU Correspondence: West Virginia, 1943–1952, Series 10: Labor Relations, 1937–1990; Bambace to William Woltz, December 6, 1944; Rosenthal to Bambace, November 18, 1957; Rosenthal to Bambace, December 10, 1947; Mary Casale to Rosenthal, December 31, 1947; Office Memo, enclosed in Bambace to Rosenthal, December 17, 1952, MC.

42. Bambace to Woltz, December 6, 1944, MC.

43. Woltz to Bambace, December 21, 1944; Rosenthal to Bambace, December 16, 1946.

44. "Maiden Form Style," *The Maiden Forum* (January 1947): 5. Maidenform jokes abounded. *The Maiden Forum* (April-May 1957): 9; *The Maiden Forum* (December 1953): 10; "Making Ends Meet," *Maiden Forum* (August-September, 1946): 4; *The Maiden Forum* (August-September, 1946): 4.

45. Joanne Meyerowitz has criticized "the conservatism-and-constraints" approach that focused on women's subordination and downplayed their agency. Joanne Meyerowitz, ed., *Not June Cleaver: Women and Gender in Postwar America, 1945–1960* (Philadelphia: Temple University Press, 1994), 3–4.

Estée Lauder

SELF-DEFINITION AND THE MODERN COSMETICS MARKET

NANCY KOEHN

INTRODUCTION

Despite rapid growth in the first two decades of the twentieth century, the U.S. beauty business remained relatively small in 1920. Most households would not have considered perfume, facial cleansers, or aftershave as essential goods. By the mid-1990s, cosmetics production was a thriving global industry, and most Americans viewed cosmetics and toiletries as routine components of the cost of living.[1]

Historian Kathy Peiss has emphasized the importance of women's identities and social roles in understanding the early development of America's beauty culture. I draw upon her research and other studies of the young beauty business, but my focus is on Estée Lauder and the decades *after* World War II.[2] To exploit the new possibilities, this entrepreneur constructed a meaningful identity for her products, one that women associated with quality, self-expression, reinvention, elegance, and control. As Estée Lauder Inc. expanded in the 1960s and 1970s, Lauder, her family, and colleagues pioneered initiatives to interest consumers and earn their trust, such as gift-with-purchase and on-site sales training, and those quickly became industry standards.

GETTING STARTED

Estée Lauder was born Joscphine Esther (Esty) Mentzer on July 1, 1908, in Corona, a section of the Borough of Queens in New York City. She was the second and last child of Rose Schotz Rosenthal Mentzer and Max Mentzer, Eastern European immigrants who had met in the United States.[3] The father, Max, had travelled to the United States from Hungary in the 1890s. He was a large, kind man with a ruddy complexion. When his youngest daughter was born, Max was a storekeeper in Corona. He and his family lived above the hardware store he owned.

Esty Lauder was a curious, active child. Like many other little girls, she enjoyed experimenting with her mother's skin creams and fragrances. But Esty's interest in beauty products and other symbols of femininity extended beyond trying them on herself. Later in life, she recalled how she had started giving what she called "treatments" to her family members and friends. Max Mentzer admonished his daughter to stop "fiddling with other people's faces."[4]

But Esty remembered that she did not obey, for she saw cosmetics as a means of self-expression for women: "I want to paint a picture of the young girl I was—a girl caught up, mesmerized by pretty things and pretty people." How, if at all, was this commitment to standards of external beauty related to Esty's upbringing in Corona? Did her interest in altering other people's faces have anything to do with a lifelong concern to reinvent herself? Lauder recalled that as a schoolgirl she was ashamed of her parents' heavy accents and European manners. She yearned "to be 100 percent American," and remembered being torn: "I loved them both so much—their beauty and their character, but I didn't love feeling different because of their old country ways."[5]

Meanwhile, after school and on weekends, she helped her father in his store. She learned to keep track of merchandise, talk with customers, and arrange tools in the display windows. And she took part in another family business as well, a small Corona department store called Plafker & Rosenthal. The store was run by two savvy, enterprising women merchants who worked to understand and meet customers' needs. They earned a reputation for being intelligent and trustworthy, and their business thrived. Young Esty took part in the commercial and social activity of Plafker & Rosenthal, running errands, laying out merchandise, and waiting on customers: "The ladies in their furs came to buy, and bought more when I waited on them. I knew it. I felt it."[6]

As Esty grew into adulthood, she explored her interests. She enjoyed retailing, but she also dreamed of being an actress. Whichever path she took, the young woman was determined to shape her sense of self without regard to existing circumstances, to become the person that she *wanted to be*, and make this identity public. Before she was 20, for example, Esther had changed her first name at least twice, from her childhood name, Esty, to Estelle and then to Estella. (She would go back to calling herself Esther before settling permanently on Estée in her early 30s).[7]

Esty continued to be intrigued by the possibilities for reinvention that cosmetics offered women. Perhaps she was also struck by the rapid proliferation of advertisements and products. Advertising expenditures for drugs and toiletries in leading magazines grew rapidly between 1915 and 1925, and with the advent of radio in the 1920s, cosmetics manufacturers began to advertise heavily on the airwaves.[8] The booming beauty busines presented numerous employment opportunities for women[9] Esty may have considered working in a beauty parlor or opening her own shop.

But in 1924, a different opportunity opened up. Her mother's brother, John Schotz, started a small business in Manhattan to manufacture and distribute beauty products and other compounds.[10] Uncle John called his company New Way Laboratories. His product list included several skin-care preparations: "Six-in-One Cold Cream," "Dr. Schotz Viennese Cream," and "Flory Anna's Eczema Ointment," which was named for his wife, Flora Anna. New Way Laboratories also made several fragrances, lip rouge, "freckle remover," poultry lice-killer, Dog Mange Cure, embalming fluid, and Hungarian Mustache Wax.[11]

The beauty side of the business fascinated Esty. At 16, she began spending all her free time with Schotz, learning from him as he worked. Her uncle, she remembered, "produced miracles." She watched "as he created a secret formula, a magic cream potion with which he filled vials and jars and flagons and any other handy container." His creams, she continued, "made your face feel like spun silk" and "made any passing imperfection be gone by evening."[12]

Esty was a fast learner. She instinctively appreciated both the science and art of the cosmetics business. She took careful note of how her uncle prepared each product, learning how to combine oils, wax, borax, lanolin, and other ingredients. She began experimenting with different formulas. As a student in high school, she became known among her peers for her cosmetic applications—what today are called "makeovers." "After school," she recalled, "I'd run home to practice being a scientist."[13] She was interested in how effective each formula was. How quickly did a particular compound clear up blemishes? How well did a given cream moisturize dry skin? Esty took the results of her school makeovers back to New Way Laboratories, where she and her uncle used them to improve his products.

Schotz reinforced his niece's interest in hands-on selling. He was an expert at demonstrating his creams and other skin-care products on customers' faces. He passed these skills on to his apprentice, teaching her to massage a woman's face quickly and soothingly. Esty learned to apply cleansing oil, cream, rouge, powder, lip color, and often eye shadow to a potential customer's face in three or four minutes.

In the late 1920s, Esty met Joseph Lauter, a gentle, down-to-earth man with a quick sense of humor. Six years older than Esty, he had a background similar to hers. The child of Austrian immigrants, Joe had grown up on the Lower East Side of Manhattan, where his father worked as a tailor. By the time he encountered Esty, Joe had been in and out of a number of commercial ventures, including silk manufacturing. In January 1930, after a three-year courtship, the couple married in a formal Jewish ceremony.[14]

For the next several years, Esty worked to balance the demands of family life with her own ambitions. In March 1933, she and Joe had a son whom they named Leonard Alan Lauter. Esty continued her involvement in the beauty business. In between making meals for her family, she tinkered with Schotz's formulas and cooked up pots of cream on her kitchen stove. She tried her skin-care creations out on anyone she could: friends, family, and even passersby.[15]

By 1933, she was listing her home-based business as Lauter Chemists in the New York telephone directory. She sold goods from her apartment, but most of her revenue was earned in Manhattan beauty parlors. In 1935 there were 61,355 beauty shops in the United States and more than 4,400 in New York City alone. Women owned the majority of these businesses, which operated primarily as hair salons.[16]

Esty herself was a regular customer at one such shop, Florence Morris's House of Ash Blondes on Manhattan's Upper West Side. She used her visits to talk with other women about her products. These one-on-one encounters convinced her that consumers, especially those who did not have extensive experience with cosmetics, needed guidance and encouragement. They also needed enough time to ask questions of the salesperson, experiment with different products, and if possible, to have a makeover. When Florence Morris, the shop owner, asked Esty about her skin-care creams, Esty brought in "four jars, on which only *everything* rested," she remembered. After applying cleansing oil, creams, powder, rouge, and lip color to the owner's face, "I showed Mrs. Morris a mirror. She was a raving beauty," Esty said.[17] That was when young Esty began getting concessions in beauty parlors.

ATTRACTING CONSUMERS

For the next several years, as Esty traveled between beauty parlors, she always carried extra supplies of her offerings and wax paper. She would leave samples with the women she met—a lipstick shaving, a dollop of her All Purpose Crème, or a spoonful of turquoise eye shadow. This was unusual at the time. But Esty already believed strongly in the power of giving women something for nothing. In dis-

Figure 9.1. Estée Lauder, shortly after her marriage in 1930. In her autobiography, *Estée: A Success Story*, she describes herself here as "[t]he smiling product of the House of Ash Blondes." Florence Morris, the owner of this New York City beauty parlor, gave Estée her first big break by offering her a concession to sell her beauty products at another Manhattan salon. Courtesy of Estée Lauder Companies, Inc.

tributing samples or applying makeup, Esty listened carefully to consumers. She was particularly interested in their opinions and adjusted products and her selling techniques to better suit her customers.

Most of Esty's early products were based on Schotz's formulas. Yet in starting her own business, she was concerned to distinguish her offerings from those of her uncle and other chemists who made cosmetics. When she began selling her offerings at New York beauty parlors, she discarded the medicinal jars and tin lids that Schotz had used, choosing opal white jars with black lids.

She debated long and hard about what to call her line. Schotz sold his beauty formulas under the Flory Anna and Florana labels, both named for his wife.[18] Esty would have none of this. Her products *had* to reflect her involvement. "I wanted to see my name in lights," she said, "but I was willing to settle for my name on a jar."[19]

She thought her formal married name, Josephine Lauter, was too long. She experimented with variants of her middle name Esther and nickname Esty. About this time, she also changed her married name from Lauter to Lauder, said to be the original spelling of Joe's family in Austria.[20] Thereafter, she would be known by the name Estée Lauder, and her products would be sold under that label.

From a marketing perspective, the name was a smart choice. Estée Lauder was distinctive. But it was also easy to say and remember. It sounded unquestionably womanly and vaguely European, an association reinforced by the mandatory accent in Estée. Feminine and worldly were connotations that Lauder wanted attached to her products, important attributes of the identity that she was creating for her offerings and perhaps for herself. She knew instinctively that how a given product looked, including what its label said, communicated a range of information to consumers. Some of this information concerned the product's functional properties. Other information was aimed at appealing to female consumers' sense of themselves. Estée believed that women in the 1930s wanted "confidence-building beauty." Lauder tailored her packaging, sales approach, and makeover techniques to these insights.

She also knew that most consumers in the 1930s had less money to spend than in the 1920s. But even in the midst of economic crisis, millions of Americans purchased small luxuries: movie tickets, candy, and alcohol. These expenditures, Estée realized, bought people moments of enjoyment, an escape from everyday problems, or just a means to pass the time. Such benefits were particularly important in economic downturns, as Estée appreciated. Per capita movie sales in the 1930s, for example, were about six times higher than in the 1990s.[21]

Going to the movies offered Americans more than a respite. As the popularity of movies increased in the 1930s, millions of women took at least some of their fashion cues from stars such as Bette Davis, Carole Lombard, and Claudette Colbert. The growth of the film industry in the 1930s and 1940s thus indirectly fed that of the cosmetics sector.[22]

Estée's work in New York City beauty parlors proved a fertile training ground. She learned more and more about producing and selling effective, attractive cosmetics. This understanding did not come through formal training. The bulk of her entrepreneurial education was a result of trial and error, of making it up as she went along.[23]

REINVENTING HER MARRIAGE

Estée's growing commitment to the business put strains on her marriage. In 1939, when she was 31, she decided to leave Joe Lauder. She was vague about her reasons. Whatever her rationale, Estée divorced

Joe on April 11, 1939, citing grounds of mental cruelty. She took custody of their son Leonard and moved to Miami Beach, Florida.

Over the next three years, she shuttled between Florida and New York City, selling her products at beauty parlors, bridge parties, and hotels. For a time, she had a concession at the swank Roney Plaza Hotel on Collins Avenue in Miami Beach. In this and other venues, Estée learned as much from certain wealthy customers as they from her, taking cues from various members of Miami Beach's high society on how to dress, speak, and comport herself. Like Elizabeth Arden or Helena Rubinstein, Estée had long dreamed of transcending her immigrant roots and acquiring the prerequisites of wealth.[24] In Florida and New York, she met scores of well-connected women. Estée kept track of these contacts, determined to build a reputation for herself as an elegant and nationally recognized socialite.

In 1942, after almost four years of being apart, Estée and Joe Lauder reunited. Although it is not clear exactly why the couple got back together, it seems likely that he never stopped loving her. Probably she reassessed her former husband, deciding that he was a good match. They were married for a second time on December 7, 1942, in a quiet ceremony. In early 1944, the couple's second child, Ronald, was born.

THE BEAUTY BUSINESS DURING WORLD WAR II

With the onset of war in 1941, writers, government officials, and others debated the role of the cosmetics industry.[25] Some, like novelist Fannie Hurst, regarded the pursuit of beauty in the midst of global conflict as frivolous. She wrote in a 1942 *New York Times* article that it was "at shocking variance with our national crisis."[26]

Others disagreed. One housewife responded that whatever "contributes to one's well-being definitely offers a service to humanity."[27] According to an editor for the *American Perfumer*, razors, toothbrushes, hand cream, and makeup were "*essential* to our way of living, just as much so as an orange or a dish of spinach."[28] Some medical authorities argued that using cosmetics had positive physiological effects for women. Efficiency experts in Britain and the United States contended that women worked more productively when they had access to cosmetics. Some companies urged women workers to look good on the job. For example, Martin Aircraft offered beauty tips for female workers. Lockheed had beauty salons and cosmetics stations installed in its factories.[29] Between 1939 and 1944, more than 3 million women entered the civilian labor force. Another 200,000 women joined the military. Many of the women who took civilian jobs had positions or responsibilities traditionally held by men.[30]

In or out of uniform, millions of working women had larger public roles and personal income than they had previously known. Many also paid more attention to their appearance. Working women purchased beauty products to help define their public identities, assert their independence, enjoy themselves, and spend some of the money they were making. In the five years starting with 1940, retail sales of makeup, fragrances, and toiletries rose from $450 million to $711 million.[31] This increase occurred despite some regulation by the federal government (not as severe as in the many other industries) and despite war-induced shortage of materials, including alcohol, various fats and oils, and packaging.

Cosmetic manufacturers continued to advertise heavily during World War II, spending about 20 percent of industry sales on print and radio messages. Estée Lauder was not yet among the advertisers. But she was planning to be.[32]

BUILDING THE ESTÉE LAUDER BRAND

As World War II ended, Estée Lauder's products were popular in a number of New York beauty shops, but she was becoming restless. She wanted a larger market than she believed she could build in these outlets and she sought to sustain a strong marriage with Joe. How was she to balance these two goals? After long discussions, the couple decided to go into the cosmetics business together. They hoped to exploit Estée's formulas, selling skills, and commercial imagination as well as Joe's financial and manufacturing knowledge to create a nationally recognized company. The couple divided responsibilities. Estée would handle product development, marketing, and sales. Joe would use his own broad business experience to oversee manufacturing and finance. They opened an office at 39 East 60th Street in Manhattan, relying on savings and loans from Max Mentzer, Estée's father. They founded their company in 1946, calling it Estée Lauder Cosmetics.[33]

The first product line was based on items that Estée had been refining and selling for years. It consisted of several skin creams, a cleansing oil, face powder, a turquoise eye shadow, and one shade of lipstick called "Just Red." The couple made most of their products in a former restaurant, mixing Estée and Schotz's formulas on gas burners, sterilizing containers, and attaching labels. In the first years of business, "we did everything ourselves. We stayed up all night for nights on end, snatching sleep in fits and starts."[34]

Using her local contacts, Estée sold their products in Manhattan and Brooklyn beauty shops. Joe staffed the small office. Revenues at the end of the Lauder's first year in business totaled $50,000. Operating expenses ate up virtually all of the company's sales.[35]

Estée remained optimistic. Surveying the postwar cosmetics business, she saw several important developments. On the supply side of the market, government rationing had ceased, and raw materials had once again become widely available. In the aftermath of the war, scores of new companies entered the industry. Established firms, such as Helena Rubinstein, Elizabeth Arden, Max Factor, and Coty, which had seen sales rise steadily during the conflict, increased production and advertising expenditures in the late 1940s. So, too, did younger companies like the Revlon Nail Enamel Company, founded in 1932.[36] Competition among cosmetics manufacturers intensified greatly. On the demand side, cosmetics consumption grew slowly in the immediate postwar years, then accelerated in the next decade. In 1946, Americans bought $758 million in makeup, fragrances, skin-care products, and toiletries. Seven years later, total purchases exceeded $1 billion. By 1957, they had risen to $1.4 billion, and in 1960, almost $1.8 billion. Figure 9.2 indicates the industry's long-term sales trend, adjusted to exclude the effects of price inflation or deflation.

Figure 9.2

U.S. Retail Sales of Toiletries and Cosmetics, 1915–1995 (in millions of 1997 dollars)

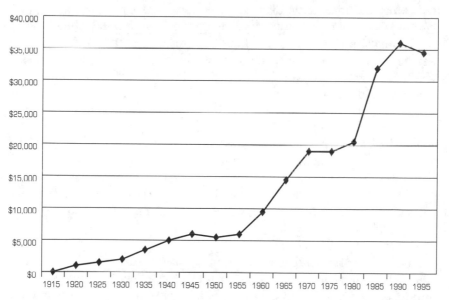

Sources: 1915 through 1935 figures from "Perfume, Cosmetic and Toilet Preparations Sales at Retail, 1914–1960," *Advertising Age* 32, no. 42 (Oct. 16, 1961), p. 88; 1940 to 1965 figures from Toilet Goods Association, "Toiletry Sales," *Oil, Paint and Drug Reporter,* (July 6, 1964, June 20, 1966), pp. 45, 50 respectively; 1970 to 1980 figures from "Cosmetics '81," *Chemical Marketing Reporter* 219, no. 9 (March 2, 1981), p. 38; 1985 to 1995 figures from Ali Khan, Kline & Company, Inc., (October 27, 1999). Recent price deflators are from the Council of Economic Advisors, *Economic Report of the President* (Washington, D.C.: U.S. Government Printing Office, 1997), p. 304.

Economic and demographic shifts underlay this consumption. In the 24 years after World War II ended, real per-capita income rose 60 percent.[37] Many Americans used their expanded means to buy things including big cars, televisions, frozen food, and toiletries. Beginning in the 1940s, the surge in U.S. birth rates, known today as the "baby boom," also enlarged long-term cosmetics markets.[38] So, too, did the growing number of women who took clerical, service, and other jobs between 1944 and 1950.[39]

In the late 1940s, Estée saw a new, much greater opportunity in the beauty business. She was pretty sure that female consumers wanted beauty offerings that made them feel feminine, sophisticated, and elegant. She was equally certain that women from a variety of social classes could and would pay premium prices for such products— but only if the advantages that buyers expected to receive from these offerings were equal to or greater than the price premium.

How were Estée and Joe Lauder to provide women with superior skin-care products and makeup that addressed consumers' desires at what they regarded as reasonable costs? How was the couple to build a national market for premium beauty products? In addressing these challenges the most important strategic tool that the couple had was the image-enhancing brand.[40]

Almost immediately, Estée selected new packaging. Her older opal-colored glass containers were "too medicinal," she decided. She was selling "pure glamour," and her products "had to be dressed for the part." For several months, she examined other cosmetics packages. She also noted the bathroom interiors of friends and colleagues. Estée eventually settled on a pale, cool, turquoise color for her jars. She was drawn to the color not only because she found it luxurious, but also because she was certain it would look elegant on most bathroom counters or medicine chest shelves. "I knew," she explained, "that women would not buy cosmetics in garish containers that offended their bathroom décor. I wanted them to be proud to display my products."[41] This signature shade eventually became known as "Estée Lauder blue." It is still used in virtually all packaging for the company's "Estée Lauder" flagship brand.

DISTRIBUTION

One of the earliest and most important decisions that the Lauders made about the brand concerned its distribution. Estée believed that *where* her products were sold would have significant consequences for the brand's future and the company's larger prospects. She ruled out drugstores, supermarkets, and five-and-tens as being at odds with the upscale image that she had already created and to which she was strongly committed. Even if they had wanted to sell in chain stores, the Lauders could not afford the large sales force necessary to service such outlets.[42]

Because she wanted to reach women who did not necessarily have extensive experience with makeup, Estée believed she could not confine the Lauder line to beauty shops and other outlets that sold only cosmetics. Equally important, she thought most consumers would rather learn to make themselves more beautiful than pay expensive beauticians to do this. She thus eschewed the early selling strategies of Elizabeth Arden, Helena Rubinstein, and other manufacturers that distributed their products through company-owned salons.

Estée decided to focus her efforts on premium department stores. Estée had spent most of her adult life marketing directly to consumers. But in the late 1940s she and her husband began to envision the family business as a wholesale manufacturing operation with a compelling reputation.

Several issues were critical in the Lauders' thinking. First, they wanted to reach large numbers of middle-class and wealthy consumers, women with sufficient means to buy premium-priced products associated with sophistication and elegance. They also hoped to locate their goods in high-traffic locations where consumers felt free to make on-the-spot impulse purchases. This meant the surroundings must be beautiful, exclusive, and comfortable for consumers. Department stores were destinations that transcended the routine stops that most women made each week to the grocery store, druggist, or dry cleaners. The Lauders hoped to use the novelty and leisurely enjoyment that women connected with upscale department stores to demonstrate their products and stimulate impulse buying.

In the late 1940s, department stores had another important advantage. Most of these retailers allowed consumers to buy on credit. Many, such as Marshall Field's, issued a store charge card to good customers.[43] Charge cards and other possibilities for buying cosmetics on credit were particularly attractive to Estée Lauder. At the beauty salon or drugstore counter, consumers had to pay for merchandise with cash. This, the entrepreneur believed, precluded a consumer from making a spontaneous purchase.[44] In the late 1940s, banks did not usually provide loans for consumer purchases other than housing. There were no universal bank credit cards such as MasterCard, Visa, American Express, or Diners Club.[45] Specific retailers, manufacturers, and sales finance companies generally issued consumer debt. Estée therefore targeted a small number of fine department stores that sold merchandise on credit, including Saks Fifth Avenue, Neiman-Marcus, Bloomingdale's, and Marshall Field's.

She was not particularly interested in middle-market department stores that competed on low prices. Her objective of working with retailers known for carrying high-quality, premium-priced merchandise probably owed something to the social aspiration that drove her. Her interest in such stores was also strategic. Estée suspected that her young brand would benefit most from association with established, prestigious retailers. In 1946, her product line met with virtually no consumer awareness outside of Manhattan.

LEADING COMPANIES

In the late 1940s and early 1950s, there were hundreds of other cosmetics manufacturers trying to sell beauty products to American women.[46] Most of these firms were small organizations with local markets. But there were also a handful of large players with brands that commanded name recognition and market shares on a nationwide basis. These leading firms fell generally into three groups: dedicated cosmetics makers, large consumer-products companies, and proprietary drug producers.

The cosmetics companies included older houses such as Avon Products, Max Factor, Coty, Elizabeth Arden, and Helena Rubinstein, and newer firms like Revlon. Each of these cosmetic firms had a significant cash flow and large advertising budget. Most of them devoted between 20 and 25 percent of net sales to advertising.[47] Consumer-products companies, such as Chesebrough-Ponds, Alberto-Culver, Helene Curtis, and Lever Brothers, produced a range of offerings, including cold creams, makeup, and hair colors. Like the established cosmetics houses, these were multimillion-dollar enterprises.[48] Large drug manufacturers that also made cosmetics included Warner-Lambert and Lehn & Fink, a company that marketed its makeup under the Dorothy Gray and Tussey lines.

The leading companies distributed cosmetics through a number of channels. Avon employed thousands of agents to sell its offerings directly to consumers. The largely female sales force traveled door-to-door to demonstrate Avon makeup and fragrances. As the suburbs expanded after the war, this tactic was hugely effective.[49]

Avon's distribution strategy, however, was unusual. Most cosmetic makers sold their products through a number of existing retail outlets, including druggists, department stores, five-and-tens, and grocers. Max Factor, Maybelline, and other lines serving the mass market were distributed in drugstores, variety stores, and supermarkets. Measured in retail sales, drugstores were the beauty industry's most important channel in the immediate postwar years, accounting for 37 percent of total sales in 1950.[50] Higher-priced, prestigious brands, such as Germaine Monteil and Lanvin, were sold primarily in department stores. And that was the road that Estée Lauder Cosmetics chose to take.

BREAKING INTO DEPARTMENT STORES

How was this young, little-known company, without a large advertising budget, to get into specific prestigious stores and thereby use their appeal to help build its brand? Beginning in the mid-1940s, Estée visited scores of department store buyers. Her methods can be illustrated by the case of Saks Fifth Avenue. That store's buyer for cosmetics, Robert Fiske, was initially not interested. When Estée told the buyer that Saks shoppers wanted her line, he responded that he and store salespeople had seen no evidence of this. "In the absence of that demand," Fiske said, "we're not going to give any further consideration to your product."[51]

Estée set out to prove him wrong, telling Fiske that she would demonstrate Saks customers' interest in her products at a charity luncheon at which she was speaking. The event was to be held at the Starlight Roof of the Waldorf-Astoria Hotel. At the same time, she donated over eighty of her lipsticks to the luncheon to be distributed as table gifts. Unlike most lipsticks at the time, these were housed in metal cases. Lunch guests noticed not only the unusual packaging but the lipstick's color and texture. As the event broke up, Fiske recalled, "there formed a line of people across Park Avenue and across Fiftieth Street into Saks asking for these lipsticks, one after another." This convinced us, he continued, "that there was a demand for the Lauder product."[52] Saks placed an initial order for $800 worth of cosmetics.[53]

The entrepreneur designed and opened the Estée Lauder counter at Saks herself. She was determined to make each sales point for the brand "a tiny, shining spa" that whispered elegance and enjoyment.[54] Her signature blue color was everywhere. She chose the lighting and mirror placement carefully so they would flatter rather than intimidate consumers. Constructing and maintaining a cosmetics counter in a department store was expensive, as were hiring and training sales representatives, buying advertising space, creating window displays, and running regular promotions. In exchange for purchasing a given beauty line and allocating selling space to it, department stores usually expected manufacturers to bear the bulk of these expenses.[55]

Over the next decade, Estée crisscrossed the United States talking to department store buyers. She hired an experienced saleswoman, Elizabeth Patterson, to work closely with her as she opened counters, made women up, and trained sales representatives. The work was frequently very hard, the days long, and the separation from her family painful. "One year," Leonard Lauder remembered, "my mother was away twenty-five weeks."[56]

Estée was obsessed with building the business. "I was unstoppable, so great was my faith in what I sold," she said describing her weeks on the road.[57] By the early 1950s, Estée Lauder Cosmetics was distributing cosmetics through Saks, Neiman-Marcus, Bonwit-Teller, and other nationally known retailers. The company also targeted department stores with a strong regional presence, such as I. Magnin in California, Himmelhoch's in Detroit, and Sakowitz in Houston. Estée quickly developed a routine at each new store. First, she tracked consumers'

Figure 9.3. Estée's personal appearances at her counters drew large crowds of consumers who came to see the entrepreneur, have a makeover, and sample her products. Courtesy of Estée Lauder Companies, Inc.

movements in the store. For example, she "stood at the door of Saks Fifth Avenue for one whole week and watched women enter. Nine times out of ten, the first place their eyes would wander would be to the right. Not to the left. Not straight ahead." Next, Estée tried to obtain the best possible space on the retailer's cosmetics sales floor. This meant placing the Lauder counter close to and to the right of the entrance to keep the brand in consumers' line of vision.[58]

She spent a week at each store in which her line was introduced, devoting most of this time to working behind the counter. This included overseeing the sales representatives, tweaking the merchandise layout, and, especially, talking with and touching potential consumers. "I'd make up every woman who stopped to look," Lauder remembered. "I would show her that a three-minute makeup could change her life." She also tried to create awareness of her brand outside the cosmetics department. She introduced herself to clerks who sold dresses, hats, and shoes, hoping to increase the likelihood of salespeople recommending Lauder products. She gave each saleswoman a sample of makeup or cream.[59]

To draw women into a store, the entrepreneur generally worked with the advertising managers. In its early years, the cosmetics company could not afford a large, mass-media campaign. Instead, Estée and department store managers sent mailings to targeted local consumers. When Lauder first began selling her products at Saks, for example, all the store's charge-account customers received a small, white, printed card with gold lettering that read: "Saks Fifth Avenue is proud to present the Estée Lauder line of cosmetics: now available at our cosmetics department."[60] Introducing her brand in Neiman-Marcus, she told Texas listeners in a radio interview, "Start the [new] year with a new face."[61] This slogan was so successful that Estée Lauder and the retailer used it for decades as part of their annual New Year's campaign.

One of the Lauders' most innovative marketing strategies involved *giving* the company's products away. Ever since she had offered beauty-parlor customers a dollop of free cream in wax paper, Estée had believed that distributing samples was "the most honest way to do business." Estée was confident that it would do more than motivate women to buy her products; it would also encourage consumers to tell others about the Estée Lauder brand. She had seen firsthand how powerful customers' word-of-mouth endorsements had been in enhancing her reputation in Manhattan beauty salons.[62]

The decision about samples was hastened by a problem with the young company's advertising budget. Early in the 1950s, the couple began looking for an ad agency. For advertising, they had earmarked $50,000 from company profits. They began to talk with specific ad agencies but were quickly rebuffed. A representative from BBD & O, which handled accounts for Revlon, Campbell's Soup, and Lucky Strike, told the Lauders that $50,000 was far too little to finance an effective advertising campaign.[63] Estée and Joe Lauder decided to plow the money into samples. This, they reasoned, might prove to be a better investment in the brand. The couple hoped sampling would create a more direct and personal connection with consumers. They ordered huge quantities of cosmetics packaged in small sizes: lipstick, rouge, eye shadow, and creams. They also had mailers printed to inform potential customers that a gift awaited them at the Estée Lauder counter at a specific department store. Most of these gifts were distributed to potential customers, to charge-account holders at major department stores, and to women who had already purchased the company's products.

In the early 1950s distributing large quantities of cosmetics samples was a completely novel idea. Some beauty executives scoffed at the female entrepreneur's efforts. "She'll never get ahead," said a manager from Charles of the Ritz observing a Lauder giveaway at Lord & Taylor. "She's giving away the whole business."[64] But the entrepreneur's sampling techniques were successful. Women visited Estée Lauder counters to receive a free gift, learn more about the brand's products, and purchase what they needed. The giveaways and the later gift-with-purchase that Estée pioneered created an opportunity to exercise her sales approach, encourage spontaneous buying, and increase customer loyalty. "People trooped in to get the free sample," explained Leonard Lauder, "liked it, and bought it again."[65] Competitors began to copy the innovation. By the late 1960s most major cosmetics regularly used the gift-with-purchase to drive traffic to their counters.

Estée focused some of her efforts on reaching consumers indirectly through the press. During the week she spent at each counter's opening, for example, she met with beauty editors from local magazines and newspapers. Most of these journalists were women. If they were impressed with a particular line, they would write about it. Estée gave them samples and offered them a makeover. Some editors and reporters were struck by her charisma, others by her natural warmth. Many liked her products and were glad to see a woman trying to make a mark in the cosmetics industry. Most thought that she and her business generated good copy for their columns.[66]

PRODUCT DEVELOPMENT

In the early 1950s Estée began to experiment with fragrances, hoping to develop a signature scent for her cosmetic line. She had always enjoyed wearing fragrance and wanted to offer one that was appealing to other women. She hoped to use a new fragrance to expand the market and enhance the brands. Besides, fragrance was more profitable than skin-care products or makeup. Gross margins—the difference between cost of the inputs and the wholesale price—for perfume and cologne ran as high as 80 percent; the margins for skin-care and makeup products, about 70 percent. If a scent were very popular, it would have a relatively large impact on the company's bottom line. In addition, a signature fragrance could be marketed with accompanying beauty products, including skin-care items and makeup. Impulse buying might increase considerably with a new fragrance introduction.

But how was she to stimulate demand among a relatively large number of women? In the mid-1950s, fragrance sales were a very small fraction of the larger beauty business, amounting to less than 1 percent of the $1 billion cosmetics and toiletries market.[67] Most female consumers viewed perfume and cologne as luxuries to be used on special occasions. Very few women actually purchased fragrance for themselves. Lauder realized that to create a successful perfume under her brand, she would have to motivate women to buy fragrance for their own use, and she would have to convince them her product was a daily necessity rather than a precious luxury.

She devised an ingenious solution to these challenges. First, she developed a sweet, diffusive scent that she thought would have broad appeal. It was discernibly more assertive and longer lasting than the leading prestige perfumes such as Chanel No. 5 or Bourjois's Evening in Paris. Second, she decided to market her fragrance not as perfume but as bath oil. This would be acceptable to women, Lauder reasoned, "because it was feminine, all-American, very girl-next-door to take baths." A woman could buy herself a bottle of bath oil the way she would buy a lipstick "without feeling guilty, without waiting for her birthday, anniversary, graduation, without giving tiresome hints to her husband."[68]

She named the dark, rich bath oil Youth-Dew. It was priced at $5 a bottle, well below prestigious scents such as Elizabeth Arden's De Luxe On Dit perfume, which sold for $65, or Rochas's "Femme" priced at $40 an ounce.[69] Unlike most French perfumes, Youth-Dew was packaged in unsealed containers. Women were free to lift any bottle's stopper and take a whiff, often leaving the bath oil on their hands. When an individual consumer left the cosmetics counter, Lauder reasoned, she would "be smelling Youth-Dew wherever she went."[70] The lingering scent, its creator predicted, would lead women back to the Lauder brand. In department stores, Estée sprayed Youth-Dew on countless women in elevators and throughout the selling areas. When women came to a Lauder counter looking for Youth-Dew, sales representatives emphasized the scent's connection to skin cream, lotion, or lipstick.

To bring consumers into the stores and up to the Lauder counters, Estée worked with individual department stores to advertise the bath oil and its availability at her counters. Some retailers inserted scented blotters into monthly statements, inviting women with charge accounts to try Estée's new fragrance. Like sampling, these were new promotional techniques in the mid-1950s.

Youth-Dew, introduced in 1953, was the beauty company's first big success. "Middle America," remembered one industry observer, "went bananas" for Youth-Dew.[71] Women flocked to Estée Lauder counters to try it. Consumers liked its strong, long-lasting scent and its dual uses as a bath oil or perfume. They also liked choosing their own perfume. As one industry observer said, "It was a whole new direction" in fragrance, and "it was affordable."[72] Women around the country sampled Youth-Dew, discovering a new scent and the Estée Lauder brand. They responded enthusiastically to both, buying not only bath oil but also other Lauder products. Over the next few years, retail demand for the cosmetics line increased rapidly, climbing from a weekly average of $300 in stores such as Neiman-Marcus to more than $5,000.[73] In helping break open the fragrance market to female consumers, the product became the foundation of the business.

Figure 9.4. An Estée Lauder Youth-Dew ad, 1960. Youth-Dew, introduced in 1953, was
Lauder's first blockbuster product. At first rejected by ad agencies because they were unable
to afford a large-scale campaign, Estée and Joe Lauder decided to promote the new product
by broad sampling and giveaways. These practices proved very successful, changing the way
cosmetics companies did business in the process. It wasn't until 1960 that the Lauders could
afford to print ads such as this one, which appeared in _Vogue_. Courtesy of Estée Lauder
Companies, Inc.

By the late 1950s, the Estée Lauder brand was a recognized name
among department store shoppers. The company was becoming,
according to Saks manager Robert Fiske, "a very dominant factor on the
cosmetics scene." The Lauder line, he added, "was probably the number three treatment line," behind those of Helena Rubinstein and
Elizabeth Arden.[74] Thousands of women understood the appeal of the
Estée Lauder brand—its combination of tangible products and intangible
associations such as elegance. Estée now had momentum toward
building one of America's leading beauty companies.

The business grew steadily in the late 1950s, but the rough division of overall managerial responsibility between Estée and Joe Lauder remained unchanged. Estée focused on expanding the company's distribution network of upscale department stores. For most of the 1950s she kept up a grueling travel schedule, visiting retail buyers, opening counters, and training sales representatives. She also oversaw promotion, merchandising, and product development, while Joe remained in New York to manage the firm's manufacturing and finances.

In 1957, Estée Lauder Cosmetic's sales totaled $800,000. In 1958, they climbed to $1 million. But the underlying organization was still a relatively small, family-run operation with a Manhattan office and production facility in nearby Nassau County. Three employees staffed the office. Ten people worked in the manufacturing plant.[75]

In 1958, the oldest son, Leonard, officially joined the business. He was 24 and had been involved in the company almost since its inception, working after school, on weekends, and during summers. Leonard made his permanent commitment to the firm after graduating from the University of Pennsylvania's Wharton School, serving a tour of duty in the navy as a supply officer on an aircraft carrier and later a destroyer, and attending evening classes at Columbia's School of Business.[76]

One of his first responsibilities was to help his mother sell. In the late 1950s and early 1960s, he worked to extend the firm's distribution network, visiting scores of department stores. Leonard was not as charismatic or outgoing as his mother, but he was a talented salesperson. He met buyers, surveyed sales floor space at new retail outlets, and evaluated the firm's existing counters. He also spent time with end consumers, taking note of what they liked and disliked. In 1959, Leonard married Evelyn Hauser, an elementary schoolteacher. After the wedding she began work in the family business, helping train behind-the-counter sales representatives and advising her husband and in-laws on product development and package design.[77]

Meanwhile the company took advantage of a good economy and the flourishing beauty market. Between 1955 and 1965 U.S. retail cosmetic and toiletry sales rose from $1.2 billion to $2.9 billion.[78] Established companies such as Avon, Revlon, and Helena Rubinstein and younger firms such as Estée Lauder and Hazel Bishop experienced strong revenue gains. Avon's annual sales, for example, more than doubled in the late 1950s and early 1960s, climbing to $168 million in 1960 and then to $352 million five years later. Estée Lauder's sales also expanded very rapidly, rising from $1 million in 1958 to $14 million in 1965.[79]

As the company grew, the Lauders recruited managerial talent. The family enterprise needed a range of capabilities, including advertising, sales, design, and production expertise. In a fast-growing market, there was no time to develop and nurture these skills solely in-house. The Lauders and their colleagues sought experienced managers from other companies and industries.

During the 1960s the company hired men and women from Saks Fifth Avenue, Bergdorf Goodman, Pan American Airlines, Bristol-Myers, Revlon, *Vogue*, and other firms. Between 1960 and 1971 the number of employees working in the Manhattan headquarters grew from eight to 225 people.[80] More than a third of these were managers.

To motivate executives, the company offered high salaries, consistent respect, and substantial responsibility. "The areas that my parents knew other people were good at," Leonard Lauder said later, "they let other people do."[81] He and his family, he explained, "look upon ourselves as winders of the clock and directors of the symphony orchestra who try to stimulate our group of talented and brilliant people to do the best we can."[82] This stimulation included creating and maintaining an ambitious company culture. Leonard said in 1973, "We believe in a hungry organization, hungry for sales, hungry for income, hungry for the amenities of life."[83]

Employee motivation, however, did not extend to any kind of equity ownership[84] (until the company's initial public offering in 1995, the Lauder family controlled all stock). Nonetheless managerial turnover in the organization remained relatively low. Some of the people hired in the early and mid-1960s stayed with the business for decades, such as Robert Barnes, who joined the company as a regional sales manager; Robert Worsfold, who headed the company's international operations; and Ira Levy, who, with Estée, oversaw package design and product esthetics.

Even as the company expanded, the Lauders were actively involved in most major decisions. Estée continued to manage product development and promotional initiatives; Joe focused on manufacturing, logistics, and finances. In the mid-1960s, the couple's younger son, Ronald, joined the company, working in its Belgian facility. Leonard shared some responsibilities with his father; with the help of other executives, the son also began to systematize the firm's expanding activities. During the 1960s, Leonard worked to devise an organizational structure, build a national sales force, create advertising initiatives, and establish long-term, professional relationships with retailers. His method of dealing with stores was considered crucial to the young firm's performance.[85]

Other companies, most notably Helena Rubinstein and Elizabeth Arden, also maintained an important presence in the evolving market for prestige cosmetics. Each of these brands was represented by its female founder, who had cultivated a glamorous image for herself and her products. Each appealed to an increasing cross section of American women who were interested in using cosmetics to express themselves and their aspirations. Each was sold in department stores, drugstores, and company-owned beauty salons. Both brands commanded wide consumer recognition, substantial price premiums, and healthy sales growth. By the mid-1960s Helena Rubinstein's annual revenues exceeded $30 million; Elizabeth Arden's were $60 million.[86]

In 1965, however, Helena Rubinstein died at the age of 95, and Elizabeth Arden died the following year at 81. Each company then struggled to define its strategic objectives and brand identity. "It's been a tradition in this industry," said the president of Helena Rubinstein in 1973, "that when the founding genius or guiding light of a company dies, the marketing structure of that company falls apart."[87] In 1970, the pharmaceutical manufacturer Eli Lilly acquired Elizabeth Arden. Consumer products giant Colgate-Palmolive bought Helena Rubinstein in 1973. Under new ownership, each cosmetics maker began concentrating on the mass market, reducing its commitment to the prestige segment.[88] In the 1980s, both companies changed corporate hands several times. At century's end, Helena Rubinstein was owned by the consumer products manufacturer L'Oréal, and Elizabeth Arden was a subsidiary of Unilever, the multinational consumer products company.

Estée Lauder Inc. benefited significantly from all these happenings. The press gave more attention to Estée's business and social activities, effectively generating free publicity for the company's flagship brand.[89] Ownership changes and strategic confusion at the two older firms provided Estée Lauder Inc. with new opportunities in the burgeoning market for upscale cosmetics. The Lauder family and its management team made huge investments in their product lines, brands, and distribution network. Sales reached $100 million in 1972. The privately held company did not release information on profits, but industry observers estimated them at between 6 and 12 percent of sales.[90] During the 1960s and early 1970s, Estée Lauder Inc. poured the vast majority of its earnings back into the business.

These efforts paid off. By 1973, when Estée relinquished the presidency of the company to Leonard, the family firm had emerged as one of the leading cosmetics makers in the United States along with Avon and Revlon. In 1973, all three players were pursuing distinct strategies. Avon, with over $1 billion in sales, sold its products door-to-door. Revlon distributed its premium lines, such as Ultima, through department stores, but the majority of its $506 million in annual sales came through drugstores and other mass-market outlets.[91] In 1973, Revlon had more than 15,000 distribution points, while Estée Lauder Inc. had 2,000 department stores and specialty stores.[92] Even in department stores, Revlon priced its cosmetics and skin-care products lower than those of Estée Lauder. For example, an Ultima II lipstick retailed for $2.85 in 1973, whereas an Estée Lauder lipstick sold for $3.50 to $4.00.[93]

Despite higher price points, Estée Lauder's profit margins were generally smaller than many of its competitors.[94] Extensive sampling, elaborate promotions, and ongoing training for counter representatives increased the premium manufacturer's selling costs. From the perspective of Estée Lauder's senior management, these costs were a necessary condition of maintaining and enhancing brand identity—brand identity that depended critically on the environment in which consumers encountered the company's products. "Sure I could pick up another million in earnings by breaking our traditional distribu-

Figure 9.5

Leading Cosmetics Firms' Net Sales Figures, 1950–1998 (in millions US $)

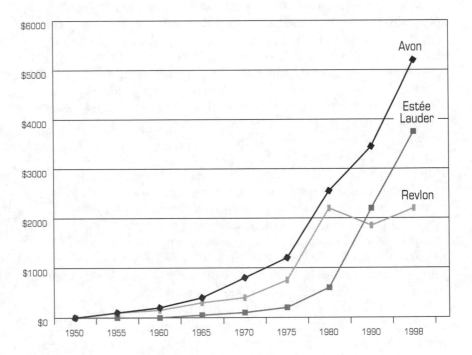

Sources: All of the total sales figures include both domestic and international sales.

Revlon figures are from *Moody's Industrial Manual* from the following years: 1956, p. 1665; 1961, p. 1983; 1966, p. 647; 1971, p. 1992; 1976, vol. 2, p. 2413; 1981, vol. 2, p. 4129; 1986, vol. 2, p.4325.

Avon figures are from *Moody's Industrial Manual:* 1951, p. 612; 1961, p. 697; 1971, p. 1535; 1981, p. 756; 1986, p. 1009; and 1991, p. 2624.

Estée Lauder figures are from Estée Lauder, *Estée: A Success Story* (New York: Random House, 1985), p. 55; *Beauty Fashion* (October 1971); *Forbes* (November 1, 1976); Lee Israel, *Estée Lauder: Beyond the Magic* (New York: Macmillan, 1985), p. 106; and *Estée Lauder Companies Annual Reports* (1996–1998).

tion pattern," Leonard Lauder said in 1973. "But we are the keystone of department store cosmetics and if we weaken that we will undo ourselves."[95]

EXPANDING THE MARKET

By 1973, millions of consumers associated the Estée Lauder name with elegance and femininity. How was the company to exploit this recognition to improve its competitive position in the market for prestige beauty products? As the market developed, how should the manufacturer respond to changing customer needs and wants?

The organization used its flagship line and other brands to deal with these issues. Senior management continued to invest substantial resources in the Estée Lauder line. Between 1965 and 1990 the company also built four new brands: Aramis, Clinique, Prescriptives, and Origins. The company developed each of these lines in response to evolving customer priorities and targeted them to distinct market segments. The firm intended each line to increase consumer interest in the company's offerings, supporting each by stringent quality control, frequent product introductions, and strategic management of people. Several of these lines lost money in their early years, but each, like the company's flagship brand Estée Lauder line, ultimately became a market leader and remains so at the beginning of the twenty-first century.

MANUFACTURING AND QUALITY CONTROL

When Estée and Joe founded their company in 1946, they made the company's skin-care products themselves, working out of a former restaurant on West 64th Street in Manhattan.[96] As the business expanded, they moved manufacturing to much larger premises in Nassau County, northeast of Manhattan. Joe oversaw operations there, including the packaging and shipping. In the late 1960s, more than 300 employees worked there.[97] By 1967, the company again needed more capacity. That year, Estée Lauder Inc. constructed a 150,000-square-foot plant in Melville, Long Island, about 33 miles east of New York City. The factory cost $2 million to build and was designed to provide manufacturing flexibility for additional product lines and fluctuations in demand. As sales rose, the company expanded plant capacity, doubling its size in 1970, after which it had 700 employees.[98]

Managers and other staff monitored quality control at the facility, ensuring that individual offerings met company and federal standards. In the early years of the business Estée and Joe had been responsible for creating new products. But in the early 1960s, Leonard established a research and development laboratory. Here chemists and other experts, in consultation with marketing executives, worked to develop

Figure 9.6. The Estée Lauder plant on Long Island, ca. 1967. The 1960s was a decade of growth for the company, and in 1967, the business built a $2 million 150,000-square-foot plant in Melville, Long Island to handle expanding production. Shortly after it opened, the plant employed over 300 people. Courtesy of Estée Lauder Companies, Inc.

beauty offerings that met consumers' needs. Once a prototype formula was developed, senior and other managers tested it with potential customers, gauging their reactions and adjusting ingredients accordingly.[99]

PRODUCT INNOVATION

The success of Youth-Dew had lasting consequences for Estée Lauder Inc. Financially, the fragrance remained an important source of company revenues. In 1985, more than thirty years after its introduction, Youth-Dew accounted for $30 million in annual sales.[100] Youth-Dew proved consistently effective in driving traffic to Estée Lauder counters, where trained sales representatives introduced customers to other cosmetics. Strategically, the scent's popularity underscored the importance of using new products—skin-care treatments, makeup, and especially fragrances—to increase consumer interest in the company's flagship brand.

Senior management relied heavily on new products to enhance the original brand, build other lines, and increase sales.[101] In 1957, for example, the manufacturer introduced Re-Nutriv, a moisturizing cream that was intended to compete with upscale European and American skin-care products such as Helena Rubinstein's Tree of Life line. Most of these treatments, packaged in 4 or 8 ounce jars, sold for under $30.[102] By contrast, the Lauders priced Re-Nutriv at $115 for 16 ounces. This pricing strategy aimed to attract consumers, move the brand upmarket, and deepen its associations with female identity and self-worth.

In the next four decades, the company launched scores of other skin-care treatments, makeup, and fragrances under the Estée Lauder name. The Lauders and their colleagues intended the innovations to enhance the organization's image and position in the prestige market, extending Estée Lauder Inc.'s reputation as a purveyor of elegant, fashionable cosmetics. A wide range of initiatives surrounding product introduction—from packaging, to the timing of a new good's arrival in specific department stores, to a focused advertising campaign—were coordinated to communicate this identity to retailers and end consumers.

New fragrances played particularly important roles in supporting the Estée Lauder brand. The launch of a new perfume provided opportunities to attract new customers. In the three decades after the debut of Youth-Dew in 1953, the company introduced seven distinct scents: Estée, Azurée, Aliage, Private Collection, Cinnabar, White Linen, and Beautiful. Senior management relied on extensive sampling, in-store events, trained sales representatives, and national advertising to promote these products. By the mid-1980s, Estée Lauder's fragrances attracted more users than those of any other U.S. company except Avon.[103]

Estée and Joe had purchased almost no national advertising in their first decade in business. But as sales increased in the early 1960s, the company embarked on an ambitious campaign overseen by the AC & R agency. A model was selected who would "personify our products" and be "the Estée Lauder woman" for consumers. Since 1962, the Estée Lauder brand has had a number of such models, each being the only advertising "spokeswoman" during her term. They were chosen carefully. In 1971, for example, Karen Graham, the third model to represent the brand, was "selected from a thousand faces" as epitomizing, in Estée's words:

a young, sophisticated woman with charm and éclat. She was sensual rather than sexy. She was strong and smart. She seemed in charge of her life, which was perceived as the good life by millions of women who identified with her.[104]

In the ensuing decades, marketing executives have tried to keep "the Estée Lauder woman" relevant to changing consumer priorities. The woman in the early ads, Estée explained, "was more formal, more involved in dressed-up elegance." Since that time, Lauder continued, the brand's representative has achieved "a more relaxed richness that reflects today's world. She's become less status-conscious. Our Estée Lauder woman is within reach."[105] (Elizabeth Hurley, an actress and model, became the brand's current spokeswoman in 1995).

Aramis In the mid-1960s, Estée surveyed the broader cosmetic market. She believed it "was barren in the men's toiletries field." The available products, she continued, "were mediocre at best and irritating at worst." She set out to develop an appealing line of toiletries for men, using Leonard and eight other coworkers as guinea pigs. Aramis was launched in 1965 around a woodsy scent, offered as a fragrance, cologne, and aftershave lotion. It was named for a Turkish root with aphrodisiac properties. To oversee the new brand, the company established a separate Aramis division.[106]

Sales at first were disappointing, and in 1967 the company relaunched a broader line of Aramis products, including aftershave moisturizers, facial masque, eye pads, cologne, and aftershave. With a vigorous advertising campaign and promotions, the brand proved popular, helping break open a growing market for men's prestige toiletries, and by 1978, Aramis sales totaled $40 million, or about 14 percent of Estée Lauder's total sales.[107]

Clinique In 1968, Estée Lauder Inc. launched Clinique, a new line of skin-care products and makeup. The firm introduced the brand as a state-of-the-art, medically sound, and accessible offering, targeting it at younger women who were knowledgeable about and interested in their skin. Sleek, pale-green casings accented with silver housed the products. Like those in the flagship Estée Lauder line, they were distributed through a controlled number of upscale department stores. Behind-the-counter saleswomen for Clinique wore white lab coats and carried penlights to examine consumers' skin and recommend a specific regime. To promote the line, the cosmetics manufacturer used extensive sampling, gift-with-purchase, and a print advertising campaign. The most famous Clinique ad, appearing first in the *New York Times Magazine* in 1974, featured a toothbrush leaning in a glass and the tag line "twice a day." The ad ran regularly for more than a decade and occasionally through the 1990s.

The company did not market the Clinique brand under the Estée Lauder name. In department stores, the manufacturer located Clinique counters far from those selling Estée Lauder products. To develop and manage the new line, senior management established a new division, hiring Carol Phillips, former managing editor of *Vogue*, to head the creative effort. Senior management, according to Estée, had three reasons for separating Clinique from its better-known sister brand:

> We didn't want to confuse the customer. We were offering something new; we didn't want her to think she'd ever tried it before. Second . . . it would have hurt Estée Lauder to have anyone make the very wrong assumption that we'd come out with a hypoallergenic line because there was something allergenic about our main line. Third, combining two different lines under one umbrella wouldn't allow for each to grow strongly as a separate entity.

Leonard was quite correct when he said we would be our own best competition. The best way of competing was with two companies, not two products under a parent name.[108]

Clinique lost money for several years, but Phillips, Ronald Lauder, who became executive vice president of the division, and other senior managers believed that the brand would ultimately succeed. In the late 1960s, the company invested millions of dollars in marketing initiatives and production facilities for the line.[109] Clinique sales increased rapidly in the mid-1970s, climbing to $80 million in 1978, almost 30 percent of Estée Lauder's total.[110] Three years later, *Forbes* magazine pronounced Clinique the "walkaway winner" among skin-care products in the prestige market. In the mid-1990s, Clinique ranked first or second in sales in virtually every U.S. outlet in which Estée Lauder products were sold.[111]

Industry experts recognized the role that managerial patience had played in creating the successful brand. The women "who bought Clinique," said a cosmetics manager in the early 1980s, "liked the scientific, therapeutic attitude behind it." Building these associations and conveying them to consumers "was costly," the executive added, "but the Lauders spent the money, took the losses for a while and nourished the business."[112] The company could do this, Leonard Lauder realized, only because it was privately held and thus relatively immune to capital market pressures for rapid growth and profits. "If we had been public, I would never have launched Clinique," he said in 1975. "We took a bath before it started paying off. The same with Aramis."[113]

Prescriptives In 1979, Estée Lauder Inc. introduced Prescriptives, another high-tech line of skin-care treatments and makeup. Like Clinique, the new brand reached buyers through upscale department stores and emphasized the science of healthy skin care, but Prescriptives' offerings carried higher prices, their image was tonier, and they were directed at consumers older than the average Clinique customer, who was typically in her twenties. Prescriptives sought its client among career women between the ages of thirty and forty-five who were interested in an individualized skin-care and cosmetics regime. Behind-the-counter salespeople for the brand encouraged customers to have a lengthy consultation, tailoring product recommendations to each woman's complexion.

Consumers were initially slow to embrace the new line. Many women found the one-hour makeover off-putting. Some thought Prescriptives products were too complicated. Others did not clearly understand the brand's distinctive benefits. In the early 1980s, Estée

Lauder's senior management tried to address these concerns, by clarifying Prescriptives' identity, streamlining its sales approach, and shifting the product mix. The manufacturer invested nearly $40 million in the brand during its first decade, and in the mid-1980s, it began to take off. By 1989, Prescriptives had become the parent company's fastest-growing brand, with estimated annual sales of $42 million.[114]

Origins In 1990, Estée Lauder Inc. introduced Origins, a line of botanics-based skin care, makeup, and sensory therapy products. The new brand was aimed at female and male consumers interested in natural, environmentally friendly offerings. It included products such as Salt Rub Smoothing Body Scrub, Clear Head Mint Shampoo, and Happy Endings Conditioner. To oversee the development of Origins the parent company created another division, headed by Leonard Lauder's son, William. He and other executives carefully controlled the line's distribution, establishing company-owned stores and "store within a store" formats in major retailers. In 1991, the first Origins store opened for business in Cambridge, Massachusetts.[115] Within five years, Origins was sold in 30 freestanding stores and more than 200 other distribution points worldwide. The brand enjoyed early success and in the mid-1990s it was one of the fastest-growing cosmetics lines in the United States.[116]

INTERNATIONAL MARKETS

In the late 1950s, Estée Lauder judged that her company's brand and supporting strategies would appeal to consumers in other countries. She decided to introduce her products in England, setting her sights on the nation's premium retailers, such as Harrods. "If I could start with the finest store in London," she reasoned, "all the other great stores would follow."[117] In 1960 the company opened its first international outlet in Harrods. As sales and brand awareness increased, other upscale retailers, including Fortnum and Mason and Selfridges, agreed to sell Estée Lauder products. Until the beauty company created an executive position to oversee British markets, Estée herself traveled from one department store to another, talking to buyers, making up customers, and training saleswomen.

In the 1960s and 1970s the entrepreneur visited other European outlets, setting up counters in Austrian, Italian, and French department and specialty stores. She was not always initially successful in convincing retailers to carry her line. For example, the cosmetics buyer at Galeries Lafayette, the Paris department store, was uninterested in the Estée Lauder line and refused to see the company's founder. To attract French consumers' interest, Estée spilled Youth-Dew on the sales floor. Over two days, shoppers repeatedly asked

Galeries Lafayette saleswomen where they could purchase the scent. Some of these conversations took place in the presence of the store's cosmetics buyer, who was impressed with women's enthusiasm for Youth-Dew. Within a few weeks, Estée Lauder opened her first counter in Galeries Lafayette.

For the next twenty years, Estée and other senior managers traveled around the world, working to expand markets. As sales grew, the company established a separate division, Estée Lauder International Inc., to manage growth outside the United States. By the mid-1990s the manufacturer was distributing its products in more than a hundred countries, including Germany, Japan, Russia, Australia, Canada, Singapore, Mexico, the Ukraine, Malaysia, and Venezuela. International revenues accounted for more than 40 percent of the company's total sales. Most of that volume, CEO Leonard Lauder noted in 1998, was "concentrated in Western Europe and Japan." As economies expand, he continued, "so do opportunities in Asia, Eastern Europe, and Latin America. We have a disciplined but aggressive approach to expanding our presence in those areas. As always, our philosophy is to have demand precede supply."[118]

CONCLUSION

In the late 1990s Estée Lauder Inc. was one of the largest cosmetics companies in the world, with 15,000 employees and annual sales of almost $4 billion.[119] The company was widely recognized for its market leadership, consistently strong financial performance, and brand management. In 1996, for example, it ranked 727 on Business Week's Global 1000 list of the world's most valuable companies. The company's founder had become one of America's wealthiest self-made women.[120] In 1998, Time magazine chose the cosmetics entrepreneur as one of the twentieth century's hundred most influential business geniuses.[121]

By the late 1990s, the organization that Estée and Joe had started fifty years earlier was one of the most important players in the worldwide cosmetics industry. Seven global corporations—L'Oréal, Procter & Gamble, Unilever, Shiseido, Estée Lauder, Avon, and Johnson & Johnson—accounted for almost half of global revenues, competing intensely with each other for market share in established and emerging markets.[122] Most of this rivalry occurred on the demand side of a given market. Companies focused their resources on trying to affect consumer priorities and decision-making, using product introductions, promotions, advertising, merchandising, service, and other initiatives.

In this competitive environment, successful brands played critical roles. They educated consumers about a particular firm's products, increasing customer confidence and reducing risk in making purchasing choices. Cosmetics brands, as Estée Lauder had long understood, also offered women and men a means of exploring and asserting their identities, social as well as individual. She and her colleagues had devoted most of their efforts to understanding these and other consumer priorities in a changing market, using this knowledge to create a series of relevant, appealing brands and the organizational capabilities that supported them. They recognized that building customer loyalty to a new product line, such as Clinique, required time as well as managerial talent and money. The Lauders and other executives were consistently willing and able to make such investments, occasionally taking initial losses on new products that they believed would become popular and earn customers' long-term loyalty. These strategic wagers on brands such as Aramis and Clinique had paid off handsomely for the business.

In the late 1990s, the company acquired several cosmetics lines, including Aveda, Bobbi Brown, *jane,* Jo Malone, La Mer, M.A.C, and Stila. The manufacturer also signed licensing agreements to make and distribute fragrances and other cosmetics under the Tommy Hilfiger and Donna Karan names. Each of these brands was targeted at a particular market segment. Each was intended to increase customer awareness of and loyalty to the line. Each was managed and promoted with rigorous quality control, strategic distribution, and imaginative marketing. Each owed its future to an organization that was founded on its ability to anticipate and respond to consumers' changing wants and needs.

NOTES

1. In 1920, cosmetics and toiletry sales totaled $130 million. By contrast, consumers spent almost $14 billion annually on food, $2 billion on recreation, and $1.1 billion on automobiles in the early 1920s. Gilbert Vail, *A History of Cosmetics in America* (New York: Toilet Goods Association, 1947), 138. Food, recreation, and automobile expenditures are from U.S. Department of Commerce, *Historical Statistics of the United States: Colonial Times to 1970* (Washington, DC: Goverment Printing Office, 1975), II, 320. In the mid-1990s, global cosmetics amounted to about $60 billion a year. Prestige cosmetics accounted for about a quarter of these. Estée Lauder Companies Inc., *Annual Report 1997,* 6; Standard & Poor's, *Industry Surveys* (September 28, 1995), T116. The average American spent about $100 annually on cosmetics and toiletries. "It's Personal," *American Demographics* 15, no. 7 (July 1993), 17.
2. Kathy Peiss, *Hope in a Jar: The Making of America's Beauty Culture* (New York: Metropolitan Books, 1998). See also, Lois W. Banner, *American Beauty* (New York: Knopf, 1983); Victoria de Grazia with Ellen Furlough, eds., *The Sex of Things: Gender and Consumption in Historical Perspective* (Berkeley: University of California Press, 1996); and Vincent Vinikas, *Soft Soap, Hard Sell: American Hygiene in an Age of Advertisement* (Ames, IA: Iowa State University Press, 1992).
3. State of New York, *Certificate and Record of Birth,* no. 3352, July 8, 1908, Municipal Archives, New York, New York. The history of Estée's family on both her maternal and paternal sides is obscure. According to one biographer, the name "Mentzer" means "the Jew from Mainz." Lee Israel, *Estée Lauder: Beyond the Magic* (New York: Macmillan, 1985), 9.
4. Quoted in Estée Lauder, *Estée: A Success Story* (New York: Random House, 1985), 12.
5. *Ibid.,* 14, 16.
6. During the 1910s and 1920s, Plafker & Rosenthal was known as "The Macy's of Corona." Israel, *Estée Lauder: Beyond the Magic,* 14.
7. When she was in her late teens and early twenties, she was known as Esther. Israel, *Estée Lauder: Beyond the Magic,* 18, 22. On her later interest in the name "Estée," see Lauder, *Estée: A Success Story,* 22. By 1937, Lauder was listed as "Estée" in the New York City tele-

phone directory. Israel, *Estée Lauder: Beyond the Magic*, 24.

8. See, for example, *A Table of Leading Advertisers: Showing Advertising Investments of Advertisers Spending $20,000 and over in Thirty-two Leading National Publications* (Philadelphia: Curtis Publishing, 1926), 220; Vincent Vinikas, *Soft Soap, Hard Sell*, 3, and Peiss, *Hope in a Jar*, 105.

9. In 1929, Helena Rubinstein estimated that women in the cosmetic industry might earn from $5 to $500 a week. Rubinstein, "Manufacturing—Cosmetics," in *An Outline of Careers for Women*, compiled and edited by Doris E. Fleischman (New York: Doubleday, Doran, 1929), 331. In the United States as a whole, 113,000 women were employed in the beauty business. Figures are for 1929 and are from Ethel Erickson, "Employment Conditions in Beauty Shops: A Study of Four Cities," *Bulletin of the Women's Bureau* no. 133 (Washington, DC: Government Printing Office, 1935), "Letter of Transmittal," by Mary Anderson, p. v; and Sophonisba P. Breckinridge, *Women in the Twentieth Century: A Study of Their Political, Social, and Economic Activities* (New York: McGraw-Hill, 1933), 134–135. See also Banner, *American Beauty*, 216; *Woman Beautiful* 3 (November 1908): 46; and Paul W. White, "Our Booming Beauty Business," *Outlook and Independent* 154 (January 22, 1930): 143.

10. *The American Druggist Yearbook and Price List* (New York: American Druggist, 1937), 69, 295.

11. John Schotz probably did not have a Ph.D, but he was generally known as "Dr. Schotz" for his experience working as a chemist. Israel, Estée Lauder: *Estée Lauder: Beyond the Magic*, 18.

12. Lauder, *Estée: A Success Story*, 18.

13. *Ibid.*, 19.

14. On Joe Lauder's professional background, see Israel, *Estée Lauder: Beyond the Magic*, 22 and Catherine Warren, "Estée and Joe," *Women's Wear Daily* (January 7, 1983), 4. Gene N. Landrum, "Estée Lauder—Impatient Overachiever," in *Profiles of Female Genius: Thirteen Creative Women Who Changed the World* (Amherst, NY: Prometheus Books, 1994), 248.

15. Marylin Bender, "Estée Lauder: A Family Affair," in *At The Top* (Garden City, NY: Doubleday, 1975), 218.

16. Israel, *Estée Lauder: Beyond the Magic*, 24. What relationship, if any, Esty's enterprise had with New Way Laboratories and John Schotz is unclear. Beauty shop statistics are from U.S. Bureau of the Census, *Census of Business: 1935, Service Establishments*, vol. 2: *Statistics for States, Counties, and Cities* (Washington, D.C.: Government Printing Office, 1935), 172.

17. Lauder, *Estée: A Success Story*, 26.

18. See, for example, *American Druggist Price Book*, 69.

19. Lauder, *Estée: A Success Story*, 27.

20. *Ibid.*, 22. In 1937, the entrepreneur first appears as Estée Lauder in the new York telephone directory. Her husband's entry that year is Joseph Lauter. Israel, *Estée Lauder: Beyond the Magic*, 24.

21. Figures for 1999 are from Patricia Keegan, ed., *International Motion Picture Almanac* (New York: Quigley, 1999), 8; 1936 information is from Terry Ramsaye, ed., *International Motion Picture Almanac*, (New York: Quigley, 1936), 6.

22. On the influence of cinematic fashions in the 1930s, see Margaret Thorp, *America at the Movies* (New Haven: Yale University Press, 1939), 90–115. Like many other consumer-goods sectors, the cosmetics industry suffered less in the Great Depression than banking, housing, and other buisnesses. Nominal cosmetic sales fell off considerably in the four years following the stock market crash of 1929. But even in 1933, one of the worst years of the Depression, dollar sales for the cosmetics industry, adjusted for price changes, were actually *higher* than they had been in 1929. Real sales rose steadily through the mid-1930s, accelerating at the end of the decade. By 1939, total retail sales were 35 percent higher in real terms than they had been ten years earlier. For industry sales figures, see "Toiletry Sales for 50 Years," *Oil, Paint, and Drug Reporter* 186 (July 6, 1964), 45. See also Vail, *History of Cosmetics in America*, 138. Price indices are from John McCusker, *How Much Is That in Real Money: A Historical Price Index for Use as a Deflator of Money Values in the Econony of the United States* (Worcester: American Antiquarian Society, 1992), 348. See also U.S. Department of Commerce, *Historical Statistics*, 1, 211.

23. Frank Stickler, "Cookbooks and Law Books: The Hidden History of Career Women in Twentieth-Century America," in Nancy F. Cott, ed., *History of Women in the United States*, vol. 8: *Professional and White-Collar Employments*, part 2 (Munich: K.G. Saur, 1993), 441–442.

24. Peiss, *Hope in a Jar*, 79–81.

25. See, for example, "Is Beauty Worth Half a Billion?" *New York Times Magazine* (December 20, 1942), 25; I. C. Furnas, "Glamour Goes to War," *Saturday Evening Post* 214, 22 (November 29, 1941), 18–19, 56–58, 60. On cosmetics sales during the war, see "Cosmetic Output Spirals," *Business Week* (August 24, 1946), 68–69; "Cosmetic Sales at New High in War Years,"

Barron's 24, no. 38 (Septemer 18, 1944): 25–29.

26. Fannie Hurst, "Glamour As Usual?" *New York Times Magazine* (March 29, 1942): 11.

27. Taking care with one's appearance demonstrated women's patriotism, according to Harrison. Would we help the brave men fighting for our country, she asked, if "we appear before them tear-stained and worn?" No, she concluded, "let's lift our heads and send them off with iron in our hearts, a smile on our red lips and a bloom in our cheeks." Mrs. Horace L. Harrison, "Glamour As Usual," Letters to the Editor, *New York Times Magazine* (April 26, 1942): section 7, 2–3.

28. Maison G. deNavarre, "Are Further Restrictions Necessary for Cosmetics?" *Advertising & Selling* (February 1943): 153 (original emphasis).

29. See, for example, "Is Beauty Worth Half a Billion?" 25; Mary Hornaday, "Factory Housekeeping," in *American Women at War* (New York: National Association of Manufacturers of the United States of America, 1942), 35–38; Laura Nelson Baker, *Wanted: Women in War Industry: The Complete Guide to a War Factory Job* (New York: E.P. Dutton, 1943), 84–95. On beauty facilities in Lockheed's plant, see Karen Anderson, *Wartime Women: Sex Roles, Family Relations and the Status of Women during World War II* (Westport, CT: Greenwood, 1981), 60–61.

30. More than 11 million Americans entered the military between 1939 and 1940. More than 7 million entered civilian jobs in the same period. U.S. Department of Commerce, *Historical Statistics,* 1, 126. On women's labor force participation during and after World War II, see Claudia Goldin, "The Role of World War II in the Rise of Women's Employment," *American Economic Review* 81; 4 (September 1991), 741–756. For a social history of working women during the war see Anderson, *Wartime Women;* Sherna Berger Gluck, *Rosie the Riveter Revisited: Women, The War, and Social Change* (Boston: Twayne, 1987).

31. On working women's interest in cosmetics, see "Face Powder and Lipstick Tops Among 'Indispensables,'" *Printer's Ink* 199, no. 4 (April 24, 1942), 13–15; and Peiss, *Hope in a Jar,* 240. Retail sales are from "Toiletry Sales for 50 Years," 45; "Cosmetic Output Spirals;" "Cosmetic Sales at New Highs in War Years;" Maurice Zolotow, "Boom in Beauty," *Saturday Evening Post* 216, no. 26 (December 25, 1943), 22–23, 58–59. Adjusted for price changes, industry sales rose 23 percent from 1940 to 1945. Price indices are from U.S. Department of Commerce, *Historical Statistics,* I, 211.

32. "Beauty Carries On," *Business Week* (May 1, 1943): 77–80; deNavarre, "Are Further Restrictions Necessary for Cosmetics?" 118, 153–154. Richard Corson, *Fashions in Makeup: From Ancient to Modern Times* (London: Peter Owen, 1972), 524.

33. Lauder, *Estée: A Success Story,* 40. See also *Estée Lauder Companies Annual Report* (1996), 2. In 1960, the company was incorporated as Estée Lauder, Inc. Sources differ on the founding dates for the company.

34. On the couple's early product lines, see Bender, "Estée Lauder: A Family Affair," 219. Quote from Lauder, *Estée: A Success Story,* 45.

35. Lauder, *Estée: A Success Story,* 55.

36. Richard S. Tedlow, "Charles Revson and Revlon," working paper 00-032, Harvard Business School, Boston, MA, 1999, 31–34.

37. U.S. Department of Commerce, *Historical Statistics,* I, 224.

38. In the ten years after 1945, birth rates climbed from 85.9 per 1,000 women to 118.5. *Ibid.,* I, 49.

39. By 1950, more than 16 million women were part of the labor force, a participation rate of almot 34 percent. *Ibid.,* I, 129, 132, 140. See also Goldin, "The Role of World War II in the Rise of Women's Employment," 748.

40. On the importance of brand names in creating strategic advantages, see Philip Kotler and Gary Armstrong, *Principles of Marketing* (New York: Prentice Hall, 1996), pp. 282–285: Kevin Lane Keller, *Strategic Brand Management: Building, Measuring, and Managing Brand Equity* (Upper Saddle River, NJ: Prntice Hall, 1998); Jean-Noel Kapferer, *Strategic Brand Management: Creating and Sustaining Brand Equity Long Term* (London: Kogn Page, 1997), 9–53; 60–65; and Leslie de Chernatony and Malcolm McDonald, *Creating Powerful Brands in Consumer, Service and Industrial Markets* (Oxford: Butterworth-Heinemann, 1998), 88–100. See also Peter Doyle, "Building Successful Brands: The Strategic Option," *Journal of Marketing Management* 5 (1989): 77–95.

41. Lauder, *Estée: A Success Story,* 41.

42. John N. Ingham and Lynne B. Feldman, *Contemporary American Business Leaders* (New York: Greenwood, 1990), 331.

43. On the early twentieth-century history of consumer debt, see Martha Olney, *Buy Now Pay Later: Advertising, Credit, and Consumer Durables in the 1920s* (Chapel Hill, NC: University of North Carolina, 1991), 95, 98.

44. Lauder, *Estée: A Success Story*, 43–44.

45. Diners Club was founded in 1949. For many years, it was used primarily by salesmen who charged meals with clients or while on the road. American Express entered the universal credit card business in 1958, as did Bank of America, which issued the BankAmericard, (later renamed Visa). In 1966, a bank consortium called Interbank issued Master Charge (later Mastercard). Lewis Mandell, *The Credit Card: A History* (Boston: Twayne, 1990), xiv, 22–51.

46. In 1954, a financial analyst estimated that there were 750 manufacturers "trying to entice women-folk to spend more" for makeup and fragrance. Faye Henle, "Beauty Parade: Cosmetics Makers Run Hard to Stand Still," *Barron's* 34: 10 (March 8, 1954): 15.

47. Avon's 1952 revenues, for example, exceeded $40 million. Coty's sales that year were $19 million, Helena Rubinstein's $18 million, and Revlon's $25 million. Henle, "Beauty Parade," 15–16; Tedlow, "Charles Revson and Revlon," 33. On advertising expenditures as a fraction of revenues, see Association of National Advertisers, *Advertising Expenditure Trends* (New York: Association of National Advertisers, 1953), appendix.

48. In 1955, for example, Chesebrough-Pond's revenues totaled $29 million. David A. Loehwing, "Search for Beauty: Cosmetics Makers Profit from an Eterial Feminine Quest," *Barron's* 36, no. 35 (August 20, 1956), 20.

49. In 1940, Avon's revenues totaled $10 million. In 1951, they exceeded $35 million. Earlier sales figure from Peiss, *Hope in a Jar*, 245. Later number from "Avon: How to Be the Biggest Cosmetic Company but Never Sell in Stores," *Advertising Age* 32; 42 (October 16, 1961): 72.

50. "Why Use TV When You Sell Door-to-Door," *Sponsor* 12, no. 8 (February 22, 1958): 34.

51. Quoted in Israel, *Estée Lauder: Beyond the Magic*, 30.

52. Quoted in *Ibid.*, 31.

53. Lauder, *Estée: A Success Story*, 44.

54. *Ibid.*, 52.

55. S. L. Mayham, *Marketing Cosmetics: A Guide for the Manufacturer in Placing His Products before the Stores and the Public* (New York: McGraw Hill, 1938), 65–73. Retailers and cosmetics companies often jointly financed newspaper and radio advertising expenditures

56. Lauder, *Estée: A Success Story*, 61–62. Leonard Lauder quoted in Bender, "Estée Lauder: A Family Affair," 219.

57. Lauder, *Estée: A Success Story*, 65.

58. *Ibid.*, 161. On consumer movements through stores, see also Malcolm Gladwell, "The Science of Shopping," *The New Yorker* 72; 33 (November 4, 1996): 66–75.

59. Lauder, *Estée: A Success Story*, 60.

60. *Ibid.*, 45.

61. Kennedy Fraser, "As Gorgeous As It Gets," *The New Yorker* (September 15, 1986): 71.

62. Lauder, *Estée: A Success Story*, 52. On the significance of consumer endorsements in expanding market share, see Thomas O. Jones and Earl Sasser, "Why Satisfied Customers Defect," *Harvard Business Review* 73 (November/December 1995): 88–99.

63. "Estée Lauder Inc.," in *International Directory of Company Histories*, ed. Paula Kepos (Detroit: St. James Press, 1997), vol. 9, 201. See also Lauder, *Estée: A Success Story*, 52; Israel, *Estée Lauder: Beyond the Magic*, 36. On Revlon's advertising expenditures, see Tedlow, "Charles Revson and Revlon," 33.

64. Quoted in Lauder, *Estée: A Success Story*, 53.

65. Quoted in Marilyn Bender, "The Beautiful World of Estée Lauder," *New York Times* (January 14, 1973): 33, 5.

66. On Estée Lauder's relationship with female journalists, see Grace Mirabella, "Beauty Queen: Estée Lauder," *Time* (December 7, 1998), 184. See also Bender, "Estée Lauder: A Family Affair," 219–200.

67. In the late 1990s, by contrast, fragrance revenues account for more than 15 percent of the market. "Aerosols Seen Spur to Perfumes," *Oil, Paint and Drug Reporter* 172; 18 (April 28, 1958): 4. Figure is from 1956. Total cosmetics sales from "Toiletry Sales," *Oil, Paint and Drug Reporter* 186 (July 6, 1964): 45. Anthony J. Bucalo, "Overview of the U.S. Cosmetics and Toiletries Market," *Drug & Cosmetic Industry* 162; 6 (1976): 26–27.

68. Lauder, *Estée: A Success Story*, 79.

69. *Vogue* (November 15, 1953): 125, 138.

70. Lauder, *Estée: A Success Story*, 79.

71. Quoted in Israel, *Estée Lauder: Beyond the Magic*, 41–42. Company sales for the new fragrance were $50,000 in its first year. Lauder, *Estée: A Success Story*, 81.

72. Quoted in Israel, *Estée Lauder: Beyond the Magic*, 42.

73. Lisa Belkin, "Man Behind Estée Lauder Image Steps Out of his Mother's Shadow," *Palm Beach Post* (November 27, 1987), 7D. See also "Look to the Future," *Beauty Fashion* (June 1956), 22.

74. Quoted in Israel, *Estée Lauder: Beyond the Magic,* 42.

75. Lauder, *Estée: A Success Story,* 99; "About the Size of It: An Interview with Leonard Lauder," *Beauty Fashion* 56, no.10 (October 1971), 34. See also Belkin, "Man Behind Estée Lauder Image Steps Out of His Mother's Shadow," 7D. Employee numbers from "About the Size of It," and author's estimates.

76. "About the Size of It," 35.

77. Lauder, *Estée: A Success Story,* 105.

78. Toilet Goods Association, "Toiletry Sales," *Oil, Paint, and Drug Reporter* (July 6, 1964, June 20, 1966): 45, 50, respectively. Price indexes are from U.S. Department of Commerce, *Historical Statistics,* 1, 210.

79. John Sherman Porter, ed., *Moody's Industrial Manual* (NY: Moody's Investors Service, 1961): 697; and Roy H. Krause, ed., *Moody's Industrial Manual* (NY: Moody's Investors Service, 1971): 1535. Sales numbers for Estée Lauder Inc. are estimated. Israel, *Estée Lauder: Beyond the Magic,"* 61. See also Kepos, "Estée Lauder Inc.," 202.

80. "About the Size of It," 35; author's estimates.

81. Quoted in Bender, "Estée Lauder: A Family Affair," 227.

82. Quoted in Bender, "The Beautiful World of Estée Lauder."

83. Quoted in Bender, "Estée Lauder: A Family Affair," 226.

84. *Ibid.,* 225; Israel, *Estée Lauder: Beyond the Magic,* 51.

85. See, for example, the comments of Richard Salomon, head of Charles of the Ritz, as quoted in Israel, *Estée Lauder: Beyond the Magic,* 95.

86. Helena Rubinstein's sales are from 1965. Frank J. St. Clair, ed., *Moody's Industrial Manual* (New York: Moody's Investors Service, 1966); 912; Elizabeth Arden's are for 1966 and are from Cat Ong, "It All Began in 1908," *The Straits Times* (December 4, 1997), Life section, 11.

87. Quoted in Lorraine Baltera, "Rubinstein Shucks Queen Bee Image," *Advertising Age* (May 21, 1974): 5.

88. Beginning in the late 1970s, Elizabeth Arden began to move its brand upmarket, trying to stake out a viable competitive position against Estée Lauder, Germaine Monteil, and other companies competing exclusively in the prestige segment. See Margaret Allen, *Selling Dreams: Inside the Beauty Business* (New York: Simon and Schuster, 1981), 101.

89. See, for example, Toni Kosover, "War of the Roses," *Women's Wear Daily* (September 26, 1969): 16–17; "The War of the Rosebuds," *Women's Wear Daily* (February 13, 1970): 26; Bender, "The Beautiful World of Estée Lauder"; Bernadine Morris, "Somehow They Survive, Unruffled by Current Social Whirl," *New York Times* (June 5, 1975): 32; Kate Lloyd, "How to be Estée Lauder," *Vogue* (January 1973): 130–131, 173–174; and "Estée Lauder's Golden Giveaways," *Forbes* (June 15, 1975): 41.

90. Estée Lauder Companies Inc., *Annual Report* (1998), 8. On profitability estimates, see Bender, "The Beautiful World of Estée Lauder," 1. See also Allen, *Selling Dreams,* 172; Estée Lauder Companies Inc. *Annual Report* (1998), 8.

91. Avon sales figures from Bender, "Estée Lauder: A Family Affair," 215. Revlon revenues from *Moody's Industrial Manual,* ed. Robert P. Hanson (New York: Moody's Investors Service, 1974), 2, 2077.

92. Israel, *Estée Lauder: Beyond the Magic,* 61; Bender, "The Beautiful World of Estée Lauder," 1.

93. Estée Lauder's fragrances, such as Youth-Dew, were often priced lower than those of the competition. This pricing strategy, which continues today, helps attract consumers to the company's counters, where they often purchase other products, including skin care and makeup. Price figures are from Bender, "The Beautiful World of Estée Lauder," 5.

94. *Ibid.,* 1.

95. Quoted in *ibid.*

96. Lauder, *Estée: A Success Story,* 45. In the first few years of the business, the Lauders probably outsourced the manufacture of makeup such as lipstick, rouge, and eye shadow to private label companies in and around New York City.

97. "About the Size of It," 35 and author's estimates.

98. "An Architectural Gem," *Drug & Cosmetic Industry* 101; 1 (1967): 39–41: see also "Packaging Flow at Estée Lauder," *Drug & Cosmetic Industry* 102; 2 (1968): 64–66; "About the Size of It," 35.

99. See, for example, *Estée Lauder Companies Inc. Annual Report* (1996), pp. 19–20.

100. Kepos, "Estée Lauder Inc.," 202.

101. In 1995, approximately 30 percent of Estée Lauder Companies' sales came from products launched in the past three years. Dillon, Read & Co., "Estée Lauder Companies—Company Report" (December 13, 1995): 5.

102. See, for example, *Vogue* (February 15, 1958): 9; *Vogue* (March 1, 1958): 12; Israel, *Estée Lauder: Beyond the Magic,* 47–48. In the late 1950s Estée Lauder's other skin care- creams

and lotions were listed at under $10.

103. "Women's Toiletries & Cosmetics," *Mediamark Research*, 305.
104. Lauder, *Estée: A Success Story*, 149–150.
105. *Ibid.*, 150–151.
106. Estée Lauder Companies Inc. *(Annual Report 1996)*, 9. See also Kepos, "Estée Lauder Inc.," 202 and Lauder, *Estée: A Success Story*, 124–126.
107. Israel, *Estée Lauder: Beyond the Magic*, 106. By the mid-1990s, Aramis had a 13 percent market share among prestige toiletries targeted at men. Dillon, Read & Co., "Estée Lauder Companies—Company Report," 7.
108. Lauder, *Estée: A Success Story*, 134.
109. According to Israel, the cosmetics manufacturer lost $3 million on Clinique before the line became profitable. *Estée Lauder: Beyond the Magic*, 75. To expedite production of Clinique products, the company built separate manufacturing facilities. "About the Size of It," 34, and Lauder, *Estée: A Success Story*, 142–143.
110. Allan G. Mottus, "Skin Care Products on Rise," *Advertising Age* 50; 9 (February 26, 1979): S-22; Israel, *Estée Lauder: Beyond the Magic*, 106.
111. Howard Rudnitsky with Janet Bamford, "Vanity, Thy Name Is Profit," *Forbes* (May 25, 1981): 48. Estée Lauder Companies Inc. *Annual Report* (1996), 4.
112. Quoted in Rudnitsky and Bamford, "Vanity, Thy Name Is Profit," 48.
113. Quoted in Bender, "The Beautiful World of Estée Lauder," 5.
114. Kathleen Deveny, "Leonard Lauder is Making his Mom Proud," *Business Week* (September 4, 1989): 69.
115. Anne-Marie Schiro, "Fresh Faces with Eye Toward Environment, " *New York Times* (September 15, 1991): sec. 1, 48.
116. Estée Lauder Companies Inc., *Annual Report 1998*, 27, Donaldson, Lufkin & Jenrette Securities, "Personal Care & Household Products Preview 1997—Industry Report" (January 30, 1997): 3.
117. Lauder, *Estée: A Success Story*, 114.
118. *Ibid.*, 120; Estée Lauder Companies Inc., *Annual Report 1996*, 3; Estée Lauder Companies Inc., *Annual Report 1998*, 6, 8.
119. Sales figure is from the fiscal year ending June 30, 1999. Estée Lauder Companies press release, www.elcompanies.com/newsroom/. Employee figure from www.globalbb.one-source.com.
120. The cosmetics corporation ranked 312th among U.S. companies in the same ranking. Kimberley N. Hunt and AnnaMarie L. Sheldon, eds., *Notable Corporate Chronologies*, 2 vols. (Detroit: Gale, 1998), 1, p. 633; Patricia Sellers, "The Billionairesses," *Fortune* (September 9, 1991): 53, 60.
121. Mirabella, "Beauty Queen: Estée Lauder," 183–184.
122. Dillon, Read & Co., "Estée Lauder Companies—Company Report," 4, and author's estimates.

Part 3

CONSTRUCTING COMMODITIES

Black Is Profitable

THE COMMODIFICATION OF THE AFRO, 1960–1975

SUSANNAH WALKER

INTRODUCTION

*I*n a recent article, activist Angela Davis complained that the Afro is remembered today only as a nostalgic hairdo, a development that, she argues, "reduces a politics of liberation to a politics of fashion." Davis cited, for example, a 1994 fashion spread from the magazine *Vibe*, which featured an actress dressed as a revolutionary Angela Davis circa 1969. Davis decried the use of her image as a "commodified backdrop for advertising" without reference to the historical and political context that gave the image its meaning and power in the 1960s. In fact, the recent revival of the Afro as "retro-chic" is only the latest development in a commodification process that began only a few years after the style first emerged as a symbol of black pride and a rejection of white beauty standards. By the late 1960s and early 1970s, the height of the Black Power movement, the Afro was as fashionable as it was political.

The African-American beauty industry, along with many black women, embraced the "natural" look but did not completely reject hair-straightening nor explicitly recognize that hair could be political. Nevertheless, the popularity of the Afro and the commercial response to that popularity contributed to a redefinition of black female beauty in the United States. Afros were part of a beauty standard that had emerged out of political struggle, whether hairstylists, cosmetics producers, and trend followers chose to acknowledge it or not. By the early 1970s, the Afro had been thoroughly commodified, but had it been completely depoliticized?[1]

This essay comes from a larger project on African-American women and commercial beauty culture in the twentieth century. The project looks at how beauty standards were created by and for black women in the United States, and how politics, gender, race, and the development of consumer culture had an impact on this process. Therefore, while this chapter contains occasional references to Afro-wearing men for the purposes of comparison, the main focus is on African-American women. Commercial beauty culture includes the hair and cosmetic preparations produced, promoted, and sold to black women, advertising and beauty advice appearing in the media, as well as the services offered by owners and operators of African-American beauty salons.

The Afro originated in the United States as a style worn by a tiny minority of cosmopolitan black women, and developed as a prominent symbol of racial pride in the mid-1960s. Responding to the Afro's grass-roots popularity, the African-American beauty culture industry mounted a largely successful effort to transform the style from political statement to fashion commodity. Black beauty businesses responded differently to the Afro depending on circumstances, timing, the nature of the business, and the demands of customers. Some beauty-salon owners complained that Afros would ruin their businesses, while others rushed to accommodate patrons desiring the new style. Hair product manufacturers produced and marketed with equal enthusiasm both hair-straightening and Afro-enhancing preparations. Advertisements for Afro products frequently invoked black pride, particularly when the company producing them was owned by African Americans. The commodification of the Afro was not exclusively a cynical exploitation of a political symbol. Rather, the selling of the Afro often entailed a complex blending of ideals, goals, and motivations based, to varying degrees, on considerations of fashion, politics, and the bottom line.[2]

ENTER THE NATURAL

As scholars such as Robin Kelley and Maxine Craig have observed, the Afro, or "natural" as it was called early on, appeared as an American hairstyle years before the Black Power movement emerged. The earliest female Afro wearers came from the fringes of African-American society. Avant-garde artists, intellectuals, and elite urban trendsetters began wearing their hair short and unprocessed as early as the late 1950s. Black men at this time commonly wore their hair close-cropped and unstraightened. (The longer, chemically straightened "conk" was actually a controversial style, often associated with musicians, young hipsters, and the "criminal element.") Black women on the other hand were rarely seen in public without hair that had undergone the ubiquitous "press and curl" treatment. As late as 1966, *Ebony* quoted a Frenchman who exclaimed, perhaps facetiously, upon seeing an

African-American woman with a natural: "I thought only Negro *men* had kinky hair!"

Women who went natural before 1965 offered a range of explanations for their decision to stop straightening. While some stressed a desire to celebrate African beauty and recognize African anticolonial movements, others cited the convenience and comfort of the new style. Women who went natural this early usually described their decision as a personal one. Unlike men and women who wore the style in the late 1960s, they had few examples to follow. Many experienced disapproval from friends, family, and community members. Regardless of why a black woman chose to wear an Afro, the style was hardly commercially popular when it first emerged and it represented a radical break from acceptable norms of African-American femininity.[3]

In the 1950s and early 1960s, virtually all black women straightened their hair. Since the early twentieth century, straightened hair had been considered an essential part of good grooming and a respectable "modern" appearance for black women. This was generally true for African-American women across class lines, whether they were Northern or Southern, whether they were rural or urban. By the mid-twentieth century, advertisers and black beauty culturists promoted straightened and elaborately styled hair as fashionable and sexually alluring. Hair that would grow long and was straight or wavy was widely considered to be "good," while hair of the extremely curly or kinky variety common to most African-American women was often described as "bad."

Having "good" hair had been a hallmark of femininity *within* black communities for generations, but of course this ideal also reflected the influence of white beauty standards in American culture. Michelle Wallace, an African-American feminist writer, recalls that in the 1950s, the line between wanting to look white and wanting to be beautiful was a blurry one. As the children of middle-class parents in 1950s Harlem, Wallace and her sister would tie scarves around their "scrawny braids," pretending it was hair like that of the actresses they had seen in the movies. Writing in 1982, Wallace observes that: "[t]here was a time when I would have called that wanting to be white." But, she continues, "the real point of the game was being feminine. Being feminine *meant* being white to us." From her post-1970s perspective, Wallace describes how notions of beauty, whiteness, and femininity were intertwined in ways that were seldom recognized, let alone articulated, by African-American women before the 1960s.[4]

In contrast, African-American beauty culturists continually insisted that hair-straightening did *not* amount to "wanting to be white." Pioneering beauty culture entrepreneur Madam C. J. Walker took great offense when people described her as a producer of hair straighteners. Even after Walker's death in 1919, company policy continued to instruct saleswomen and beauty culturists not to use the word "straightener" or say that they "straightened" hair. Guidelines printed in the Walker newsletter in 1928 told agents not to ask the customer if "she wants her hair straightened" but instead to say "treated." Marjorie Joyner, a hairstyling demonstrator and promoter for the Walker Company, stated in a 1980 interview that Madam Walker's approach should be viewed as "a method to beautify rather than thinking about making a woman look white."[5]

African-American beauty culturists stressed that both black and white women needed to have their hair groomed and styled if it was to look "good," and downplayed the racially sensitive nature of their business. Proprietors of the large beauty shops that sprang up in African-American neighborhoods after World War II emphatically highlighted this point. Rose Morgan, co-owner of a famous Harlem beauty salon employing dozens of operators, debunked the notion that black women had "bad hair." "All hair is bad if it isn't well-styled and groomed," Morgan told an *Ebony* interviewer in 1946. Margaret Cardozo Holmes, proprietor of a large beauty salon in Washington, DC, explained in 1947 that her shop was successful because she recognized that: "colored people have far better hair than they ever thought they had," and that all it required to look good was "proper treatment."

Nevertheless, until the mid-1960s, "well-groomed" and "properly treated" hair for black women was always straightened, unless the natural texture of a patron's hair rendered straightening "unnecessary." Black beauty culturists never challenged the idea that kinky hair, or, to use a popular professional euphemism, "excessively curly hair," was undesirable. Both Morgan and Holmes took pride in the innovative methods they had devised to take the kinks out of black women's hair so that it looked smoother and more "natural" than hair straightened with heavy pressing oils and hot combs. Through the early 1960s, no one in the African-American beauty industry, from the neighborhood hairdressers to the producers and advertisers of mass-produced products, questioned the aesthetic of straight or softly waved hair. The weekly trip to the beauty parlor was assumed to be a regular part of most black women's lives.[6]

Early natural wearers were therefore operating outside and to a great extent in opposition to both the African-American beauty industry and dominant beauty standards in black society. Nevertheless, these women were not, for the most part, challenging the beauty industry as deliberately or openly as later Afro wearers would. Women who stopped processing their hair before the mid-1960s did so largely on their own. The decision was often a personal one, whether it involved a desire for convenience, an attempt to forge a cultural connection to Africa, or consciousness inspired by Civil Rights activism. Women made the change on their own or within very small groups of like-minded individuals. Mostly students, writers, and musicians, they could afford eccentricity in their appearance because of their particular occupations and circumstances. Early Afro wearers were viewed as anomalies by the popular black press and were barely acknowledged by the African-American beauty culture industry.

African-American dancers Ruth Beckford, Katherine Dunham, and Pearl Primus were some of the first female Afro wearers. Beckford, for example, claims to have worn the style as early as 1952. These women chose to wear their hair short and unstraightened so they could dance and perspire without having to worry about pressed hair reverting to kinkiness after every performance or rehearsal. In addition, these dancers incorporated traditional African dance movements into their routines, and natural hair was therefore part of their image as performers. In her dissertation on the Black Is Beautiful movement, Maxine Craig notes that women like Dunham and Primus had artistic license to wear a hairstyle few black women would have felt comfortable with at the time. Other artists, such as the American blues singer Odetta and South African folk singer Miriam Makeba, caught attention for their unprocessed heads, and were often cited as inspirations by the earliest wearers of the natural. At Howard University, a few young women involved in the Civil Rights movement began wearing their hair natural in 1961 despite loud disapproval from a conservative Howard community. One of the first of these women was Mary O'Neal, who had been encouraged by Stokely Carmichael, her boyfriend at the time, to stop straightening her hair. As Maxine Craig's oral interviews with O'Neal and others show, the decision to stop straightening was to these women a natural outgrowth of their political commitment. For other black women, those who were not student activists, artists, or otherwise living at the fringes of mainstream, middle-class, black life, wearing a natural was not an easy choice.[7]

Many women who decided to "go natural" early in the 1960s experienced personal conflict and faced considerable opposition from the more conservative segments of African-American society. Michelle Wallace recalls first wearing an Afro to school in 1964, a time when few women wore the style. Wallace received a few compliments from people in her building, but, she writes: "others, the older permanent fixtures in the lobby, gaped at me in horror." Once on the streets of Harlem, the thirteen-year-old faced catcalls from men on corners and later learned that it was because her hair made her look like a "whore." Wallace decided to fix her hair back to "normal" and did not wear an Afro again until 1968. She explained in retrospect that while the natural look: "appealed to my proclivity for rebellion, . . . having people think I was not a 'nice girl' was The War already and I was not prepared for it." In her attempt to counter "white" standards of beauty and look unconventionally attractive, Wallace had unwittingly challenged African-American conventions of feminine respectability.[8]

Other women who began wearing natural hair in the early 1960s may not have received quite the negative reaction Wallace did, but they often described their decision as a difficult one. *Jet* associate editor Helen Hays King withstood "disapproving stares" in her South Side Chicago neighborhood and "have you gone crazy" looks from coworkers when she decided to stop straightening after twenty years. Describing herself as a "terribly conventional woman," King wrote in 1963 that she wore the new style because it looked and felt better, not out of any concern for the "neo-African aspects of the 'au naturelle.'"

Writer Margaret Burroughs described her rejection of the straightening comb in 1961 as a "revolt," but one that "came about as a result of five or more years of pondering and wondering about the state of my hair." It took her that long to overcome her own hair insecurities, ignore the disapproval of family, friends, and coworkers, and finally believe that kinky hair could be beautiful. "My search for a type of hair conditioning particular to me was in essence an effort to reject adherence to white standards of beauty in the grooming of hair," she wrote. "Mine was a determination to become aware of myself and to aid other Negroes to become aware of themselves as a beautiful contribution to the human race." For Burroughs, like King, wearing a natural was initially a personal choice, one that suited her better than straightening. Unlike King, Burroughs came to appreciate the political dimension of her choice, and embraced the natural in the end as a symbol of racial consciousness as well as a comfortable and attractive hairstyle.[9]

While a handful of black women were wearing their hair short and unstraightened by the early 1960s, the style was not widely popular. Nevertheless, a few prominent women did try to encourage African-American women to give up the straightening comb. One of the most famous wearers of natural hair as a political statement was jazz singer Abbey Lincoln. Lincoln explained that media depictions of her as a "glamour girl," rather than a serious singer, led her to change her image. She declared in 1961: "I have viewpoints, outlook, and values . . . I'm not anybody's symbol." But Abbey Lincoln's new look was not, for her, simply a personal choice. She hoped to use her image and music to celebrate black womanhood. "I think now that the black woman is most beautiful and perfectly wonderful," she said. "I am proud of her." Lincoln's efforts to celebrate black womanhood included the "Naturally '62" and "Naturally '63" fashion shows. The shows featured the Afro-wearing "Grandessa" models who toured cities across the United States and received considerable attention in the black press. The use of a fashion show to promote the natural suggests no one was really questioning the idea that it was a woman's ultimate desire and "duty" to be beautiful. "All women want to look beautiful," Lincoln told the Nation of Islam organ *Muhammed Speaks* in 1963, "Now it is up to our men to let our women know that they are beautiful as they are." At the same time, however, show director Cecil Braithwate stressed that the show was "designed to dignify the Negro image and present racial standards which promote dignity, class and pride." Grandessa model Rose Nelms observed: "nationalism does go deeper than natural hair . . . but nationalism has to be practiced on many levels."[10]

Black newspapers that covered the Grandessa fashion shows paid little attention to the political dimension. While the shows featured much more than natural hair, including African fashions as well as drama, music, and dance "dedicated to the Dark Continent," media attention focused mostly on the "fuzzy 'au naturelle' coiffure" on the head of each model. Articles speculated extensively on whether or not the new hairstyle would catch on, often concluding that it was too controversial to gain widespread acceptance. Typical pieces characterized the natural as a passing fad. In an article headlined "Will 'Natural' Style Be the New Hair-Do?" the *Amsterdam News* acknowledged that the women choosing to wear Afros tended to "lean toward the Black Nationalist group." Still it characterized Afros as "just another style," along with the Jackie Kennedy coiffures and blond dye jobs then in vogue. It was a fad with little social significance, no different from the "white-shoes-all-year style of the Harvard fellows . . . or a thousand and one styles and fashions that might strike one's fancy."

Other newspapers reported on African-American women's negative reactions to the style. An Associated Negro Press account of the Naturally '63 show in Chicago highlighted controversy among the 300 attendees. The article stated that everyone agreed the models in the show "would have looked good with any kind of hair style . . . or no hair at all." It then quoted Cecil Braithwate predicting a "lucrative new market" available to hairdressers willing to learn the various natural styles. Nevertheless, the article quickly moved on to the naysayers. Alma Pryor, an African-American model, said: "I think the styles are beautiful, and there are some women who can wear them . . . but in my line of work it is doubtful if they would be acceptable." Bessie Bridey, another woman present at the show, also liked the styles but said that: "it will be some time before the American Negro women in general will accept the natural hair styles." One anonymous woman was overheard saying only "it's horrible," while another claimed to have been fired from her Cook County Credit Bureau job because she wore her hair unstraightened. The mainstream black press treated the style as an anomaly, a fad, appropriate only for daring artistic types.

While some gave passing acknowledgment to the political message of the Afro, it was portrayed mostly as a rather exotic and obscure fashion statement with little significance and doubtful staying power or commercial significance.[11]

BLACK POWER AND THE AFRO

Indeed, *very* few African-American women wore their hair natural before about 1965 or 1966. By the mid-to-late 1960s, however, as part of the developing Black Power movement, the natural began to emerge as one of the most familiar symbols of racial pride for male and female activists. Earlier, only small numbers of politically conscious students and artists had sported the style; by the late 1960s, it was common among Civil Rights workers, college students, actors, musicians, and even some professionals. That said, it must be noted that the Afro was worn by a minority of African Americans, and was favored mostly by young urban dwellers who were, after all, the strongest advocates of the Black Power movement. Furthermore, the increased popularity of the style did not resolve conflicts black women faced about their hair, beauty, and femininity. As with the earlier "naturelle" fashion shows, black women could not escape the question: Can one wear an Afro and still be attractive? While the decision to "go natural" was no longer such a lonely one, it continued to be complicated by long-standing, commercially promoted standards of beauty. At the same time, the growth of the Afro opened the door to later efforts by the black beauty industry to turn natural hair into a moneymaking proposition.

In his history of the Black Power movement, William L. Van Deburg points out that at the height of the movement's popularity, only about 10 percent of African Americans supported political separatism, approved of the Black Panthers, or favored figures such as Stokely Carmichael or Rap Brown as leaders. While studies of the inner cities revealed greater support for Black Power, even there the NAACP, Martin Luther King, and integration were consistently favored. Nevertheless, Van Deburg makes the important point that Black Power's *cultural* dimension received considerably more support from black Americans than its political agenda. Promotion of African language, history, and culture, the creation of Black Studies programs in colleges and high schools, and the adoption of "distinctive hair styles, clothing, cuisine, and music" were broadly popular developments in African-American society.

The Afro, then, was one of many cultural symbols and practices in the late 1960s that had a powerful political message to convey about racial pride and solidarity. It was much the same message Abbey Lincoln and others had attempted to communicate a few years earlier, but the victories and disappointments of the Civil Rights movement had created a new racial climate. The same developments that led to the creation of the Black Power movement spurred a much wider acceptance for Black Power's cultural symbols than would have been likely just five years earlier. When Stokely Carmichael declared in 1966 that "black is beautiful," African Americans rallied to his words, transforming them into one of the most familiar political slogans of the 1960s. While Afros were common for activists by 1965, a year or two later the style had been widely adopted as a symbol of pride and resistance to oppression by many African Americans who had not participated directly in political activities.[12]

By the second half of the decade, natural hair was widely popular with African Americans whether they were politically active or not. In 1966, Robyn Gregory beat her "processed" rivals to become Howard University's first Afro-wearing homecoming queen. On a conservative campus where only 300 of 11,000 students were said to wear naturals, Gregory's victorious campaign stressed black pride and offered a new image of the beauty queen. Nevertheless, the style continued to attract controversy among African Americans. Letters responding to a 1966 *Ebony* article about the natural look offered a range of reactions to the style, from the man who denounced Afro-wearing women as "lazy, nappy-haired females," to the writer who gushed over the beauty of the women photographed in the article and proclaimed: "May we all become more natural . . . in every way!"

By the end of the decade the style seemed to enjoy extensive, if not entirely overwhelming popularity. A 1969 *Newsweek* poll of black Americans revealed strong support for Afros. While it is not surprising that 75 percent of Northern blacks under thirty liked the style, it must be noted that a majority of all Northern blacks and a full 40 percent of all Southern blacks liked "the new natural hair styles." Moreover, by this time the style was no longer limited to a short halo of unprocessed hair around the head. The larger, rounder versions of the style had fully taken hold among the ranks of activists as well as the merely trend-conscious. Late in the 1960s, Southern Civil Rights leader Ralph Abernathy expressed approval for the natural as a generational marker and symbol for how far the movement had come. Mentioning his wife's straightened hair, Abernathy declared that his children: "wouldn't do that in a million years. They've got their Afros. That's the difference these fifteen years have made for blacks—they look black, they think black, and they want freedom now."[13]

AFROS AND AFRICAN-AMERICAN WOMEN

But what did the Afro mean to black Americans, and how did the style evolve from a political statement to a beauty culture commodity? African-American men commonly wore their hair very short and natural in the 1960s. The longer Afro style, which quickly came to symbolize "militant" rebellion, could only enhance the masculine image of the male wearer. At the same time, unprocessed hair was a direct challenge to well-established images of African-American femininity. Young, politically conscious black women had hoped "black is beautiful" would help them to escape the commercial beauty industry along with the white beauty ideal. Nevertheless, they frequently found that it was still their duty as women to be beautiful, and that the beauty industry continued to play a role in shaping the new beauty standards.

Beauty businesses may have been wary of the Afro at first, but many were quick to recognize the profit potential of the popular new style. Some felt natural hair threatened to close beauty salons and cripple the black beauty culture industry, but by 1969 savvy salon owners and cosmetic companies were offering black women an array of products and services to help them achieve the new, racially conscious hairstyle. Whatever else the Afro might have represented, it was youthful, urban, and symbolized the questioning of authority, all highly marketable qualities in the 1960s. Advertising copy and beauty culture literature trivialized, ignored, or downplayed the political meaning of the Afro, portraying it as a hip, modern style that could be adopted or abandoned at will. By the early 1970s the Afro was commonly promoted by the beauty industry as just another popular style — another example that rebellion was "in." Beauty professionals assumed that like any fashion trend, the style would inevitably run its course. It might not die out completely, but it would always be one among many hair choices, including straightened ones.

This commercialization of the Afro stood at odds with the ideals of those African-American women who had adopted the style for political reasons. For many, natural hair represented an abandonment of commodified beauty culture as much as it expressed a rejection of a white esthetic. This paralleled critiques of American capitalism coming from the Black Power movement (particularly from the Black Panthers), but it also echoed challenges to the beauty industry leveled by feminists around the same time. Michelle Wallace, who let her hair go natural for a second time in 1968, lumped her new hairstyle together with a multitude of other commercial and cultural trappings of femininity. Along with wearing an Afro, Wallace discarded "makeup, high heels, stockings, garter belts," and supportive underwear in favor of "T-shirts and dungarees, or loose African print dresses." Maxine Craig notes that women who went natural in the mid-1960s were delighted to find "ways of looking beautiful that simply had not existed a few years earlier." While these women saw the Afro as a symbol of political resistance, they also felt a communal sense of pride in themselves as "naturally" beautiful women. A 1966 *Ebony* article interviewed several women on why they had chosen to go natural. Suzi Hill, a Southern Christian Leadership Conference field-worker expressed the opinion that African-American women "must realize that there is beauty in what we are, without having to make ourselves into something we aren't." Another woman pointed out that the standard of straight hair forced poor women to forego necessities in order to afford trips to the beauty salon. For many black women, then, embracing the natural did not only mean rejecting white beauty standards; it also meant shunning commercially promoted beauty products and services of any kind.[14]

In fact a crucial part of the political ideology behind the Afro, particularly by the mid-1960s, was the indictment of white beauty standards, the embrace of African traditions, and a return to simple, natural hair. People who expressed an opinion on the subject portrayed the Afro as a simple style that required little formal maintenance. The Afro was meant to demonstrate one's political commitment and an appreciation of one's cultural heritage. In a 1962 essay, Eldridge Cleaver declared that black liberation would prove impossible unless African Americans could claim their "crinkly" hair as their own. Not all black nationalists took such a drastic position. Black nationalist Eleanor Mason allowed that while natural hair had "its place," it did not in itself amount to a celebration of black women. Mason contended that the American mass media would never accept black women as beautiful, and she claimed furthermore that African women had for centuries used irons on their hair and cosmetics on their faces. Given these facts, she argued, the issue was not "naturalness" so much as black consciousness. Whether a woman straightened her hair was not the point, she wrote: "nationalism demands only one thing from the black woman—that she think black."[15]

Nevertheless many advocates of the Afro explicitly connected their chosen hairstyle with "authentic" blackness, enthusiastically proclaiming that they were abandoning artifice and simply letting their hair do what it was going to do. Lee McDaniel and Joyce Gere, Chicago-based designers of African-inspired clothing, declared that they had stopped "trying to look like Doris Day and Elizabeth Taylor." Saying that she "never really liked elaborate curls, an art student interviewed by *Ebony* remarked: "I just feel more black and realistic this way." In response to the assertion that the style was "primitive," Afro barber Ernest X of Los Angeles retorted: "What's wrong with being primitive? The word primitive simply means primary or original. So, the black man is returning to his original state and is no longer being artificial." In his 1973 book, *400 Years without a Comb*, Willie Morrow traced the history of African-American hair, claiming that under slavery, African Americans had been robbed of the tools, particularly the wide-toothed comb, they needed to groom their hair, were made to feel ashamed of their kinky locks, and turned to straightening as the only way to keep their hair neat and attractive. Where once black hair had been "put to sleep through years of denial," now it was, according to Morrow, "alive and growing and freely and naturally on the scalps of black people all over the world." A rejection of old beauty processes and products and the reintroduction of the simple Afro comb were for Morrow a promising sign of a return to African traditions.[16]

THE NATURAL GOES COMMERCIAL

Even as the Afro reached the height of its popularity, some questioned the style's "naturalness" and its African credentials. In 1970 a group of Africans denounced the Afro as a "cultural invasion from America." While African women wore their hair closely cropped or elaborately plaited, commented Tanzanian writer Kadji Konde, the "wild oiled bushes on the skull" popular in the United States were as American as "soul music, jeans, drug trips and cowboy boots." Essentially Konde was recognizing how much a part of American popular culture the Afro was. Nevertheless, a central element of natural hair to its most vocal advocates was the abandonment of all but the most essential commercial hair products—except for combing, shampooing, and the occasional trim, black people essentially ought to leave their hair alone.

In view of this, and given the array of hair goods and services traditionally available to African-American women, how did the black beauty culture industry respond to the growing popularity of the Afro? A 1969 *Ebony* article observed that hairdressers were initially among the most vocal opponents to the style, and that "perhaps through wishful thinking," they were eager to predict its demise. A "mid-western stylist" was quoted as complaining that the natural hair "fad" threatened to weaken one of the bastions of African-American economic independence. "People do all this talking about black power and going 'natural,'" she said, "but they don't stop to think that it might all backfire. . . . If they go all the way with this thing, they'll be putting people out of work." One journalist observed in 1965 that New York City hairdressers were in dire straits, primarily due to the "ever increasing legions of black women who are no longer convinced that they must straighten their hair to be beautiful," and who choose to wear their hair "au natural." In 1970, *Jet* cited a study by the National Beauty Culturist's League, the main trade organization for African-American beauty culturists, suggesting that this was a national trend. The study revealed that there had been a 20 percent decline overall in the black beauty-shop business in the past year alone, and that the decline was more like 30 or 35 percent in cities such as New York, Chicago, and Los Angeles.[17]

By the late 1960s the beauty culture industry could no longer ignore the Afro. Instead it responded by commodifying it. Many hairdressers and beauty companies insisted that natural hair still required professional care, and took pride in offering the most up-to-date hairstyles and treatments to black women. Increasingly black beauticians' services included creating and maintaining Afros. As the style became more popular, black and white hair-care companies quickly developed products designed specifically for the care of Afros. Advertisements for Afro products began to appear in magazines around 1969. These ads, particularly the ones promoting products made by black-owned companies, deliberately invoked themes of racial pride and black beauty. Nevertheless, advertisers and hairdressers alike portrayed the natural as just one among many styles available for sale. Natural hair was promoted as young, hip, and trendy, but representatives of the beauty culture industry did not suggest that all women ought to stop straightening. On the contrary, professional beauticians offered the Afro as a choice—a style that could be worn all the time, sometimes, or not at all. What was important, the beauty-culture industry continued to insist, was that regardless of the hairstyle a black woman chose, she needed to be beautiful and she required commercial products and services to achieve that beauty.

Was the black beauty-culture industry merely trying to protect itself from the threat of business lost to Afro wearers? Was it cynically co-opting a powerful political symbol for its own economic gain? The answers to these questions vary. The motivations of salon owners were often different from those of cosmetics companies, and black-owned companies often promoted Afro products differently from white companies. Beauticians were fiercely protective of their businesses, but this came as much from the sincere belief that they performed an essential service for black women as it did from fear over lost revenue. Beauticians countered the idea that natural hair could simply be washed, combed, and left to "do its thing." They argued that black women who wore Afros still needed to visit the beauty shop and follow a careful maintenance process at home. Failure to do so would result in damaged, unhealthy hair.

Many beauticians represented their trade as a health service. Like going to the doctor or dentist, going to the beauty shop was, according to one barber, "not a luxury but a necessity." A Chicago beautician observed that her business had decreased because "many people misunderstand the natural and think they don't have to keep it groomed." Beauty culturists maintained that combing out Afros potentially caused hair breakage, and argued that people could not maintain scalp health at home. "When a person shampoos at home, he can never get to the scalp properly," a New York salon owner told *Jet* in 1970. The "constant picking of the Afro," particularly the bigger versions of the style, was blamed for breaking hair shafts and causing potential early baldness.[18]

After the initial shock of natural hair, black hairstylists worked to add it to their repertoires. The Afro, it seemed, could be seamlessly adopted into the world of commercial beauty culture after all. In the words of a prominent black male stylist: "women who came to the salon every week to have their hair styled still do so, after they've gone 'natural.'" "Its not simply a matter of looking nice," said Mr. Paul, owner of a salon in Chicago's Hyde Park, where a quarter of the middle-class clientele had gone natural in 1969: "Women like to be pampered, to have someone do something for them instead of having to do for others all the time." Beauty-advice columnist Marie Cooke recommended periodic trims, frequent shampooing, and deep conditioning to protect natural hair. In a 1969 editorial in the African-American trade magazine *Beauty Trade*, industry leader Marjorie Joyner assured beauticians that they could weather the Afro trend. "This Virgin hair must be kept clean, cut and styled," she wrote: "The scalp needs treatments before and after a shampoo—then the hair shows its Natural Beauty." Joyner added that beauticians could get "$5 and up to shampoo, cut and dress a Natural."

Older and established beauty shop owners may not have liked the Afro—they certainly would never have chosen it for themselves—but for the most part they were happy to accommodate the women in their communities who did like the style. In oral interviews in the 1970s and 1980s, prominent salon owners Rose Morgan of Harlem and Margaret Cardozo Holmes of Washington, DC, expressed no distaste for the look that diverged so sharply from the glossy, waved coiffures they had spent their careers refining and promoting. Reflecting upon 1960s criticisms of hair-straightening, Morgan said that the natural did not hurt her business at all because women still needed to have their hair shampooed, cut, and treated. Margaret Holmes agreed; when the natural came along, the hairdressers in her shop "got busy right quick and learned how to do that."[19]

The difference between women like Morgan and Holmes and women who wore Afros to reject commercial beauty and express black identity was perhaps more generational than political. Beauty culturists had always placed themselves at the forefront of African-American struggles for racial equity and advancement. Beauty-culture pioneers Madam C. J. Walker, Annie Malone, and Sara Washington were famous for their philanthropic endeavors and their support of political causes. African-American beauty culturists always emphasized their role as independent entrepreneurs who did not have to rely on whites for business or income. It was this economic independence that, as

Tiffany Gill so effectively demonstrates, allowed many Southern black beauty parlor owners to participate actively in the Civil Rights movement. Black beauty professionals saw no conflict between supporting racial causes and making money caring for black women's hair, no matter what style they chose.

That politically motivated advocates of natural hair did see such a conflict speaks to the generational as well as ideological differences between Black Power activists and supporters of earlier civil rights movements. Black Nationalists rejected straightened hair outright and were often critical of the middle-class, capitalist, and integrationist proclivities of pro–civil rights entrepreneurs. African-American consumers of beauty culture fell somewhere in the middle of this dichotomy. In spite of the reported decline in the black beauty salon business, most African-American women continued to get their hair professionally done. At the same time, increasing numbers of black women admired Afros and appreciated "black is beautiful" both as a political idea and as a fashion statement. These women had not necessarily given up trips to the beauty parlor and were prime targets for commercial marketers of the "radical" new style.[20]

By the late 1960s, there was a wide array of goods and services available to the woman who wanted to "go natural." Early female Afro wearers had to go to men's barbershops to get their hair done, and some barbers became specialists in women's natural styles. Before too long, however, black women could get their Afros cut and cared for in women's beauty shops. Beauty parlors catering exclusively to persons wanting the "natural look" sprang up in cities such as New York, Los Angeles, Washington D.C., and Chicago. These establishments did not merely accommodate the Afro, they celebrated it and deliberately emphasized the style's political significance. At the same time, Afro stylists frankly played up the fashion angle. Ernest X, an Afro barber at the Magnificent Brothers salon in Los Angeles, expressed the opinion that black people should abandon "artificial" hair-straightening and be proud of their natural appearance. Still, he saw a role for professional beauty experts like himself, promising that "in the future there will be better and more beautiful natural hair styles."[21]

Advertisements for Afro hair-care products began to appear in African-American magazines around 1969. Among the most prominent producers and advertisers for these new products were black-owned companies. Murray's Superior Product Company, for example, marketed Natural Sheen hair conditioner as "New for the Natural" while promoting the same hair pomade it had produced for decades as perfect for enhancing the look of the new Afro styles. The black-owned Johnson Products Company was a top seller of African-American hair products in these years. While continuing to promote the Ultra Sheen brand of straightening products, the company also marketed the popular Afro Sheen line of conditioners, shampoos, and sprays. Advertising campaigns featured explicit appeals to racial pride. "Natural Hair hangs out. Beautiful!" declared a 1969 Afro Sheen ad featuring a large photo of a man and woman wearing impeccably groomed Afros. Other ads touted Afro Sheen as "A Beautiful New Hair Product For A Beautiful People" and "soul food for the natural." One Afro Sheen ad pictured a woman and girl above the Swahili caption "Kama mama, kama binti (Like mother, like daughter)."

Black-owned companies such as Murray's, Johnson, and Supreme Beauty Products enthusiastically used the politicized image of the Afro to sell Afro products. At the same time, these companies did not abandon the hair-straightening products of their businesses, nor did they shy away from producing mass-market hair relaxers, which were gaining a foothold in the women's beauty-culture market. Obviously these companies wanted to make money whether they were selling hair straighteners or Afro enhancers. The use of black pride as a selling tool was nothing new for African-American beauty-culture industries, which had consistently invoked themes of economic independence and the celebration of black female beauty in their advertising. That black-owned companies played a role in commodifying the Afro represents a continuation of this trend—with the recognition that popular images and definitions of black pride had changed and diversified by the late 1960s.[22]

Many white beauty companies also promoted products for use on Afros and depicted models with natural hair in their advertisements. Clairol and Nice 'n Easy both used Afro-wearing models in ads for hair coloring in the early 1970s. Clairol had actually been courting African-American women since the early 1960s, placing ads for its hair coloring in *Ebony*, conducting research on potential black markets for its products, and sending representatives and demonstrators to black hair shows. Drawing from a long-standing relationship with black female consumers, Clairol was well prepared to take advantage of the Afro trend.

While Clairol did not develop new products specifically for Afros, it did promote established items for use on natural hair. For example, the company marketed its "Hair So New" creme rinse in African-American magazines using a picture of a black woman with a huge Afro and the caption: "Don't beat around the bush. Get *hair so new*." The ad promised that the spray would make: "life easy for your pick, your hair, and your head. It's a fine mist of creme rinse that lets you spray away snarls and tangles. So you can pick out your hair as fast and full as you like. Without all that ripping or breaking . . . or leaving a lot of it in the sink."

Avon was another white-owned company with established ties to the black cosmetics market. Avon ads began appearing in *Ebony* in 1961, and African-American Avon representatives had been working in black neighborhoods at least since the 1940s. In 1974, rather late in the game, Avon began to offer Natural Sheen products specifically for Afros. The company marketed them through print ads and radio commercials, using the black advertising firm Uniworld to develop ad campaigns aimed at the African-American consumer.[23]

Promotion of the Afro differed across gender lines. Magazine articles that discussed women and the Afro often broached the issue of how the style ran counter to established standards of female beauty. A 1966 *Ebony* article observed that: "like all women, those who wear naturals are concerned about male response and recognize that short hair might detract from their femininity." Earrings and makeup were cited as essential accessories for those who did not want to be mistaken for teenage boys. A 1969 article, also in *Ebony*, noted the social significance of natural hair for black men and women, but maintained that: "all along, the 'change' has been a more drastic step" for black women "due to the greater emphasis placed on women as sexual objects" and women's innate desire to "look good." Advertisements for Afro products frequently stressed the glamour of the style. One company in particular, Supreme Beauty Products, offered separate product lines for men and women, with highly gendered sales pitches. Duke Natural products were for men, and portrayed the Afro as an appropriate symbol of masculine strength and independence. Raveen Au Naturelle products were designed for the "Natural woman, free, at last, from rollers, hot combs, sticky dressings." While the actual products, conditioning spray and a spray for "sheen," were identical, the ad copy expressed different meanings for the Afro according to gender. One ad juxtaposed the "bold" (male) with the "beautiful" (female) Afro wearer, while another declared simply that "Sisters are different from brothers."[24]

THE "ARTIFICE" OF THE COMMODIFIED NATURAL

As sold to women, Afros were generally larger and more complex in shape, and required more maintenance than those of men. Beauticians, once they had become adjusted to the popularity of the Afro for women, devised ever more complicated "natural" styles. The earliest naturals had been simple—unprocessed hair trimmed about two or three inches from the head. By the late 1960s, hair designers were promoting elaborate versions of the style. Afros that were impossibly large and domelike (continuing the ideal of long hair for women), Afros with multiple "puffs" and "braids," and Afros with decorative attachments were offered as examples of how chic and elegant natural hair could be.

By the late 1960s and into the early 1970s, *Beauty Trade*, a trade journal for black beauticians, regularly featured Afro styles in its pages. The journal featured the first ever Natural Competition at the African-American beauty culturists' and barbers' trade show in 1970. The winning style was a high, round Afro with a sculpted widow's peak at the forehead. Styles were said to have lost points with judges if "proportions were out of balance for the face." The designer of the winning style remarked that he was concerned with "form more than anything else," although he did admit that his mission was also to express "the beauty in 'Blackness.'" The second-prize winner created the big "African Queen" Afro, which might be worn for evening with a jewel at the forehead, and which was designed to "fit the facial features and contour of the heads of black women." The Afro category became a regular part of trade show contests in the early 1970s, and the pages of *Beauty Trade* were full of suggestions and models for creating beautiful, intricate, and high-maintenance natural hairstyles.[25]

A 1971 book, *All about the Natural*, by hairdresser Lois Liberty Jones and journalist John Henry Jones, featured a stunning array of Afro styles from which to choose. The book, interestingly, was published by Clairol and endorsed Clairol shampoos, conditioners, and coloring products. The text traced the history of African and African-American hair traditions and criticized hair-straightening methods as damaging to black women's hair. While the writers took the perspective that natural hair was a symbol of black pride, they also reassured readers that the style was trendy. They stated, for example, that "Afro-American is in," and that pressing and processing were on their way "out." "Fortunately," they declared, "the 'fashion of the moment' is the natural hair style." The Joneses asserted that the natural was for everybody, but that it was not a "do it yourself thing. There is the 'primitive' Natural and there's the well groomed coiffure." The remainder of the book featured multiple "high fashion" Afro styles. There was the Delta Magic, with a medium Afro above a band of braids, the demure Teen Twist, the Miss Zanzie, described as a "burst of Natural beauty," the Soul Love, and the Freedom Burst.[26]

In this way the Afro was constructed by beauty culturists as a "fashion statement." This was not entirely new, of course; among the earliest promotions of the natural style were Abbey Lincoln's Au Naturelle fashion shows. Nevertheless, these early shows always put the hairstyle in a distinctly political context and featured relatively simple versions of the style. Afro stylists in the late 1960s and early 1970s were certainly promoting the "black is beautiful" ideal, and in this way they were at the forefront of creating a new and elegant beauty standard for black women. Nevertheless, it must be noted that the beauty-culture industry insisted that black beauty could include straightened as well as natural hair. Also, these complicated Afro styles left by the wayside the notion of simplicity and the freedom to let one's hair "do its thing." Women in particular were faced by new images of black beauty that were probably as difficult to achieve and maintain as straightened hair.

Michelle Wallace makes this very point from a black feminist perspective. By 1968 she had embraced natural hair as a symbol of her commitment to "Blackness" and her emancipation from commercial beauty standards. Nevertheless, within a few years she found herself in a new femininity trap. "No I wasn't to wear makeup but yes I had to wear skirts that I could hardly walk in," Wallace wrote. "No I wasn't to go to the beauty parlor, but yes I was to spend countless hours cornrolling my hair." Wallace observes that even black women who were part of "The Movement" were expected to be beautiful. "Whatever that was." "So I was again obsessed with my appearance," Wallace recalls, "worried about the rain again—the Black women's nightmare—for fear that my huge, full, Afro would shrivel up to my head." (Parenthetically, she adds that: "despite Blackness, Black men still didn't like short hair.") Whether one felt compelled to wear the big, full Afro of feminine black consciousness, or one followed the latest spectacular Afro trends promoted by the beauty industry, natural hair offered little escape, it seems, from the admonition that black women needed to work hard—and spend money—to be beautiful.[27]

Manufacturers of hair products and black beauticians in particular insisted that black women who went natural would have to continue to spend money on their hair. Magazine advertising and articles about the Afro paid particular attention to women and the "dilemma" of how women could wear their hair natural and still be feminine and beautiful. Advertisers and hairdressers took special care, as well, not to alienate the majority of women who chose to continue straightening their hair. Advertising for black hair products frequently portrayed the Afro as merely one choice among many, downplaying its political significance. Typical were ads such as that for Raveen Conditioner, which featured a woman with straightened hair and one with an Afro: "Whatever Hairstyle You Choose, NEW RAVEEN Is the Hair Conditioner To Use." Posner, another black-owned company, exhorted black women to: "Go smooth. Go curly. Be a 'natural,'" but use Posner's conditioner for "smooth and pretty hair." An ad for Tintz hair color declared: "Natural or Straight? . . . Color it Black, Baby, But By All Means Color It." This ad observed that the natural looked good "on those who can wear it," highlighting the commercial characterization of the style as primarily a fashion choice.

Some ads exhorted women to use chemical relaxers in order to achieve a bigger, better natural. An ad for Perma-Strate hair relaxer told women that whether they wanted: "smoothly straight hair, soft curls . . . or a sweeping Afro . . . they'll look their best only if you *first straighten, then style!*" An Ultra Sheen ad pictured a woman in an Afro and two others with straight hair, telling female readers: "You can change your hair style as easily as you change your mind—with Ultra Sheen Permanent Creme Relaxer." *Beauty Trade* freely promoted the use of relaxers to "improve" the Afro, and suggested women alternate between straight and "kinky" styles. The March 1969 issue featured a method allowing "the patron who wants both permanent and natural" to "have her cake and eat it too." "There's no need for you to lose important revenue," the article stressed. Hair could be permanently straightened then cold-waved on small rods to achieve a "tight frizzy curl." Such a process, in theory, allowed hair to be blown straight, or set in tiny curlers for the "Curly 'Fro' look." The "blow out" involved using a hair dryer to create the bigger Afro look, and *Beauty Trade* advocated the use of a relaxer cream before drying to create an even bigger Afro. In this commercialized context, the natural was not natural at all. It was promoted as a bold new look, but one virtually devoid of its original political meaning.[28]

By the late 1960s, black women could easily have an Afro without going natural. Advertisements for Afro wigs crowded the pages of black magazines. In 1971, the Summit Company launched its Afrylic line of wigs, "designed specifically for the black woman." The Brown Skin Baby wigs, which featured "scalps" tinted to match African-American skin tones, were touted as the only wigs with "brown skin, baby!" In obvious conflict with the original goal of the Afro, one Afrylic ad promised that the wigs were "so natural" they would "make you hate your own hair." Beauty culturists embraced the Afro wig, which had long made up a part of their business, as a way of recouping the loss of business due to the natural trend. Salons owners could conceivably straighten and style a woman's hair, *and* sell that same woman an Afro wig for when she felt like going a little "wild."

Rose Morgan maintained that the popularity of the Afro created an entirely new market for her line of wigs. *Beauty Trade* championed the Afro wig as a revenue-maker compatible with established black beauty processes. Model Cynthia Archer, featured in an Afro wig on the December 1968 cover of the industry magazine, said that she straightened her hair but wore the wig as a "change of pace." "This is the way us Professionals like our Customers," commented *Beauty Trade*. "We endorse Afro Wigs. But we also endorse Professional Care at all times." The designer of Ms. Archer's wig, a prominent New York salon owner, touted the Afro wig as ideal for black women "who don't want to cut their hair for the natural because then they are stuck with it," *and* for the beautician who can both sell the wigs and provide care for the hair under them. Another New York salon owner commented in 1969: "Naturally, we push the Afro Wigs to try to protect the Permanent business. One can help the other, if it's sold correctly." By the late 1960s and early 1970s, then, the black beauty culture industry was actively endorsing the Afro as a fashion easy to put on and just as easy to take off. The Afro was no longer recognized as a permanent lifestyle choice that denoted racial consciousness or as an outright rejection of hair straightening, either for the sake of convenience or as a political statement. From the perspective of black beauty professionals—if not politically active black women—the Afro truly was "just another style" to be bought and sold.[29]

CONCLUSION

Did the commodification of the Afro rob it of its political meaning and its power to convey a message of racial consciousness? By the mid-1970s few would have argued that the style was rebellious or revolutionary. Natural hair no longer had the shock value it did ten or fifteen years before. Certainly the prominence of the commercialized version of the style helped blunt the militant edge of the natural look. Nevertheless, hairdressers and hair-product manufacturers who promoted the Afro did not necessarily see any conflict between supporting images of Black Power and making a profit. For black business owners these were likely seen as complementary rather than antithetical goals.

It must be recognized, too, that commodification was not the sole or primary reason for the popularity of the natural look. Widespread acceptance of the Afro in black communities developed *before* efforts to sell the style were in full swing. Into the 1970s, the Afro continued to be viewed as a symbol of pride and an assertion that black was indeed beautiful. Many politically active black people were still wearing Afros in the 1970s as a badge of their commitment to racial progress. As late as 1973, magazine articles portrayed the Afro as a controversial style. Indeed, African-American women who wore natural hair in the 1960s and early 1970s potentially faced real threats to their livelihoods. Articles about the Afro "trend" written in the late 1960s mentioned that some women wore wigs over their naturals when at work in order to avoid trouble with white employers. In 1971, *Jet* reported that the Philadelphia Commission on Human Rights had received several complaints from black women who had been sent home from work, or even fired for wearing Afros. Even as the Afro was gaining prominence as a "chic" and "daring" new look in fashion circles, wearing the style could still be problematic for ordinary black women.[30]

By the mid-1970s, the Afro was featured less frequently in magazines like *Beauty Trade* and *Ebony*, while advertising for Afro products in black magazines also waned. Like any successful fashion commodity, the style had been heavily promoted and elaborately developed, and then quickly faded from prominence. By the end of the decade, the Afro was likely seen by the style-conscious as passé. Nevertheless, the natural look remained a choice for black women. In the absence of widespread commodification, it is possible that the Afro regained some of its political significance for the few who continued to wear it. Furthermore, the Afro was merely the first of several "natural" hairstyles to gain prominence after 1960. At the height of the Afro's popularity in the late 1960s and early 1970s, cornrows, braids, and other African-inspired hairstyling methods emerged as attractive alternatives for women who felt Afros were too commercial and not authentically "African." While the bigger versions of the Afro were out of style by the mid- to late 1970s, "natural" or unprocessed hair (whether in the form of braids, short hair, or dreadlocks) is still a popular way for black women to denote racial pride, show political consciousness, or just make a fashion statement. African-American women who today wear what are sometimes termed "extreme" hairstyles continue to be subjects of controversy and criticism at work, school, and in the media. Thus, even in its absence as a popular style, the Afro leaves us with an important legacy: the widespread and *conscious* use of hair by many African-American men and women to signify political loyalties and commitments. Whether they were politically motivated or not, hairdressers and beauty-product manufacturers who provided goods and services for the natural played a vital role in supporting the "black is beautiful" principle. In these ways the black beauty-culture industry did not rob the Afro entirely of its political meaning. Ultimately the Afro had a symbolic power and a material influence on African-American women's style and beauty standards that went beyond the narrow meaning commodification gave it.[31]

NOTES

1. Angela Y. Davis, "Afro Images: Politics, Fashion, and Nostalgia," in *Soul: Black Power, Politics, and Pleasure*, ed. Monique Guillory and Richard Green (New York: New York University Press, 1998), 23, 28.
2. For my purposes, "beauty" itself is the commodity being sold, whether by product manufacturers, by beauty "experts" writing in popular magazines, or by the owners of neighborhood beauty salons. The transformation of beauty into something that can be "achieved" through consumption of the right goods and services has been thoroughly explored by Kathy Piess in her recent book: *Hope in a Jar: The Making of America's Beauty Culture* (New York: Metropolitan Books, 1998).
3. Phyl Garland, "The Natural Look," *Ebony* (June 1966): 143; Robin D. G. Kelly, "Nap Time: Historicizing the Afro," *Fashion Theory: The Journal of Dress, Body & Culture* 1 (December 1997): 341; Maxine B. Craig, "Black Is Beautiful: Personal Transformation and Political Change," Ph.D. dissertation, University of California, Berkeley, 1996, 75; Maxine Craig, "The Decline and Fall of the Conk: or, How to Read a Process." *Fashion Theory* 1 (December 1997): 404–409.
4. Michele Wallace, "A Black Woman's Search for Sisterhood," in *All the Women Are White, All the Blacks Are Men, But Some of Us Are Brave*, Gloria T. Hull, Patricia Bell Scott, and Barbara

Smith, eds. (Old Westbury, NY: Feminist Press, 1982), 5. A good popular overview of the origins of the preference for straight hair among African Americans can be found in Kathy Russell, Midge Wilson, and Ronald Hall, *The Color Complex: The Politics of Skin Color among African Americans* (New York: Harcourt Brace Jovanovich, 1992). See especially chapters 2 and 3.

5. Nolewe Rooks, *Hair Raising: Beauty, Culture, and African American Women* (New Brunswick, NJ: Rutgers University Press, 1996), 63; Former hairdressers interviewed in Stanley Nelson's documentary "Two Dollars and a Dream, A Film" Diversity Video Project, New York, 1980; and "The Newest in Beauty Culture Language," *Walker News* (September, 1928), Madam C. J. Walker Collection, Indiana Historical Society.

6. "House of Beauty: Rose-Meta Salon is Biggest Negro Beauty Parlor in the World," *Ebony* (May 1946): 27; Woody L. Taylor, "Here's a $31,000 Beauty Enterprise," *Afro-American* (Baltimore) (November 15, 1947): M5.

7. Craig, "Black Is Beautiful," 78, 80–84.

8. Wallace, "A Black Feminist's Search for Sisterhood," 5–6.

9. Helen Hays King, "Should Women Straighten Their Hair?—No!" *Negro Digest* (August 1963): 65, 68–71; Margaret Burroughs, "Down the Straight and Narrow," *The Urbanite* (May 1961): 15ff.

10. June Lirhue, "The New Abbey Lincoln: A Voice of Protest," *Courier* (Pittsburgh) (May 27, 1961): sec. 2, 20; "The Natural Look is Reborn in Brilliant New Show, " *Muhammed Speaks* (February 9, 1963): 12; Associated Negro Press release printed under the headline: "Many Negro Women Favor New African-Type Hairdos," in *Muhammed Speaks* (April 1963): 17; Rose Nelms, "Natural Hair Yes, Hot Irons No," *The Liberator* (July 1963): 13.

11. "Will Natural Style Be the New Hair-Do?" *Amsterdam News* (March 10, 1962): 12; Associated Negro Press article: "'Au Naturelle' Revue Sparks Controversy," appeared in the *Courier* (Pittsburgh) (March 9, 1963); *Muhammed Speaks* ran most of the above material under quite a different headline: "Many Negro Women Favor New African-Type Hairdos," *Muhammed Speaks* (April 1963): 17.

12. William L. Van Deburg, *New Day in Babylon: The Black Power Movement and American Culture, 1965–1975* (Chicago: University of Chicago Press, 1992), 17; Craig, "Black is Beautiful," 101.

13. E. Fannie Granton, "Pride in Blackness and Natural Hair-Do Led to Spirited Campaign," *Jet* (November 10, 1966): 48–53; "Letters to the Editor," *Ebony* (August 1966): 12. Female writers also expressed both negative and positive views; Peter Goldman, *Report from Black America* (New York, 1969), 157. Nevertheless, the percentages of people actually wearing Afros, particularly those over the age of thirty, was probably much smaller. This was particularly true outside cities such as New York, Chicago, Los Angeles, and San Francisco For example, in her ethnography of a Seattle beauty shop, Leatha Chadiha observed that in 1969 the Afro was not worn in the community, or in Washington State as a whole. "A Study of Black Beauty Culture and Values About Beauty in Black Society," MA Thesis, Washington State University, 1970, 13.

14. Wallace, "A Black Feminist's Search for Sisterhood," 6; Craig, "Black is Beautiful," 93–94; Phyl Garland, "The Natural Look: Many Negro Women Reject White Standards of Beauty," *Ebony* (June 1966): 143.

15. Elinor Mason, "Hot Irons and Black Nationalism," *The Liberator* (May 1963), 22; Eldridge Cleaver, "As Crinkly As Yours," *The Negro History Bulletin* 30 (March 1962): 127–132.

16. Garland, "The Natural Look," 144, 146; "Los Angeles Goes 'Natural,'" *Sepia* (January 1967): 60; Willie Morrow, *400 Years Without a Comb* (San Diego, 1973), 19, 86.

17. "Afro Hairdo Upsets African Writer," *Jet* (October 15, 1970). Cultural critic Kobena Mercer makes a similar point, arguing that the Afro was neither African, nor was it natural. Mercer maintains that the style's claims to "naturalness" and "Africaness" were part of a political rhetoric that framed white beauty standards and commercial beauty culture as artificial and antithetical to the project of black liberation. Kobena Mercer, "Black Hair/Style Politics," in *Out There: Marginalization and Contemporary Cultures,* Russell Ferguson, Martha Gever, Trinh T. Minh-ha, and Cornel West eds., (Cambridge, MA: MIT Press, 1990); "The Natural Look—Is It Here To Stay?" *Ebony* (January 1969): 108; Sylvester Leak, "The Revolution in Hair Grooming—Is the Black Beautician Losing Fight For Life?" *Muhammed Speaks* (February 26, 1965): 21; "Beauty Shop Business Suffers 20% Decline," *Jet* (March 26, 1970): 48.

18. "Beauty Shop Business Suffers 20% Decline," 49, 50; "The Afro: A Natural Groove Or A Natural Mess? *Jet* (July 13, 1972): 16.

19. "The Natural Look—Is It Here To Stay?" *Ebony* (January, 1969); Marie Cooke, "Wear Your Natural Beautifully and Proudly," *Dawn Magazine* (May 25, 1974): 12; Marjorie Joyner, "Naturals Paying Off!" *Beauty Trade* (May 1969): 12; Rose Morgan Interview, 1988 (video-

taped interview with Jame Briggs Murray), Shomburg Center for Research in Black Culture, New York; Margaret Holmes Interview, 1977, transcript, p. 112, Ruth Edmonds, ed., *The Black Women's Oral History Project*, Arthur and Elizabeth Schlesinger Library on the History of Women in America, Radcliffe College, (Westport, CT: Garland, 1991).

20. Tiffany Gill, "'Emphatically Our Race is Interested in Beauty': Beauty Salons, Hairdressers and the Creation of African American Female Identity, 1930–1960," paper presented at the "Beauty and Business" Conference, Hagley Museum and Library, Wilmington DE, March 1999.

21. Garland, "The Natural Look," 146; "Los Angeles Goes 'Natural,'" 60.

22. Natural Sheen ad, *Ebony* (February 1970); Murray's Pomade ad, *Ebony* (March 1971); James F. Forkan, "Who's Who in $350,000,000 Black Grooming Market," *Advertising Age* (November 20, 1972): 96; Afro Sheen Ads: *Tuesday Magazine* (April 1969); *Tuesday Magazine* (June 1968); *Ebony* (June 1971); *Ebony* (April 1971).

23. Raymond Oladipupo, "All-Out Marketing Keeps Clairol Ahead With Negro Women," *Media-Scope* (September 1969): 18; Clairol ad, *Tuesday Magazine* (October 1972); Mrs. Willie Miller was profiled in *Outlook,* Avon's promotional magazine for representatives. She was a black woman who started with Avon in 1947. *Outlook* 15 (1970), Avon Collection, Hagley Museum and Library, Wilmington, DE; Offprints of print ads and radio ad scripts, 1961–1980, Record Group I, boxes OS-37, OS-38, and OS-39, National Black Advertising, Avon Collection.

24. Garland, "The Natural Look," 146; "The Natural Look—Is It Here To Stay?" 104; Supreme Beauty Products ad, *Ebony* (October 1969); Supreme Beauty Products ad, (December 1969).

25. "Big Show—Natural Competition," *Beauty Trade* (December 1970): 12–14.

26. Lois Liberty Jones and John Henry Jones, *All About the Natural* (1971).

27. Wallace, "A Black Woman's Search For Sisterhood," 6–7.

28. Raveen ad, *Jet* (March 2, 1967); Posner Bergamot ad, *Ebony* (May 1971); Tintz ad, *Ebony* (April 1969); Perma-Strate ad, *Ebony* (July 1972); "From Permanent to Natural the Easy Way," *Beauty Trade* (March 1969): 24; Edward Clay, "Blow-Out Technique For Men and Women," *Beauty Trade* (July 1972): 22–23.

29. Press Release, 1973, box 2, folder 8, Agency Records, Kenyon and Eckhardt, Caroline Jones Collection, National Museum of American History, Archives Center, Smithsonian Institution; Afrylic Wig ad, *Jet* (May 11, 1972); Rose Morgan interview, 1988, Schomburg Center; Cover Description, *Beauty Trade* (December 1968): 9; "Afro Wigs Are Good Money-Makers," *Beauty Trade* (December 1968): 19; Minnie Easley, "The Natural Will Be Around For Awhile," *Beauty Trade* (April 1969): 16.

30. *Encore Magazine,* a short-lived African-American news/issues/arts publication, featured a "Point/Counterpoint" article in which one writer criticized the political message of natural hair as "nonsense," while another writer affirmed the political significance of hair. Carl Rowan, "Hair Ain't Where It's At," versus Lillian Benbow, "Hair *Is* Where It's At," *Encore Magazine* (October 4, 1973): 38–39; Garland, "The Natural Look," *Ebony* (June 1966): 146; "Los Angeles Goes 'Natural'," *Sepia* (January 1967): 60; "Afro Hair Styles, Attire Cause Bias Complaints," *Jet* (January 7, 1971) 25.

31. Phyl Garland, "Is the Afro on Its Way Out?" *Ebony* (February 1973); I do not mean to suggest that there was no political meaning in African-American hair before the Afro, but I do think that the conscious use of hair to "make a statement" becomes much more widespread and deliberate as a result of the Civil Rights movement and the concurrent popularity of the Afro style in the 1960s.

"Loveliest Daughter of Our Ancient Cathay!"

REPRESENTATIONS OF ETHNIC AND GENDER IDENTITY IN THE MISS CHINATOWN U.S.A. BEAUTY PAGEANT

JUDY TZU-CHUN WU

*I*n February 1958, seventeen young women came to San Francisco from throughout the country to compete in the first Miss Chinatown U.S.A. beauty pageant. Sponsored by the San Francisco Chinese Chamber of Commerce (CCC) as part of the Chinese New Year celebration, the competition sought to find "the most beautiful Chinese girl with the right proportion of beauty, personality and talent." The organizers promised that "honor, fame and awards . . . is [sic] ahead for her majesty in this, the most Cinderella-like moment of her young life." June Gong, a twenty-one-year-old senior majoring in home economics at the University of New Hampshire, captured the title of the first Miss Chinatown U.S.A. Although she expressed surprise at winning, Gong had a history of competing successfully in beauty contests. She had won the titles of freshman queen and football queen at college. In 1957, she placed second in the Miss New Hampshire beauty pageant, a preliminary for the Miss America competition. She also won the 1957 Miss New York Chinatown title, which provided her with the opportunity to compete in the national pageant. Years later, she explained that the Miss Chinatown U.S.A. pageant was not "a beauty contest"; it was "more like a matter of ethnic representation." Having grown up in Miami, Florida, with only a few Chinese families, Gong's participation in the San Francisco event provided her with the opportunity to come into contact with the largest community of Chinese people outside China and to learn about her ancestral culture.[1]

The popularity of the first Miss Chinatown U.S.A. beauty pageant made the event one of the highlights of the Chinese New Year celebration, which it continues to be today. Without it, one organizer explained, there would be no focus to the celebration: no pageant, no coronation ball, no Miss Chinatown float for the annual parade, and no fashion show. These Chinese New Year events draw hundreds of thousands of tourists into San Francisco's Chinatown, serving the dual purposes of educating the public about Chinese-American culture and attracting business for Chinatown merchants.

The Miss Chinatown U.S.A. beauty pageant has served as a beauty competition, a promotional event to attract tourism, and a means for exploring and celebrating ethnic identity. Because of its multiple purposes, an analysis of the pageant provides insights into Chinese-American efforts to construct both gender and ethnic identities during the post–World War II era. In defining the ideal woman to represent Chinatown, pageant organizers responded to developing cultural, economic, and political tensions within the Chinese-American community and the broader American society. In turn, these efforts to represent Chinese-American womanhood generated a variety of responses that reflected community conflicts surrounding not only gender roles and ethnic identity but also class divisions and international politics.[2]

Using pageant publications, oral histories, and Bay Area and Chinese-American community newspapers, this essay analyzes the Miss Chinatown U.S.A. beauty pageant from its origins and popularization in the late 1950s and the 1960s through the growing controversy that surrounded it in the late 1960s and 1970s. During the height of the Cold War and the era of racial integration, pageant supporters successfully balanced tensions within the Chinese-American community and with the broader society by depicting their ethnic identity as a nonthreatening blend of Eastern Confucian and modern Western cultures. However, with the rise of social movements during the late 1960s and 1970s, this conception of ethnic identity came under attack for presenting an outdated and exotic image of Chinese Americans in general and women in particular. Critics argued that Miss Chinatown did not represent the "real" Chinatown women, who tended to be working class, or the revolutionary Asian women in the Third World. Pageant supporters responded by emphasizing the importance of beautiful and articulate Chinese-American women as role models for promoting respect for the community.[3]

Ethnic beauty pageants, a subject rarely explored by scholars, provide an opportunity to examine how idealized versions of womanhood reflect broader concerns about power and culture. In a recently published collection of essays devoted to the study of beauty pageants, *Beauty Queens on the Global Stage*, the editors, Colleen Ballerino Cohen, Richard Wilk, and Beverly Stoeltje, argue that pageants: "showcase values, concepts, and behavior that exist at the center of a group's sense of itself and exhibit values of morality, gender, and place. . . . The beauty contest stage is where these identities and cultures can be—and frequently are—made public and visible." In studying the formation and evolution of a community ceremony, I had the opportunity to examine not only how the pageant publicly and visibly reflects the community's identity and culture, but also how the event shaped and developed community values. In other words, the history of the pageant and the community dialogue that the event generated provide insight into evolving conflicts concerning ethnic and gender identity as well as class divisions and international politics.[4]

Furthermore, the study of the Miss Chinatown U.S.A. beauty pageant suggests the need to reevaluate dichotomous models of gender and ethnic systems. Beauty pageants do not simply victimize women through male domination; both women and men supported as well as criticized the pageant. Similarly, the cultural content of the pageant cannot be evaluated in terms of ethnic assimilation versus retention. Rather, both pageant supporters and critics defined ethnic identity by synthesizing elements of both Chinese and American traditions. While contending groups questioned their opponents' cultural authenticity and commitment to women's advancement, their conflicts often arose because they advocated different strategies to advance similar goals of gender and racial equality.

"A MELTING POT OF THE EAST AND THE WEST"

From the very beginning of the pageant, organizers had an ideal image of Miss Chinatown contestants as the perfect blend of Chinese and American cultures. Businessman and community leader H. K. Wong, who is credited with coming up with the idea of the pageant, explained that contenders for the crown must have the "looks that made China's beauties so fascinating" as well as the language skills to answer "key questions" in their own native dialect during the quiz portion of the competition. In addition to these Chinese attributes, contestants had to display modern American qualities. They needed "adequate education, training and the versatility to meet the challenge of the modern world." The cheong-sam ("long gown") dresses that contestants wore symbolized this theme of "East meets West." First introduced by Manchu women of the Qing dynasty, the cheong-sam, "the figure-delineating sheath dress with high-necked collar and slit skirt," became "the national costume of Chinese women." For the purposes of the pageant, modern dressmakers modified the design of the cheong-sam to emphasize the cleavage area, creating "the 'poured-in' look so highly desired." Furthermore, the slit up the side of the dress was increased "to endow the basically simple Cheong-sam with a touch of intrigue . . . [,] a tantalizing suggestion about the beauty of its wearer." This conception of Chinese-American identity as a blend of East and West allowed pageant supporters to negotiate cultural, economic, and political tensions within the Chinese-American community and with the broader community during the late 1950s and 1960s.[5]

Organizers argued that the beauty pageant demonstrated both the assimilation of the Chinese-American community and their need to preserve Chinese culture. CCC leaders explained that they wanted to organize "something western" to attract the interest of the American-born generations as they became more assimilated. After nearly a century of racial exclusion and segregation, Chinese Americans became increasingly integrated into American society during the post–World War II era. Because of the alliance between China and the U.S. during the war, Chinese Americans for the first time gained the right to become naturalized citizens. With changes in segregationist residential restrictions after the war, middle-class Chinese Americans began moving out of Chinatown. They also gained access to white-collar jobs as occupational racial barriers decreased. These opportunities encouraged college-educated Chinese-American women to join the labor force. The pageant provided a means for Chinese Americans to demonstrate their assimilation by inviting young, educated women to participate in an event that was becoming popular in American society during the postwar era—the beauty pageant.[6]

At the same time, the pageant also sought to preserve Chinese culture among those who were merging into the mainstream. For contestants like June Gong, San Francisco Chinatown represented their first contact with a large population of Chinese Americans. She exclaimed upon her arrival in San Francisco, "I had never seen so many Chinese people." Her unfamiliarity with Chinese culture made the event exciting and educational. She recalled that "it was even fun discovering Chinese food." Other contestants expressed similar sentiments about the pageant. One contestant from Glendale, Arizona, explained that she came to San Francisco to catch "her first glimpse of Chinese life." She told a reporter: "When you're born and raised in Glendale, China doesn't mean too much to you. . . . To me, San Francisco's Chinatown is China."[7]

In addition to promoting awareness of Chinese culture among contestants, organizers pointed out that the beauty pageant fostered a more cohesive sense of identity among Chinese Americans across generations and throughout the country. Because the pageant successfully attracted young Chinese-American women and encouraged their interest in Chinese culture, the event helped bring together generations that might have been separated by cultural differences. One organizer explained that H. K. Wong thought of the pageant as: "a joyful event to get the families and the parents involved in the New Year show." In addition, the pageant fostered cooperation among Chinese Americans nationwide. In order to attract contestants from diverse geographical regions, pageant organizers sought the assistance of Chinese chambers of commerce, merchant organizations, and families' associations in other cities. Some areas that already had community beauty pageants began sending their representatives to San Francisco. Others initiated contests in order to participate in the Miss Chinatown U.S.A. beauty pageant. The solidification of these networks helped foster a sense of a national Chinese-American identity.[8]

The pageant and the New Year festival not only promoted an awareness of ethnic identity among Chinese Americans but also educated the general public about the value of Chinese culture. As the embodiment of the positive aspects of ethnic identity, Miss Chinatown U.S.A. held symbolic importance in promoting greater acceptance of Chinese Americans. Historically, the white community viewed Chinatown as a disease-ridden society populated by unattached men. The stereotypes of Chinese-American women as exotic slave girls or sequestered women with bound feet symbolized the moral corruption of the community. The pageant offered an alternative view of Chinese-American women, which in turn emphasized the progress of the community. First, the pageant demonstrated the demographic changes of the community from a "bachelor society" to a "family society." By presenting beautiful, charming, and intelligent Chinese-American women the competition also paid tribute to the families of these contestants, as implied by the lyric from the official pageant song, "loveliest daughter of our Ancient Cathay." Second, the pageant also demonstrated the modernization of Chinese-American gender roles. One pageant booklet charted the advances of women "from dim memories of wee bound-feet to present day stiletto heels." In this statement, the accessory of high heels is supposed to symbolize the advancement and independence of Chinese-American women. While bound feet suggests the enforced debilitation of women by outdated cultural practices, the ability to wear high heels suggests women's economic power to purchase modern commodities. Chinese-American women, like their American counterparts, were becoming part of a commercialized world.[9]

These images of Chinese-American women and the conception of ethnic identity as a blend of the East and the West not only served to educate the broader American public but also helped draw tourists to Chinatown. While the pageant was usually attended by Chinese Americans, the proceeds from the event helped fund the annual New Year parade, which attracted hundreds of thousands of non-Chinese people. In addition, pageant contestants served as models for advertisements for the festival, and their presence at various New Year events helped attract tourists who shopped in Chinatown stores and ate in Chinese restaurants.

The developing commercial viability of Chinatown coincided with broader social interest in Asian culture following World War II. The military presence in the Pacific theater during the war and the political, commercial, and military interest in Asian countries during the Cold War led to increased contact between Western and Asian peoples. American popular culture reflected this fascination with the "Orient," which also included "orientals" in the U.S.; San Francisco officials and business leaders actively supported the Chinese New Year festival and the Miss Chinatown U.S.A. beauty pageant for commercial purposes. As early as 1957, political and civic leaders expressed interest in promoting the festival as a distinctively San Franciscan cultural event that would draw tourists into the city. They wanted a festival "to rival Mardi Gras." The presence of ethnic beauty queens constituted an important component of the plan to encourage tourism. One non-Chinese festival organizer envisioned that "we'll have floats from Siam, Japan and Korea and we'll have pretty Chinese girls from all over the world . . . [and] I really think we will have an attraction to equal the Mardi Gras in five years."[10]

The joint interests of the CCC and city officials in promoting the commercial benefits of Chinatown fostered tensions as well as cooperation. Ironically, while Chinatown organizers sought to promote the compatibility of East and West through their events, white organizers cautioned Chinese Americans against overassimilation. In a speech to the Chinese Historical Society of America, journalist Donald Canter, who regularly covered the Chinese New Year festival and Miss Chinatown U.S.A. beauty pageant, explained that the annual parade had become so Americanized that: "I wasn't quite sure whether I was viewing the Rose Parade in Pasadena or a New Year's parade of the largest Chinatown outside the Orient." To promote more tourism for the community, he encouraged organizers to highlight Chinese cultural practices. Instead of having the Miss Chinatown queen and princesses ride in floats for the parade, he suggested the: "possibility of having the Queen, and possibly her court, carried in sedan chairs with the carriers performing their chore in relays." He argued that this practice would be "much more Chinese" and would appeal:

> much more to the imagination of the hundreds of thousands viewing this annual spectacle. . . . Wouldn't they write their folks and friends across the country about that eerie spectacle of a Chinese Queen and Chinese princesses being carried in Chinese sedan chairs? . . . And consequently, with a proper Chinese sense for reality, wouldn't [that] lure more tourists and their dollars into San Francisco and Chinatown?

To attract white tourists interested in seeing the "bizarre," Canter encouraged CCC leaders to emphasize an "orientalist" image of Chinatown by creating cultural practices that were not relevant to Chinese Americans.[11]

CCC leaders did not entirely disagree with this approach of portraying Chinatown as something "exotic" and "foreign" in order to maintain its commercial viability. Pageant publications regularly invited tourists to visit San Francisco Chinatown because of its resemblance to "the Orient." The souvenir booklet explained that: "if you have not been to the Orient, your trip to Chinatown will be as if you were visiting Formosa or Hong Kong." At the same time that pageant organizers promoted a positive conception of Chinese-American identity to encourage self-pride and cultural awareness, they also consciously promoted an exotic image to fulfill the expectations of white tourists.[12]

The CCC efforts to balance its agenda of ethnic representation and commercial viability were further complicated by the international political context of the Cold War, which ignited immense hostility toward Communist China. The *San Francisco Chronicle* regularly placed its coverage of the New Year events next to articles on the People's Republic of China (PRC). To distance themselves from the negative images of "Red China," pageant and festival organizers emphasized a nonaggressive conception of Chinese culture. One CCC publication explained that the Chinese:

> seldom express their passion, particularly in public. This, combined with the
> Confucian doctrine of the dignity of man, makes them a calm and pacific
> race. Fatalism plays an important role in the Chinese mind. Generally they
> are quite content with their station in life. For this reason, the western sense
> of the word "revolution" has no appeal to the Chinese mind.

This portrayal of Chinese-American identity as orderly and content with the existing order also encompassed Cold War conceptions of gender identity. Pageant founder H. K. Wong explained that the pageant represented a quest by: "Chinatown Elders . . . for [a] Queen with Ancient Virtues of Chinese Womanhood." He defined the ideal Chinese woman as obeying the patriarchal figures of the Chinese family. She must respect: "first your father, than your brother, then your husband." This emphasis on female submissiveness is part of a more general portrayal of Chinese people as culturally passive. Both conceptions of ethnic and gender identity were consciously promoted to counter the notion that all Chinese were potentially red subversives. Furthermore, pageant supporters also implied that their version of Chinese culture was more authentic than the changes taking place in the PRC, because they traced their cultural origins to "Confucian" doctrines.[13]

CCC organizers simultaneously claimed Chinese cultural authenticity and emphasized their loyalty to America. They argued that the ability to celebrate their culture in the U.S. demonstrated the superiority of American society. According to James H. Loo, president of the CCC in 1962:

> In the turmoil of the world situation, we citizens of Chinese ancestry want to take this opportunity to demonstrate to the peoples of the world, particularly those who are living behind the iron and bamboo curtains, how American democracy really works. . . . We, like many Europeans, who came to settle in this free land, are also proud of our ancient culture and endeavor to retain the best of our heritage. The New Year celebration exemplifies the expression of such a love of freedom and liberty.

The close affiliation of the Taiwanese government, the Republic of China (ROC), with the pageant and the festival reinforced CCC antagonism toward Communism. Members of the ROC Consulate participated regularly in the festival and the pageant. Officials were presented as dignitaries during the beauty pageant and the New Year parade. The wife of the consul also served several times as a judge for the Miss Chinatown U.S.A. contest. Chow Shu-Kai, ROC ambassador to the U.S., explained that his country supported the pageant and the festival as a reminder to: "our compatriots on the mainland of China, who do not have the means to celebrate nor the freedom to commemorate occasions significant and meaningful according to the traditions of the old country." The ambassador as well as CCC officials emphasized the freedom of Chinese Americans to celebrate their culture and the authenticity of their version of Chinese culture compared to Communist China.[14]

To support their argument that the beauty pageant represented an expression of authentic Chinese culture, organizers pointed to a Chinese tradition of appreciating female beauty. Although the more conservative Chinese philosophers emphasized female modesty and advocated the seclusion of women to the inner quarters of the home, poets, playwrights, as well as folk storytellers celebrated the beauty of famous women. H. K. Wong drew on these literary traditions to describe the standard of beauty used to select Miss Chinatown. He suggested that:

> the elusive memory of ancient China's greatest beauties might lurk in the judges' minds as they ponder their decision. Their thoughts might linger on the centuries-old Chinese concept of beauty such as melon-seed face, new moon eyebrows, phoenix eyes, peachlike cheek, shapely nose, cherry lips, medium height, willowy figure, radiant smile and jet black hair.

Interestingly, the modern beauty pageant did resemble certain Chinese cultural practices. During the Northern Sung, Ming, and Qing dynasties, the imperial court instituted a female draft to select palace maids, consorts, and wives. Choices were based on both the girl's personal appearance and on her family status. Pageant organizers used these Chinese traditions of appreciating feminine beauty to justify the Miss Chinatown U.S.A. competition as an expression of Chinese, as well as American culture.[15]

The conception of ethnic and gender identity promoted by the Miss Chinatown U.S.A. pageant and Chinese New Year festival during the 1950s and 1960s emphasized the blend of the exotic, passive, Confucian East and the modern, democratic West. This interpretation of Chinese-American culture allowed pageant supporters to negotiate tensions within the community and with the broader society during the post–World War II era. Reacting to the integrationist impulse among Chinese Americans, Chinatown organizers used an "American" event to attract the interest of the younger generation and to encourage the maintenance of Chinese culture. The pageant's emphasis on modern Chinese-American women also served to educate the broader public about the "progress" of the community, even as the exotic foreignness of the events attracted tourists to Chinatown. The community's ability to celebrate its ancestral culture demonstrated the freedom that existed within democratic societies, while the pageant's emphasis on a nonrevolutionary, Confucian notion of Chinese culture allowed Chinese Americans to claim cultural authenticity while also distancing themselves from the negative images of Communist China.

The formulation of gender and ethnic identity presented by the Miss Chinatown beauty pageant suggests the vulnerability of the Chinese-American community during the 1950s. While the aftermath of World War II had brought increased economic and social opportunities, Chinese Americans also sensed the possibilities of community dispersion and political persecution. In this context, the pageant represented a means to promote a sense of community among Chinese Americans and between Chinese Americans and the broader American population.

The ability of the Miss Chinatown U.S.A. beauty pageant to reconcile tensions within the Chinese-American community and with the broader society helped the event achieve widespread popularity. Throughout the 1960s, spectators annually filled the Masonic Auditorium, which seated over 3000. One organizer for the New Year parade recalled that the pageant was the premier event for Chinatown, attracting the "who's who" of the community. Because of the popularity of the pageant, people often complained of the difficulties of obtaining tickets for the event. Those who could not get tickets either watched the pageant as it was televised to another auditorium or else listened to the program on the radio. By the 1960s, then, the pageant had become a recognized tradition in the community.[16]

"CHINA DOLLS" AND "IRON GIRLS": CONTENDING IMAGES OF CHINESE-AMERICAN WOMEN

During the late 1960s and 1970s, a generation of Chinese Americans who became involved with grassroots social movements increasingly criticized the popular Miss Chinatown U.S.A. beauty pageant. Influenced by the Civil Rights, Black Liberation, antiwar, and Women's movements, college-educated and community youth began organizing to address social problems within Chinatown. While some advocated social reform, others questioned the fundamental assumptions of American capitalism and sought inspiration from Third World and socialist movements. Their criticisms of the Miss Chinatown U.S.A. beauty pageant and the Chinese New Year festival demonstrated their attempts to redefine the ethnic and gender identities of Chinese Americans.

The rise in political consciousness among a young generation of Chinese Americans coincided with changing demographic trends in the Chinatown community. In 1965, the U.S. Congress abolished discriminatory national-origins quotas, allowing immigrants from Asian countries to come to the U.S. in the same proportions as Europeans. The new Chinese immigrants followed preexisting demographic patterns. Educated professionals and technicians settled in areas outside of Chinatown, while unskilled workers and those with limited English facility became part of the older community. The heavy influx of working-class immigrants into San Francisco's Chinatown, estimated at "two to four thousand new residents" annually, both revitalized the community and exacerbated its social problems. With this rise in population Chinatown's poverty level increased, its housing conditions deteriorated, and health and social services became inadequate. Both parents in Chinese immigrant families were likely to work long hours in service and light-manufacturing jobs for low wages. Immigrant women also worked a "second shift," which included taking care of children and doing housework. Because of the crowded conditions in Chinatown and the poor quality of housing available, immigrant families were likely to live in small tenement rooms with inadequate plumbing facilities, no central heating, and communal kitchens and bathrooms. These poor and overcrowded living conditions increased the health risks among community residents.[17]

Like other ghetto communities, however, Chinatown lacked the resources to respond to the needs of its residents. Government agencies such as the San Francisco Equal Employment Opportunity Commission were reluctant to allocate funds to assist immigrants or to address systemic problems within the community. Chinese Americans also lacked the political clout to combat the widespread belief that Asian Americans constituted model minorities who could succeed solely through hard work and perseverance.

In reaction to the ghettoization of Chinatown, young activists advocated new solutions to address these problems. They sought to educate themselves and the broader public about the needs of the community and they demanded the reallocation of government and community resources for social services. During the 1960s and 1970s, liberal and radical activists formed agencies to serve the economic, educational, cultural, and social concerns of Chinatown residents. They also initiated grassroots campaigns to mobilize Chinese Americans to demand better living and working conditions. As part of their broader agenda to change fundamentally the existing social structure, they began criticizing the popular Miss Chinatown U.S.A. beauty pageant. The new generation of activists questioned the role of tourism in the community, the images of Chinese-American women promoted by the pageant, and the appropriateness of the Confucian values and the ROC in representing Chinese culture. For them, Miss Chinatown represented a symbol of a commercialized, antirevolutionary, middle-class Chinese-American identity, exactly what reformers, radicals, and feminists sought to change in the community.

During the 1960s and 1970s, critics of the pageant and New Year festival increasingly questioned the use of community resources to promote tourism and the educational benefits provided by tourism. *East West*, a liberal Chinese-American newspaper, noted that Chinese New Year:

> is the time when people near and far come to visit the Chinatown. . . . But would the visitors be able to see the real Chinatown? Would they have a chance to meet our residents? Would they begin to understand our many community problems? At the moment, what we are showing the visitors are the rides in the carnival, beauty contestants, an occasional cherry bomb, and busy restaurants where service could best be described as chaotic.

Because of the enormous crowds that the Chinese New Year attracted, keeping peace and order proved difficult. While the city's fire chief annually threatened to ban firecrackers to lessen chances of injury and fire, the police chief increased security during Chinese New Year to prevent fights and public disturbances. In 1969, a full-fledged riot broke out, resulting in thirty-five arrests and eighty-nine injuries. An observer's account suggests that Chinese New Year did not necessarily inspire greater appreciation of Chinese culture. George Chu, who described himself as "a square middle-class Chinese," explained that Chinese New Year was a particularly volatile time in the community. Because of racial tensions, fights between Chinese and whites had the potential to escalate. These tensions were exacerbated by the behavior of white tourists, who indiscriminately threw firecrackers without watching for people around them. Others strolled through the community, "tearing posters and paper lanterns from the booths for souvenirs, [acting] as if Chinatown was theirs for the picking." Police security for the festival did not help the situation, since officers tended to ignore these incidents. When they did intervene, they tended to assume the Chinese were at fault. Even Chinese Americans who volunteered to help patrol the streets were warned that: "when the cops come, stay out of it; they can't tell the Chinese apart." Some Chinese Americans, angry about the racist treatment by the police and the disrespect of tourists, criticized the CCC for promoting the festival.[18]

The tensions between business leaders and activists came into focus when the Holiday Inn decided to build a hotel to provide luxury accommodations for tourists in Chinatown. As part of the hotel's promotional campaign, it sponsored a contestant, Celeste Wong (alias), for the Miss Chinatown U.S.A. beauty pageant. As a publicity stunt for the gala grand opening of the Holiday Inn, Wong jumped out of a giant fortune cookie. Across the street, members of the Red Guard Party, a radical organization of Chinatown youth, and other Asian Americans staged a rally protesting the "invasion of Chinatown's territory" by the Holiday Inn. Citing the crowded conditions of San Francisco's Chinatown, protesters asked: "How many of our people have had to move out of their shops and homes to make way for the growing financial district?" Questioning the displacement of Chinatown people for commercial enterprises like the Holiday Inn, the protesters demanded "low cost housing for our people!" During the New Year parade, some protesters went so far as to throw eggs at Celeste Wong for representing the Holiday Inn. In the end she had to be removed from the float because of public hostility. Activists criticized the Miss Chinatown U.S.A. beauty pageant for helping to promote a false commercial image of Chinatown in order to attract tourism. One community activist highlighted the contradictions between the tourist image of Chinatown and the actual experiences of its residents:

> In Holiday Inn . . . there is a swimming pool on the roof and a grand view of
> the city . . . there is the plush of soft carpets, bright lights, and spacious quar-
> ters . . . there are bell boys in smart uniforms . . . there are hostesses in mini
> skirts and cheong sams . . . there is . . . Miss Holiday Inn, and now Miss San
> Francisco Chinatown . . . there are tourists and business men with their
> briefcases . . . it's all there, across from Portsmouth Square, where the poor,
> the old, and the very young while their time away before the sun goes
> down.[19]

The growing awareness about racial and class oppression also fostered critiques of the Miss Chinatown U.S.A. beauty pageant for objectifying Chinese-American women. Beginning in the late 1960s and escalating throughout the decade, Chinese Americans criticized the pageant for judging women based on physical standards and portraying them as "China dolls." Their criticisms were partly inspired by the broader movement for women's equality. In 1968, women involved with the budding feminist movement conducted a widely publicized protest of the Miss America pageant in Atlantic City. They crowned: "a live sheep to symbolize the beauty pageant's objectification of female bodies, and filled a 'freedom trashcan' with objects of female torture — girdles, bras, curlers, issues of *Ladies' Home Journal*." Although no bras were actually burned, the media referred to protesters as "bra-burners," which then became a simplistic derogatory term to refer to feminists.[20]

Chinese Americans concerned about women's issues echoed white feminist criticisms of beauty pageants. Although Miss Chinatown contestants were supposedly judged according to their intelligence, "talent, beauty, charm and knowledge of Chinese culture," critics argued that physical appearance tended to be the main criteria. Pageant observers pointed out that many "would-be queens" displayed a "sad lack of 'talent.'" Others commented that the interview session of the contest did not really demonstrate the contestants' knowledge of Chinese culture or their intelligence. After attending her first Miss Chinatown U.S.A. beauty pageant, Judy Yung criticized the candidates for obviously memorizing their responses to the Chinese portion of the interview session: "But even with preparation, their answers don't always make sense, since they speak Chinese with a heavy American accent." Because of these problems, the Chinese portion of the interview eventually became optional in 1980. Yung further complained that the English portion of the interview did not challenge the intelligence of the contestants, for judges asked questions such as:

> (1) If you saw your best friend cheating, what would you do? or (2) If you dressed informally to a formal party, what would you do? or (3) If you found your hem falling during a public appearance, what would you do? Evidently, the judges are more interested in finding out how you can get out of difficult situations than what your knowledge and opinions are on current events and social problems.

Other critics of the pageant pointed out that the main purpose of the event was to display a "parade of flesh." One documentary filmmaker portrayed the 1973 Miss Chinatown beauty pageant, which took place during the year of the Ox, as a "Livestock Show."[21]

Chinese-American feminists expanded beyond mainstream criticisms that beauty pageants objectified women by pointing out the racial implications of certain female images. Critics argued that despite the flowery language used to invoke Chinese standards of beauty, the Miss Chinatown U.S.A. beauty pageant actually used white standards to judge Chinese-American women. One community member stated her belief that the contest "shows that the closer you look like the Whites, the prettier you are." Another critic agreed that Asian Americans internalized "white standards" of beauty promoted by mass media. These images emphasized that: "a beautiful woman has a high-bridged, narrow nose, a large bosom, and long legs." She pointed out that while "these and many other physical traits are not inherent in most Asian women," beauty pageants like the Miss Chinatown U.S.A. contest encouraged women to achieve that ideal. Asian women "can compensate by setting our hair, curling our eyelashes, or wearing false ones, applying gobs of eye make-up, and going to great lengths to be the most 'feminine' women in the world." In attempting to achieve this feminine image, Chinese-American women perpetuated the stereotype of Asian women as "exotic-erotic-Susie Wong-Geisha girl dream of white American males." As white women became active in demanding social equality, Asian women became associated with the sexuality and the submissiveness of the "ideal" woman.[22]

Contestant statements and articles on the beauty pageant support this notion that white standards of physical beauty were used to judge the competition. Some candidates, organizers, and observers believed that judges preferred tall contestants. One entrant, who was five feet two inches tall complained that "it was obvious those girls with height had it." Other evidence suggests that "Caucasian" eyes represented a standard of beauty for Chinese-American contestants. When one 1973 entrant was asked if she had any special attributes that might make her stand out, she said that her eyes might be an advantage, because they were "larger than [those of] some of the girls." Large eyes with double eyelids and longer eyelashes have traditionally been associated with a "Western look," as opposed to small eyes with single eyelids. During the late 1960s, the double-eyelid look gained increasing popularity among Asians in Asia and the U.S. To achieve that look, women resorted to various methods. While teenagers "place[d] scotch tape or a gluey substance over their eyelids overnight," those with more resources paid for "plastic surgery to westernize Oriental eyes." One pageant souvenir book even carried an advertisement for cosmetic surgery by a Dr. David Wang, who invented a special technique for converting "'oriental eyes' with single eyelids into 'Caucasian eyes' (with double-eyelids)." Wang developed this technique through experiments done on volunteers who tended to be female "movie actresses, singing stars and participants in beauty contests."[23]

This emphasis on physical appearance placed psychological and emotional burdens on the contestants. In preparing for the competition, entrants experienced subtle and overt pressures to alter their physical appearance through cosmetics, dieting, and even plastic surgery. This emphasis on viewing women as sexual objects may have led to more abusive forms of behavior, such as sexual harassment. Celeste Wong remembered that: "alot of the people who directed the activities in Chinatown were older men who took advantage of the situation. . . . You'd be in a taxi or car with somebody and all of a sudden you'd feel a hand slipping under your dress." Her sponsor, the Holiday Inn hotel, provided her with a white male escort and required her to attend various functions to promote their business projects. Once, when the Holiday Inn flew her to Memphis for the opening of a hotel, her escort reserved only one room for both of them. Only sixteen years old at the time, Wong responded to these advances by ignoring them or escaping from the situations. However, she did not have the words or confidence to expose the treatment she received. Wong later interpreted these incidents as a result of the beauty pageant, which encouraged young women to present themselves as physically desirable. The sexual harassment "had to do with the contest and had to do with being a young woman who's supposed [to] just win based on what you looked like." The men who harassed her translated the accessibility of her body image for commercial and cultural purposes as an accessibility of her body for their sexual purposes.[24]

In addition to exposing the personal and psychological effects of beauty pageants, community activists also criticized the pageant for promoting an elite image of Chinese-American women. Because the competition sought to highlight educated, accomplished, poised, and beautiful Chinese-American women, critics considered the image of contestants "bourgeois." They argued that: "most of the contestants come from wealthy and influential backgrounds and know very little about Chinatown, the ghetto." Because the competition sought to present "the most 'beautiful' Chinese women in their fine clothes and just perfect make-up, pranc[ing] around the stage," critics did not consider this image as representative of Chinese-American women. They pointed out that: "the majority of Chinese women are hard-working, either with jobs or full-time family responsibilities, and in most cases it's both. They are not women of leisure and their 'beauty' is not in their 'made-up, worked on for hours' physical outward appearance." Instead of promoting exceptional women as representative of Chinese-American womanhood, critics sought further recognition of the problems facing women as workers and family members.[25]

Activists preferred to promote an image of Chinese-American women as protesters of injustice. Challenging the CCC's portrayal of

Chinese culture as passive and nonrevolutionary, the critics pointed to the growing militancy of women in Chinatown and throughout the Third World. Just as some Chinatown publications regularly featured women from beauty contests, papers with more liberal and radical agendas emphasized women's activism in movements for social justice. For example, articles in the latter papers frequently covered the struggles of garment workers striking for better working conditions and wages. The photographs of middle-aged women holding picket signs represented a dramatic departure from the images of young women in cheong-sams and makeup. Community members concerned about working women's issues also began celebrating International Women's Day in Chinatown during this period. Occurring in early March, this annual event could be interpreted as a symbolic alternative to the Miss Chinatown U.S.A. beauty pageant, which usually took place in late January or February.

These images of women as protesters rather than beauty queens were directly inspired by Third World female revolutionaries. Radicals criticized the CCC's emphasis on Confucian values as representative of Chinese culture. Instead, they sought inspiration from the new socialism forming throughout Asia. *Getting Together*, the newspaper for an Asian-American Marxist-Leninist organization, regularly featured images of female cadre and revolutionaries transforming patriarchal family structures and building new socialist societies in the PRC, Vietnam, the Philippines, and North Korea. Community radicals sought inspiration from the image of China's "Iron Girls," a group of women "who took on the most difficult and demanding tasks at work" and who developed legendary reputations for exerting superhuman energy. Community activists who promoted the Third World revolutionary women as role models for Chinese-American women criticized the involvement of the ROC in the Chinese New Year Festival. As an alternative, pro-PRC supporters organized a noncommercial celebration of Chinese New Year. Rather than emphasizing China's Confucian tradition, their Spring Festival highlighted "the creative and innovative aspects of Chinese culture," as represented by developments in the PRC.[26]

The criticisms leveled against the Chinese New Year festival and the Miss Chinatown U.S.A. pageant during the late 1960s and 1970s represented a contest over the definition of ethnic and gender identity. Influenced by radical social movements, a new generation of Chinese Americans began advocating new forms of interracial, gender, and class relationships. Instead of promoting a commercial image of Chinatown to attract tourists, the activists demanded support from city officials and community leaders to address social issues. Instead of encouraging women to achieve certain standards of beauty or personal advancement, they advocated community responsibility and political activism. Instead of seeking cultural inspiration from a Confucian past and political legitimation from nationalist Taiwan, they turned to Communist China. The vociferousness of community debates regarding gender and ethnic identity reflected the high degree of conflict within San Francisco's Chinatown during the late 1960s and 1970s.

THE REFORM TRADITION OF RADICALISM

The responses of pageant supporters to their critics demonstrate the diverse and often contradictory strategies available to advance racial and gender equality. On the one hand, pageant organizers and contestants expressed fundamental disagreement with the agenda of community reformers, radicals, and feminists. They questioned the cultural authenticity of their critics and disagreed with their views on tourism, the class bias of the pageant, and the gender roles portrayed through the image of Miss Chinatown. At the same time, pageant and New Year festival supporters also proclaimed their commitment to community service, accurate portrayals of Chinese culture, and women's achievements. While their critics sought to expose the contradictions involved in the Miss Chinatown U.S.A. beauty contest, pageant supporters revealed the contradictions embedded within the social movements that advocated racial and gender equality.

Reacting to criticisms of the pageant and the Chinese New Year festival, supporters questioned the ability of their critics to speak on behalf of Chinatown. One observer of the Holiday Inn rally suggested that the young radicals protesting for the good of the "community" did not necessarily understand the community. He pointed out that when one journalist asked the protesters what some older female residents were talking about in Chinese, "all the youths could respond was, 'I don't understand Chinese.'" Just as pageant critics questioned the ability of the CCC and other establishment leaders to represent the community, the ability of the liberals and radicals to speak on behalf of Chinatown also came into question.[27]

Claiming that they had the interest of the community at heart, pageant and festival supporters argued for the benefits of tourism. They suggested that "there's nothing wrong in bringing in large crowds" to Chinatown. Tourism provided an economic lifeline by supporting the restaurants and stores, which, in turn, employed Chinatown residents. Furthermore, the public exposure gained through the Miss Chinatown U.S.A. pageant and Chinese New Year festival helped Chinese Americans gain national and international attention. Some community members agreed that "in spite of the commercialization of Chinese New Year, it does help remind us that we belong to a unique culture." New Year festival supporters further suggested that those who wanted a less

commercial version of Chinese New Year should turn to private celebrations. One organizer explained that: "you have to understand the private and public celebrations are two very different things. . . . People
will go on having the traditional New Year family reunions, feasts and
gift-giving regardless of the parade." Pageant supporters thus downplayed their power to define ethnic identity by emphasizing the community's ability to celebrate cultural events in diverse ways.[28]

Pageant supporters also argued that the beauty competition transcended class divisions and helped promote upward mobility. They
pointed to the enormous popularity of the pageant among the working
class in Chinatown and the opportunities that the contest provided for
women. Cynthia Chin-Lee, a 1977 contestant from Harvard University,
agreed with this argument. She remembered that the pageant was
more of a casual, fun experience for her, because "I was going to
Harvard and I knew I had a different type of career ahead of me."
However, other contestants who "didn't have real high power careers"
approached the competition more seriously, because it offered an
opportunity for social recognition and career advancement. The experiences of Rose Chung, Miss Chinatown 1981, illustrate the argument
that beauty pageants provided opportunities for working-class women.
Growing up in a single-parent household, Chung remembered that she
stayed home to take care of her four siblings while her mother worked
as a seamstress. The pageant offered an opportunity to gain public
exposure and participate in a glamorous event. After winning the Miss
Chinatown title, she received a $2,000 scholarship and free trips to
locations in the U.S., Canada, and Asia. Chung also became an instant
celebrity, receiving recognition from the Chinatown community. She
recalled that because of her sheltered childhood, she "always wanted
to participate in community activities." After she won the Miss
Chinatown title, Chung served as the president of the women's auxil-
iary group of her family association, as president of the San Francisco
General Hospital Chinese Employee Association, and as a member of
the Republican County Central Committee. She traces these accomplishments to her victory in the Miss Chinatown U.S.A. pageant.[29]

Pageant defenders also countered their critics by challenging the
goals and methods of the Women's Movement. They disagreed with
feminist critics on issues concerning the importance of beauty, marriage, and radical protest. Although supporters acknowledged that
beauty pageants objectified women and fostered their feelings of inse-
curity, they believed that the competition provided overriding benefits. Because of the racial discrimination against minorities in
mainstream pageants such as the Miss America contest, the Miss
Chinatown U.S.A. and other ethnic pageants gave women of those
backgrounds the opportunity to achieve recognition. The experiences

of Sandra Wong, Miss Chinatown U.S.A. 1973, demonstrated this function of ethnic beauty pageants. Prior to entering the Miss Chinatown pageant, Wong competed twice in the local Miss San Leandro contest. Had she won, she would have been the first Asian American to be represented in the Miss California contest, a preliminary for the Miss America pageant. Although Wong won both the talent and swimsuit contests during her first attempt, she did not win the competition. During both years, she placed as first runner-up. She did not publicly protest these results as racially motivated, but others did. Journalist John Lum's exposé of Wong's experiences concluded that: "discrimination doesn't only extend to housing, education, and jobs, it extends to beauty 'contests,' too." Because of racial discrimination in mainstream beauty pageants, as well as in careers involving modeling, acting, and performance, pageant defenders argued that the Miss Chinatown U.S.A. competition was important for promoting positive images of Chinese Americans. These supporters disagreed with feminist critics who argued that emphasis on external appearances necessarily degraded women.[30]

Pageant backers also explained their disregard for feminist criticisms by proclaiming their support for more traditional female roles. When questioned about their thoughts on "women's lib" and on their future plans, many contestants discussed their dual commitments to career and marriage. Contestants during the late 1960s tended to view the two goals in conflict and prioritized marriage over careers. For example, 1967 contestant Irene Ung acknowledged gender discrimination against women in her field of international marketing when she remarked that "being a woman can be a handicap when you're looking for a man's job in a man's world." However, Ung did not necessarily aspire to "a career of working." "Like any other girl," Ung explained, "someday I'll want to get married and have children," goals that presumably set her apart from the feminist movement. Other contestants also voiced their preference for more "gentlemen-like" behavior from their male companions. One contestant explained that she "still enjoys having her cigarette lit and having somebody hold the door for her." She interpreted these desires as antagonistic to the feminist agenda. Still other contestants expressed their dissatisfaction with critiques of beauty pageants by emphasizing the radical image of feminists. Sandra Wong explained that she did not believe in the Women's Liberation movement's members "protesting and burning their bras." By explaining that feminists and beauty contestants operated in separate worlds and held different values, pageant supporters could partly explain their disregard of feminist criticisms.[31]

Even as they questioned their critics' authority and disagreed with the radical agenda, pageant defenders also professed similar goals of racial and gender equality. In response to criticisms raised during the 1960s and 1970s, organizers and participants altered the pageant and the New Year festival to assist community service projects and to project a less "plastic" version of Chinese culture. They also argued that the pageant promoted the goal of gender equality by emphasizing the importance of female bonding, women's achievements in the public realm, and sexual liberation. Pageant defenders argued that they, like their critics, shared the goals of advancing the Chinese-American community and Chinese-American women.

These reform efforts were often initiated by a new generation of pageant supporters who had activist credentials. Gordon Yaw provides one example. Yaw's family moved out of San Francisco when he was a young boy, but he returned to attend Chinese school. Because he grew up in an Oakland neighborhood where the Black Panthers had a positive influence, Yaw became involved with the Berkeley Third World Strike during the late 1960s. Through his protest activities, he met many Asian-American students who criticized the CCC and other Chinatown establishment leaders for ignoring the needs of the community. They also condemned the Miss Chinatown U.S.A. beauty pageant as a symbol of the status quo. Rather than just criticize the event, however, Yaw became involved and encouraged others to volunteer in order to change the pageant and the Chinese New Year festival. *East West* editors applauded these efforts, pointing out that: "as presently arranged, most of the New Year activities are organized by and for only a small segment of the community. Changes are needed to involve the young and those in the middle years, as well as the elderly, with meaningful activities."[32]

The involvement of younger people altered some of the content of the New Year festival. Through the lobbying efforts of Chinatown youth organizations, the CCC consented to include a community-sponsored street fair as part of the celebration in 1969. Rather than having a "traditional carnival organized by professional concessionaires," members of thirty youth organizations came together to create a street fair to raise funds for community services. The events, which included a run through Chinatown, ping-pong tournaments, cooking, and shadow-boxing demonstrations, were intended to "inform the public about Chinese culture, history and tradition" as well as to involve community members in recreational social activities. The organizers of the street fair wanted to use Chinese New Year to benefit the community directly. Beauty pageant contestants also demonstrated a growing consciousness about the need for social service. While pageant queens previously helped to raise funds and generate publicity about community projects, such as playgrounds for children, contestants in the 1970s also expressed career ambitions to serve the community. As one 1974 entrant explained, her life goal was "to be a social worker."[33]

In addition to emphasizing ways to contribute to community service in the New Year festivities, the new generation of organizers and participants also sought to alter the cultural content of the events. Sensitive to charges that the festival projected an artificial, tourist-oriented version of Chinese culture, organizers sought to revitalize the image of the celebration. For example, David Lei, one of the younger generation of organizers, traveled to Taiwan to research Chinese culture and purchase artifacts. To encourage tourists to look beyond "the old 'chop suey image' where people have a very superficial idea of what's Chinese culture," he "included a block-long bridal procession of the Han period" in the 1977 parade. Organizers of the beauty pageant also sought to incorporate Chinese culture into the event. One year, pageant organizer Louella "Lulu" Leon scripted the pageant in the form of a Chinese opera. The demographic changes in the Chinese American population also helped revitalize cultural aspects of the pageant. As immigrants from Hong Kong and Taiwan entered the pageant, contestants demonstrated greater knowledge and familiarity with Chinese language and culture.[34]

In addition to promoting community service and cultural education, younger pageant supporters also expressed their commitment to women's accomplishments. Like contemporary Women's Rights activists, they emphasized the importance of "sisterhood," women's achievements in the public realm, and sexual liberation. Almost all the contestants explained that their desire to meet other Chinese women constituted an important motivation for their decisions to enter the pageant. Jennifer Chung, a 1967 contestant, expressed her hope for "everlasting friends[hip]" with the other contestants. In their parting statements, Miss Chinatowns frequently invoked the rhetoric of female friendships. These expressions of "sisterhood" may not have reflected real experiences. When asked if she had developed any close friendships with other contestants, Chung admitted that her busy schedule preparing for the pageant did not allow her time to do so. Competition among contestants and the unequal treatment of winners and losers after the pageant presented obstacles as well. Despite the unevenness of women's relationships with one another, the use of rhetoric emphasizing female bonding suggests that pageant supporters viewed sisterhood as an important value that helped to justify the competition.[35]

Whatever the obstacles to female friendships, the beauty competition promoted female achievements, according to organizers. Participating in the Miss Chinatown U.S.A. beauty pageant provided contestants with an opportunity to acquire poise, grace, confidence, and public-speaking experience. These skills provided an important foundation for activities in the public realm. As one community member remarked, the pageant: "gives Chinese girls an opportunity to meet people and get into things. Too many of them sit at home and don't do anything." In fact, many contestants viewed the pageant as a stepping-stone to other challenges. In contrast to late-1960s contestants, who prioritized marriage over their careers, the 1970s contestants mainly discussed their future work plans or else emphasized the compatibility of marriage with careers. Jeannie Fung, Miss Chinatown U.S.A. 1975, expressed her desire to "be a medical technician and eventually to teach in junior college." Arleen Chow, a 1972 contestant, discussed the complementary roles of worker and mother. She believed that: "a girl can do a man's job, mentally and physically, if trained properly. . . . The wife should be both a parent and a supporter." For these contestants, participation in the pageant did not conflict with goals for women's social equality. Many contestants explained that they supported women's liberation to the extent that they believed in equal access to jobs and in "equal pay for equal jobs." In fact, the description of pageant contestants as "intelligent, ambitious, and mature women" matched the image of "modern" career women.[36]

Perhaps in response to feminist criticisms, the Chinese Chamber of Commerce also began to promote female leadership among pageant organizers. Although women had always participated in organizing the pageant, the leadership positions had previously been male-dominated. In 1974 the CCC selected Carolyn Gan as the first female editor-in-chief for the annual souvenir book. In 1979 a woman was elected to the CCC board of directors. The all-female fashion-show committee also made some adjustments in 1976 that appeared to respond to feminist critiques. In the midst of community debates about the exploitation of women, the fashion committee decided to include male models and men's fashions in the traditionally all-female fashion show. While these changes could be interpreted as responses to the growing criticisms of the pageant, their limited nature also demonstrates the difficulty of fundamentally changing the pageant or the CCC. The numbers of women in recognized leadership roles remained small, while the inclusion of male models and fashions occurred for only one year.

In addition to these attempts to integrate the leadership and content of the pageant, some proponents further claimed that their support for sexual liberation demonstrated their commitment to women's equality. In 1974, the fashion-show committee included a "feminist fashion" selection that emphasized revealing clothing. One of the "Women's Lib" outfits was described as "a black full-length evening gown with neckline in back swooping to the waist." Others associated female activists with wearing miniskirts. These interpretations of "feminism" emphasized women's willingness to express their sexual desirability in shocking ways. Ironically, this emphasis on physical exposure reinforced the objectification of female bodies that feminists criticized. For example, 1972 contestant Patricia Moy decided to give a speech on free love as her talent presentation. She argued that:

a) No one objects to free love, love meaning everything excluding the physical act of sex, which can be considered love. . . .
b) Virginity shouldn't be a prerequisite for marriage.
c) Homosexuality is not necessarily "bad" as society has always labeled it.

The main points of her speech coincided with developing feminist critiques of socially constructed heterosexual ideals and represented a radical departure from more conservative Chinese notions of sexuality. However, the manner of her presentation during the pageant suggests that she may have reinforced traditional sexual roles for women rather than transcended them. She began her act "by stripping off the top half of her pantsuit to reveal a bikini top, and then proceeded to deliver her original speech on free love, virginity, and homosexuality." Moy's decision to expose her body expressed her sexual freedom but also encouraged audience "gawkers" to view her as a sexual object.[37]

This relationship between increased sexual freedom and sexual exposure offers one explanation for the introduction of the swimsuit component to the Miss Chinatown U.S.A. beauty pageant. When the competition first began in 1958, organizers prided themselves for not having their contestants parade around in bathing suits. However, organizers introduced a "playsuit" portion in 1962, in which contestants displayed themselves in short-skirted outfits. In 1967, the bathing suit replaced the playsuit. One organizer claimed that the new requirement responded to the contestants' interest in displaying their beauty through wearing swimsuits. Although this explanation is not confirmed by other sources, his comment suggests that arguments for sexual liberation may have been used to justify sexual exploitation.[38]

During the 1960s and 1970s, pageant participants and supporters responded to critics both by disagreeing with them and by expressing their own commitments to gender and racial equality. The ability of pageant organizers to use the same concepts to refer to different strategies demonstrates the tensions within movements promoting social equality. By emphasizing the importance of individual role models to inspire Chinese Americans, women, and members of the working class, pageant supporters negated arguments calling for systemic structural changes. By stressing the importance of promoting beautiful images for Chinese Americans because of racial discrimination, pageant defenders downplayed the danger of encouraging women to use their physical appearance to gain social acceptance. Their arguments reveal the multiple and often contradictory strategies that could be used to advance racial and gender equality.

THE MODERN CHINESE AND CHINESE-AMERICAN WOMAN

The debates surrounding the Miss Chinatown U.S.A. and Chinese New Year festival demonstrate the complex struggles to define Chinese-American identity through gender images. The intensity of criticisms against the pageant coincided with the degree of community conflict surrounding issues of ethnic representation and gender roles, as well as class divisions and international allegiances. During the Cold War, organizers of the Miss Chinatown U.S.A. beauty pageant successfully balanced tensions within the Chinese-American community. By representing the Chinese community as a blend of the East and West, sponsors were able to address growing generational and cultural conflicts at a time when Chinese Americans sought to integrate into the broader community while also maintaining their cultural values. This conception of Chinese-American identity as embodied by Miss Chinatown also served cultural, economic, and political purposes in the community's relationship with the broader society. However, as social movements of the 1960s raised fundamental critiques of existing racial, sexual, and economic hierarchies, the Miss Chinatown pageant also came under attack. Pageant and festival supporters disagreed fundamentally with their critics on the importance of tourism, the evaluation of women based on physical standards, and the role of the ROC in the pageant. However, a new generation of organizers did reform certain aspects of the pageant in response to the criticisms. By emphasizing the importance of individual role models, organizers justified the pageant as a means to promote gender and ethnic equality.

While the overt conflict surrounding the pageant decreased in the 1980s with the decline of radical social movements, the process of negotiating gender and ethnic identity continues both internationally and domestically. Both the PRC's changing attitudes toward commercial images of women and the motivations of Miss Chinatown U.S.A. contestants in the 1980s demonstrate the ambiguous benefits of beauty pageants.

With the normalization of relations between Communist China and the U.S. in 1979, political pressure was placed on CCC leaders to lessen its pro-Taiwan stance and extend a hand of welcome to the PRC. Pageant and festival supporters did so reluctantly. In the 1979 Chinese New Year parade, Chinese school marching bands and an airline sponsor of the Miss Chinatown U.S.A. beauty pageant displayed the Nationalist flag, even after Mayor Dianne Feinstein asked for assurances from organizers that this would not occur. In 1980, after Feinstein applied political pressure, the CCC reluctantly issued a last-minute invitation to the envoy of the PRC and then quickly withdrew the invitation to both the Communist and Nationalist representatives. Pageant organizers chose to distance themselves from both countries rather than be forced to extend friendship to Communist China.

Despite the reluctance of the CCC to establish relations with the PRC, China was shifting its public image to accommodate the political, economic, and social changes that occurred following the Cultural Revolution. Ironically, even as Chinatown radicals promoted Third World socialist role models of working and revolutionary women, the PRC was commercializing the image of women to promote economic development and trade with the West. According to historians Emily Honig and Gail Hershatter: "adornment and sexuality, topics that had been off-limits to the generation of the Cultural Revolution, dominated publications for young women in the 1980s. Attention to beauty and fashion was part of a growing concern with the quality of personal life, and clearly captured the public fancy." Some state-owned businesses in China began instituting beauty requirements to hire women for service jobs. Beauty pageants have reportedly become very popular throughout China. Ironically, the living Chinese culture that community radicals promoted was evolving to adopt Western practices of commodifying women's beauty.[39]

Just as Communist China recognized the commercial uses of women's bodies in promoting its national economy, Chinese-American women in the 1980s and 1990s continued to use the pageant as a means for personal and community advancement. According to filmmaker Valerie Soe, Miss Chinatown 1984 Cynthia Gouw first entered the Los Angeles pageant as part of an undercover reporting assignment for a school newspaper. Gouw was supposed to "expose the contest from a feminist, leftist, socialist point of view . . . [and uncover] the oppression of Asian American women." However, after Gouw won the Miss L.A. and then the Miss Chinatown U.S.A. titles, she decided not to criticize the event. Gouw argued that there was no contradiction between the pageant and her feminist and political beliefs: "I didn't feel exploited at all. . . . I want to show people that I can be very articulate and assertive as opposed to a stereotypical beauty pageant winner. . . . What I want to represent to the Asian population is that I am very concerned about the community." Gouw suggested that her personal advancement reflected upon the entire community, because groups who have traditionally been disadvantaged, women as well as racial minorities, need role models and spokespersons. After she won Miss Chinatown U.S.A., Gouw entered and won the Spokesmodel competition for Star Search. Since then, she has appeared in films and TV commercials and worked as a news reporter. For her, the pageant opened up numerous opportunities, allowing her to achieve, in the words of Valerie Soe, the "American Dream." The question of whether Gouw in fact transcended stereotypes of Chinese-American women, or merely benefited from perpetuating them remains unanswered.[40]

The history of the Miss Chinatown U.S.A. pageant, from the early years of success through the years of controversy, demonstrates how idealized roles of womanhood represent broader concerns about power. Activists of the late 1960s and 1970s, like commercial leaders of the late 1950s, recognized the significance of gender roles in defining the identity of a community. The intensity of their debates about the pageant reflected a contest over ethnic and gender identity as well as international politics and class relations. The persistent success of the Miss Chinatown U.S.A. beauty pageant into the 1980s and 1990s suggests its unique ability to reconcile conflicting impulses within the Chinese-American community. The competition continues to provide a means for exceptional Chinese-American women to use their physical appearance and personality skills to achieve recognition within the existing commercialized society. The cultural event promotes recognition of disadvantaged groups without threatening the fundamental American values of individualism and meritocracy. The continued popularity of beauty pageants combined with the decrease in vocal opposition suggests the decline of alternative strategies that advocate structural change and group-based solutions to achieve gender and racial equality.

ACKNOWLEDGMENTS

The *Journal of Social History* kindly gave permission to reprint this article. My thanks to those who shared their experiences with the Miss Chinatown U.S.A. beauty pageant and to the many who offered helpful criticisms of this essay. In particular, I want to mention Gordon Chang for recommending this research topic, Estelle Freedman for fostering a supportive intellectual community, the members of the 1993–1994 seminar "Women, Family, and Sexuality" for "coauthoring" this paper, and Shawn Lahr for his willingness to read drafts, no matter how rough the quality. A big hug for Mark Walter, who gave up valuable gardening and squirrel-chasing time over Labor Day weekend to proofread this article. Earlier versions of this essay were presented at the Stanford History Gender and Sexuality Workshop (1995), the Association for Asian American Studies National Conference (1996), and the American Historical Association, Pacific Coast Branch Conference (1996).

NOTES

1. *Miss Chinatown U.S.A. Pageant Program* (February 21–23, 1958); "June Chin," *California Living Magazine* (February 17, 1985): 9; The overall Chinese American population in 1960 was 237,292. Of the 29,000 Chinese living in San Francisco in 1960, 18,000 lived in Chinatown.

2. Although the pageant held symbolic value for Chinese-American communities through-out the country, I focus on San Francisco and Bay Area responses to the competition as part of the annual Chinese New Year celebration. On the one hand, San Francisco's Chinatown could be considered unique because of its large Chinese population, its histor-ical relationship with the nationalist Republic of China, and its exposure to local social movements. On the other hand, the tensions in San Francisco's community, the unoffi-cial capital of American Chinatowns, were often representative of the conflicts in other Chinese-American communities.

3. The main newspapers used for research include *East West, San Francisco Journal*, and *Getting Together*, all bilingual Chinese-American publications based in San Francisco's Chinatown; *Chinatown News*, a Chinese-Canadian publication based in Vancouver, B.C.; *Asian Week*, an Asian-American publication based in San Francisco; and the *San Francisco Chronicle*. Because of my limited Chinese reading skills, I was not able systematically to access Chinese-language materials. Consequently, the experiences and perspectives of Chinese Americans who felt more comfortable expressing themselves in Chinese will not be represented as well as those who wrote in English. The perspectives of the former are not less valuable but are nevertheless not accessible to me at this point. Fortunately, the staff of the bilingual newspapers did publish translations of some Chinese articles on the Miss Chinatown U.S.A. beauty pageant.

4. Colleen Ballerino Cohen, Richard Wilk, Beverly Stoeltje, eds., *Beauty Queens on the Global Stage: Gender, Contests, and Power* (New York: Routledge, 1996), 2. This collection exam-ines a variety of beauty contests throughout the world for their significance concerning not only gender roles but also ethnic, class, and national identity formation. Prior to the publication of this collection, most scholars of beauty contests tended to focus on the Miss America pageant, which involves predominantly white contestants. See Frank Deford, *There She Is* (New York: Viking, 1971); A. R. Riverol, *Live from Atlantic City* (Bowling Green, OH: Bowling Green State University Press, 1992), and Lois W. Banner, *American Beauty* (New York: Random House, 1983). A few scholars have analyzed state or local beauty pageants and their significance in terms of community representation. See Frank Deford, "Beauty and Everlasting Faith at the Local Level," *Audience* (1971, 1:5); 56–72; Geoffrey Dunn and Mark Schwartz, directors, *Miss . . . or Myth?* (Distributors: Cinema Guild, 1986), film; Robert Lavenda, "Minnesota Queen Pageants: Play, Fun, and Dead Seriousness in a Festive Mood," *Journal of American Folklore* 101:400 (1988): 68–175.

   For the most part, scholars of Chinese-American women have not analyzed the Miss Chinatown U.S.A. beauty pageant. Their studies tend to focus on the emergence of women from the private realm of family concerns to the public realm of political organiz-ing and work. See Huping Ling, "Surviving on the Gold Mountain: Chinese American Women and Their Lives," Ph.D. diss., Miami University, 1991; Stacey G. H. Yap, *Gather Your Strength, Sisters: The Emerging Role of Chinese Women Community Workers* (New York: AMS Press, 1989); and Judy Yung, *Unbound Feet: A Social History of Chinese Women in San Francisco* (Berkeley, CA: University of California Press, 1995). One exception is Judy Yung's paper entitled "Miss Chinatown USA and the Representation of Beauty." She pre-sented it at the 1992 Association for Asian American Studies national Conference in San Jose, but it is not available to the public at this time.

5. The title for this section is quoted from James H. Loo, "Who Are the Chinese?" in *San Francisco Chinatown On Parade*, ed. H.J. Wong (San Francisco: N. P., 1961), 6–7.

   Beginning in the 1910s, San Francisco Chinatown organizations sporadically sponsored community pageants as fund-raisers for social services, such as the Chinese Hospital. In 1948, various merchant, family, and civic organizations initiated an annual Miss Chinatown pageant. Inspired by the earlier tradition of fund-raising, the winners were determined by the contestants' ability to sell raffle tickets to benefit a social cause. H. K. Wong is credited with proposing the joint sponsorship of the beauty contest and the pub-lic celebration of the Chinese New Year festival in 1953. In the late 1950s, the CCC altered the format of the pageant so that a panel of judges selected winners based on such criteria as beauty, personality, and poise. Lim P. Lee, "The Chinese New Year Festival," *Asian Week* (February 5, 1981): 4; and "The Chinese New Year Festival II," *Asian Week* (February 12, 1981): 2; H. K. Wong, "Miss Chinatown USA Pageant," *San Francisco Chinese New Year Festival*, souvenir program (February 4–7, 1960); Alice Lowe, "Concealing—Yet Revealing," *San Francisco Chinatown On Parade*, 26–27.

6. Julie Smith, "A Little Tiff at the Chinese New Year," *San Francisco Chronicle* (February 18, 1977): 2. The proportions of Chinese-American women in the labor force exceeded white women during the decade of the 1940s. Whereas 39.5 percent of white women worked for pay compared to 22.3 percent of Chinese women in 1940, 30.8 percent of Chinese women compared to 28.1 percent of white women worked in 1950. In 1960, 44.2 percent of Chinese women worked in the labor force compared to only 36.0 percent of white women. The gap in labor participation between the two groups continued to increase. Huping Ling, "Surviving on the Gold Mountain: Chinese American Women and Their Lives," 134–135.

Following the war, the Miss America pageant increasingly gained popularity, culminating in its first national televised broadcast in 1954. Whereas previous pageants held significance mainly for the local audience of Atlantic City, television made the event a truly national one, so that by 1959 every state was finally represented at the "Miss America" pageant. A. R. Riverol, *Live From Atlantic City*, 56.

7. "June Chin," *California Living Magazine*; Donald Canter, "In New Year of the Boar: Chinatown 'Moves West,'" (February 9, 1959), clipping from Chinese Historical Society, San Francisco, box 3, folder 16. The collection is located at the Asian-American Studies Library of the University of California, Berkeley. hereafter cited as CHS-SF.

8. Lim P. Lee, "The Chinese New Year Festival," *Asian Week* (February 5, 1981): 4.

9. Pageant souvenir booklets regularly included informational pieces explaining Chinese culture to audiences unfamiliar with the community.

Victor and Brett de Bary Nee use the terms "bachelor society" and "family society" to characterize the evolution of the San Francisco Chinatown community; see *Longtime Californ': A Documentary Study of an American Chinatown* (Stanford: Stanford University Press, 1972). The development of the beauty pageant coincided with the balancing of sex ratios among Chinese Americans. In 1890, when the Chinese population reached a nineteenth-century peak of 107,488 in the U.S., men outnumbered women 26.8 to one. Due to the combined influence of natural birthrates and immigration, the sex ratio became 1.3 to one by 1960. (Huping Ling, "Surviving on the Gold Mountain," 127.) For further discussions of Chinese American family and community life in the late nineteenth and early twentieth centuries, see Peggy Pascoe, "Gender Systems in Conflict: The Marriages of Mission-Educated Chinese American Women, 1874–1939," in *Unequal Sisters: A Multicultural Reader in U.S. Women's History*, ed. Ellen Carol DuBois and Vicki L. Ruiz (New York: Routledge, 1990); and Sucheng Chan, "The Exclusion of Chinese Women, 1870–1943," in *Entry Denied: Exclusion and the Chinese Community in America, 1882–1943* (Philadelphia: Temple University Press, 1991).

Lyrics to "Miss Chinatown" by Charles L. Leong and Kenneth Lee, 1964, published in *Miss Chinatown U.S.A.*, Chinese New Year festival souvenir program, 1975. Robert H. Lavenda makes a similar argument that contestants of community pageants tend to represent "the community's daughters." Lavenda, "Minnesota Queen Pageants: Play, Fun, and Dead Seriousness in a Festive Mode," *Journal of American Folklore* 101 (1988): 169. Daisy Chinn, "Women of Initiative," *San Francisco Chinatown On Parade*, 64.

10. For an examination of how international relations influence portrayals of Asian Americans in popular culture, see *Slaying the Dragon*, directed by Deborah Gee (San Francisco: NAATA/Cross Current Media, 1987). In the late 1950s, C. Y. Lee's *Flower Drum Song* (New York, 1957), a love story about intergenerational and cultural tensions set in San Francisco's Chinatown, became a best seller. Rogers and Hammerstein subsequently turned the book first into a Broadway musical hit and then into a motion picture, leading Hollywood and Broadway to declare 1959 the "year of the oriental." Chinatown organizers cashed in on the publicity by honoring and promoting the author of the book during the New Year festivals in the late 1950s and early 1960s.

As part of the city's efforts to promote the Miss Chinatown U.S.A. beauty pageant and the Chinese New Year festival, mayors, police commissioners, and supervisors regularly appeared in the annual parade. Politicians and their wives served as judges for the pageant, and in 1963 the San Francisco Convention and Visitors Bureau became a cosponsor of the festival. "To Rival Mardi Gras? Mayor Urges Big Chinatown Festival," January 24, 1957, CHS-SF, box 3, folder 16; Arthur Hoppe, "Festival Overture, Opus I: Montgomery St. Hails Chinese New Year," clipping from CHS-SF, box 3, folder 15.

11. Donald Canter, "Speech," Chinese Historical Society of America, 1965, CHS-SF, box 3, folder 27.

12. T. Kong Lee, President Chinese Chamber of Commerce, "Welcome to Chinatown," *San Francisco Chinatown On Parade*, 2.

13. James H. Loo, "Who Are the Chinese?" *San Francisco Chinatown On Parade*, 6–7; W. K. Wong, "Interview," *Longtime Californ'*, 244–245.

14. *San Francisco Chinatown Souvenir Annual*, 1962.
15. H. K. Wong, "Concept of Beauty," *San Francisco Chinatown On Parade*, 79; Evelyn S. Rawski, "Ch'ing Imperial Marriage and Problems of Rulership," in *Marriage and Inequality in Chinese Society*, ed. Rubie S. Watson and Patricia Buckley Ebrey (Berkeley: University of California Press, 1991), 180. Although pageant organizers argued that the beauty pageant drew inspiration from Chinese as well as American cultural practice, scholars attribute the growing popularity of beauty pageants in Asian countries following World War II to the commercialization and Westernization of those countries. Corporations in Taiwan, Hong Kong, Japan, the Philippines, and Southeast Asia increasingly sponsored pageants as a way to help advertise their products and to promote tourism. Some scholars further suggest that businesses "actively promote[d] Western-style sexual objectification as a means of ensuring employee loyalty" by channeling the energy of female workers towards self-beautification through purchasing commodities. Barbara Ehrenreich and Annette Fuentes, "Life on the Global Assembly Line," in *Feminist Frameworks*, ed. Alison M. Jaggar and Paula S. Rothenberg (New York: McGraw-Hill, 1984), 285.
16. David Lei, telephone interview, San Francisco, November 23, 1993; Shirley Sun, "Jumbo Banana Split Proves Too Much for Beautiful May Chiang," *East West* (February 21, 1967): 5.
17. In 1971, 41 percent of Chinatown's population fell below the federally defined poverty level partly because of the low wages paid to immigrant workers. Immigrant men commonly found service jobs, such as waiters, and tended to work "ten hours a day, six days a week, for wages that average from $350 to an occasional high of $700 a month." Immigrant women usually worked as garment workers, receiving pay not by the hour but by the piece. These low wages as well as the lack of cultural familiarity made it unlikely that immigrant families would move out of Chinatown, despite the fact that 77 percent of its housing was considered substandard by city codes. In 1970, the population density of the community was the second highest in the country, with 120 to 180 persons per acre. These crowded conditions created enormous health risks, as demonstrated by the fact that Chinatown had the highest tuberculosis and suicide rates in the nation. To service its population of over 40,000 people, Chinatown had only one hospital with sixty beds. Nee, *Longtime Californ'*, xxi-xxv.
18. "The Most Visible Event," *East West* (February 14, 1973): 2; George Chu, "A Wild Night in Old Chinatown," *San Francisco Chronicle* (March 9, 1969): 18, 21; The racial tensions between Chinatown residents and white tourists and police officers were not necessarily new. However, the growing numbers of Chinese-American youth in the community as a result of immigration and the increased awareness of racial injustice during the 1960s raised the volatility of intergroup contact.
19. "Liberate Holiday Inn," *Getting Together* (February 1971): 2; Jade Fong, "The CHI-am Corner," *East West* (February 3, 1971): 3.
20. Sara Evans, *Personal Politics: The Roots of Women's Liberation in the Civil Rights Movement and the New Left* (New York: Vintage, 1979), 214, and "No More Miss America! August 1968," in *Sisterhood Is Powerful*, ed. Robin Morgan (New York: Random House, 1970), 521-524.
21. "A Queen for the Year of the Canine," *East West* (December 10, 1969): 1; Ben Wong-Torres, "Miss Chinatown—a Few Immodest Proposals," *East West* (March 11, 1967): 3; Judy Yung wrote in the pen-name Jade Fong, "The CHI-am Corner," *East West* (March 1, 1972): 3; Mabel Ng, "The Chinatown Pageant . . . A Miscarriage of Grace," *East West* (January 30, 1974): 10; Wei Chih, "Queen Contestants," trans. from the *Chinese Pacific Weekly* (January 16, 1975) printed in *East West* (January 22, 1975): 2; Curtis Choy, *The Year of the Ox: The 1973 Livestock Show* (Oakland, 1985), film.
22. Lisa Fangonilo, quoted in "What Do You Think about the Miss Chinatown USA Beauty Contest?" *East West* (January 27, 1971): 9; Pam Lee, "Letter to the Editor," *East West* (April 13, 1970): 2.
23. Louella Leon, conversation with author. As of 1987, "the average height of Miss Chinatown U.S.A. winners is 5 feet 5.3 inches." *Miss Chinatown U.S.A. Pageant Souvenir Program 1987*; Paul Hui, "Alice Kong Also Ran . . ." *East West* (February 20, 1974): 5; Curtis Choy, *The Year of the Ox*; "Oriental Eyes Get Western Look," *Chinatown News* (December 3, 1969): 4; "Dr. David Wang—Face-Lifting Surgeon," *Chinatown News* (December 18, 1969): 10–15.
24. The experiences of Nathele Sue Dong, reported in a promotion piece for the pageant, demonstrate the importance of cosmetics for helping contestants compete successfully. When Dong decided to run for the Miss Chinatown U.S.A. pageant in 1961, one of her supporters encouraged her to seek the advice of Helen Lew, the director of the Patricia

Stevens modeling agency. Lew taught Dong the importance of cosmetics, clothing, jewelry, and hairstyling for creating the image of a beauty pageant contestant:

Helen told the girl the only reason her face was shiny was because she'd never worn makeup, corrected it with a color that blends with Nathele's skin. Two pencil strokes and Nathele's eyebrows were intriguingly accentuated and slightly higher; a green Chinese dress (because green is very becoming with the Oriental skin) brought out the red pigment in her face. Nathele's first pair of earrings (rhinestone drops) a visit to the hairdresser (her hair shaped in closer) and you can see for yourself how Nathele has acquired the poise, personality and good looks required of a candidate for Miss Chinatown USA. ("They Look Twice Now," *San Francisco News-Call Bulletin* [February 17, 1961], CHS-SF, box 3, folder 20.)

One Miss Chinatown contestant reportedly had a face-lift operation prior to the pageant. Manchester Fu, "Manny and the Celestial 5," *East West* (January 21, 1970): 3. Many observers noted the disappointment of candidates who did not win a title in the pageant. Ronda Wei Jeyn-Ching, Miss Chinatown 1980, commented that "many young girls develop a poor self-image after failing to win a pageant title." "A Parting Queen's Reflections," *Asian Week* (February 26, 1981). This feeling of inferiority partly arose from their failure to fulfill the expectations of parents and sponsors. Pageant organizer Louella Leon recalled that one contestant who did not win a title began crying backstage. She became even more traumatized when her mother yelled at her for making mistakes and not presenting herself in the best light during the competition. Because of what occurred, organizers decided to ban family members from backstage areas of the pageant. (Louella Leon, conversation with author.)

Celeste Wong (pseudonym), interview, San Francisco, December 8, 1993; Wong had lied about her age to enter the Miss Chinatown U.S.A. beauty pageant, which required contestants to be between the ages of seventeen and twenty-six.

25. Pamela Tau, *East West* (February 3, 1971): 5; Pam Lee, "Letter to the Editor," *East West* (April 13, 1970): 2; "Reflections on Chinese New Year—2 Views," *Getting Together* (February 3–16, 1973): 3.
26. Emily Honig and Gail Hershatter, *Personal Voices: Chinese Women in the 1980s* (Stanford, CA: Stanford University Press, 1988), 24; "Public Invited to Spring Festival Celebration," *San Francisco Journal* (February 9, 1977).
27. Stan Yee, "Notes of a Chinese Bum on Holiday Inn," *East West* (January 20, 1971): 2.
28. Ann F. Nakao, "A Hard Look: The Fires behind Chinatown's Parade," *San Francisco Examiner* (February 15, 1977): 8; Carole Jan Lee, "Carole's Barrel," *East West* (February 18, 1970).
29. Cynthia Denise Chin-Lee, telephone interview, Palo Alto, February 20, 1994; Rose Chung, telephone interview, San Francisco, December 2, 1993.
30. John Lum, "The Miss San Leandro Contest: There's No Point to It," *East West* (May 17, 1972): 6. Y. C. Hong, a judge for the 1965 competition, explained that if he had a daughter, he would not wish her to enter the contest because he sympathized "with the heartaches of many beautiful girls who failed to get within the 'magic circle' and the disappointments of their parents and sponsors." Despite these reservations, he applauded the contestants for entering the competition and demonstrating the positive aspects of Chinese-American culture. He believed that "it is a good thing for our Chinese in showing the peoples of the world that we do have many beautiful and talented Chinese girls from all parts of the country." Y. C. Hong, "Letter to the Editor," *East West* (March 21, 1967): 2.
31. Irene Ung, "Irene Ung Satisfied with Simple Things in Life," *East West* (February 21, 1967): 7; "Interviews with Two Bay Area Beauty Pageant Contestants," *East West* (February 4, 1976): 11; Doris G. Worsham, "There is a 'There' for Her," *Oakland Tribune* (February 17, 1973), clipping found in "Beauty Contests—CA" folder at UC Berkeley's Asian-American Studies Library.
32. Gordon Yaw, telephone interview, Oakland (February 7, 1994); "Consider the Alternatives," *East West* (January 30, 1974): 2.
33. "Only a 'Fair' Fair," *East West* (March 19, 1969): 2; Katie Choy, "E-W Interviews 'Miss Chinatown' Contestants," *East West* (January 23, 1974): 6.
34. Nakao, "A Hard Look," 1, 6.
35. Shirley Sun, "Tall & Lissome Jennifer Chung Fulfills Her Childhood Dream," *East West* (February 21, 1967): 6. Thanking the other contestants, Miss Chinatown U.S.A. 1976 Linda Chun wrote that we "are all dear friends and I shall cherish our moments together always." Linda Sue Kwai En Chun, "Reflections," *Chinatown San Francisco*, souvenir program, 1977, 42; Celeste Wong recalled that after she won the title of Miss San Francisco Chinatown, her fellow contestants were not as friendly towards her. (Celeste Wong, interview.)

36. Melanie Feng, "What Do You Think about the Miss Chinatown USA Beauty Contest?" *East West* (January 27, 1971): 4; Katie Choy and Paul K. Hui, "3 Beauties Interviewed," *East West* (January 22, 1975): 5; Judy Quan, "Three Queen Contestants: The Person behind the Face," *East West* (February 16, 1972): 7; Worsham, "There Is a 'There' for Her"; Fang Wei Lyan, "Under Those Plastic Smiles," *East West* (January 21, 1967): 1–2.

   In some cases, the pageant provided more opportunities for women to gain exposure to certain public sectors. Women interested in modeling, movie, or public-relations careers viewed the pageant as a good way to gain recognition. After winning the Miss Chinatown U.S.A. title, Sandra Wong auditioned for a movie role opposite Clint Eastwood. Contestants who won trips to Asia gained some exposure to international politics through meeting such dignitaries as ROC President Chiang Kai-shek. Contestants might also learn about international finance, for the Chinese Chamber of Commerce used these "goodwill tours" to build trade relations with Taiwan, Hong Kong, and other Asian countries. The participation of recognizable national and state politicians, such as Anne Chennault and March K. Wong, as pageant judges also provided models of successful Chinese-American women who transcended traditional female roles. In other words, pageant supporters argued that they, like their feminist critics, sought to promote female achievements in the public realm.

37. Mary Jew, "Fantastic Turnout at Fashion Show," *East West* (February 13, 1974): 5; "Come Alive," Editorial, *East West* (August 28, 1968): 2; Judy Quan, "Three Queen Contestants: the person behind the face," *East West* (February 16, 1972): 7. Moy did not win the pageant; Wally Lee, "Wahine stewardess Miss Chinatown USA," *East West* (February 23, 1972): 1,10.

38. Hing C. Tse, interview, San Francisco (November 12, 1993).

39. Honig and Hershatter, *Personal Voices*, 335; "China Wants Good-Looking Stewardesses," *Chinatown News* (January 18, 1980), reprint from *New York Times*.

40. *Cynsin: An American Princess*, video by Valerie Soe, 1991; Lorena Tong, "Miss Chinatown Cynthia Gouw Insists She Is Not the 'Beauty Pageant' Type," *East West* (December 5, 1984): 8.

Hiding the Scars

HISTORY OF BREAST PROSTHESES AFTER MASTECTOMY SINCE 1945

KIRSTEN E. GARDNER

*B*reast-prostheses production and distribution in the United States is a small but growing segment of the multimillion-dollar prostheses industry. As advertisements for breast forms and mastectomy bras reveal, the product is closely aligned with contemporary notions of an ideal female beauty. A quick review of marketing strategies, the material culture of "mastectomy boutiques," and the inclusion of this product in lingerie departments and on Web sites that sell the forms suggests the deliberate association between notions of beauty and this prosthetic part. Pastel images surround images associated with the product, flowers appear next to the breast forms, and many companies emphasize the vital role of the artificial breast in restoring a woman's sense of beauty after a mastectomy. Obviously these sources also feature pictures of smiling, full-figured women, presumably comfortable wearing a prosthetic breast. These sources gloss over any discussion of the medical and surgical nature of the product and instead constantly stress attractiveness. They echo the messages ubiquitous in women's magazines that place the center of women's value in her physical and feminine appearance. When and how did a "surgical appliance" that catered to a narrow and specific consumer base evolve into a beauty product?

This essay traces the changes in breast prostheses production, sales, and rhetoric from the post–World War II era to the present. Since 1945 popular women's magazines, sales catalogues, and businesses have made increasingly public reference to artificial breasts and the breast-prostheses industry. Responding to a culture that revered large breasts and an era of affluence that encouraged mass consumption of beauty products, the prosthetic breast became a medical device that could deliver a sense of beauty and femininity.[1] Since World War II, a typical breast replacement after surgery has evolved from a "foam rubber form" priced at $2.98 to silicone breast forms that sell for several hundred dollars; some forms today cost in excess of $3,000. Moreover, in this ever-growing and expanding market, innovators insist that a more perfect replacement breast can still be achieved.

Cultural values about beauty have influenced advertisements, the breast prosthetic industry, and marketing strategies that conflate medical issues and notions of beauty. American advertisements for breast forms are shaped by cultural values that emphasize the female ideal of a double-breasted figure. Women who have had mastectomies recognize the plethora of postmastectomy products available to consumers today, evoking both praise and criticism of this multimillion-dollar industry. Although the expansion of this industry has ushered in a host of choices for women regarding postmastectomy care, its emphasis on beauty has also fostered a sense that the surgical, physical, and emotional scars of breast cancer should remain hidden from the public eye.

The transformation of this industry from a small craft to a corporate interest has also shifted more attention to profit. Beginning at mid-century, corporations started to enter a business once controlled by individuals. Between 1950 and 1970, as silicone became the standard material for breast forms, artificial breast production became increasingly commercial. Although American suppliers influenced the packaging and marketing for the products and distributed silicone breast forms, manufacture moved to cheaper overseas locations. The prostheses business is informed by a profit motive that recognizes prostheses as commodities that serve both a medical and cosmetic function. As a speaker at a mastectomy fitter clinic told her audience: "When I say price it is a very important issue. Owners need to make money."[2]

HISTORY OF ARTIFICIAL-BREAST MANUFACTURE

In 1872 Frederick Cox earned the first United States patent for an artificial breast. Since then, the continuous stream of patent applications for breast forms suggests that inventors and entrepreneurs acknowledged a market for artificial breasts. To date, the U.S. Patent Office has issued 182 patents within the subclass "breast," under the class title "Prosthesis (i.e. artificial body members), parts thereof, or aids and accessories therefore."[3]

Early patent applications stressed the nature of breast forms meant to augment existing breast size. The "breast pads," "bust pads," and "artificial breasts" often included a cavity to accommodate the breast and used rubber, down, cotton, and other miscellaneous fill material to reproduce the feel of breast tissue. A 1919 patent application for a "surgical breast substitute" marked the first explicit recognition of a medical application for breast forms. The actual distinction between this one and earlier ones is vague—except for the title, the "substitute" noted little about breast surgeries of this era—but the patent's title articulated its purpose. Some years later, in 1935, a woman sought a patent for her "Breast Adapter" and made the first reference to mastectomy in an application. She described the purpose of her invention as to fill "bodily depressions caused by the removal of female breast and pectoral muscles." Stressing the uniqueness of her invention, she stated that earlier breast forms had "not been adaptable to take the place of bodily injuries that have resulted in the removal of the breasts, muscle and flesh of the human body in the vicinity of the chest."[4]

Throughout the early decades of the century, the vast majority of patent applications for artificial breasts stressed design. For instance, the essence of Helen Perl's 1944 application was her idea regarding the sewing and manufacture of the part. As suggested in her title "Pattern and Method of Forming Breast Forms," she offered direction to individuals who might make this form. As she instructed, a form could be made by:

> attaching a sheet of material over the human breast to be duplicated, cutting the sheet to form end and intermediate portions that remain united at the central portion of the sheet, then folding the end portions over onto the respective intermediate portions and securing the parts together in such overlapping relation so as to cause the pattern to conform to the shape of the breast, then indicating on the pattern the outline of the breast, then removing the formed pattern from the person's body, and using the pattern as a model from which a breastform may be sculptured.[5]

Like Perl, throughout the early decades of the century most inventors imagined their product as a means to breast augmentation and thereby a product to enhance beauty. Inventors that recognized a post-surgical application for their design usually described the medical application as an addendum that expanded the purpose of their augmentation product. Claims of medical application for the breast form tended to focus on the shape of the form and assertions that the invention offered a more realistic breast replacement for women whose breast had been amputated.

Until 1945, individuals or teams of two to three people filed patents for artificial breasts; in that year, however, companies began filing for these patents. The growing importance of corporations and business in the prostheses industry in the second half of the twentieth century cannot be understated. Before 1945 individuals filed 100 percent of the granted artificial breast patents; since 1970 50 percent of the 124 patents filed have been granted to companies. As breast-prostheses manufacture moved beyond the realm of individual innovations, more and more inventors aligned with companies when filing a patent. This shift in ownership from individual to corporate reflected a larger trend of increased commercial interest in this product. Moreover, patents filed by companies in the latter half of the century frequently included manufacturing specifications that reflected a move in production to factories and assembly plants.[6] Company willingness to sponsor an inventor and file a patent reflected its vested interest in ownership claims and its recognition of a burgeoning market.

SELLING ARTIFICIAL BREASTS

Since early in this century businesses have tapped into the artificial-breast market, using advertisements to promote the product. Throughout the early decades of the century, the Sears, Roebuck Catalogue regularly featured various "breast forms" meant to augment a woman's breast size. These advertisements ignored the potential use of breast forms among women who had had mastectomies. Similar to patent applications from the first part of the century, advertisers expressed the purpose of an artificial breast as augmentative. For example, throughout the 1940s Charmode marketed Flatterettes, foam and breast-shaped inserts "for under-developed breasts." For 77 cents women could choose one of three Flatterettes that offered women a "new, attractive figure" in a culture that placed value on women's breast size.[7]

At mid-century Sears, Roebuck expanded the artificial breast market. Starting in 1946, it introduced a line of products for postmastectomy care. They were also manufactured by Charmode and, like earlier artificial breasts, indexed under the title "bust pads," but advertisements noted a new purpose for the product. The "Surgical Bust Forms" could "restore bust contours after surgery." The advertisement further promised potential buyers that they could "avoid any self-conscious feeling." As the advertisement read: "Your clothing will fit better for these forms give you a natural looking silhouette." In 1951 the marketing rhetoric continued to stress the surgical nature of this product and promised restoration of the female form. In addition it emphasized an easy application for the form: "Just slip foam rubber forms into bra."[8]

The simple instructions for wearing a breast form and reminders that it did not require "expensive fittings" suggested that the mail-order catalogue industry faced competition from other retailers that sold breast forms. By mid-century women might buy a breast form from Sears, Roebuck, local pharmacies, hospitals, or department stores. If they bought a form in person, often a trained fitter would recommend a postoperative bra and fill. Sears, Roebuck regularly implied that profession fittings were time-consuming, unnecessary, and expensive.

The "NEW CHARMODE Post-Operative Bras" described in Sears' 1954 catalogue reflected the quick expansion of the postmastectomy care market. Advertisements deliberately highlighted the medical nature of this product. For example, an emblem was stamped on the advertisement that read: "accepted for advertising in publications of the American Medical Association." The advertisement listed corrective functions of the postoperative bra, such as its ability to restore a sense of balance after surgery. It pushed women to wear this bra immediately and constantly after a mastectomy:

> Amazing *Inflatable* "COMPENSATION" surgical bra comfortably restores your figure balance after surgery. No long, drawnout fittings; little if any alterations—yet it defies detection as if it were made just for you. Actually looks like part of you . . . permits wearing sleek fitting apparel. Best of all "Compensation" bras can often be worn home from the hospital![9]

At the same time that the prosthetic breast advertisement emphasized the medical benefits of the part, it also suggested its applicability to fashion and implied that a woman should immediately replace her amputated breast.

The early advertisements for surgical breast forms from Sears, Roebuck tended to emphasize the medical usefulness of this product. Advertisements alluded to the beauty aspect of this business, most evident in the constant emphasis on "realistic appearance," yet primarily stressed the medical purpose of the form. However, as early as 1949, some retailers started to shift attention to the cosmetic nature of this product. For instance, in 1949 Chesterman-Leeland published a promotional folder, "SECRETS: For Restoring Female Beauty." A sensual, nude, female figure hidden in shadows graced the front cover of the folder designed to promote "sales on 'Chesties,' a Latex down-filled bust form." Unlike the titles Sears, Roebuck attached to forms, such as "Surgical" or "Post-operative," Chesterman-Leeland's product "Chesties" downplayed the medical function of the part and emphasized its relation to notions of female beauty. Moreover, Chesterman-Leeland openly stated that the prosthetic part was applicable "for both amputation cases and general figure improvement," thereby conflating any distinction that existed between the surgical purpose and cosmetic function of artificial breasts.[10]

Despite moves by other companies that emphasized the cosmetic function of artificial breasts, the Sears, Roebuck Catalogue continued to focus on the medical nature of these products well into the 1950s. In 1958 Sears advertised "Scientifically Designed Post-Operative Bras."

Although these bras did not include an innovation that warranted the label scientific, the text that accompanied the advertisement offered an extended discussion of mastectomy. The text was clearly informed by knowledge of the Halsted radical procedure and the extensive nature of this operation, which often included removal of the breast, connecting tissues, and pectoral muscles. The operation often left indents in the chest, underarm, and back. The advertisement read: "These inserts are pre-shaped to give natural-looking contour, may be inflated to the degree you want . . . reach well back into the arm."[11]

POSTWAR CULTURE AND PROSTHESES

The optimism that pervaded postwar culture influenced public perceptions of science and medicine. As an article in *Women's Home Companion* asserted: "World War II taught one lesson of incalculable importance. The lesson: that with unlimited money to spend we can buy answers to almost any scientific problem."[12] For the prostheses industry, the postwar years ushered in a new level of sophistication. The industry used a range of new materials and worked to create more realistic artificial parts. Perhaps more significant to the breast-prostheses market, cultural attitudes in the postwar years emphasized the value American society placed on notions of femininity. Moreover, throughout this era psychologists recognized the category of "normal" femininity that offered a standard to which other categories might be compared. As Kathy Peiss explained: "In the postwar years, sexual allure and desire were celebrated as key attributes of the normal female psyche."[13] Cultural assumptions of the 1950s implied that breast prostheses offered a woman a means to restore a normal physical appearance after breast cancer surgery and thereby improve her mental health.[14]

The Sears, Roebuck advertisements suggest the specific market for prosthetic breasts that emerged in the postwar years. This market resulted, at least in part, from a broadening discussion of breast cancer in the latter half of the century. To be sure, popular periodicals had discussed breast cancer as early as 1913.[15] However, the public discussion of treatment options for women with breast cancer, ranging from surgery to radiation, received little attention in popular women's magazines until mid-century. As magazines began to address treatment options, readers learned more about the mastectomy procedure. Authors encouraged women to wear a prosthetic breast after mastectomy. Notions of healing seemed to depend on a woman's willingness to overcome her surgery and disguise it from public view.

In 1955 *Woman's Home Companion* published "If the Verdict Is Cancer," outlining various stages of the postdiagnostic procedure. Its subtitle read: "What will happen if your doctor finds you have cancer?

Here for the first time a cancer expert leads you through this dreaded experience step by step." As the author, Emerson Day, explained about the 1950s woman: "She had been warned to catch signs of cancer early but she had never been told what would happen to her if cancer were discovered."[16]

Day spelled out what a woman faced after she discovered a suspicious lump in her breast, including the biopsy procedure, overnight stay in the hospital, and needle-prick's-worth of pain that rendered a patient unconscious for the biopsy and potential mastectomy procedure. He then explained that the biopsy specimen was sent immediately to pathology. If deemed benign, the woman returned to her room to recover. If it was cancerous, however, a radical mastectomy was performed:

> Working slowly and carefully, the team of surgeons first separate the breast tissue from the chest wall. Although all of the inside of the breast is removed, a portion of its surface skin is retained to help cover the area. Then they remove the two muscles in the hollow of your shoulder and the lymph glands of the armpit which have been found to be a common path for cancer cells to follow in spreading from the breasts to other parts of the body.

Day also described the expected size, shade, and shape of the scar and details about when it might heal. He dealt briefly with the psychological aspects of mastectomy but tended to rely on stereotypical generalizations about women and their response to losing a breast:

> Reactions are never the same in each patient—all of us are individuals. But most women, to a greater or lesser degree, develop the fear that their femininity has been endangered. If you are married, you may worry that your husband will not accept your "mutilated" state. If you are single you may envision yourself no longer able to compete with other women for a husband.[17]

Day assumed heterosexuality in women faced with breast-cancer surgery, an assumption echoed in most discussions of breast-cancer treatment. Likewise, the value women attached to their "femininity" was defined by their physical appearance, more specifically their figure.

Breast-cancer support programs also offered advice for women who had a mastectomy. Reach to Recovery, founded by Therese Lasser, published a 1952 manual that addressed issues women faced after a breast-cancer diagnosis. Lasser wrote the manual after her own breast cancer diagnosis and surgery. She sensed a common reaction among women who lost a breast: anxiety, feelings of unattractiveness, and fear about the changes in the body. Lasser wanted to assure other breast-cancer survivors that they could look and feel normal again after a mastectomy.

She asked physicians to allow her to speak to women recently treated for breast cancer, share her emotions with them, and offer advice about breast prostheses. She distributed her Reach to Recovery manual to hundreds and eventually thousands of women treated for breast cancer. Its popularity led to several reprints in 1954, 1955, and 1957. It was revised and reprinted in 1960 and again in 1963. The American Cancer Society absorbed the Reach to Recovery society and continues to publish editions of the manual today. Throughout the 1950s and 1960s this small organization, started by the activism of one woman, expanded to include thousands of members in all fifty states. This network of women exchanged information about their diagnosis, treatment, and recovery, creating a support network. Moreover, the group provided both emotional and physical advice on issues that cancer literature had previously ignored.[18]

The manual recommended: "Just as soon as your doctor gives permission, arrange to be fitted with one of the many kinds of prosthetic devices which are available in almost all department stores and specialty shops."[19] Lasser explained:

> A prosthesis should do three things for a woman: first, give weight to the side of the operation, go around a little on the side and on the top when necessary, thus helping to take the place of the lost muscles; third, give back her figure. Unless it does all three, it is not fulfilling its purpose.[20]

Emphasizing the third function of the breast prosthesis, she stressed that a mastectomy could remain hidden from public view. She provided women with a list of prostheses suppliers and stressed the crucial role an artificial breast played in recovery. In fact, Reach to Recovery volunteers were required to maintain a groomed appearance and to wear a properly fitted breast form. Today, a Reach to Recovery volunteer often visits women in the hospital immediately after surgery. She offers support to patients concerned about their diagnosis and treatment. The volunteer also delivers, or the ACS sends, a package that includes a foam breast form meant to fulfill a replacement function until a better form can be purchased, as well as a list of wig and breast-prostheses suppliers.

In 1958, the Oregon Division of the ACS produced a twenty-minute film, *After Mastectomy,* that echoed many of the themes of the Reach to Recovery program. The film opens with a close-up of a woman, Kay Elliot, who has recently had a mastectomy. As she gardens, she also articulates the thoughts occupying her mind: "That Sylvia couldn't keep her eyes off me. Trying to figure out which one was mine and which came from the emporium." Elliot then experiences a flashback that is located in the doctor's office. Typically, in the 1950s, breast-cancer diagnosis and treatment was a one-step process. Women entered surgery for biopsy, but if cancer was present, the woman remained unconscious while the mastectomy was performed. Therefore, upon waking from the procedure women were uncertain if their breast had been amputated. In Elliot's flashback scene, she recalls waking to the news that her breast had indeed been amputated. She stares at a photograph of her husband and wonders how this will affect her future. A narrator asks: "How can a patient be helped from the fear, depression, and pain so normal during the first day or so following the removal of a breast?" The narrator explains that unmarried women face a particular worry regarding their attractiveness to single males after a mastectomy. Finally, after discussing the disfigurement that accompanies breast-cancer treatment, the narrator recognizes a common fear among women about whether or not the doctor was able to remove all the cancer.

As the film proceeds, a nurse appears to console Elliot: "Nothing helps more than putting your face on. Want some makeup?" The nurse reminds Elliot that she needs to move her arm to restore mobility, and demonstrates how applying makeup and brushing hair can serve as exercises that increase mobility. When the doctor enters the scene, Elliot asks him about her medical concerns, including the results of her surgery and the likelihood that the cancer has spread. The doctor recounts the details of the surgery, including the fact that her pectoral muscles were removed, and offers a hopeful prognosis.

Soon, Elliot is reading an ACS pamphlet, "Help Yourself to a Recovery."[21] A narrator comments:

> With the help from their doctors, nurses, and families, the Kay Elliots of this world will recover with a few scars from their mild depressions and anxieties. There are others, however, who will be disturbed, even profoundly disturbed. These will need more time and help. Even to those with the greatest inner strength, appearance is important.

As this film demonstrated, cancer educators insisted that all women needed to maintain a certain standard of appearance after mastectomy. A breast prosthesis became the critical component to the restoration of a female shape and thereby a crucial step toward healing.

In the final scenes of the film, the nurse teaches Elliot how to insert cotton into the bra to give the appearance of a breast: "I've got cotton. Let's see what we can do to fool the public." A Reach to Recovery volunteer, Mrs. Evans, enters and shows Elliot her prosthetic breast, reminding Elliot to shop until she finds one that really fits. She bluntly states that there is "nothing easy about readjusting after the shock of losing a breast."[22]

EXPANSION OF THE MARKET

The concern for developing a "perfect" breast prosthesis that incorporates modern material and technology is not a recent phenomenon. In fact the model for the contemporary external breast prosthesis, the casing form, was designed in the early years of this century. This model consisted of an envelope or casing of soft material meant to resemble the skin, filled with a soft cushioning material meant to simulate the human breast. However, since mid-century there have been dramatic innovations in the material substances used to make breast prostheses. Slick plastic shells with tapered edges have replaced early casings of silk and cotton. Simple fill products such as hair, birdseed, cotton, and sponge have been replaced with silicone, the contemporary standard material for breast prostheses that offers a close resemblance to human tissue. Since World War II, and largely as a result of the scientific innovations that occurred during the war, synthetic chemicals have been added to rubber, altering its behavior and ultimately leading to the creation of a more realistic breast substitute.

Perhaps spurred by the publicity directed to breast cancer in the postwar era, retailers published comments about the breast-prostheses market. In 1963, when Jean Gordon Goldman recounted decades of work in the intimate-apparel industry, she discussed breast-cancer survivors as one segment of this market. As a public relations officer, Goldman devoted her adult life to the promotion of the corset and bra industry and obviously appreciated the commercial aspect of this field. She perceived a broad base of customers that included women whose breast had been amputated as treatment for cancer. As she explained to readers in *Profitable Corset & Brassiere Merchandising: A Guide for Retailers, Manufacturers, and Fitters*, "With over 50,000 cases of mastectomy, [fitting prosthetics] is a problem that we must face daily."[23]

In the 1960s, the prosthetic breast industry was still in its early stage of development, and many corset companies had only recently expanded their production capabilities to include breast prostheses production and sale.[24] Most manufactured breast prostheses used foam, rubber, or cotton to replicate breast tissue. Some prostheses could be inflated to various sizes, and others were built into postoperative bras. Silicone had yet to be widely marketed in the external-breast industry, and breast prostheses usually cost consumers a few dollars.

To be sure, silicone was invented as early as the 1930s. A compound that combined quartz and sand, it has several useful properties such as its flexibility, durability, and temperature resistance. Some also argued that silicone was a biologically inert substance. Dow Corning owned the patent to silicone and used the material for a variety of applications in the 1940s and 1950s. It could be found in war machinery, proved useful as a cleaning material, and made a wonderful caulking substance. Other random by-products of silicone included the creation of Silly Putty.[25]

Rumors suggest that Japanese doctors recognized the usefulness of silicone for breast augmentation during the war years. By the 1950s, Americans were experimenting with silicone and breast augmentation, and the press reported stories of silicone injections and larger breast sizes. Dow denies any involvement in this early implant business. Eventually, silicone would replace cotton and foam as the most popular replacement for breast tissue in artificial breast forms, but Goldman's book confirms that cotton and foam still dominated the industry in the early 1960s.[26]

Popular magazines, advertisements, and American Cancer Society literature taught women recently treated for breast cancer that the artificial breast served medical functions. It restored women's emotional health and physical shape after breast-cancer treatment. Goldman's comments to retailers who sold postmastectomy products underscored these assumptions: "To understand this customer you must realize that she has gone through several emotional and physical changes. Sometimes she feels that she is only 'half a woman.'" Goldman further commented that if a "breast amputee" customer was married, "She will be worrying about her husband's reaction to her figure change."[27]

Goldman also spoke about the effects of the most common surgical treatment for breast cancer, the radical mastectomy: "There is usually more scar tissue than just across the breastline. If the cancer spread through the ligaments, there will be deep indentations under the arm, into the rib cage and sometimes into the arm itself." Assuming women would want to hide the scars of this operation, Goldman reminded the reader that both the side and the breast would need to be fitted with artificial fill. Goldman's analysis of this market suggests that the contemporary notions that link a woman's emotional recovery from breast cancer to her willingness to reconstruct her body to its premastectomy form have been fostered by a consumer market that profits from the sales of these artificial parts.[28]

The emphasis on buying an artificial breast with a proper fit, articulated by popular magazines, American Cancer Society literature, cancer education films, and public relations officers, was answered in part when Dow Corning introduced its silicone breast prosthesis in the late 1960s. In addition to redefining reconstructive surgery, silicone redefined the external-breast-prostheses industry. Corning approached Airway, a noted external-breast-prostheses manufacturer, to promote silicone as a better breast substitute. As Airway described it: "We took it to market as the first 'premium quality' breast prosthesis, called that because the retail price—$150.00 in late 1960s dollars, was over two times the cost of other breast forms on the market at that time."[29]

As companies such as Dow Corning recognized a wider market for their innovations in synthetics that had been discovered thirty years earlier, marketing departments assumed the responsibility of convincing customers and health insurance companies that the improved product was worth the new and significantly higher price tag.[30]

At the same time that Dow Corning was entering the external-prostheses market, women started to report that internal silicone breast implants had long-term harmful effects on the body. Within a decade of Dow Corning's 1963 introduction of sealed silicone gel packs intended for surgical replacement or augmentation of breasts, women with breast implants complained of medical ailments. *Ms.* magazine published one of the first exposés on the subject in a two-article series that included "Beauty and the Breast: A 60% Complication Rate for an Operation You Don't Need" and "A Shot—or Two or Three—in the Breast." As Larned revealed in her history of liquid silicone as a breast replacement:

> Though never clinically tested, silicone liquid nonetheless became widely used for cosmetic purposes in Japan during the fifties; small doses injected in the face removed wrinkles, and larger doses injected directly into breast tissue transformed a 34A into a 34C "instantly"—and without apparent problems. Shortly thereafter however health problems became apparent. Silicone implants masked indications of breast cancer, leaked or spread during breast palpitation, and the "migrating and infection-producing tendencies of silicone were also becoming evident."[31]

In addition, a range of less definite health problems emerged among women with implanted silicone.

The risks associated with implants ensured the survival and expansion of the external-breast-prostheses industry. Since the 1970s the external breast form has evolved enormously, and contemporary forms offer a wide range of colors, sizes, and shapes to women seeking a breast replacement. Marketing departments produce literature and images that stress the superiority of their product in this competitive market. The breast-prostheses industry is not unique in this recent expansion. The entire prostheses industry has been shaped by innovations in science, medicine, and technology that have fostered new, better, and more expensive products. In a 1978 *Forbes* article, "Spare Parts for Humans," author Steven Solomon commented that an industry "virtually nonexistent" a couple decades ago was now estimated to be worth $700 million, with projections for financial expansion at 15 percent per year.[32] Silicone was used in an array of prosthetic parts. As John Byrne described one Dow employee's career throughout the 1970s: "Armed with a briefcase filled with artificial finger joints, ears, noses, chins and breast implants, Barley would deliver a canned presentation dubbed 'Spare Parts for the Body' to women's and civic groups, radio and television talk shows."[33]

Throughout the 1980s criticism contending that implanted silicone was unsafe escalated, again fostering increased sales for the external-breast business. Court battles in the 1990s drove Dow Corning to bankruptcy, and although it settled the lawsuits for a phenomenal sum, it never accepted responsibility for the health problems experienced by so many women who used their product. Another indication of the continual expansion of the external-breast-prostheses market is the stream of new companies joining the market. For instance, Ruth Handler (best known as the inventor of Barbie) launched her breast-prostheses company at the height of the surgical implant craze. Her company, Nearly Me, produced a breast form of "liquid silicone enclosed in polyurethane with a rigid foam backing" that sold for $116 to $154 in the 1970s. By 1980 the company had exceeded sales of $1 million. It used a variety of marketing ploys to launch its product, including store promotions, handwritten invitations, seminars, and talk-show appearances. Like most breast-prostheses companies, it continues to launch new products today.[34]

A 1990S MARKET: BREAST PROSTHESES

According to the 1999 American Business Index, 1,439 companies in the United States are currently associated with artificial breast production and sales. Of these, approximately half have sales under $500,000 per year and employ fewer than five people. A handful of prostheses companies exceed $1 million of sales, and larger umbrella companies with sales in excess of $1 billion list prostheses sales as one of their subdivisions. These numbers suggest the diversity of business interests in a market that appeals to large corporations and small business owners alike. The breast-prostheses market is clearly sizable and expanding.

The culture of the 1990s has also led to a burst in the opening of specialty shops that cater to cancer-related products. For instance, under the headings "breast forms" or "breast prostheses," telephone directories in most U.S. cities today list local specialty shops that sell external breast prostheses. Many of these shops dub themselves "boutiques" and, in addition to breast forms, often sell wigs for women who have lost their hair due to chemotherapy treatment for cancer and clothing such as bathing suits and nightgowns tailored for women who have had mastectomies and wear breast prostheses. More recently, specialty shops in larger U.S. cities cater to African-American and Hispanic women and maintain a large stock of products in different skin tones. The contemporary breast-prostheses industry produces dozens of styles every year in a variety of sizes, shapes, and skin tones, in materials that range from silicone to cotton, and in forms designed to accommodate all surgeries, including radical, modified-radical, lumpectomy, and partial mastectomy. Women searching for a breast prosthesis device after a mastectomy literally have hundreds of choices for a replacement breast form.[35]

The common theme in marketing the external prosthetic breast, among at least six major manufacturers of the artificial part, links the breast form to images of beauty. Some companies establish this association when deciding on their corporate name. BFI, Butterfly Images, a breast-prostheses supplier, explains that its acronym stands for "Beautiful, Feminine, Image." A larger manufacturer, Amoena, explains in its advertisements that: "Amoena seeks to be the embodiment of the Latin meaning of its name: 'the beautiful, the lovely.'" Most suppliers and manufacturers identify the purpose of their companies as restoring women's sense of beauty after a mastectomy. For example, one supplier, Close to You, states its dedication to "helping women feel beautiful again." Naturalwear Camp promises that its "soft and feminine styles keep every woman looking and feeling beautiful."[36]

Not surprisingly, the artificial breast has also been gendered feminine. The packaging of the product, advertisements, and explanatory literature rely on symbols often associated with women and beauty, including pastel colors, floral images, flowing and cursive lettering, and lacey bras. The rhetoric and images of beauty throughout these advertisements reinforce the notion that a positive physical appearance defined by normalcy is a critical component of healing after a breast-cancer diagnosis and surgery. Even a mid-1970s Sears, Roebuck advertisement adopts the rhetoric and claims its prosthesis will "give you a beautiful, natural-looking bustline."[37] This industry blurs the distinction between a prosthetic part and a cosmetic product; replacing an amputated body part is presented as a way to enhance feminine beauty.

As Goldman's book for lingerie retailers indicated, the association between lingerie and prostheses is not new. Until the recent invention of an artificial breast that can adhere directly to the chest, a brassiere made up a critical component of the prosthesis. Postoperative brassieres included pockets for prostheses. Most prosthetic-breast retailers offered options in both breast forms and postmastectomy brassieres. As more boutiques open throughout the country, larger department stores that occupied a larger section of this market before the advent of specialty stores have sought to reclaim their niche in this market.

Many department stores are currently expanding their selection of specialty bras, and some offer a selection of artificial breasts. As retailers explain, early detection of breast cancer and the fear of reconstructive surgery have created a larger market in recent decades. Department stores are tapping into the "potential market" of the future as more women survive breast cancer and live longer with a prosthetic breast. As lingerie retailers begin to play a more active role in selling breast forms, they too depend on notions of femininity and beauty to bolster sales.

Trade journals introducing new designs in breast prostheses refer to women who have had breast cancer surgery as the "postmastectomy market." They introduce the product line with frequent reference to the diverse needs of women and reminders about new products that cater to every woman's need. This literature, geared toward breast-prostheses retailers, epitomizes the blurring of boundaries between the role a prosthetic part plays in replacing a lost body part and its position in the retail market as a product that influences profit margins. A recent trade article suggested that: "Too often a woman may be led to believe that she should commit to one type of breast form and not deviate from her choice. In reality, a woman's breast form collection might, and perhaps should, contain a variety of forms, from silicone to lighter fiberfill forms."[38] As this comment suggests, while suppliers and retailers are offering a larger product line for women, they are bene-fiting from the increase in sales and fostering the perception that women both need to and should wear prostheses at all times, includ-ing their trip home from the hospital after surgery, while they sleep, and during sporting activities.

Marketing for external breast prostheses continues to assume that women will want to hide the effects of their surgery from public view, that women desire perfect breasts, and that women's mental wellness and health is dependent on a sense of external beauty. Moreover, many cancer support groups, most notably the American Cancer Society and its affiliate Reach to Recovery, make similar assumptions. The medical profession also links women's decision to wear a prosthe-sis as a critical step toward healing after a surgery. While many med-ical studies have focused on the benefits of wearing a prosthesis, few if any case studies examine the benefits of *not* wearing a prosthesis. Instead, this subject has been addressed by individuals, often outspo-ken activists and feminists.[39] Artist and author Matuschka was made famous when her controversial photographic self-portrait graced the cover of the *New York Times Magazine* on August 15, 1993. Since her breast cancer diagnosis in 1991, much of her artistic expression has focused on her body, revealing the scars of her mastectomy. As she explained about her decisions to locate her work on her body and pub-lish it in a widely circulated magazine:

I have always adhered to a policy that one should speak and show the truth, because knowledge leads to freewill, to choice. If we keep quiet about what breast cancer does to women's bodies, if we refuse to accept women's bodies in

whatever condition they are in, we are doing a disservice to womankind. . . .
In publishing my photograph, my intention was never to harm or embarrass
women who, like me, have gone through the painful and humiliating ordeal of
mastectomy.

Matuschka wants to present images of her scars and feature her sense
of beauty after her mastectomy in a society that offers very few images
of disfigured women as beautiful, normal, and acceptable.[40]

Julie Friedeberger expressed another critique of prostheses, but
directed it toward a medical audience in "The False Breast: Should We
Go for It So Quickly?" published in the *British Medical Journal* in 1996.
Friedeberger explained that after her mastectomy, medical staff and
cancer support groups encouraged her to wear a prosthesis, suggesting
that it would be her first step toward recovery. Friedberger felt that
wearing the artificial breast was a psychological way of avoiding her
mastectomy, and she lacked a desire to wear one immediately after
surgery. Moreover, she criticized the assumption, from all the people
and cultural images she knew, that she needed to replace her missing
breast. As she explained to the medical profession:

After mastectomy we need time to accept what has happened and to realize
that we are now different, not deformed; transfigured, not disfigured.
Prosthesis and reconstruction cannot help us do that, but once we have done
it they can take their place as the useful, practical assets that they are, rather
than as instruments of concealment and denial.[41]

Clearly artificial breasts serve practical purposes. In addition to
replacing a body part that has been amputated, the breast prosthesis
corrects a sense of imbalance that might follow surgery. For many
women, the prosthetic breast is an integral component of healing,
offering a variety of psychological benefits. Moreover, it offers a safe
alternative to reconstructive surgery for women who have had mastectomies and want a replacement form for their breasts.

The prostheses business is also a beauty business, however, and the
breast form serves a cosmetic purpose. Therefore the evolution of this
business and industry has benefited from the emphasis American society places on female beauty and more specifically on images of perfect
breasts. The images and text published in breast prostheses pamphlets,
brochures, and advertisements reflect these cultural values and reinforce them. Although it seems fairly logical that manufacturers would
exploit notions of female beauty to advance sales, it is less clear why
there seems to be such a consensus in contemporary society that
women who have had a mastectomy need to have reconstructive
surgery or wear a prosthesis. Specifically the American Cancer Society
and Reach to Recovery, who approach women within days of their mas-

tectomy, offer newly diagnosed breast-cancer patients a cotton breast form and explain the options after the surgery: wear a prosthesis or have reconstructive surgery. The option of living as a single-breasted woman is virtually ignored. Likewise, the number of medical studies that examine the benefits of prostheses far outnumber those that examine the effects of not correcting a surgery. In addition, the medical profession supports the ACS/RTR effort by encouraging newly diagnosed patients to meet the volunteers and to wear a prosthetic breast.

The evolution of the prostheses industry marks shifts in production, changes in who controls production, and an ever-changing material culture of the product. Clearly, the expansion of the industry has offered useful and very lifelike replacements for breasts. The goal of manufacturing a prosthetic part that matches the remaining breast has been very nearly realized. Moreover, recent innovations such as the wider selection of skin tones in breast prostheses reflect a concern for all women and the long-overdue recognition that the "flesh tone" of standard production models does not match the skin tones of many women, including African-American and Hispanic women. New product lines also reflect designer's attention to shifts in surgery and accommodate a variety of operations.

At the same time, the breast-prostheses industry has merged its concerns for replacing an amputated body part with American culture's obsession with the female breast and standard notions of beauty. In its efforts to assure women that a prosthetic breast can restore a sense of beauty after surgery, the industry—along with the medical profession, cancer support groups, and many others—has exaggerated the therapeutic value of the prosthetic part. It offers no recognition that the part fails to restore sensation and cannot erase the memory of surgery. Nor does it diminish the cancer diagnosis that a woman will deal with for the rest of her life. Audre Lorde perhaps described this best when she recorded her first memory of a breast prosthesis in *The Cancer Journals*. Shortly after her mastectomy, a volunteer delivered "a wad of lambswool pressed into a pale pink breast-shaped pad." As Lorde explained:

> Her message was, you are just as good as you were before because you can look exactly the same. Lambswool now, then a good prosthesis as soon as possible, and nobody'll know the difference. But what she said was, "*You'll* never know the difference and she lost me right there, because I knew sure as hell *I'd* know the difference.[42]

CONCLUSION

The rise of the breast-prostheses industry in mid-century reflected increased attention to the high incidence of breast cancer, scientific and technological innovation, and corporate venture into medical sales. Clearly, women who had mastectomies created a demand for the product and the industry responded by creating a larger niche in the market. Production of breast prostheses gradually shifted from the home to factories. While this shift has certain obvious benefits, it also marks the demedicalization of the prosthetic part and its entrance into the competitive market of beauty and business.

NOTES

1. Kathy Peiss, *Hope in a Jar: The Making of American Beauty Culture* (New York: Metropolitan Books, 1998), 245. As Peiss demonstrated, after World War II, " the beauty industry entered a rococo period and, like other consumer industries, began to produce a limitless array of goods, colors, and styles." See also Elizabeth Haiken, *Venus Envy: A History of Cosmetic Surgery* (Baltimore, MD: Johns Hopkins University Press, 1997), 185. Haiken suggests how the postwar emphasis on beauty influenced cosmetic procedures: "World War II gave new impetus to the link surgeons had forged between outer appearance and inner peace or lack of it."
2. This conference, "Orthotic Fitters Training Programs," was held in the Cincinnati area October 18–23, 1999. Surgical Appliance Industries, the parent company for Airway, sponsored the meeting.
3. United States Patent Directory.
4. "Breast Adapter" by Blanche E. Wiggers (September 24, 1935); and "Surgical Breast Pad," by Abe Silverman (December 30, 1947).
5. "Pattern and Method of Forming Breast Forms," by Helen N. Perl (May 8, 1944).
6. John Byrne, *Informed Consent: A Story of Personal Tragedy and Corporate Betrayal . . . Inside the Silicone Breast Implant Crisis* (New York: McGraw-Hill, 1996). In addition, most manufacture has now moved outside the United States and prosthetic breasts are imported products.
7. The *Sears, Roebuck Catalogue* (Chicago: 1942–1943), 185.
8. *Sears* (1946–1947), 218; and *Sears* (1951), 341.
9. *Sears* (1954), 409.
10. *American Surgical Trade Association Journal* 36 (April 1949): 18, in Max Wocher Papers, box 1, folder 6, Max Wocher and Sons Manuscript Collection, Cincinnati Historical Society, Cincinnati, Ohio.
11. *Sears* (1958), 300.
12. "We Could Cure Cancer Now!" *Woman's Home Companion* (November 1946): 35.
13. Peiss, *Hope in a Jar*, 248.
14. Susan Jahoda also offers a discussion of the postwar notion of "normal" in "The Anthropometry of Barbie: Unsettling Ideals of the Feminine Body in Popular Culture" in *Deviant Bodies: Critical Perspectives on Difference in Science and Popular Culture*, Jennifer Terry and Jacqueline Urla, eds. (Bloomington, IN: Indiana University Press, 1995). Elaine Tyler May commented on increased American obsession with female breasts after World War II in *Homeward Bound: American Families in the Cold War Era* (New York: Basic Books, 1988). See also Robert Westbrook, "'I Want a Girl, Just Like the Girl that Married Harry James': American Women and the Problem of Political Obligation in World War II," *American Quarterly* 42 (1990): 587–614; and Vicki Howard, "At the Curve Exchange," Hagley Conference on Beauty and Business, March 1999, included in this volume.
15. Samuel Hopkins Adams, "What Can We Do About Cancer," *Ladies Home Journal* (May 1913): 21–22. Deemed both a quintessential muckraker and a "superb" health educator, Adams published extensively on public health issues such as cancer, tuberculosis, medical fraud, and drug addiction. See James H. Cassedy, "Muckraking and Medicine: Samuel Hopkins Adams," *American Quarterly* 16 (Spring 1954): 85–99.
16. Emerson Day, "If the Verdict Is Cancer," *Woman's Home Companion* (January 1955): 32.
17. *Ibid.*, 43.
18. Terese Lasser, *Reach to Recovery* (New York: privately printed, 1953); *Reach to Recover: A Handbook for Women Who Have Had Radical Breast Surgery* (New York: Reach to Recovery Foundation, 1963); *Reach To Recovery: After Mastectomy: A Patient Guide* (New York: American Cancer Society, 1982).
19. *Ibid.*, esp. 15.
20. *Ibid.*, 89.
21. Although this pamphlet is featured in *After Mastectomy*, I cannot find any copies of it, nor am I sure it was ever published for audiences.
22. *After Mastectomy* (New York: American Cancer Society, 1958). A copy of this film is pre-

served at the Library of Congress Film Division.

23. Jean Gordon Goldman, *Profitable Corset & Brassiere Merchandising: A Guide for Retailers, Manufacturers, and Fitters* (New York: Fairchild Publications, 1963), 36. Goldman started her career in fashion as a salesperson in Rochester, New York. She then worked as a buyer for the B. Forman Company and wrote a column for female shoppers in the *Rochester Times Union*. She later worked for Warner Brothers Company as an advertising copywriter and public relations director. She also lectured on the corset and brassiere industry, organized fashion shows, and taught classes on the subject at the Fashion Institute of Technology. See "About the Author," first page.

24. At least two of the largest American breast-prostheses businesses today started as corset companies. Camp Health Company evolved from the S. H. Camp and Corsette Company near mid-century, and Airway (now a branch of Surgical Appliance Industries), was once Airway Corset Company.

25. John Byrne offers a comprehensive history of Dow Corning and the evolution of silicon in *Informed Consent*, 1996. Elizabeth Haiken also offers a good chronology of the evolution of the silicone industry for breast augmentation in *Venus Envy*, 1997. See esp. chap. 6, "Beauty and the Breast." Haiken persuasively argues that the "vocal minority" of women who needed breast reconstruction for medical purposes propelled the rapid evolution of breast-reconstruction procedures and demanded they be safe. As she explained: "Women wanted physicians to take seriously their need to put the experience of cancer behind them and begin life again with a reconstructed breast," 259. J. Franklin Hyde invented silicone in the 1930s. His obituary dubbed him "father of silicones." "J. Franklin Hyde, 96, the 'Father of Silicones,'" *New York Times* (October 15, 1999).

26. See Byrne, *Informed Consent*, and "This Man Sounded the Silicone Alarm—in 1976," *Business Week* (January 27, 1992): 34.

27. Goldman, *Profitable*, 36.

28. *Ibid*. I recognize that wearing a prosthetic breast is a critical component of healing for many women after a mastectomy. I am merely suggesting that the prostheses market has reinforced this notion of health and restoration to improve sales of its product.

29. Airway Marketing Department, Cincinnati, Ohio, correspondence with author, October 7, 1999.

30. Every year insurance companies adjust coverage benefits. In 1999, Medical agreed to cover six postmastectomy bras and one artificial form per year.

31. Marjorie Nash and Mimi White, "Beauty and the Breast," *Ms.* (September 1977): 53–54; and Deborah Larned, "A Shot—or Two or Three—in the Breast," *Ms.* (September 1977): 55.

32. American Business Disc offers the most comprehensive information on the size of the current prostheses industry. Several companies that sell orthopedic and prosthetic devices, such as Cobe Laboratories Inc. and United States Surgical Corp., exceed $1 billion in sales per year. However, available sales figures do not distinguish how much of these sales are derived from the prostheses branch of their industry compared to their other business interests. The figures also do not distinguish between sales of breast prostheses versus other artificial body parts.

33. Byrne, *Informed Consent*, 39.

34. "From Barbie to Real Life," *Fortune* (September 8, 1980): 88.

35. For example, see Rebecca Tollen, "Prosthesis Store Gives Special Care to Minorities: Imani Breast Care Helps Cancer Stricken," *Oakland Tribune*, (May 4, 1997): D4; Karyn Monget "New Products, Fresh Outlook," *WWD* 164 (October 8, 1992): 9.

36. For examples see "Breastcare," CAMP Healthcare, 1997 catalogue; "Helping You Stay in Top Form," Amoena, 1998 Coloplast Corporation pamphlet; advertisements on the internet, including www.Closetoyou.com; www.bfi-ia.com.

37. *Sears* (1975), 193.

38. Teresa Wolff and Sarah McLeod, "A Delicate Subject: Postmastectomy Equipment Overview," *Independent Living Provider* (March 1996): 54ff.

39. For example, see Hendel N. Siverstein, et al., "Reasons Why Mastectomy Patients Do Not Have Breast Reconstruction," *Plastic Reconstructive Surgery* 88 (December 1990): 1118–22; R. C. Sadove and E. R. Scherl, "Immediate Breast Reconstruction at the Time of Mastectomy for Breast Cancer," *Journal of Kentucky Medical Association* 90 (May 1992): 225–231; G. Georgiade, et al., "Rationale for Immediate Reconstruction of the Breast Following Modified Radical Mastectomy," *Annual of Plastic Surgery* 8 (January 1982): 20–28.

40. Matuschka, "Why I Did It," *Glamour* (November 1993).

41. Julie Friedeberger, "The False Breast: Should We Go for It So Quickly?" *British Medical Journal* 7063 (October 19, 1996): 313ff.

42. Audre Lorde, *The Cancer Journals* (Argyle, NY: Spinsters Ink, 1980).

Notes on the Contributors

Nancy Bowman is a member of the faculty at The Bishop's School in La Jolla, California, and a Ph.D. candidate in history at the University of Maryland. This piece represents a portion of her dissertation, "Cultural Identities and Smoking Taboos in the United States, 1880–1930."

Jill Fields is an assistant professor of history at California State University, Fresno. She is the author of the forthcoming book *The Production of Glamour: A Social History of Intimate Apparel in the Twentieth Century*.

Kirsten E. Gardner is assistant professor of U.S. history and gender studies at the University of Texas, San Antonio. Her dissertation was on female cancer awareness efforts in the United States from 1913 to 1980.

Tiffany Mclissa Gill is a doctoral student in American history at Rutgers University. She is currently working on her dissertation, "Civic Beauty: Beauty Salons, Beauty Culturists, and the Politics of African-American Female Entrepreneurship, 1900–1960."

Sarah A. Gordon is a graduate student at Rutgers University in American and women's history.

Vicki Howard is a Woodrow Wilson Postdoctoral Fellow in the Humanities at the Hagley Museum and Library and Rutgers University, Camden. She received her Ph.D. from the University of Texas at Austin. Her dissertation is titled "American Weddings: Gender, Consumption, and the Business of Brides."

Nancy Koehn is associate professor of business administration at the Harvard Business School. She is the author of *The Power of Commerce: Economy and Governance in the First British Empire* (1994) and a contributor to *Creating Modern Capitalism: How Entrepreneurs, Companies, and Countries Triumphed in Three Industrial Revolutions* (1997). Her current research focuses on the history of entrepreneurs who built strong relationships with consumers.

Katina L. Manko is a doctoral candidate in the Department of History at the University of Delaware. Her dissertation, "Ding Dong! Avon Calling!: Gender and Business in Door-to-Door Selling, 1886–1962," is a business and cultural history of Avon Products, Incorporated and Avon Ladies.

Kathy Peiss teaches American women's history and cultural history at the University of Massachusetts, Amherst. She is the author of *Cheap Amusements: Working Women and Leisure in Turn-of-the-Century New York* (1986) and *Hope in a Jar: The Making of America's Beauty Culture* (1998).

Philip Scranton is Board of Governors Professor of History at Rutgers University and director of the Center for the History of Business, Technology, and Society at the Hagley Museum and Library. He co-edits Routledge's Hagley Perspectives on Business and Culture series with Roger Horowitz, associate director of the Hagley Center.

Carole Turbin is professor of sociology and history at SUNY/Empire State College. She is the author of *Working Women of Collar City* (1992) and coeditor of a forthcoming collection of essays on the social history of fashion and textiles. She is currently working on a book on changes in men's fashions, visual culture, gender ideology, and social class in the early twentieth-century United States.

Susannah Walker is working on a Ph.D. in social and cultural history at Carnegie Mellon University in Pittsburgh. Her dissertation is about African-American women and commercial beauty culture from the 1920s to the 1970s. She teaches undergraduate courses in women's history and the history of advertising.

Judy Tzu-Chun Wu is an assistant professor of history at the Ohio State University. Her areas of specialization include U.S., Asian-American, and women's histories. She is currently writing a thematic biography of Dr. Margaret Chung (1889–1959), the first American-born Chinese female physician.

Index

labor strikes, 116, 195, 205
labor unions, 102, 177, 181, 203, 210–11
Ladies' Home Journal, 30, 36, 47, 67, 69, 290
Langer, Suzanne, 9
Larned, Deborah, 320
Lasser, Therese, 315–16
Lauder, Estée, 217–20, 222–33, 235–37, 242–46
  business strategies of, 225–33, 242–43
  education of, 218, 219, 220, 222, 223
  family of, 217–18, 219, 220, 222–23, 224, 234, 235, 236
  as hands-on entrepreneur, 229–30, 232, 233, 235, 244–45
  sold to beauty shops, 220, 222, 224, 227, 231
  see also Estée Lauder, Inc.
Lauder, Leonard Alan, 220, 223, 229, 232
  in family business, 235, 236, 237, 238–39, 242, 243, 245
Lauder, Ronald, 223, 236, 243
Lauder, William, 244
laundering, 68, 87–88, 100, 103
Lauter, Joseph, 220, 222–23, 224, 235, 236, 239
Leach, William, 68–69
Lei, David, 298
Lever Brothers, 15
Leyendecker, Joseph Christian, 87, 92–93
Life Boat clubs, 176
Life magazine, 53–55, 77
Lincoln, Abbey, 259–60, 271
Lockheed Aircraft Co., 205–223
Lombard, Carole, 222
Loo, James H., 285
Lorde, Audre, 325
L'Oreal, 237, 245
Luce, Henry, 17
Lum, John, 296

magazines, 12, 13, 19, 25, 30, 67, 93, 96, 201, 203, 219, 232, 270, 309, 319
  (for individual publications, see titles)
Maidenform company, 199–200, 210, 212
  advertising of, 199–203, 206, 212
  newsletter of. See *Maiden Forum, The*
  piecework system in, 203
Maidenform employees, 200, 203, 206, 210
  as beauty contestants, 203–5
  satirized beauty culture, 211–12
  as union members, 203, 211
  upheld gender ideals, 195–97, 206, 208–9
Maiden Forum, The, 203–10, 211–12
  focused on romance, 208–9, 210, 212

  Pin-Up Girls in, 195, 203, 205–6, 208
  reflected employees' interests, 207–8
Malone, Annie Turnbo, 174, 177, 191n16, 267
Malone, Regina, 66–67
management, 16, 211, 235–7, 239–41
  sales 127–8, 143, 148–54, 156–63
  scientific 125
Manko, Katina L., 142
Manning, Marie, 60, 64, 66
Marinello, 12, 16
marketing and sales, 8, 14, 18–19, 101, 112, 128, 212, 222, 227–32, 237–9. 268–70, 309
  direct, 142–65, 174–6, 220–1
markets, 7, 103, 131, 153, 317, 323
  art 9–10
  rural 147–50, 175–6
marriage, 10, 57, 67–8, 197–8, 201, 295–6, 315
Martin, Ella Mae, 183, 187
masculinity/manhood, 28, 55–6, 59, 87, 90, 91–2, 93–5, 104, 171
  and critiques of men, 99
  and critiques of women, 27–9, 40, 53, 61
Mason, Eleanor, 264
mastectomies, 311, 314–15, 316–17
  Halsted radical procedure, 314, 315, 319
  healing from, 317, 319, 322, 323, 324
  see also breast prostheses
Matuschka, 323–24
Max Factor, 16, 146, 225, 228
Maybelline (cosmetics), 146, 228
McConnell, David, Jr., 152, 153, 155, 156, 165
McConnell, David H., 142, 147–50, 159–60, 164
  sales strategies of, 147, 152, 157
medical conditions and treatment, 28, 59, 103, 125–6, 314–17, 321
  see also physicians, surgery
men, 93–94, 241–42
  Afro-wearing, 255, 262–63, 264, 270
  in black businesses, 170–71
  cigarette-smoking, 53, 59
  working-class, 91–92, 98, 102
  see also Arrow Man; middle-class men
Mencken, H. L., 64
men's clothing, 89–90, 95–96, 98–99
  blurred class distinctions, 96, 97, 101–2, 103–4
  informal styles of, 98–100, 102–3
  See also collars, detachable
Metropolitan Museum of Art, 31, 34–35, 39, 46, 47